CW00674008

Lord Liverpool

LORD LIVERPOOL

A Political Life

William Anthony Hay

THE BOYDELL PRESS

First published 2018
The Boydell Press, Woodbridge

ISBN 978 1 78327 282 2

The Boydell Press is an imprint of Boydell & Brewer Ltd
PO Box 9, Woodbridge, Suffolk IP12 3DF, UK
and of Boydell & Brewer Inc.
668 Mt Hope Avenue, Rochester, NY 14620–2731, USA
website: www.boydellandbrewer.com

A CIP catalogue record for this book is available
from the British Library

The publisher has no responsibility for the continued existence or accuracy of URLs for
external or third-party internet websites referred to in this book, and does not guarantee that
any content on such websites is, or will remain, accurate or appropriate

This publication is printed on acid-free paper

Printed and bound in Great Britain by
TJ International Ltd, Padstow, Cornwall

To

Margaret Hampton Hay

Contents

Illustrations

Acknowledgements

Samuel Johnson's remark about turning over half a library to make one book may seem an exaggeration, but historians realize it understates the work involved. I am delighted to acknowledge the help from both individuals and institutions with my biography of Lord Liverpool. Material from the Royal Archives at Windsor is cited by gracious permission of Her Majesty the Queen. I would like to acknowledge permission to consult their collections of manuscripts granted by Earl Barthust, the Earl of Harewood, Viscount Sidmouth, and the Earl of Harrowby. Chris Woolgar provided access to the Wellington MSS at the University of Southampton, along with insights on Wellington's career and his relationship with Liverpool. Staff at the British Library, National Archives at Kew, West Yorkshire Archive Service, and Devon Record Office helped tremendously during repeated visits. Indeed, the British Library's manuscript room became a home away from home. Their counterparts with the Kent History and Library Service and Suffolk Record Office assisted with reproductions from those collections.

Research fellowships at the William L. Clements Library at the University of Michigan, where Brian Dunnigan has been an indefatigable guide, and the Beinecke Rare Book and Manuscript Library at Yale facilitated research in the United States. Although a different project had brought me to Yale's Lewis Walpole Library in Farmington, Connecticut, Cynthia Roman showed me a George Humphrey shop album of print satires from 1820 that provided several of the book's illustrations. She and Susan Walker could not have done more to make my time there a pleasure. The Department of Prints and Drawings at the British Museum and the National Portrait Gallery in London granted permission to use images from their collections I am pleased to acknowledge.

The Earhart Foundation supported my work from an early stage. Its closing in 2015 was a great loss to scholars. David Kennedy, Montgomery Brown, and especially Ingrid Gregg at Earhart merit special thanks. Bill Campbell of the Philadelphia Society, who introduced me to Earhart, showed great enthusiasm for my project on Liverpool and kindly shared insights on political economy and conservative thought. The College of Arts amd Sciences and Department of History at Mississippi State University also provided funding at different points along the way. I am especially grateful to Gary Myers and Rick Travis as Deans of the College, and to Alan Marcus as History Department head. Work on Liverpool's career coincided with my work on other projects with the Foreign

Policy Research Institute and its quarterly journal *Orbis*. Scholars and staff there offered insights and perspectives that inform my work. The late Harvey Sicherman, FPRI's president until 2010, taught me much about how government works from the inside and the complex process of making policy as events rapidly change. His untimely death was a deep loss. James Kurth and Walter McDougall are colleagues who became valued friends. Their conversation shaped my approach to the present book. Alan Luxenberg, FPRI's current president, has long facilitated work by other scholars.

Stephen Schuker at the University of Virginia has been a friend since my days as his graduate student in the 1990s. Crossing paths with him and his late wife Lisa on research trips in London was a real pleasure. His scholarship on the intersection of foreign and security policy with economics and domestic politics has guided my own approach. W. Brown Patterson at Sewanee introduced me to church history and the varieties of Anglican theology. Sam Williamson also provided welcome encouragement. Charles Perry has been a longtime mentor and friend. I particularly appreciate his thoughts on nineteenth-century historiography and how later generations viewed the Age of Reform as I revised the present book.

Jennifer Siegel and Matthew Davis helped with access to sources unavailable in Mississippi. Robert Ingram patiently fielded questions on religion over the long eighteenth century. John Severn, Rory Muir, and Huw Davies shared thoughts on Wellington and his career. David Bell answered questions on the French Revolution and Napoleon. David Brown, John Bew, Richard Gaunt, Mark Lester, Douglas Hurd, Andrew Lambert, Brian Holden Reid, Angus Hawkins, and Michael Bentley helped on other specific points. Conferences, especially the 2015 Wellington Congress, the Waterloo 200 commemoration held at King's College London, and Jeremy Black's symposium on Tory approaches to foreign policy at the University of Exeter, provided valuable feedback and the chance to share ideas. Jeremy Black, James Sack, Richard Davis, and Jonathan Clark have shaped my perspective on the eighteenth century. I appreciate their help from the very start. Jim Sack kindly read the entire manuscript, as did Karl Schaffenberg and Gerald Russello who set aside other responsibilities to comment helpfully. Robert Messenger has been a helpful sounding board. Working with Erich Eichmann over the past decade has sharpened my prose. His perspective on writing and argumentation guided revisions of the final manuscript. Any errors remaining, of course, are mine.

My late father Norman Hay saw the book finished, but he died before its publication. I appreciate his encouragement and miss his company. My wife Carolyn Jane provided valuable support. She and our three children Margaret Hampton, Wills, and Sarah Jane have also lived with Lord Liverpool. It is a pleasure to dedicate the book to Margaret Hampton, who has many of Liverpool's best qualities, none of his flaws, and meets life with a grace and flair all her own.

Note on Personal Names

Important figures in this biography, including its subject and his father, changed their names as they either received or inherited titles of nobility. Since those changes might confuse readers, explaining them helps track some central protagonists.

- Charles Jenkinson became Baron Hawkesbury in 1786 and Earl of Liverpool in 1796.

- Robert Banks Jenkinson took the courtesy title Lord Hawkesbury in 1796 on his father's promotion in the peerage and inherited the title Earl of Liverpool in 1808.

- Henry Addington became Viscount Sidmouth in 1805.

- Robert Stewart held the courtesy title Viscount Castlereagh from 1796 as heir to the Marquis of Londonderry in the Irish peerage. He inherited his father's title as Lord Londonderry in 1821. Holding an Irish title enabled him to remain in the House of Commons.

- Sir Arthur Wellesley received the title Viscount Wellington of Talavera in 1809 and successive promotions in the British peerage as Earl (1812), Marquess (1812), and then Duke of Wellington (1814).

Key Events 1756–1848

DATES	PERSONAL	DOMESTIC POLITICS	INTERNATIONAL POLITICS
1756	Charles Jenkinson (Robert Banks Jenkinson's father) unpaid secretary to Lord Holderness.		Seven Years War began.
1760	Charles Jenkinson granted a pension.	Accession of George III. Lord Bute prime minister.	
1761	Jenkinson appointed Undersecretary of State. Elected MP for Cockermouth.		
1762	Jenkinson made private secretary to Lord Bute as prime minister.	Massacre of the Pelhamite Innocents.	
1763	Joint secretary to the Treasury.	Bute resigned as prime minister. George Grenville prime minister. John Wilkes prosecuted for seditious libel.	Seven Years War ended.
1764	Jenkinson advised George Grenville on Stamp Act.		
1765	Jenkinson left office with Grenville.	Stamp Act passed. Grenville resigned.	
1766	Jenkinson opposed Stamp Act repeal. Appointed to the Admiralty Board.	Stamp Act repealed following colonial protests. Declaratory Act asserted parliament's authority over colonies.	

Bold text indicates events in the life and political career of Robert Banks Jenkinson, who later became Lord Hawkesbury, and then Lord Liverpool (the 2nd Earl of Liverpool).

DATES	PERSONAL	DOMESTIC POLITICS	INTERNATIONAL POLITICS
1767	Elected MP for Appleby. Appointed to the Treasury Board.		
1768		Riots in London over John Wilkes' imprisonment.	
1769	Married Amelia Watts February 9.		
1770	**Robert Banks Jenkinson born June 7.** Amelia Jenkinson died July 7.	Lord North prime minister. Edmund Burke published *Thoughts on the Causes of Present Discontents.*	
1772	Jenkinson elected MP for Harwich.		First Partition of Poland.
1773		Boston Tea Party.	
1775		American Revolution began with fighting at Lexington and Concord.	
1776		Adam Smith published *An Inquiry into the Nature and Causes of the Wealth of Nations.*	American Declaration of Independence.
1778	Jenkinson appointed secretary at war.		France entered American War of Independence.
1779	**Robert Banks Jenkinson started preparatory school at Albion House.**		Spain joined war against Britain as France's ally.
1780		Anti-Catholic Gordon Riots in London.	Russia backed league of armed neutrality against Britain.
1781	Charles Jenkinson declines to replace Lord George Germain as colonial secretary.		British surrendered at Yorktown.
1782	Charles Jenkinson resigned office in March and marries Catherine Cope on June 22.	North resigned as prime minister.	

DATES	PERSONAL	DOMESTIC POLITICS	INTERNATIONAL POLITICS
1783	**Robert Banks Jenkinson started at Charterhouse.**	Fox–North coalition in office April through December. East India Bill defeated in Lords. William Pitt the Younger prime minister.	Treaty of Paris recognized United States of America's independence.
1784	**Robert Banks Jenkinson confronted by a highwayman.** Charles Jenkinson named to the Board of Trade.	Parliamentary elections. Pitt's India Act reorganized oversight of British East India Company with a Board of Control.	
1785			Eden Treaty signed reducing trade barriers with France.
1786	Charles Jenkinson created Baron Hawkesbury on August 21. He was named President of the Board of Trade August 23 and Chancellor of the Duchy of Lancaster in September.		
1787	**Robert Banks Jenkinson matriculated at Christ Church, Oxford on April 27 and met George Canning in November.**		
1788		George III's illness sparked Regency Crisis.	United States constitution ratified.
1789	Robert Banks Jenkinson spent July through October in Paris.		French Revolution began.
1790	**Robert Banks Jenkinson completed studies at Oxford. Then elected MP for Rye and began grand tour in July.**	Parliamentary Elections. Burke published *Reflections on the Revolution in France*.	

DATES	PERSONAL	DOMESTIC POLITICS	INTERNATIONAL POLITICS
1791	Lord Hawkesbury entered the cabinet. **Robert Banks Jenkinson returned from grand tour.**	William Wilberforce introduced a bill to abolish slave trade. Edmund Burke and Charles James Fox break over French Revolution.	
1792	**Robert Banks Jenkinson's maiden speech on February 29. Travelled to Coblenz and met the Duke of Brunswick.**	Wilberforce's second bill against slave trade.	France declared war on Austria on April 20 and invaded Belgium. Battle of Valmy September 20.
1793	**Robert Banks Jenkinson appointed to India Board on July 3.**		Louis XVI guillotined January 20. Britain joins war against France. Second Partition of Poland.
1794	**Robert Banks Jenkinson made colonel of the Cinq Ports Fencible Cavalry. He called for a march on Paris in a Commons debate on April 10.**	Portland Whigs joined Pitt's government with Duke of Portland as home secretary.	
1795	**Robert Banks Jenkinson married Louisa Hervey on March 25.**		Third Partition of Poland. Jay Treaty signed between Britain and United States.
1796	Hawkesbury created 1st Earl of Liverpool in May. **Robert Banks Jenkinson took the courtesy title Baron Hawkesbury.**	Parliamentary elections in May and June.	
1797			Treaty of Campo Formio ended first coalition against France.
1798			Napoleon's expedition to Egypt. Second Coalition against France. Battle of the Nile on August 1–3.

DATES	PERSONAL	DOMESTIC POLITICS	INTERNATIONAL POLITICS
1799	**Lord Hawkesbury (Robert Banks Jenkinson) appointed Master of the Mint in March. Chaired parliamentary committee on regulating bread production.**		*Coup d'état* in France brought Napoleon to power as First Consul.
1800	Lord Liverpool effectively retired from public life.	Act of Union with Ireland.	Second league of armed neutrality formed against Britain with Russian support.
1801	**Lord Hawkesbury appointed Foreign Secretary on February 20. Began peace talks with Louis-Guillaume Otto in April. Reported defeat of a Russo-Danish league of armed neutrality in May. Announced preliminary peace terms with France on October 1.**	Pitt resigned and Henry Addington became prime minister. Parliamentary elections.	Treaty of Luneville. Battle of Copenhagen. League of armed neutrality collapses. Tsar Paul assassinated. Alexander I took Russian throne.
1802	Peace of Amiens concluded on March 21.		Peace of Amiens.
1803	**Lord Hawkesbury announced defensive preparations against France on March 9. Summoned to the Lords as leader of the house on November 15.**		Louisiana Purchase by United States in April. Britain declared war on France on May 18.
1804	**Lord Hawkesbury made home secretary with leadership in the Lords in May. Quarreled with Canning over a public slight in June. Hawkesbury brokered a reconciliation between Pitt and Addington in November and December.**	Addington resigned and Pitt returned as prime minister.	

DATES	PERSONAL	DOMESTIC POLITICS	INTERNATIONAL POLITICS
1805	Lord Hawkesbury declined a move to the Admiralty in April. Gave major speech against Catholic Emancipation on May 10.	Addington joined Pitt's cabinet with a peerage as Viscount Sidmouth on January 14. Lord Melville censured by Commons and forced from the Admiralty. Sidmouth resigned July 10.	Battle of Trafalgar, October 21. French captured Vienna in November. Battle of Austerlitz, December 3. Austria withdrew from the war.
1806	Lord Hawkesbury declined George III's offer of the premiership in January and advised sending for Lord Grenville. Hawkesbury appointed Warden of the Cinq Ports by George III.	Death of Pitt in January. Grenville appointed to lead a government of "All the Talents" with Fox and other Whigs. Parliamentary elections October through December.	Holy Roman Empire dissolved. French occupy Prussia after victory at Jena-Auerstadt on October 14. Napoleon's Berlin Decree on November 21 forbade import of British goods.
1807	Lord Hawkesbury summoned by George III to broker formation in March of a new government led by the Duke of Portland. He returned to office as home secretary with leadership in the Lords and managed War Office in the autumn during Castlereagh's illness.	Slave trade abolished. Fall of Talents Administration in March. Portland became prime minister. Parliamentary elections in May through June.	HMS Leopard attacked USS Chesapeake on June 22. Treaty of Tilsit in July allied France and Russia. British attacked Copenhagen in August through September and seized Danish fleet. British Order in Council restricted French trade and blockaded France's ports in November. Portuguese court fled to Brazil under British protection. Napoleon's Milan Decree on December 17 forbade all British trade with Europe. Embargo Act on December 22 closed United States ports to foreign trade.

DATES	PERSONAL	DOMESTIC POLITICS	INTERNATIONAL POLITICS
1808	**Lord Hawkesbury declined to replace Portland.** **He managed War Office again in Castlereagh's absence.** **Lord Hawkesbury's father, Lord Liverpool, died in December and his son acceded to the earldom.**		French troops occupied Madrid in March. Spanish revolt began on May 2. Napoleon's brother Joseph made King of Spain in June. Britain pledged support to Spain and Portugal in June. British expedition to Portugal in August. Convention of Cintra. Napoleon led an army into Spain during the autumn.
1809	**The new Lord Liverpool worked to keep the cabinet together July through September, but rejected Spencer Perceval's suggestion he return to the Foreign Office. Instead made War Secretary with management of military strategy.** **Lord Liverpool promised Wellington in November his support for campaigns in Portugal.**	Duel between Canning and Castlereagh. Portland resigned, Spencer Perceval became prime minister.	Battle of Corunna followed by British withdrawal from Spain in January. Austria declared war on France in April. Napoleon defeated at Aspern-Essling in May. Austria defeated at Wagram in July and compelled to end the war. Failed British expedition to the Scheldt Estuary in July–December.
1810	**Lord Liverpool defended efforts in the Peninsular War in parliamentary debates. He moved proposals for a regency with the king's incapacity through the Lords in December.**	George III's illness brought his final incapacity. Parliament debated regency bill in December.	Wellington defeated French invasion of Portugal.
1811		Prince of Wales became regent in January. Prince Regent confirmed Perceval and his administration in May.	

DATES	PERSONAL	DOMESTIC POLITICS	INTERNATIONAL POLITICS
1812	Lord Liverpool appointed prime minister to succeed Perceval, but his efforts failed to recruit Canning and Lord Wellesley. Liverpool announced the cabinet's neutrality on Catholic Emancipation. The government withdrew Orders in Council and Liverpool managed passage of the Little Toleration Act in June.	Perceval assassinated on May 11. Parliamentary elections in October and November.	United States Congress declared war on Britain. Napoleon invaded Russia. Battle of Borodino on September 7.
1813		Canning dissolved his parliamentary following.	Napoleon retreated from Russia. Sixth coalition formed against France.
1814	Lord Liverpool invested a knight of the Garter in June. He defended peace terms in parliament during autumn and supervised peace negotiations with United States at Ghent.	Allied monarchs visited London. Princess of Wales went abroad.	Castlereagh arrived at allied headquarters to represent Britain. Treaty of Chaumont. Napoleon abdicated. French monarchy restored under Louis XVIII. Treaty of Paris. Congress of Vienna began. Struggle for Independence of Spanish America began. Treaty of Ghent.
1815	Lord Liverpool approved Castlereagh's alliance with France and Austria in January.	Corn Law passed in March.	Battle of New Orleans. Napoleon returned from exile. Congress of Vienna final act signed. Battle of Waterloo. Allied occupation of France. Napoleon exiled to St Helena. Louis XVIII restored. Second Treaty of Paris.

DATES	PERSONAL	DOMESTIC POLITICS	INTERNATIONAL POLITICS
1816	Lord Liverpool's wife Louisa unwell during summer.	Property tax defeated in Commons on March 18. Canning joined cabinet. Cold wet weather brought "year without a summer." Violent protests spread through summer and autumn. Spa Fields Riot on December 2.	
1817		Habeas Corpus temporarily suspended. Pentridge Rising in June. Princess Charlotte died November 6	Allied occupation army in France reduced.
1818	**Lord Liverpool passed Church Building Act.**	Parliamentary elections in August. Milan Commission arrived in Italy to gather evidence on Princess Caroline's conduct for divorce proceedings. Wellington joined cabinet as Master of the Ordnance.	Congress of Aix-la-Chapelle. Allied occupation of France ended in November.
1819	**Lord Liverpool's administration won a vote of confidence on a finance measure in Commons, June 7.**	Parliament agreed on a return to cash payments by 1822. Plebeian unrest revived over summer. Peterloo massacre on August 16. Parliament recalled in late November to address unrest. Six Acts passed in late December.	Carlsbad Decrees issued.

DATES	PERSONAL	DOMESTIC POLITICS	INTERNATIONAL POLITICS
1820		Death of George III on January 29. Cato Street Conspiracy to murder the cabinet exposed on February 23. Parliamentary elections in March and April. Cabinet backed Liverpool against George IV on a royal divorce in an April 24 memorandum. Queen Caroline arrived in England on June 5. Evidence against her presented to the Lords. Queen Caroline's Trial began August 17. Proceedings against Caroline dropped November 10. Lord Grenville declined an invitation to form a government on November 25. Canning resigned office in December.	Military revolt in Spain. British state paper in May rejected intervention. Revolution in Naples. Congress of Troppau.
1821	**Lord Liverpool's wife Louisa died on June 11.**	Death of Queen Caroline on August 7. George IV reconciled to Liverpool in November. Sir Robert Peel joined cabinet as home secretary and Grenville faction backed government.	Austria suppressed revolution in Naples and unrest in Piedmont. Revolt in Danubian Principalities. Revolt in Greece.

DATES	PERSONAL	DOMESTIC POLITICS	INTERNATIONAL POLITICS
1822	**Lord Liverpool married Mary Chester, his late wife's friend, in September.**	Castlereagh committed suicide August 12. Canning returned to the cabinet as Foreign Secretary on September 21.	Ferdinand VII appealed for intervention in Spain. Monroe Doctrine proclaimed by US. US recognized independence of Spanish American republics. Conference at Vienna. Congress of Verona.
1823		Budget in February cut taxes while lowering public debt. Daniel O'Connell founded Catholic Association in Ireland.	French army occupied Spain and restored Ferdinand VII. Polignac Memorandum marked Anglo-French de facto acceptance of South American independence.
1824	**Lord Liverpool helped establish the National Gallery.**	Church Building Act provided a second parliamentary grant.	
1825	**Lord Liverpool honored by Bristol merchants and civic leaders in January. He contemplated resigning in May over Catholic Emancipation.**	Parliament banned Catholic Association and other "unlawful societies" in Ireland. Catholic Emancipation rejected by Lords following Lord Liverpool's May 17 Speech against it. Economic Crisis hit in December with a series of bank failures.	Nicholas I succeeded Alexander in Russia. Britain formally recognized Spanish American republics. Egypt intervened in Greece.

DATES	PERSONAL	DOMESTIC POLITICS	INTERNATIONAL POLITICS
1826	**Lord Liverpool quarreled with Wellington over clerical preferment for Gerald Wellesley.**	Lord Liverpool rejected the Bank of England's demand to suspend cash payments and sever tie between sterling and gold. Parliamentary elections in June and July. Corn Laws temporarily suspended to relieve shortages in summer. Proposals for Corn Law reform circulated in cabinet.	Conflict between Portugal and Spain.
1827	**Lord Liverpool suffered crippling stroke on February 17. He relinquished the premiership on April 9.**	Canning succeeded Liverpool and the party split. Canning died August 8. Lord Goderich became prime minister.	Britain, France, and Russia agreed to intervene jointly in Greece. Battle of Navarino.
1828	**Lord Liverpool died on December 4, buried at Hawkesbury Church in Gloucestershire beside his first wife Louisa on December 18.**	Goderich resigned and the Duke of Wellington became Prime Minister. Test and Corporation Acts repealed. Daniel O'Connell won by-election for County Clare in Ireland.	Andrew Jackson elected president of the United States.
1829		Catholic Emancipation passed.	
1830		George IV died on June 26, William IV succeeded to throne. Parliamentary elections. Wellington's administration resigned. Earl Grey formed a Whig-dominated government committed to parliamentary reform.	July Revolution in France. Revolution in Belgium with demands for independence from the Netherlands. Polish Revolution.

DATES	PERSONAL	DOMESTIC POLITICS	INTERNATIONAL POLITICS
1831		Reform bill introduced in Commons on March 1. Parliamentary elections in April and May on reform. Reform Bill passed Commons in September. Lords rejected the reform bill, riots followed.	Polish Revolution suppressed.
1832		New reform bill introduced and passed by Commons. Wellington urged Lords to drop opposition. Reform Act became law on June 7, 1832.	Treaty of Constantinople recognized Greek independence.
1833		Slavery abolished in British Empire.	Netherlands accepted Belgian independence.
1834		Sir Robert Peel became prime minister on December 10.	
1835		Peel resigned April 8. Parliamentary elections. Municipal Corporations Act reformed local government.	
1837		Death of William IV. Victoria succeeded as queen. Parliamentary elections.	
1839			Netherlands formally recognized Belgium. Great powers guaranteed Belgium's neutrality.
1841		Peel formed Tory government on August 30.	

DATES	PERSONAL	DOMESTIC POLITICS	INTERNATIONAL POLITICS
1846		Corn laws repealed. Peel resigned on June 29.	
1848			Revolutions across Europe.

Abbreviations

AC	*Correspondence of Charles Arbuthnot.* Ed. Arthur Aspinall. Camden 3rd ser. 65. London: 1941.
Add MSS	British Library Additional Manuscripts Collection.
AJ	*The Journal of Mrs. Arbuthnot, 1820–1832.* Ed. Francis Bamford and the Duke of Wellington. 2 vols. London: 1959.
BD	*British Diplomacy, 1813–1815: Select Documents Dealing with the Reconstruction of Europe.* Ed. Charles K. Webster. London: 1921.
Canning MSS	Harewood (Canning) Papers, West Yorkshire Record Office.
CC	*Memoirs and Correspondence of Viscount Castlereagh, Second Marquis of Londonderry.* Ed. Charles William Vane, 3rd Marquis of Londonderry. 12 vols. London: 1848–53.
Colchester	*The Diary and Correspondence of Charles Abbot, Lord Colchester.* Ed. Charles, Lord Colchester. 3 vols. London: 1861.
Cookson	J. E. Cookson. *Lord Liverpool's Administration: The Crucial Years, 1815–1822.* Edinburgh: 1995.
Croker MSS	John Wilson Croker Papers, William L. Clements Library. University of Michigan.
Croker Papers	*The Croker Papers: The Correspondence and Diaries of the Late Right Honourable John Wilson Croker, Secretary to the Admiralty from 1809 to 1830.* Ed. Louis J. Jennings. 3 vols. London: 1885.
Dangerous People	Boyd Hilton. *A Mad Bad Dangerous People? England, 1783–1846.* Oxford: 2006.
EA	William Smart. *Economic Annals of the Nineteenth Century.* 2 vols. London: 1910 and 1917.
Farington	*The Farington Diary.* Ed. James Grieg. 8 vols. London: 1923–8.
Foreign Policy	Charles K. Webster. *The Foreign Policy of Castlereagh.* 2 vols. London: 1963.
Fortescue	*Correspondence of King George III from 1760 to December 1783. Printed from the Original Papers in the Royal Archives at Windsor Castle.* Ed. J. W. Fortescue. 6 vols. London: 1927–8.
George IV	*Letters of George IV.* Ed. Arthur Aspinall. 3 vols. Cambridge: 1938.
Greville	*The Greville Memoirs.* Ed. Roger Fulford and Lytton Strachey. 8 vols. London: 1938.
Harrowby MSS	Harrowby Papers. Sandon Hall, Staffordshire.

HMC   Historical Manuscripts Collection.
Hobhouse   *Diary of Henry Hobhouse, 1820–1827.* Ed. Arthur Aspinall. London: 1947.
LC   *Later Correspondence of George III.* Ed. Arthur Aspinall. 5 vols. Cambridge: 1962–70.
Leveson-Gower   *Lord Granville Leveson-Gower (First Earl Granville) Private Correspondence, 1781 to 1821, Edited by his Daughter in Law Castalia Countess Granville.* 2 vols. London: 1916.
Loan   British Library Loan Manuscripts.
Muir, *Napoleon* Rory Muir. *Britain and the Defeat of Napoleon, 1807–1815.* New Haven: 1996.
Muir, *Wellington* Rory Muir. *Wellington: The Path to Victory, 1769–1814* and *Wellington: Waterloo and the Fortunes of Peace, 1814–1852.* New Haven: 2013 and 2015.
PH   *Cobbett's Parliamentary History.*
PD   *Hansard's Parliamentary Debates.*
P of W   *Correspondence of George, Prince of Wales, 1770–1812.* Ed. Arthur Aspinall. 8 vols. New York: 1963–71.
RA   Royal Archives. Windsor Castle.
Regency Memoirs Duke of Buckingham and Chandos. *Memoirs of the Court of England during the Regency, 1811–1820.* 2 vols. London: Hurst and Blackett, 1856.
Sidmouth MSS   Sidmouth Papers. Devon Record Office. Exeter.
TRHS   *Transactions of the Royal Historical Society.*
Ward   *Memoirs of the Political and Literary Life of Robert Plumer Ward.* Ed. Edward Phipps. 2 vols. London: 1850.
WD   *The Dispatches of Field Marshall the Duke of Wellington, during his Various Campaigns in India, Denmark, Portugal, Spain, the Low Countries and France.* Ed. Colonel Gurwood. 8 vols. London: 1844.
WND   *Dispatches, Correspondence and Memoranda of Field Marshall Arthur, Duke of Wellington K.G.* Ed. his son, the Duke of Wellington in continuation of the former series. 8 vols. London: 1857–80.
WSD   *Supplementary Dispatches, Correspondence and Memoranda of Field Marshall Arthur, Duke of Wellington K.G.* Ed. his son, the Duke of Wellington. 15 vols. London: 1858–72.
Yonge   *The Life and Administration of Robert Banks, Second Earl of Liverpool, K.G. Late First Lord of the Treasury. Compiled from Original Documents.* Ed. Charles Duke Yonge. 3 vols. London: 1868.

Introduction

Robert Banks Jenkinson, 2nd Earl of Liverpool and prime minister since 1812, joined his colleague and eventual successor George Canning at a civic banquet held to honor them in Bristol on January 12, 1825. Canning told his wife that the mayor and council really wanted Liverpool and "would take no denial." Sheriffs met the party and escorted them in procession to the Mansion House. Notables from surrounding counties joined Bristol merchants and tradesmen to honor the visitors. The Whig-leaning *Bristol Mercury*, which excoriated what it called the Tory system of William Pitt the Younger and gave Canning only cautious praise, acknowledged Liverpool's talents, while calling his father "one of our most able financiers." The event congratulated ministers for reviving trade and bringing the country through a difficult transition to peace after the long struggle with Revolutionary and Napoleonic France.[1]

Amidst the plaudits, Liverpool thanked Bristol's Merchant Venturers for conferring upon him the freedom of their society. Britain owed commerce its prosperity, which gave the landed interest its present revival. No interest, Liverpool declared, stood alone, "*all were links in a great social chain*, all connected and all dependent on each other for that mutual welfare he was pleased to witness and believed to be increasing."[2] Deliberately pitched to flatter his listeners, Liverpool's words expressed his sincere commitment both to trade and a conception of social relations that guided his public life. With trade the mainspring of British prosperity, he viewed society as an interlocking network of interests governed by a patrician elite acting for the public interest. Its leadership upheld the ordered liberty that secured property and lawful authority while allowing private initiative the widest possible scope. When toasted after dinner, Liverpool replied that his merits lay in good intentions and best efforts for the country. Neither would have succeeded without "the talents of my excellent and able colleagues."[3] Their united efforts, backed by commercial and other great interests, had brought peace and a prosperity that he fervently hoped would continue to increase. A rhetorical flourish captured Liverpool's habit of downplaying his own part and sharing credit with colleagues.

Born in 1770, Liverpool had entered public life with high expectations. Despite his later title, his family were part of the gentry. His father Charles Jenkinson, a political fixer and commercial expert with close ties to George III, had risen to a peerage and seat in Pitt's cabinet. The younger Jenkinson had the eye of both king and prime minster from the start. Early skill in parliamentary debate brought junior office with the respect of opponents and colleagues. As foreign secretary in Henry Addington's government at the age of thirty, Liverpool negotiated the brief peace of Amiens with France. He later served as home secretary (1804–6 and 1807–9), handling Irish unrest and communication between king and cabinet along with the whole range of domestic policy. Reports from magistrates attuned him to concerns of the local political establishments that collaborated with ministers in governing the realm. As war secretary (1809–12) Liverpool guided British strategy and became Wellington's essential partner at home. Leading the House of Lords for seven and a half years under three prime ministers, he defended the government's conduct and managed legislative business. Liverpool's experience made him especially well prepared when he succeeded Spencer Perceval as premier in June 1812.

Overcoming political challenges at the start of his tenure, Liverpool directed the endgame of the struggle against Napoleon and a new war with the United States. He worked closely with Castlereagh to settle a peace that gave Britain unprecedented security. But rather than enjoying political dividends from victory over Napoleon in 1815, Liverpool and his colleagues faced an escalating cycle of conflict. Recession followed the long wars, reviving parliamentary opposition and sparking plebeian unrest in a dangerous cycle. While governments typically face the most strain at their start or end, the hardest period for Liverpool was those middle years between 1815 and 1822.[4] Scandal in 1820, when George IV sought to divorce his long-estranged wife, almost brought down the government. Withstanding those challenges and then recapturing the initiative enabled Liverpool to press his own agenda. Lowering taxes and reforming trade regulations to encourage commercial expansion brought the government out of the extended postwar gloom. Administrative reform met charges of elite parasitism and reduced the cost of government. Success allaying discontent reduced pressures for the organic political change Liverpool sought to avoid. It also vindicated his claim to govern in the interest of the nation as a whole.

The Bristol celebrations thus marked a high point in the halcyon years of Liverpool's administration. Neither private scandal nor personal unpopularity tainted the accomplishments it acclaimed. Liverpool quietly provided the keystone of Britain's political architecture. Not only did he enjoy the personal confidence of cabinet members, but he repeatedly contained differences that risked pulling them apart. His tenure saw an important shift toward collective responsibility as colleagues made clear their resignation would follow his dismissal or departure.[5] Lord Bathurst praised him in 1825 for leading "the most popular administration which this country has for some time had." That popularity rested upon weathering the postwar storm and implementing reforms beyond the scope of those Pitt earlier had envisioned to establish a conservative policy with lasting effect.[6] Holding together an administration for nearly fifteen years amidst considerable upheaval itself marks a noteworthy feat. Only Sir Robert Walpole and William Pitt the Younger among Liverpool's predecessors exceeded his uninterrupted tenure in office. No successor has yet matched it. Prime ministers before and after him dealt effectively with either major foreign crises or equally sharp domestic and economic problems. Liverpool handled both with greater success than most. His long tenure as prime minister in 1827 ended at the height of his popularity in the country and prestige with king and parliament.

Nevertheless, Liverpool faded quickly from public view after a stroke in February 1827 forced his retirement. Why was he largely forgotten over the ensuing decades? Conflicts among the colleagues who succeeded him and the 1832 Reform Act overshadowed Liverpool's memory. Quarrels Liverpool had kept in check overwhelmed his successors. A crisis over parliamentary agency involving contention between the Established Church, Protestant Dissenters, Catholics and politicians eventually focused on reforming the structure of parliamentary representation. Repealing the Test and Corporation Acts and Catholic Emancipation severed an essential link between Church and state even before a Whig-dominated administration led by Lord Grey passed the parliamentary reform Liverpool always opposed. What the Tory politician and writer John Wilson Croker lamented as "a revolution gradually accomplished *by due form of law*" transformed the political order.[7] A relic of that displaced world, Liverpool seemed out of step. Critics ignored his support among dominant groups in the 1820s to frame what became the dominant narrative that he had opposed the ultimately triumphant forces behind reform. Benjamin Disraeli's famous dismissal of Liverpool in 1844 as "the Arch Mediocrity who presided rather than ruled over this Cabinet of Mediocrities" passed substantially unchallenged. Other hostile accounts of his era by Harriet Martineau and Lord Brougham reinforced it. The three-volume biography Charles Duke Yonge compiled from Liverpool's papers in 1868 served to entomb its subject more than enshrine him as a leading statesman.[8]

No circle of protégés upheld Liverpool's posthumous reputation or tried to shape a favorable historical narrative. Canning enjoyed a personal following that carried on his reputation as the standard bearer of liberal Toryism. Sir Robert Peel drew sympathy as a reformer easily cast as a precursor to Gladstonian Liberalism, not least by William Gladstone himself after the Conservative Party split over repealing the Corn Laws in 1846.[9] Byron and Shelley made Castlereagh a caricatured symbol of reaction. The Duke of Wellington's stature as a national hero and his longevity established him as an iconic figure by Victoria's day, albeit one whose early biographers stressed pithy anecdotes and quotable remarks that cast the great man as a comic turn.[10] Liverpool, by contrast, faded into the background. His self-effacing manner and a willingness to share credit, rare among politicians in any age, lowered his profile. More importantly, Liverpool's political management as prime minister consciously diverted attention – and controversy – from himself. What Boyd Hilton aptly calls his "political arts" hid his role.[11]

Not surprisingly, he appeared more the chairman of a cabinet dominated by stronger personalities than its guiding force.

Historians were slow to challenge that verdict. Norman Gash rehabilitated Liverpool with the first complete scholarly biography in 1984. It cast him as first in a line of innovative premiers who shaped the Victorian state despite leading the last great eighteenth-century administration. Earlier scholarship touched on parts of this larger story. W. R. Brock's *Lord Liverpool and Liberal Toryism: 1820 to 1827* (1941) had stressed economic policy to show him as the Tory architect of liberal reform. John Cookson, a New Zealander who studied with Gash at St Andrews University, published *Lord Liverpool's Administration: The Crucial Years, 1815–1822* (1975), a detailed, close study of high politics that brings out the premier's resilience under pressure. Boyd Hilton's *Corn, Cash, Commerce: The Economic Policies of the Tory Governments, 1815–1830* (1977), which examined pragmatic reforms that favored commerce and industry over agriculture, had been revised from a 1973 Oxford doctoral thesis on which Gash had been an examiner.[12] Like Gash's biography, these specialized works focused on Liverpool's tenure as prime minister.

Gash dominated the study of political history of the 1810s through 1850s much as E. P. Thompson set an agenda for social historians. Where Marxism shaped Thompson's outlook, Gash had a conservative temperament and party allegiance that made him sympathize more than most academics with governing elites. His close analysis of political practice transcended an older form of "constitutional history" through a definitive biography of Peel and studies of early Victorian politics.[13] Turning to Liverpool's era after his own long career he noted conservative policies adumbrating a recognizably Conservative party formed under Peel. Liverpool, rather than Castlereagh or Canning, had laid the foundation. Developing those points and trying to uncover more about Liverpool as a personality set Gash's agenda for his biography.[14] Hilton challenged its take on Liverpool in 1987 by contrasting the premier's reputation as a conciliatory figure with the reality of a touchy man quick to take offense. He countered that Liverpool's effectiveness rested upon tactics that kept conflict out of the cabinet and shifted responsibility away from policymakers. When substantive policy differences entered the cabinet after 1822, political discord followed. Hilton raised important questions about how Liverpool governed that he returned to in *A Mad Bad Dangerous People? England, 1783–1846* (2006). The volume also stressed how a fragmented civic culture – "the normative set of values to which most privileged sections of society subscribed" – made consensus elusive and public opinion hard to read.[15] But with no biography of Liverpool published since 1984, the task Gash had noted of producing a fuller study using manuscript sources beyond Liverpool's own papers remained incomplete.

I treat Liverpool from a different vantage point, taking his background and early career as a guide also informed by older, eighteenth-century currents.

Experience with unrest dating from the 1790s, as Malcolm Chase points out, prepared Liverpool and his colleagues to handle disorder in the 1810s and 20s. Attending to concerns local political establishments raised helped them understand problems and forged relationships to manage them.[16] Liverpool himself had faced rioters as a young officer commanding yeoman cavalry and later grappled with issues relating to the food supply before deeper involvement with domestic policy as home secretary. Roger Knight has shown how wartime pressures from the 1790s forced administrative efficiencies and made officials and ministers alike raise their performance. Britain's political system and economy almost buckled under strain twice between 1796 and 1798 and then again in 1807 and 1812. The prolonged struggle with France forced a sharp learning curve in civilian and military affairs that made postwar governance more effective.[17] Liverpool gained essential lessons while building a reputation that secured him the premiership.

Other influences also shaped Liverpool's outlook. Alexis de Tocqueville shrewdly observed how "habits of heart and mind" shaped political societies more deeply than laws. Beliefs and sentiment guided individuals just as they animated the constitutional arrangements, public values, and political organizations within which they operated. Eighteenth-century assumptions that formed Liverpool differed significantly from the ones that set the lineaments of Victorian political culture during the 1820s and 30s.[18] Sympathetically addressing the immediate and recent past to which he responded – a period that included his father's career – brings key factors into sharper focus. Besides offering language and analogies to discuss political issues, the world of Liverpool's youth and preceding generation framed concerns in ways that a stress on day-to-day governance overlooks. If liberal Toryism aimed to uphold the established order, understanding that order and what motivated its defenders becomes all the more important. Hence the need to recover influences that shaped how Liverpool acquired his political arts and determined the ends to which he turned them.

Engaging those points presents Liverpool's life as a study in statesmanship, a term best understood as reconciling principle with circumstance in pursuing the national interest. Showing what Liverpool and other protagonists thought they were doing and why they tried to do it recreates political culture in operation by recovering the density of action in critical periods. The narrative engages larger questions tied with Liverpool's statecraft: the nature of executive government and its relationship with parliament and public opinion; the development of a party system from parliamentary factions and the expansion of national politics to engage provincial interests; shifts in British geopolitical strategy driven by wartime imperatives and efforts to create a stable post-Napoleonic order; and the transition from mercantilist policies to a liberal trading system intended to raise living standards and national prosperity. Public discourse – in language and image – offers another important theme, along with shifts in political culture and expectations. If, as an observer remarked, whoever writes England's history must necessarily write Liverpool's biography, his life and career offer a revealing palimpsest for a pivotal era in British history.[19]

Liverpool defended a constitution in Church and state which had taken form over the eighteenth century. An older family tradition and George III's example served as a lodestar. The king's accession in 1760 provided a single, undivided focus of loyalty that reconciled many alienated during the era of Whig supremacy (1714–1760) to a disposition that favored order, rank, and subordination. The Church of England served as both moral guide, teaching what adherents believed the purest form of Christianity, and an institutional pillar upholding the temporal order. Combined with freedom of worship for other denominations, its ascendancy checked sectarian rivalries that had brought upheaval over the previous century.[20] Crown, parliament, and Established Church together secured ordered liberty and property while uniting disparate interests. Ideas of a balanced political order drew upon Cicero and Polybius through Aristotle to reinforce more recent British custom and practice. Parliament joined principles of monarchy, aristocracy, and democracy in a dynamic equilibrium while ensuring representation for the estates of the realm. Balance checked usurpation, whether by royal tyranny, aristocratic faction, or the people. William Blackstone, Jean de Lolme, and William Paley made mixed government canonical in their successive writings. Representing major interests supplanted the older concept of social orders, but that shift merely formalized longstanding assumptions.[21]

What Brock saw as "a curious mixture of High Toryism and the new ideas of 'economists' and 'philosophers'" reflected Liverpool's conservatism.[22] In opposing parliamentary reform in 1793, he echoed his father's insistence decades earlier on maintaining "that true mediocrity" or equipoise to uphold both due authority and freedom. Extending democracy, aristocracy, or monarchy beyond its proper sphere would unbalance, not improve the constitution. The problem that reforming parliamentary representation sought to address, Liverpool insisted, rested with human nature and not institutions.[23] He also upheld the liberties of an uncensored press and distanced British policy from the authoritarian tendencies of Continental European states after 1815. Neither reactionary nor repressive, Liverpool sought to defend Britain's social and political order along with institutions that he believed gave them expression. He consequently sided with liberal Tories in the 1820s on economic questions and foreign policy while resisting steps like Catholic Emancipation that he feared weakened vital parts of the larger edifice. Sensing that judicious readjustment could be handled safely set him apart from Tories like Lord Eldon, along with his belief that authoritarian policies defeated themselves over the longer term.

Liverpool distinguished speculative theories built upon "ideas of perfection that do not exist" from adapting human institutions to the passions and weaknesses of mankind.[24] The latter had ample precedent in a political system that long accommodated reformist tendencies. Veneration for the institutional edifice and the habit of piecemeal adaptation over radical renovation persisted.[25] Liberal Toryism worked to show that a political system able to initiate reforms in spheres that included law and economics did not itself require change. It adapted Pitt's approach in the 1780s, which had successfully reasserted elite authority in the face of significant outside pressure.[26] Liverpool followed the logic of taking credit for reforms while designing them to limit the innovation rather than make hopeless efforts to defend what is established merely on that ground. Adapting institutions also strengthened the established order by drawing new, rising interests to its side and thereby denying their support to advocates of sweeping change. The conservative policy Gash discerned as a foundation for Peel's achievements sprang from Liverpool's defense of the eighteenth-century constitution.

Liverpool's personal attributes shaped how he developed and implemented policy. Rhetorical skill helped tremendously. Wellington called Liverpool and Pitt the only debaters he had seen who knew exactly what they were going to say before addressing parliament. Besides defending measures or policy, he could provide what Croker called "that *flow* of ideas and language which can run on for a couple of hours, without on the one hand committing the government or, on the other, lowering by commonplaces or inanities the status of a cabinet minister."[27] Opponents credited his fairness in stating their own views. Church of England clergy provided support beyond Westminster that reflected Liverpool's moral propriety and his political principles. A shift in political culture to value a discreet manner, personal reserve, and an image of the statesman as orator and legislator played to his strengths.[28] Mastery of parliamentary and administrative procedure helped deflect pressure and guide deliberations. Knowledge and experience enabled Liverpool to operate strategically, often anticipating problems to deflect them where possible. He grew from slips and errors in his early career. Judgement forged by experience helped him delegate effectively while retaining ultimate control. Liverpool thus quietly imposed a clear lead on his cabinet that Pitt and North before had not managed which made his administration far stronger despite facing much greater pressures.[29]

Personal reserve and a temperamental aversion to publicity, however, masked that authority. Lacking anything like charisma, Liverpool had neither the charm to conciliate and persuade nor the forceful personality to overawe. Contemporaries in the 1790s thought him shy and awkward. Early friends mocked his serious demeanor, often playing jokes at his expense. A wit later described the tall, gaunt young politician as always looking "as if he had been on the rack three times and saw the wheel preparing for a fourth."[30] Satirical prints depicted him with a worried, careworn expression. Colleagues during his premiership complained of his nervous fidgeting. Often misreading social cues, he handled direct personal interactions awkwardly. Liverpool's chance actions had "the knack of becoming grotesque" in a way that indicates a lack of self-awareness and an awkward manner that has to be set alongside other qualities.[31] Partly for that reason, Pitt described him in 1804 as better suited to give wise counsel than decide any great question. Growing confidence muted the anxieties of youth by 1808, but his acute nervousness returned with successive crises and growing ill-health from 1817.

Other factors compensated. Formidable determination stood behind his diffident outward manner. As a boy returning to school at Charterhouse, he faced down a highwayman and later testified against the man in open court. Although a dutiful son, he stubbornly resisted his father's opposition to his marriage to Louisa Hervey and eventually won approval for the match that made their relationship stronger. A colleague's observation that "he always quotes his father" reflected filial piety along with the elder Jenkinson's deep expertise.[32] Loyalty built trust, not least from George III with whom Liverpool became close. Indeed, he held fast to their legacy differing with Pitt only when the premier was at odds with his father or the king. He also showed loyalty to friends, even when, like his occasional rival Canning, they gave scant ground to deserve it. Pitt's other protégés noted Liverpool's willingness to subordinate personal interest or ambition to their collective service. Collegiality along with competence strengthened his standing. It came as no surprise when the cabinet turned to Liverpool after Perceval's death. Nor did his insistence on sharing credit during the 1825 Bristol celebration with his "able and excellent colleagues."

With their help, Liverpool guided Britain through a turbulent age. Looking back decades later, the Reverend Sydney Smith remarked on the "old fashioned, orthodox, hand-shaking, bowel disturbing passion of fear" prevalent in the 1810s and 1820s. The threat had been so great, he told the Bishop of London, that you would have gladly given up half your property to secure the rest.[33] Incidents from the Spa Fields Riot in 1816 to the Cato Street Conspiracy in 1820 heightened unease. Memories of the French Revolution cast a long shadow. Rather than the lurid imagining of plebeian insurrection satirists lampooned, the danger involved a more subtle erosion of the legitimacy that upheld government authority. Liverpool had seen the dynamic unfold in France as a young visitor in 1789. Spiraling disorder and the collapse of France's governing institutions enabled ambitious men to grasp at power that few managed to hold for long. Liverpool and his colleagues feared a similar cycle in Britain if a Whig cabinet, unable to resist or accommodate popular demands, replaced them. Sweeping political reform might endanger Britain's entire governing structure. Liverpool's ambitious exercise in political managerialism to prevent or postpone constitutional reform confounded opposition Whigs and radicals alike.[34] He reconciled interest groups within the social chain he invoked at Bristol and vindicated the established political order by showing it could adapt on its own terms. Changes that followed his death came more smoothly because of his success.

CHAPTER I

Antecedents and Upbringing

WILLIAM WORDSWORTH FAMOUSLY described the child as "father of the man," wishing for his days "to be / Bound each to each by natural piety."[1] Childhood, with a generous portion of filial piety, set the course for Robert Banks Jenkinson's life and career. Early loss of his mother, the world of his Jenkinson relations, and his father's political connections bent the twig from an early age. His family history highlights aspects of British politics and culture that influenced the future prime minister, along with particular differences that set him apart from contemporaries and colleagues. The Jenkinsons sprang from the provincial gentry that had governed England for a century or more. Charles Jenkinson took a common path for ambitious gentlemen without an estate to inherit by pursuing an administrative career that led him into parliament, while his wife's family used a fortune made in India along with ties forged there as a bridge into English society. Young Robert was raised to enter public life. Connections gave him an advantageous start.

Amelia Jenkinson gave birth to her only child at Hawkesbury in Gloucestershire on June 7, 1770, roughly sixteen months after marrying the rising politician Charles Jenkinson. Childbirth proved too much for the nineteen-year-old mother who died within a few weeks of her son's christening at St. Margaret's Westminster in London on June 29. Shattered by Amelia's death, Charles Jenkinson sought advice from the noted physician Anthony Addington, who also attended the Pitt family and occasionally served as Lord Chatham's spokesman in society, before spending three months in solitude to recover. His mother Amarantha Jenkinson took the baby into her care promising that "should God spare my life the loss of a mother I will endeavor to supply to the best of my power." She hoped that "time, religion, and good sense" would carry Jenkinson through his loss.[2] The pathos of an infant left without his mother struck a resonant chord in the age of sensibility, but it also underlined the predicament father and son faced. The forty-two-year-old widower devoted himself entirely to his son's upbringing and his own official career. Those two sides of his life fit closely together as the ambitious Jenkinson invested future hopes in his son.

Charles Jenkinson had married Amelia Watts at St. Marylebone in February 1769 after reportedly courting in secret.[3] Prudential considerations made Jenkinson take a wealthy heiress as his bride, but the evident sorrow of a highly reserved and unexpressive man on whom her loss fell hard suggests they enjoyed an affectionate marriage. Amelia had been born in India to William Watts, a Scottish protégé of Robert Clive, and his Anglo-Indian wife Frances. Watts served as chief of the East India Company factory at Cossimbazar and planned the overthrow of Siraj Ud Daulah in Bengal, for which he received a £114,000 grant from the nawab's treasury and appointment as governor of Ft. William in Madras. Watts' published account of the story, entitled *Memoirs of the Revolution in Bengal*, went through several editions.[4] Having shaken the pagoda tree to great effect, he returned to England with his family in 1759, purchasing a house in Hanover Square and later making arrangements to acquire an estate at Hanslope in Berkshire that remained incomplete upon his early death aged forty-two in 1764. That year Jenkinson had observed the company's activities had "become much too big for the management of a body of merchants" and would likely "end in a parliamentary enquiry." His responsibilities as Secretary of the Treasury had drawn him deeply into its political and financial matters. Later he would serve on successive committees that laid the foundation for Pitt's India Act in 1784 which established a system to oversee the company's operations.[5] Jenkinson's involvement with Indian policy drew him into the Anglo-Indian network that included the Watts family.

Amelia's mother, Frances, had a more exotic background as the daughter of East India Company official Edward Croke and Isabella Beizor, whose Portuguese surname belied Eurasian descent. Frances Croke had grown up at the intersection of Indian and European society when neither race nor culture drew sharp boundaries.[6] Her marriage to Watts was the third of four unions, and the most successful and long-lasting of them all. Frances's close relationship with Siraj Ud Daulah's mother, the Begum Amina, had enabled her to remain safely with her children in Cossimbazar when her husband surrendered the fort there before moving to French-controlled Chandernagore. She and the children thereby escaped the sack of Calcutta. Later reminiscences about her protector eventually led Frances Watts to be known as the Begum Johnson. England never suited her. She returned to India after Watts' death, where marriage to William Johnson ended with estrangement, and became a noted society hostess who entertained Warren Hastings, Lord Cornwallis, and the Wellesley brothers at her Calcutta house on Clive Street. Charles Jenkinson helped with her affairs, including the effective dissolution of her last marriage. He kept her apprised of her grandson's progress. The Begum Johnson's relationship with the Jenkinsons, which included correspondence with her grandson, lasted until she died in 1812.

Robert Banks Jenkinson had a connection with India that went beyond what a biographer called "a tincture of Indian blood through his mother's side of the family."[7] Her family participated in an Anglo-Indian world that bridged a cultural gap during the eighteenth century while playing a central part in founding the British Raj. Charles Jenkinson's long involvement with Indian affairs from London made his son's appointment to the India Board in April 1793 a natural step. Young Jenkinson's parentage interestingly drew no public comment. Perhaps most contemporaries did not know the details of his mother's background. Few let George Canning forget his mother had been an actress. Ethnic stereotypes provided a commonplace shorthand. Henry Dundas often appeared in a kilt or plaid to highlight his rough Scots manner, while depicting Edmund Burke with whiskey, potatoes, and rosary associated him with Ireland.[8] A later generation would not have ignored the fact that a politician had a Eurasian mother. Ideas of racial hierarchy emerged from the late 1780s with restrictions on employing Anglo-Indians. East India Company officials increasingly sent Eurasian children to make their careers in Britain.[9] Tensions leading to the Indian Mutiny raised further barriers. Lord Salisbury notoriously called Dadabhi Naroji in 1892 a "black man" English voters would not accept as an MP. The world that formed young Jenkinson worked on very different premises.

Although the Jenkinson family had a less exotic pedigree, their story also reflects deep currents. Originally Welsh, the name derived from a patronymic for Shenkin. Anthony Jenkinson, the Lancashire-born younger son whose prosperous father owned several inns and other property, was the first Englishman to penetrate into Central Asia. Edward VI, Mary I, and Elizabeth employed him as an agent to the Turkish Sultan and Russian Tsars.[10] As a founding member of the Muscovy Company, Jenkinson's father-in-law John Marshe promoted his career, including four expeditions – in 1558, 1561, 1566, and 1571 – to negotiate on the company's behalf. The first was a journey through Kazan and Astrakhan to the Caspian Sea and Central Asia. Jenkinson wrote a detailed account Richard Hakluyt later published. Described as having been further into Asia than any Englishman had previously ventured, he became a freeman of the Mercers Company in November 1560. His narrative provided one of the first European reports on Central Asia and the Caspian since trade with that region had declined as new oceanic routes opened.[11] The second expedition introduced Jenkinson to Tsar Ivan IV, and he returned in 1572 at the tsar's request.[12]

Granted armorial bearings in 1568–9, Anthony Jenkinson solidified his family's status with land in Oxfordshire and Gloucestershire that included the manor of Hawkesbury.[13] Education and property gave families a springboard for social advancement over generations. Local status bolstered by metropolitan connections and wealth derived from trade or the professions helped consolidate or extend their position among the county elite. Profits from land often then facilitated further advancement. Such aristocratic families as the Cecils, Spencers, and Russells began their rise under the Tudors. More broadly, the successful gentry became the foundation of England's governing elite. Anthony Jenkinson's travels

set him apart, but his family followed a common path among those who served
the state and dominated local government.

Subsequent generations stayed closer to home, extending their landholdings
and ties within local society. Robert Jenkinson's marriage to the daughter of Sir
John Banks, a Dorset gentleman whose family would represent Corfe Castle from
1660, brought the Banks name into the family.[14] Their son Robert Jenkinson
stayed neutral during the civil wars of the 1640s, albeit with difficulty. He served
on local commissions from 1647 and represented Oxfordshire in three parliaments under Oliver Cromwell before he was created a baronet in 1661.[15] Sir
Robert's son attended Oxford University and then held county office and entered
parliament. Friendship with Henry Hyde, second Earl of Clarendon, provided
connections at court. A High Churchman opposed to excluding the future James
II from the throne, Jenkinson lost office in 1688 after refusing consent to James
II's plans to remove penal laws or religious tests. Elected as MP for Oxfordshire
in 1689 with backing from the Tory magnate Lord Abdingdon, he held the seat
until he died in 1710.[16]

The Jenkinson family operated within an emerging Tory tradition that determined their position under the first two Hanoverians. Serving in parliament
helped to promote local interests – and claim status in Oxfordshire society –
rather than provide the path to an official career. Contentment "with playing a
spectator's role in the Commons" typified country gentlemen while distinguishing an active from a passive political class.[17] Passivity, however, never meant indifference. As Tory gentlemen of High Church principles, the Jenkinsons held a
distinct place in the political landscape. Robert Harley called the second baronet
in 1791 a "country" supporter with a hardening anti-court stance. His successor
was later a "worthy patriot" and "Tory patriot." Jenkinson's name appeared on a
1712 list of the October Club that demanded peace with France. He shared the
resistance to excise taxes, government expense, and interference with trade and
local affairs that made Tory views resonate beyond the elite.[18]

Toryism joined loyalty to the Church of England and popular patriotism to
link gentlemen politicians with the crowd. It distrusted Roman Catholics and
Protestant Nonconformists, with the latter blamed for the upheaval of the 1640s
and 50s. The second Sir Robert Jenkinson not only voted against impeaching
Dr. Henry Sacheverell for attacking non-conformists as a danger to Church and
state, but also entertained the High Church cleric during a local tour.[19] Oxford
University was a center of high churchmanship that educated both clergy and
gentlemen, including the Jenkinson family. High church principles joined an
elevated view of monarchy with commitment to a religious establishment and
belief in the state's duty as a divinely ordained entity to protect and promote the
Church 's interests. Other theological premises involving the apostolic succession, qualified primacy of dogma, and the emphasis on sacramental grace set high
churchmen apart from latitudinarian Anglicans as well as reformed Protestant

churches that had abandoned episcopacy.[20] The Jenkinsons' persistent commitment to Church and king principles epitomized eighteenth-century Toryism.

Although Sir Robert's narrow ambitions limited the effects, George I's accession set the Jenkinsons on the wrong side of the political divide. Harley had recognized in 1707 that the days had passed in which a mixed administration of Whigs and Tories might work. He anticipated in its place a self-regulating two-party system operating "like a door which turns both ways upon its hinges to let in each party as it grows triumphant." The Hanoverians slammed the door, however, and Sir Robert Walpole then established a system that kept it bolted shut.[21] Old Corps or Court Whigs who dominated national politics and government until the 1750s thought it entirely legitimate for the crown to rely upon men like themselves who had proven their commitment to the Hanoverian dynasty and the political settlement forged out of the Glorious Revolution. They had no concerns over the consolidation of government authority during the long decades of Whig supremacy as they believed it provided firm, decisive leadership while preserving public liberties.[22] Their rivals and many in the country disagreed.

Lord Shelburne thought confounding Tories with Jacobites loyal to the Stuarts distorted their character and principles. Tories were

> the landed interest of England who desired to see an honorable, dignified government conducted with due economy and due subordination, in opposition to the Whigs who courted the mob in the first instance and the next the commercial interest.[23]

His view carried little weight for a king who thought them skeptical at best of his claim to the throne. Suggesting the nation largely shared Tory prejudices merely convinced Whigs they could maintain control over parliament only if the king provided them the necessary "ways and means."[24] Political stabilization after 1715 meant checking the influence of popular opinion generally as the middling classes and others were marginalized along with Tories who picked up the demotic mantle Court Whigs abandoned to uphold oligarchy.[25] Given the resources available to Whigs and the scope for Whig sheriffs and justices of the peace to exert influence during elections, why the Tory party declined seems less a question than how it survived at all.[26]

It did survive, but exclusion reinforced a mentality forged in opposition. Tories kept to their estates, only briefly coming to London for meetings of Parliament. They retained ideological cohesion, capacity for concerted political action, and considerable economic power.[27] A subculture persisted among squires, parsons, and at Oxford University, where ministers abandoned hopes of support before the first decade of Hanoverian rule ended. Besides the literary power sustained by the university, clergy it educated became formidable propagandists in parishes.[28] Popular Toryism aligned gentry, tradesmen, and skilled artisans behind "Church

and king" language which set communal solidarity against grasping individualism.
Its festive, communal, and royalist culture marked one side of the divide created
by seventeenth-century religious and political differences.[29] Tories opposed all the
trends of the age – a party machine, moneyed men, efforts at centralization and
the fiscal–military state that emerged in consequence of Britain's rise as a great
power – and they survived at the local level and in the world of ideas. Certain
patterns of argument retained their appeal. Faced with the duty of supporting
established authority, even some Whigs borrowed doctrines on kingship that
resonated more than the cooler idioms of natural law, contract, and coordinate
powers. Shifting sovereignty from the crown alone to the crown-in-parliament
made Tory arguments palatable to a wider section of the elite. Thoughtful Court
Whigs adapted some of them to defend the balanced constitution forged after
1688 as a repudiation of both the republican anarchy and monarchial tyranny
that had plagued the seventeenth century.[30] A synthesis that emerged by mid-
century would shape Robert Banks Jenkinson's outlook as he entered public life.

The Jenkinsons remained political outsiders. Two of Sir Robert Jenkinson's
three sons served in parliament and succeeded to the baronetcy. Besides sharing
their father's Tory views, the two elder brothers lacked ambition for a political
career. Sir Robert Banks Jenkinson, was named to the Stuart pretender in 1722
as a probable supporter, the same year he returned to parliament unopposed. His
younger brother Charles was more willing to accommodate the Hanoverians and
joined the Royal Horse Guards Blue, then called the Oxford Blues, through the
influence of General Sir John Cope. Colonel Jenkinson commanded the Blues
at Dettingen in 1745, where his gallantry earned George II's admiration.[31] He
had married Amarantha Cornwall, who gave birth to Charles Jenkinson in 1729.

Intended for a career in the Church, Jenkinson attended Charterhouse
School, where he began a long friendship with William Jones, later noted as a
high church theologian and controversialist, before matriculating at University
College, Oxford. He became friends there with George Horne, another important high church figure whose career intersected with Jenkinson's own. The Duke
of Marlborough and Lord Macclesfield won the young gentleman to the Whig
interest. Abandoning his clerical ambitions, Jenkinson declined the offer of a
church living from an uncle with Whig connections to pursue a political career.
Family tradition describes him as writing "electioneering verses and squibs for the
Whigs" as Sir William Blackstone did for the Tories. Mocked as Squire Lickspittle
and Tall Boy, Jenkinson faced charges of apostasy in the press suggesting that his
own attacks stung as much as the change in party.[32]

Given family tradition, Charles Jenkinson's move to the Whigs seemed to
match in conceptual terms at least the distance Anthony Jenkinson had travelled two centuries before. The reality proved more complex. Advancement
meant aligning with a political interest that could offer a talented man preferment. Horace Walpole's quip that "all the sensible Tories I ever knew were

Jacobites or became Whigs; those that remained Tories remained fools" under-lined the limited opportunities available even to Hanoverian Tories.[33] As heir to a younger son, Charles Jenkinson had to make his own way. He secured through Marlborough an unpaid position as private secretary to Lord Holderness, an experienced diplomat and secretary of state, that introduced Jenkinson to depart-mental business and foreign affairs.[34] On George Grenville's recommendation, Lord Bute appointed Jenkinson his under-secretary in 1761 with responsibility for his correspondence, circulating letters with the king and cabinet and drafting replies. He drew up a paper for Bute, a political novice, outlining a secretary of state's duties in both domestic and foreign matters, along with subordinates' work and the office's general management.[35] Where instructions had been given verbally, the tidy minded Jenkinson began making a précis to improve efficiency and ensure that clerks completed their tasks.

Jenkinson moved to the center of power as private secretary to Bute who became First Lord of the Treasury in 1762. Managing relations with the press and London merchants broadened his contacts. Jenkinson compiled the list of Whig officeholders Bute used to retaliate against political opponents with the "massa-cre of Pelhamite Innocents" that purged dependants from lesser office as well as Grafton and Rockingham. Alluding to The Duke of Newcastle's role in securing the Hanoverian succession, some quipped that Bute "had turned out every man brought in by his Grace except the king." Jenkinson thought the patronage the ministry's opponents had enjoyed "properly disposed of will now make others more firmly attached to us." [36] As observers saw his hand in Bute's actions their reputations became entwined.

When George Grenville succeeded Bute in April 1763, Jenkinson went to the Treasury to manage patronage, elections, and parliamentary business. Colonial and financial policy also became his métier with work on the Molasses and Stamp Acts, plus research on the laws of navigation and trade that led to the Revenue Act of 1764.[37] He left office with Grenville in 1765, but their relationship had already frayed. When Jenkinson accepted appointment to the Admiralty board in December, Grenville declined to answer his note and "forbid his porter ever to let him into his house again."[38] The break said more about the prickly Grenville than Jenkinson, who thereafter avoided tying his fortunes too closely to any political figure or faction. He became instead the "longest-lived and most abused" among a group known as the king's friends who contributed expertise and administra-tive skills to carry on government business along with continuity over a succes-sion of short administrations in the 1760s. Loyal primarily to the Crown, they developed an ethos of executive government amidst the ebb and flow of politics. George III, praising their "uniform attachment to his person," found a kindred spirit in their diligence, efficiency, and attention to duty.[39] What John Morley later called "the assumption that a benevolent providence created the people of England in order that they might be governed by a select number of patrician families" also inclined Jenkinson – and other able men proud of their talents – to align with the king rather than an aristocratic patron.[40]

Critics, however, deemed a threat both their commitment to royal prerogative and the administrative continuity they provided. Bute and Jenkinson were denounced as "ministers behind the curtain" who did not account to parliament for their advice. Jenkinson increasingly replaced Bute in opposition demonology, and Horace Walpole called him by 1770 the "director or agent of all His Majesty's secret councils." An almost legendary dislike seems to have derived from something like physical repulsion. Jenkinson's personal reserve and humorless manner did not help. Admitting he was "eminently ugly," Hester Piozzi still found him "a very particularly agreeable man, unaffectedly good humored, and pleasant in his voice and manner." Others likened him to a dark lantern, claiming that "something impervious and inscrutable" marked his demeanor.[41] Justified or not, the image set the touchy Jenkinson's public reputation. He curtly told Thomas Townshend in 1770 during a Commons debate that he sprang from a family "as antient [sic] and as good as" Townshend's own.[42] Burke's son would write facetiously in 1791 of having dined with "secret influence" in *propria persona*. Jenkinson's image as a player among gentlemen in the political game became a sore point that missed his true role.[43]

Jenkinson began his career at the start of a watershed decade. George III's accession shifted politics as the whole disposition in favor of order, rank, and subordination, which included the intelligentsia and many common people along with the elite, now found a single object for their loyalty. His ardent commitment to the Church of England helped reconcile Tories to the Hanoverian dynasty. Besides consolidating the social elite, it appealed to others, including Samuel Johnson, who recognized George III as they had not done his two predecessors. Dissenters showed less enthusiasm, often seeing the king's Anglican piety as a mark of Toryism.[44] Although he sought partnership with ministers rather than the personal rule critics alleged, George III broke with his predecessor's willingness to let Whig leaders monopolize office and develop policy among themselves.[45] The political reconfiguration for which he bore partial responsibility brought "country party" Whig complaints against party government, Hanover, and the Old Corps Whig system together with an older Toryism of personal loyalty and prerogative rights.[46]

George III sought to safeguard the constitution from oligarchy by ruling independently of party, but removing Newcastle opened what Horace Walpole called an "era of faction." Conflicts over taxes, debt, and colonial policy following the Seven Years War, which paralleled discontent after 1815, made forming stable governments difficult. The reconfiguration of politics created space for views associated with hitherto marginalized country party Whigs or Tories.[47] Some independent Whigs, however, appealed to groups outside parliament which demanded other changes to further extend the revolutionary settlement of 1688.

Drawing arguments from Robert Gordon and John Trenchard's *Cato's Letters* that attacked monopolies in trade, politics, and religion, they framed a critique that went beyond attacking the oligarchic system of the Old Corps Whigs to challenge elite authority generally. Agitation fueled by John Wilkes, the libertine publicist excluded by the Commons as MP for Middlesex, mobilized plebeian support that prefigured agitation in the 1790s. Jenkinson and many others saw Wilkes' idea of liberty as a dangerous brand of political licentiousness which challenged both social and political order.[48] Polarization on principle complemented the fragmentation and reworking of allegiances in the 1760s. "Tory" returned to use as an opposition epithet for those who backed ministers and showed deference to royal prerogative. Since this usage involved principles more than pedigree, Tory often became a label for apostate Whigs.[49]

Jenkinson's opinions reinforced perceptions of his political role to cast him as a Tory. His part in framing colonial policy and reforming the East India Company's management taught how interests could manipulate public opinion to serve their own ends. Jenkinson opposed publishing the report of a parliamentary committee on India in 1773 as likely to hinder gathering information for legislation. Secret committees, he had argued earlier, were the most efficient way to act quickly. Publishing an inquiry into expenditure during the American War risked mischief by disseminating ill-founded charges which only fueled malicious opposition.[50] Jenkinson tied deference to executive government with upholding parliamentary supremacy in America. Failing to exercise powers claimed in theory meant losing them. He saw American opposition as resistance not to a particular tax, but to parliament's legislative authority.[51] The seemingly fragile basis of political order in the 1760s and the American crisis only heightened his suspicion of those like Wilkes who challenged it. While Jenkinson told the Commons in 1778 that "the principles of liberty always diminish the force of government," he also praised Britain's balanced constitution which maintained "that true mediocrity which is the support of all due authority on the one hand, and of true freedom on the other." Upholding authority, however, took precedence now because challenges at home and abroad showed the danger that weakness posed.[52]

Political theology shaded Jenkinson's views as the Established Church's supporters rallied against threats. An implicit elite consensus had extended divine right beyond the sovereign's person to sanction the social and political hierarchy as a whole. High Churchmen went further in their view of the state as a divinely ordained entity with responsibility to protect the church.[53] Jenkinson publicly defended William Laud, architect of Charles I's religious policy, while attacking "the despicable tribe" of David Hume, Viscount Bolingbroke, and Jean-Jacques Rousseau, whom he called an ingenious madman. Unsurprisingly, he lamented how "under the notion of religious liberty, the solemn truths of religion itself are treated with contempt and skeptical infidelity abounds."[54] His resistance to ending the requirement that Oxford students subscribe to the Thirty Nine Articles reflected a particularly Tory view of the 1630s and 40s that resonated long into the next century. Citing the dangers of kindling theological disputes, he defended the ecclesiastical polity as it stood and urged that MPs "stir not the plague from the pit in which it is buried" by undue concessions to dissent.[55] Doing so threatened both the church's integral part in the constitution and the subordination drawn from theological principles that upheld social and political order. Extending toleration beyond its present limits in England – which provided dissent more indulgence than under any other well governed state – threatened the peace of civil society and its governing framework.[56] With such High Church clergy polemicists as George Horne and William Jones, who had kept alive the positive usage of "Tory," Jenkinson's patronage network suggests that if he had different principles before joining the Whigs in 1754 he never quite shed them.[57]

During his early tenure, North "wielded the House of Commons in all its moods as no minister since Walpole," but his position weakened as the American crisis grew. Effective as a peacetime minister, he lacked the assertiveness to direct a war. Ministers handled their own business within a "government of departments." North admitted lacking "vigor and resolution" to end the situation despite realizing the ministry needed a single figure "to govern the whole and direct every measure."[58] Jenkinson stood beside North with his ally John Robinson, as "two sturdy inelegant figures" who drew antipathy while serving as hard-working props to the faltering system.[59] If Burke and Horace Walpole accused him of subverting the constitution through secret influence with the king, Jenkinson privately insisted that his aid "was never called for but in emergencies when they cannot do without me."[60]

Jenkinson became secretary at war in late 1778, a post outside the cabinet with responsibility to defend army estimates in parliament and direct access to the king. Reporting on politics and policy to George III drew him into giving advice which fueled the impression of illegitimate influence. Jenkinson publically denied that the king was his own minister with his servants hiding behind the throne.[61] Nonetheless, he worked with him and Robinson to keep a demoralized North in place. A hostile newspaper indeed had called North in late 1775 "the humble slave of the Junto controlled by Charles Jenkinson."[62] Twice North proposed giving Jenkinson the exchequer and thought him "by much the fittest person in England" to direct the finances. George III, however, feared North might then retire. Jenkinson often referred to North's "low spirits." He came to view the prime minister's vacillation with contempt and thought his indecisive transaction of business hurt the public service.[63] Their relations became equivocal, even though North had promoted his brother-in-law Charles Cornwall's election as speaker of the Commons and offered Jenkinson a cabinet post when Germain left office. With the significant exception of Dundas, Jenkinson was the only man in the Commons by January 1782 that North thought willing or able to defend government policy.[64]

News of defeat at Yorktown brought a crisis in early 1782 when support evaporated for an administration that hitherto had more lives than a cat.[65] Jenkinson and other advisors sought to form a broad government after North's fall, but George III yielded to the inevitable in calling Rockingham to form an administration in March 1782. Having lost office, Jenkinson thought it best to absent himself from the Commons, unless "friends should desire my attendance." Even before Rockingham's administration fell after his death on July 1, Shelburne approached the king about bringing Jenkinson into office.[66] Shelburne's government, with William Pitt the Younger at the exchequer, lacked stability because its leader had no personal following. His notoriously difficult personality blighted his career. Leading a ministry pieced together out of dissidents from other factions, Shelburne felt compelled to broaden his support with overtures to North. While Jenkinson, along with Robinson and Dundas, pressed their former chief to back Shelburne, William Eden urged instead an alliance with Charles James Fox, who now led the Rockingham Whigs. Robinson complained that North seemed to acquiesce, but "afterwards somehow or other it is drawn back and nothing gets done."[67]

Shelburne told George III on February 24, 1783 that he had determined to resign after a series of defeats in the Commons. Despite the king's urging, Pitt declined to fill Shelburne's place. Jenkinson worked to build an alternative ministry, but talk that he, Dundas, and Lord Gower might form the basis for an effective administration proved impractical. When Thomas Coke rose before the Commons on March 24, Jenkinson intended to oppose any address calling upon the king to appoint a ministry likely to enjoy public confidence as a violation of the royal prerogative. Pitt, however, made no objection to the motion and declined stepping forward himself. His conduct, which Jenkinson called inexplicable, squelched an alternative to coalition. George III thought Pitt had acted falsely, leaving him to be treated by the Commons as a puppet and Jenkinson without the means to avoid it. Deeply frustrated, the king turned to North who insisted on a coalition with Fox and the Duke of Portland as its nominal head.[68]

George III never truly accepted the Fox–North coalition. The pressures of forming a government prompted him to draft a statement in late March abdicating the throne in favor of his eldest son. By "storming the closet" Fox and North usurped the king's prerogative to choose his own ministers and rendered him "a cipher in the trammels of any self-created band." The need to end a conflict which disrupted government had brought George III to the brink of retiring to Hanover. Having openly worked to avoid the coalition he described as "this thralldom," the king hoped that only a few months would elapse before "men of abilities and character will relieve me."[69] Others also found the combination of quondam adversaries unnatural. If Jenkinson and Dundas joining with Shelburne, Pitt and others of Lord Chatham's party struck North and Burke as a "union of Jacobites and Tories with Republicans," Fox and North themselves were an even sharper contrast. Pitt landed a telling blow in noting how "gentlemen talked of forgiving animosities and altering their political opinions with as much ease as they could change their gloves." As an independent Whig like his father, Pitt was closer to Fox than North who had fought Rockingham and Burke through the 1770s.[70] While rhetoric had long invoked an ethos of public virtue, politicians increasingly recognized that their character rested upon principled consistency and disinterested service to the public good. The Fox–North coalition seemed a triumph of self-interest over principle.

Jenkinson worked with Robinson and others to undermine its foundations, reporting in September that "a certain personage has not in the least altered in his disposition to the present ministers… He grants whatever he can take from them again, but nothing permanent." Fox, Portland, and North realized that "the king is personally stronger and themselves weaker," while Fox built his hopes "on the present disunited state of opposition."[71] Indian affairs gave the coalition's enemies their chance. Fox introduced a measure to reform the East India Company in November after Shelburne's defeat prevented Dundas from moving forward on a bill. The proposal included replacing the existing proprietors and directors with seven commissioners nominated by parliament for set terms. Giving commissioners who could not be dismissed control over subordinate appointments put Indian patronage at the disposal of ministers whose influence would last after they left office.

Even before Robinson openly broke with North, he and Jenkinson mobilized resistance to the bill. George III secretly gave authority to state that any peer voting for the India Bill that reached the House of Lords "is not *his* friend."[72] Not since Walpole's abortive Excise Bill in 1733 had a measure excited such controversy. The young Spencer Perceval, a future prime minister, thought it erected an aristocratic power over the state. Another observer warned against the boldest and most artful effort any subject had attempted since the Glorious Revolution of 1688.[73] Pitt described the India Bill as forcing the king to "take the diadem off own head and place it on the head of Mr. Fox" by transferring to him the immense patronage of the East India Company. Jenkinson's role, however, led a coalition supporter to call the real question "whether Charles Fox or Charles Jenkinson should be minister." An answer of sorts came on December 17 when the Lords rejected Fox's bill. Two nights later, a messenger from the king required Fox, Portland, and North to deliver their seals of office "as audiences on such occasions must be unpleasant."[74]

Wondering if "it be not a dangerous discovery that that king can keep his favorite minister against a majority of the House of Commons," Gibbon called the struggle between king and coalition a revolution.[75] Jenkinson framed it as a majority in the House of Commons opposing the king, Lords, and the people. Pitt offered merely the vehicle "to support the king, who has I think been personally ill-treated by some & whose authority and rights have been invaded."[76] Where Burke had famously justified party action during the 1770s as a brake on executive power, Jenkinson believed overthrowing the coalition defended the balanced constitution against aristocratic faction. The outcome, however, remained unclear for months. An opposition wit called Pitt's ministry a "minced pie administration" fit only for the festive season. Jenkinson helped Robinson and Dundas keep it in office by counting votes and planning for debates. Despite overtures to Fox for a junction at North's expense – and many saw Pitt and Fox "as formed to act together" from shared principles and abilities – the government held on until a spring election won a Commons majority that rendered it unassailable.[77] George III had helped recreate a political world that accorded with his aspirations on taking the throne. Despite the electoral management to secure Pitt's majority in 1784, popular sentiment clearly backed the king against Fox. The struggle tapped continuities reflected in Jenkinson's own career along with a loyalist backlash that continued into the 1790s.[78] Even before the French Revolution presented a new threat, Pitt and his friends prided themselves on having defended king and constitution against factionalism.

Jenkinson remained on the periphery despite his efforts on Pitt's behalf and standing "ready to accept office, to support without office, as is most agreeable to the wishes and opinions of those who are at the head of the Government."[79] Robinson liked Pitt whom he described as "a delicate, high spirited mind, beset by *Boys*, theoreticks, & prejudiced persons, but which by gentle training, civil treatment & address will be led to what *is right*." Dundas would soon guide the premier as Jenkinson might wish.[80] Pitt, however, anticipated efforts to manage him. Having been forced to accept Lord Thurlow as Chancellor, he resisted other representatives of court influence. Preferring a Whig reunion. Pitt made early overtures to his father's surviving friends. He only looked further when that plan failed and remained suspicious of the king's friends.[81] Jenkinson's reputation brought difficulties. Aiding the government made no difference. He supported ministers from loyalty to the king, but could not grant implicit confidence "till I have seen more of their behavior." Revealingly, given his reputation for intrigue, Jenkinson remarked that "I always hated the character of a political adventurer" disposed too readily to change his party.[82]

Despite his complaints of neglect, Jenkinson did not give up. Appointment to a newly constituted Board of Trade, in March 1784, acknowledged his position as an expert on commercial and imperial matters. Publication in 1785 of his *Collection of Treaties between Great Britain and the Powers from 1648 to 1783* and consultation with Pitt on Irish commercial proposition underlined his value. While his brother-in-law anticipated "every possible attack that envy or malice could suggest," he also thought that once Jenkinson secured a peerage "there is no situation in the government you will not command in three months." Pitt forwarded Jenkinson material in 1786 from William Eden regarding trade negotiations with France for his advice on the proposed terms.[83] Because Pitt had determined not only to be in charge of the government but to be seen clearly as such, the king's former confidants only joined on his terms. Talk circulated in June 1786 of a dispute in the cabinet with Pitt threatening to resign over Jenkinson coming into office with a peerage. The reality proved quite different.[84] Pitt told his mother that news of Jenkinson's peerage as Baron Hawkesbury and accession to the government would "sound a little strange at a distance, and with reference to former ideas, but he really has fairly earned it and attained it at my hands."[85]

Hawkesbury's peerage drew comment, not least from the *Rolliad* which urged

> Jenky, pursue Ambition's task
> The king will give whate'er you ask.
> Nor heed the frowns, of Pitt;
> Though proud, he'll truckle to disgrace,
> By feudal meanness keep his place
> And turn the royal spit.[86]

But as Pitt noted, Hawkesbury's accomplishments earned his place in the cabinet rather than the oft discussed "secret influence" associated with his name. An earlier satire alluding to the Irish commercial propositions described Pitt concerting with Jenkinson "to crush the poor and save the Rich." The author had Pitt further tell Jenkinson that

> To secret influence I owe
> The power I possess
> Twas you that shew'd me the back stairs,
> And duty I profess.[87]

The jibe's premise came from an incident when Pitt and Dundas rode through an open turnpike gate on their way to Wimbledon from an evening at Addiscombe that had "left their reason drowned in Jenkinson's champagne" only to be mistaken as highwaymen and fired upon by the keeper.[88] Exaggerated for effect, the story shows a growing relationship, though one that never became personally warm.

Fox's attack on Jenkinson in June 1786 charging him with backstairs authority reflected an outdated view seized upon by satirists that missed the real basis for Hawkesbury's return to office.[89] His administrative skills and knowledge were too useful to be ignored. Hawkesbury stood alongside Dundas as a pillar of the government and entered the cabinet itself in 1791. The historian Piers Mackesy claimed Hawkesbury had taught Dundas, who managed Indian business for Pitt, all the Scot knew about the subcontinent.[90] Joking about Pitt's reliance on his friends, North quipped that whenever Lords Carmarthen and Sydney, the government's two leading peers, were called upon "they will both arise, and like the two mutes in *The Mourning Bride*, point to Lord Hawkesbury."[91]

Illus. 1.   Charles Jenkinson by George Romney (1786–8). A commercial expert and political fixer acknowledged as leader of "the king's friends," Old Jenkinson raised his son for public office.

Robert Banks Jenkinson's early years coincided with his father's rising importance. They also accompanied a conservative turn first seen in a backlash against Wilkes and then responses to the American and French Revolutions that tapped deeper strains of opinion seen in the Jenkinson family. Hawkesbury bridged the transition between the first and second Tory parties; just his son's career shaped the revival of Toryism around Pitt's political heirs. The elder Jenkinson educated young Robert for a political career, training him to become a cabinet minister if not premier. As the diarist Nathaniel Wraxall noted, Jenkinson lived to see his son's rise to the cabinet, unlike the Elder Pitt and Lord Holland who both died too early. Lord North's father shared his son's triumph in gaining office, but he also witnessed the subsequent fall and the short-lived coalition with Fox that seemed to sacrifice principle for a second chance in office. No such disappointment marred Jenkinson's view of his son's career.[92]

Despite his situation as the orphaned son of an active politician, young Jenkinson grew up in the 1770s around an extended family that filled the gap left by his mother's death. Sophia Watts, Amelia's sister, lived with Amarantha Jenkinson as a paying guest and helped with the baby.[93] Charles Jenkinson kept close watch on his young son. Letters chronicle the boy's health. A smallpox outbreak around Oxford in October 1771 prompted Jenkinson to fetch him from a visit with his godfather Banks Jenkinson and have him inoculated. Grandmother and uncle later expressed dismay at the thick clothes in which the boy was bundled even for a June visit. Such incidents suggest more than a hint of protectiveness, but the child fared no worse for it.[94] Charles Wolfram Cornwall, Jenkinson's brother-in-law and political associate, often had young Robert as a visitor to his house in Winchester. Like Amarantha Jenkinson, his wife Elizabeth provided maternal care. Indeed, Robert briefly attended school there.[95] Six months before his eighth birthday he left this heavily female world to enter the care of Monsieur du Rosell in Chelsea where he learned deportment, manners, and dancing. Cornwall thought the experience improved the boy. Rosell, he reported, "says everything of him you could wish."[96]

Deportment mattered in a world where politeness set the standard for elite behavior. Politeness conveyed patrician norms of gentility, enlightenment, and sociability to members of the wider elite seeking to advance their status. Those norms made genial, inoffensive sociability the chief condition and bond for civil society. Poised self-comportment determined social and moral standing, checking boisterous laughter among other forms of expression.[97] A brisk trade in conduct books showed a preoccupation with manners later generations found difficult to comprehend. The pursuit of superior gracefulness Lord Chesterfield urged on his son existed as both an ideal and a code of elite behavior.[98] Although Samuel Johnson famously observed that Chesterfield's *Letters* "teach the morals of a whore, and the manners of a dancing master," Johnson also distinguished between exterior grace and honor. Confusing licentiousness with honorable manners sprang from the tendency Adam Smith noted of finding the vices of the great agreeable and the virtues of the inferior ranks mean and disagreeable.[99] While Charles Jenkinson had no tolerance for licentiousness, he knew the value of exterior grace as a mark of culture and refinement.

If a child's early years fell within a female purview, decisions on education remained a father's prerogative. As Robert grew older, his father's influence became more pronounced. Peter Waldo, a noted High Church critic of latitudinarianism in Jenkinson's circle, had recommended Albion House, a preparatory school at Parsons Green near Fulham.[100] Beyond its academic repute, the prominent families from which the school drew pupils cannot have escaped Jenkinson's notice. Upon consideration he judged it suitable. Robert began in September 1779. An early letter with copious misspellings brought a sharp enough rebuke that Robert apologized again for it as late as May 1781.[101] He clearly strove to win approval from a demanding and distant but affectionate father. School suited Robert well. His progress impressed the masters who thought him well-behaved and likely "to make a good scholar." Charles Jenkinson told the boy's grandmother in Calcutta that he "grows & improves every hour." Want of attention, "very common to children of good parts," may have been lacking from the father's serious-minded perspective, but it was the only apparent defect in a child not yet ten.[102]

Even accounting for the inevitable partiality among friends and relations, Robert drew praise as an exceptionally docile and well-mannered child. Accounts describe him as eager to please and be pleased. Cornwall, who enjoyed his nephew's visits, thought him "the best tempered & best disposed boy I ever knew." A music teacher praised him as not only "perfectly disposed to learn," but also taking "great pains to correct all the bad habits."[103] Robert picked up his father's seriousness at an early age. When John Jenkinson had invited his young nephew to help in building his house, the four-and-a-half-year-old later feared his absence had caused his uncle to have only two rooms. He accordingly wished to do "his duty" in rectifying the situation. Sir Bankes Jenkinson told a similar story about Robert at age nine, when he expressed deep alarm about a report of his father's neighbor and colleague Sir Grey Cooper being sent to Newgate prison "for carrying on a Treasonous correspondence with the French." Concern for Lady Cooper's plight showed the boy's generous nature, along with a gullibility he retained into early maturity.[104]

Failure to recognize teasing went deeper than a child's tendency to read things literally. Young Jenkinson missed social cues and failed to pick up on non-verbal communication from an early age. Clumsy behavior and poor social skills without impaired language or cognitive development suggest that Robert's lifelong quirks were more than eccentricity. Overcoming them required effort, along with emotional support from those closest to him. Diligent study and the capacity to focus intensely on a particular interest served him well in acquiring knowledge, but he also lacked poise or ease. He certainly showed both personal empathy and heightened sensitivity. The result made him a figure of fun among contemporaries well into adulthood. As child he held back from other boys, but a warm family circle may not have inclined him to reach beyond it.

At age thirteen, in September 1783, Robert entered Charterhouse as a foundation scholar or gownsboy, following his father's footsteps forty years earlier. The school still remained on its original site of the Carthusian monastery in London near Smithfield, Newgate, and the Old Bailey. Its establishment included an asylum for elderly men known as "old Codds." The location, dusty in summer and foggy in winter, was less than salubrious, but Charles Jenkinson saw other advantages in the school.[105] He described it as "a much better school than it was in my time." Besides teaching "nearly as much Latin and Greek" as the other public schools of the day, Charterhouse offered algebra and mathematics while encouraging general reading. Just as importantly for Jenkinson, "the fashionable vices are kept at a greater distance, and as the master allows only two boarding houses, he is able to pay more attention to the morals of his pupils."[106] High Church sentiments and a straitlaced personality underpinned Jenkinson's concern that his son avoid dissolute habits, while experience made him recognize the importance of knowledge beyond the classics.

For all their limitations, public schools during the late eighteenth century served a key role in both socializing and educating the English elite. Among ministers of state between 1775 and 1800, 87 percent had attended a boarding school. Eton or Westminster educated 72 percent of them. Residential establishments taught boys at the most social of ages to get along with their fellows and look after themselves. The robustly egalitarian culture within them, along with their austere furnishings, discouraged the exaggerated sensitivity a privileged child might have developed, especially at home in as doting a circle as young Jenkinson enjoyed. Boys had to adjust to "the tempers and talents of others." Doing so forced them to develop ways of making life satisfactory that went beyond money, power, or inherited respect. Regardless of wealth or rank, English gentlemen formed in this environment shared a common equality as part of a cultural elite.[107]

Gibbon thought public schools gave their pupils more practical experience of the world than they could acquire from education at home, while teaching them to measure birth and riches by the standard of personal merit.[108] Formal instruction revolved around Latin and Greek, which meant grammar and rhetoric as well as literature. Training in composition and declamation sharpened oratorical skills. Teaching methods that seemed rote to critics enabled senior pupils to reach beyond the grammatical skeleton and engage the substance of classical works. Studying the ideals of classical antiquity in such depth reinforced the social formation that prepared readers to take their place within a patrician world. Reason took precedence over the passions. Cicero's emphasis on the complexity of political life and the consequent need to exercise prudential judgment particularly influenced students. It underlined the importance of pragmatic wisdom to engage with the world as it existed over speculative theorizing. Even setting aside the personal connections made, public schools offered future statesmen an impressive schooling.[109]

Charterhouse's greater degree of supervision over students and broader curriculum fit Jenkinson better than the fashionable alternatives of Eton and

Westminster. Its headmaster, Samuel Berdmore, had built on his predecessor's efforts to improve the school and reported very favorably on his charge's progress. Charles Jenkinson observed that he "becomes everyday more manly & robust, without losing that native & natural modesty which is his distinguishing characteristic." More importantly, young Robert showed promise as a scholar with a translation from a Greek epigram that expressed "all the neatness & force of the original."[110]

Jenkinson took a sharper tone with his son, insisting on diligent study; "you should not be satisfied in doing your exercises just so as to pass without censure, but always aim at perfection, to be assured, that in doing so, you will by degrees approach to it." Applying "every leisure moment" to algebra and mathematics would master them while inculcating "a habit of reasoning closely & correctly on every subject." Robert should use hours not otherwise employed to read history and criticism. The boy's knowledge of French furnished many excellent books for that purpose. Like many fathers of the day, Jenkinson warned against novels as a waste of time better devoted to serious endeavors.[111] Robert became exceptionally well read on a range of subjects including modern history and European politics. He received a catalog – possibly drafted by George Chalmers, the Board of Trade's chief clerk and an Edinburgh-trained admirer of Adam Smith – of the best writers on political economy with a selection of works emphasizing commerce and finance. Without neglecting "more abstract departments of knowledge," father and son emphasized practical studies to prepare for a public career.[112]

Poise and deportment also mattered. Jenkinson warned his son to "pay proper attention to your person" as "every failing in this respect excites disgust or exposes a man to ridicule in such a manner as to defeat the advantages he would otherwise derive from his parts & lineage & other accomplishments." Without careful effort, improper manners and tastes might become a habit.[113] Did such advice reflect the mixed reputation Charles Jenkinson's own social experience had brought him? He certainly appreciated the need to project the dignity and pleasing manner expected of a gentleman along with a manly countenance. Robert had been a sickly child, notably thin and pale, but his aunt insisted that despite appearances he was healthy as any boy. At one point, his dancing master suggested a cure for worms "which devour him," but later described Robert as well made and not at all as clumsy as his appearance suggested.[114] A damning hint of faint praise captured a physical awkwardness that followed him into adulthood. While age and growth would solve much, as Sir Bankes Jenkinson remarked, Charles Jenkinson insisted on close attention to speech and manners. Speaking too slowly, he warned, "always gives an air of dullness."[115] As with his studies, Robert applied himself dutifully to strive for continued improvement.

One incident from his days at Charterhouse stands out. As a fourteen-year-old returning to school from a visit with family at Addiscombe, young Jenkinson encountered a highwayman who took his watch and some money. That Robert showed "no extraordinary alarm" pleased his father who nonetheless sought assurance he was well and sent money to replace what had been lost.[116] Called a year later to testify at the highwayman's trial, Robert gave his father a detailed account. "Not the least confused or perplex'd" by the proceedings, he spoke well. The thief had been arrested trying to pawn his watch, and the constable who had seized him found plans and tools for housebreaking. While Robert identified the watch under oath and had no doubt the man in question had robbed him, he lacked "a sufficient view of him before to be able to be able to swear to him."[117] The story highlights characteristic attributes. Having not seen the highwayman's face directly, Jenkinson declined swearing to the fact despite his certainty it was the same man. Unruffled by either the robbery itself or the subsequent appearance in court, he showed both nerve under pressure and a surprising care as a witness at fourteen. Firmness and self-possession underlay the boy's willingness to please, along with an ability to carry himself in public.

The elder Jenkinson had become an important figure by the 1780s whose position as a recognized expert who could speak authoritatively on a range of issues had revived his career. Remarriage on June 22, 1782 to Catherine Cope, widow of Sir Charles Cope, brought two further children along with connections among the English establishment that solidified Hawkesbury's position. His part in overthrowing the Fox–North coalition and establishing Pitt's government in office coincided with young Jenkinson's schooldays at Charterhouse. The new peer's ambitions shifted to his son, who showed great interest in political news and gossip. F. W. Cornwall, a relation of his uncle Charles Cornwall, brought young Jenkinson to a levee in 1786 where he met George III, who showed the boy marked attention and later inquired of his progress.[118] By the time Robert left Charterhouse for Christ Church, Oxford, in April 1787, his father was particularly well situated to help launch a political career. That task became Hawkesbury's primary focus.

Hawkesbury chose Christ Church, Oxford on similar grounds for selecting Charterhouse for his son. Although a graduate of University College, he thought Christ Church had the best discipline and was least likely to give a young man of rank improper indulgence.[119] University life broadened horizons while forging valuable relationships and offering practice in oratory and other essential skills. Friendships and rivalries forged at university – and for some, though not Jenkinson, at public school – often lasted through later life. Cyril Jackson, who became Dean of Christ Church in 1783, had seized opportunities presented by the college's access to crown patronage to take a decisive political and academic lead at Oxford. It quickly became a forcing house for aspiring public men who made a mark in coming decades, including William Grenville, Charles Arbuthnot, and William Wickham. Sir Robert Peel was the most famous of the generation that followed Jenkinson. Jackson's efforts doubtless caught Hawkesbury's notice, but friendship with Dr. George Jubb, Regius

Professor of Hebrew and Canon of Christ Church, helped Robert secure well-furnished rooms from Lord William Russell.[120] Robert's introduction to Jackson and his tutor, Henry Hall, by Sir Bankes Jenkinson on April 26 began his experience at Christ Church.

Not wishing to rely upon his own testimony, Hawkesbury urged Jackson to judge his son's academic proficiency for himself, while insisting the dean would not find him deficient in moral character, temper, and discretion.[121] Jackson replied that while Jenkinson had mastered Latin, his Greek only sufficed "to have carried him beyond the first tedious drudgery even of the Grammar." Competence to engage texts properly would demand resolute effort. Jackson thought his charge's knowledge of algebra a good start for developing style in composition, but acerbically observed that Jenkinson "has been more accustomed to talk English than to write it."[122] The new student set himself to make up the deficiency with five hours of Greek each day and the remainder devoted to pursuing other subjects in his rooms. Not required to attend lectures, he progressed rapidly and passed examinations in Homer and algebra. Jackson urged his student to press on with those two sciences – "since indeed I may with propriety call Homer a science" – until the long vacation, after which he might begin ancient history and Euclid. Vacations provided more time for concentrated work. Jenkinson told his father that with a few months he would master Greek. The same proficiency with algebra would enable him to attend the rhetorical lectures during the coming term.[123]

The diligent Jenkinson took full advantage of the opportunities he found. Critics disparaged eighteenth-century Oxford as almost completely indifferent to its educational mission and saddled with an outdated curriculum. Gibbon famously lamented the consequences of being "steeped in port and prejudice among the monks of Oxford" whose cloistered milieu left students "ignorant of the life and language of Europe."[124] The stereotype conveniently ignored the ancient universities' purpose as guardians of a body of traditional learning upon which religious orthodoxy, political obedience, and social order rested. Beyond training clergy and cushioning other students' entry into the responsibilities of adult life, Oxford and Cambridge were trustees of orthodoxy in the Established Church. They existed to preserve and transmit knowledge rather than foster innovation. A curriculum grounded in classics, mathematics, and theology did not preclude intellectual rigor. Christ Church saw a growing emphasis on Greek and mathematics, particularly under Jackson's leadership. Students engaged a wider range of texts than their predecessors. Even at its worst, the curriculum provided rigorous training in formal logic, construing texts, and rhetoric that students could apply to other endeavors.[125]

Life at Christ Church drew Jenkinson out of the reserve that characterized his earlier interactions beyond the family circle. He retained what a fellow student called a "conciliatory temper and benign manner in ordinary society."

Lady Stafford, mother of Granville Leveson-Gower, thought Jenkinson spoke
well when she encountered him on a visit home from Oxford the month after
he entered Christ Church, but observed that, if he were her son, she "should
have wished him to be more inclined to listen to what the Chancellor and Mr.
Pitt said, than to express his own opinions." Early exposure to leading public
men bred a confidence that put him at ease in their company. Others, especially
contemporaries or adults not inclined to dote on him, read it as presumption.
Rather than a personal flaw in Jenkinson, however, Lady Stafford considered his
manner simply how bright scholars at Oxford "contract high ideas of themselves,
which wear off when they come to live with the rest of the world."[126]

A more notable social occasion came when Jenkinson received an invitation to
Blenheim Palace through his fellow student Lord Henry Spencer. Their families
had longstanding ties through Oxfordshire politics that made it logical for the
Duke of Marlborough to show interest in Jenkinson, but he expressed unease at
the prospect of joining in amateur theatricals planned during his visit.[127] Plays
had been a standard entertainment at Blenheim for decades, beginning as an
amusement for the first duke after he had suffered repeated strokes. The custom
fit broader patterns of elite sociability, though Blenheim differed in having a
large theatre seating two to three hundred spectators plus two boxes.[128] Jenkinson
wondered how far his straitlaced father would approve his son's acting, especially in what amounted to a public performance. While he pleaded "inability
as an excuse for not acting" to his hosts, the performance being "on a much
more private plan than before" offered an excuse for Hawkesbury. Jenkinson later
reported that he acted only in one play and "declined in a very proper manner
any further engagements." The performance drew compliments. Nathaniel
Whetherell told Hawkerbury that it showed how well his son spoke, an important accomplishment in a world that valued oratory. But Jenkinson decided that
while acting on a particular occasion might cause no harm, inconvenience might
arise from engaging as one of the company.[129]

Public life involved performance with polite culture providing the script.
Internalizing that script was an important part of education. Hawkesbury
noted rumors of his son "disputing in company" since his arrival in Oxford, but
Jenkinson insistently denied any grounds to them beyond envy and malice. As
before at school, he bowed to his father's advice, but the touchiness of his reply
hints at a growing independence. He carefully followed guidance, not least his
tutor's injunctions against getting carried away with general ideas and failing to
weigh a book sufficiently, but struck a less docile note than as a schoolboy.[130]
Ironically, few undergraduates at any time would have been less in need of such
injunctions. Jenkinson's letters to Hawkesbury charting his reading in the classics
give the impression of a remarkably sober young man. He failed to spend the
whole of his £200 annual allowance during his first year at Christ Church, an
achievement for an undergraduate in any age. Later memories often shade actual

experience, but Jenkinson's recollections in 1824 of having had the good fortune to live in a very quiet and orderly set at Oxford ring true.[131]

Relationships Jenkinson made at Christ Church lasted through his life, especially his friendship with George Canning who later became a political rival and ally. Canning arrived at Christ Church in November. He and Jenkinson at once took to each other. They had much in common, not least the loss of a parent at a very early age. Talent and scholarly interests were another bond. Differences stand out too, along with the remarkable intertwining of their careers. Where Liverpool had been raised by a strong-minded, ambitious father with political connections, Canning's widowed mother had become an actress before his uncle removed him from her care. The stigma of having a mother in a life barely distinguished from prostitution contributed to Canning's haphazard childhood and later cast a shadow over his career. Unhappy at first when sent to Eton, Canning found his feet and became a prodigy as one of three contributors to the *Microcosm*, a student magazine that drew the king and queen's notice.[132] His reputation made Canning a man to watch, but one, unlike Jenkinson, not trained for a political career and needing much help securing patrons to smooth his way.

Canning thought Jenkinson "very clever and remarkably good natured." Along with a few others – notably J. F. Newton and Lord Henry Spencer – they formed a debating society with a distinct uniform of brown coats with cuffs and collars in velvet and buttons adorned with the initials of Pitt, Fox, Demosthenes, and Cicero calculated to excite curiosity. The group met Thursday evenings to debate current political issues, with Canning presenting the Whig side and Jenkinson that of the government. Canning's uncle had Whig sympathies – Richard Brinsley Sheridan was a family friend – and he remarked that since "we might be ranged against each other on a larger field, we were perhaps neither of us without the vanity of wishing to obtain an early ascendancy over the other."[133] Though Canning obviously sought to test his mettle, the comment grossly misjudged his amiable friend. When the club aroused curiosity within the college, Jackson urged Canning to resign lest suspicions of political ambitions prejudice his hopes for a legal career, which he did to the dismay of others in the group. Talk about the debating club may also have fed rumors of Jenkinson disputing in company that prompted his father's concerns in early 1788.[134]

Though lasting, the friendship between Canning and Jenkinson proved uneven. A biographer aptly described it as an attraction of opposites in which Canning's high spirits and crystalline mind paired with Jenkinson's amiable nature and broad reading. They shared an interest in learning along with a sensitivity expressed in different forms. Despite the acclaim won at Eton, Canning's upbringing and parentage left an insecurity that made him seek the upper hand in relationships. The boast to Newton that crushing Jenkinson in debate "cost me some pains" offers a case in point, though the admission that Jenkinson's "good now blazes; all his bad is in the grave," takes away some of its sting.[135] Sharp wit staked Canning's claim to attention, even if it came at another's expense, but he lacked prudence to check himself. Cyril Jackson, who befriended Canning, later warned him against "flippancies of wit which are beneath you & make more enemies than even serious warfare."[136]

Many who met Jenkinson found his serious demeanor and precocious knowledge pompous. Awkward mannerisms invited mockery. When Jenkinson brought friends to a levee to meet the king, Canning rather cruelly likened the scene to a Putney boarding school on a Sunday walk with their writing master. Credulity and taking things literally made Jenkinson an easy target for teasing. Indeed, Lord Boringdon, their slightly younger contemporary, first knew of Jenkinson through tales of horseplay and teasing. Leveson-Gower spoke of his friend as "continually rowed and laughed at, but he takes it all very good naturedly."[137] Jackson later described the Christ Church set around Jenkinson and Canning as perpetually quarreling and making up. The pattern continued when they entered politics during the 1790s.

Politics remained a preoccupation at Oxford. Through his father Jenkinson heard inside news and gossip. He reported back the universal sorrow over the king's illness with party prejudice entirely forgotten. The greatest alarm arose from "the uncertainty of the consequences."[138] Not everyone beyond Oxford agreed. Whigs led by Fox sought a back door to power by granting their friend the Prince of Wales an unrestricted regency. Hawkesbury anticipated the king would recover, but also realized that given a chance the prince would dismiss Pitt's ministry. The "happy revolution" of the king's recovery, as Hawkesbury phrased it, made the government stronger than before from public disgust at the opposition's conduct. By aggressively pressing the Prince of Wales' claims to an unrestricted regency with high Tory arguments completely at odds with their declared principles, Fox and the Whigs appeared self-interested. The episode reinforced impressions left by the Fox–North coalition. Only the king's differences with his sons marred his strong recovery. Hawkesbury pronounced him by March 1789 "as well as he ever was in his life."[139] Jenkinson rejoiced, though he saw the dangerous consequences a regency might have had. Hearing the Commons discuss the "great & important question" raised by the king's illness, had been his aim since November.[140]

A foray into the turbulent world of electioneering came in 1789 when Jenkinson and some friends joined the efforts of a government ally, John Pitt, to win election to parliament for Gloucester. Sir Charles Barrow's death in January forced an election that set Pitt, who had local ties, against the Duke of Norfolk's nephew, Henry Howard, standing with support from the town recorder and corporation. Although Jenkinson thought their canvass had not found much support, despite straining every nerve for votes, they sent to the poll all they had secured. Pitt won by a single vote, even though he spent only half the £20,000 his opponents devoted to the contest. Jenkinson rejoiced at Oxford on the news of his victory.[141]

Jenkinson focused primarily on his studies. Diligent effort brought improvement that drew praise. His abstract of Plato's *Gorgias*, a work the young scholar called "the finest discourse on moral obligation ever written," won the dean's commendation in February. Jackson had had him read his themes weekly since the vacation and Jenkinson believed the distinction had raised his standing within the college. Progress in Latin enabled him to inform his father that Livy's history of the Roman Republic "may always serve as a <u>lounging book</u>."[142] Roman history had a lasting impact on Jenkinson's thinking by reinforcing the value of a balanced constitution drawn from Polybius and Cicero. It also showed the pitfalls of civil strife driven by factionalism. The section on Rome in Sir Walter Raleigh's *History of the World*, along with Plutarch and Caesar's *Gallic War*, featured among his reading. Style learned from works "remarkable for the beauty of the writing" provided a lesson no less valuable than the general ideas and facts such reading provided. Jenkinson's tutor, Hall, reported to Hawkesbury on his son's attentiveness to business. By July, he praised manners and conduct that approached settled manliness."[143] The closing steps in his education pointed to a new chapter as the aspiring statesman entered the world.

CHAPTER 2

Apprenticeship and Public Life

JENKINSON'S EARLY POLITICAL education continued through his studies at Christ Church. As that period closed, he began an apprenticeship in public life that continued through the 1790s. Travel took him to Continental Europe as the French Revolution unfolded. Seeing its violent upheaval at first hand had a lasting impact. Entering parliament gave Jenkinson the chance to apply his training in rhetoric and take a place among his father's political colleagues. Debate tested his mettle among established men by engaging questions that shaped his intellectual development. Jenkinson's first years in public life went beyond the standard *cursus honorum* among the English elite. Responsibilities as a promising junior MP on Pitt's side prepared him for higher office while lending a confidence apparent in his growing self-assertion. Jenkinson also gained experience beyond politics at Westminster as he returned to Europe and then commanded volunteer soldiers on policing duties in Scotland. Lessons from those experiences guided his later career.

A four-month visit to Paris from July through October 1789 marked the next step in Jenkinson's education. Confident of its cultural superiority and the tone it set, old regime France was the "middle kingdom" of Europe. Fluent command of French brought access to ruling circles across the Continent and opened a cosmopolitan world of ideas and the arts. Hawkesbury had encouraged his son to use his French to read history and criticism at Charterhouse. The grand tour gave young men something to do that encouraged cultivation between ending their formal education and settling into adult responsibilities. A rite of passage meant to shape an individual resolutely British but knowledgeable in classical antiquity, modern taste, and other European nations, it cultivated a disposition to see the world through the prism of classical ideas acquired by study that reinforced earlier stages of elite education. Despite the common preoccupation with sex, gambling, and drink – which Jenkinson avoided on both his ventures abroad – travel facilitated the acquisition of social graces and an education beyond what reading alone could provide.[1] An Irish clergyman, Martin Sherlock, who wrote a guide to Italy where Jenkinson later spent an extended visit, remarked that

Nothing is so useful as travelling to those who know how to profit by it. Nature is seen in all her shades, and in all her extremes… If the traveler has the seeds of one or of several talents, he will find men of the first merit in every line, who will think it a pleasure to encourage and unfold those seeds, and to communicate knowledge….The traveler has, besides, the advantage of making continual comparisons which strengthen his judgment extremely.[2]

His words capture Jenkinson's experience both in Paris and during later journeys.

Hawkesbury had extensive contacts in France, and he approached a Monsieur Boutin to help find accommodation for his son and secure an introduction to Parisian society. He aimed to perfect Jenkinson in the French language and enable him to learn French manners and politeness. For that purpose Hawkesbury wished his son to "confine himself wholly to French society" rather than English expatriates.[3] Indeed, he asked the British ambassador, the Duke of Dorset, who later married the daughter of Hawkesbury's second wife, not to invite Jenkinson to his table for company beyond immediate family until his son was fit for the better sort of French society. A four month sojourn among the Paris elite would further Jenkinson's education while adding the polish to "make a complete gentleman of him."[4] Although evidence leaves unclear which of the Boutin brothers, Charles-Robert or Simon-Robert, Hawkesbury approached, both were leading financiers and administrators whose standing in France paralleled his own. Their ties to the court and the world of culture, art, and design, made them a natural guide for young Jenkinson.[5]

As a close watcher of French affairs, Hawkesbury thought an unsettled government that kept it from any great foreign exertions served Britain best.[6] His informed commentary illustrated an emerging loyalist critique of unfolding events that looked back to earlier upheavals in both France and Britain, though he wrote that not even the wisest man would venture to foretell the outcome of French events. Dorset had reported provincial violence in February 1789 amounting to "little less than a civil war," with two convents in Provence attacked and the nuns raped, an experience less jolly than Dorset's flippant tone supposed.[7] Tensions grew when the meeting of the Estates General in May led to the formation of a National Assembly the next month that forced its demands on Louis XVI. Hawkesbury believed abandoning privileges of the noblesse fatally undermined monarchy. Doubting matters would end there, he thought revolutionaries would find it easier to destroy an old government than to form a new one. England's experience in the 1640s and 50s suggested that "violent changes are never permanent" and "generally revert nearly to the point whence they started." As French nobles took refuge in England, he predicted more would follow.[8]

Jenkinson watched events at first hand from his arrival in Paris on July 7. He saw the storming of the Bastille where rioters, including women, murdered many of the surrendered garrison. Bernard René de Launay, governor of the Bastille, tried to avoid bloodshed with an honorable surrender only to be paraded before the mob and stabbed to death. A pastry cook decapitated him to display the head as a trophy.[9] Jenkinson drew a profound lesson from these events. Without lapsing into cynicism, he completely avoided the error of idealistic contemporaries who welcomed the French Revolution as a triumph of liberty.[10] Jenkinson thought the National Assembly had squandered the esteem it had earlier acquired by its folly, not least in accepting Necker's financial plan on August 4 solely *de confidence en M. Necker* and without deliberating upon its details. By September, he concluded the French nation's contest for liberty would prove ineffectual and end in "either a restoration of despotism or the ruin of the country." Jenkinson reported ongoing confusions in Paris with *milice bourgeoise* driven from the Palais Royale and a probable declaration of state bankruptcy. The course of events seemed "more and more difficult every day to determine," and he believed "the nobility and men of property would readily consent to pay part of their fortune for the positive security of the rest."[11]

Four revolutions unfolded beneath the surface of events Jenkinson saw. An aristocratic revolt against Louis XVI's ministers paralleled a bourgeois protest against noble privileges. Urban workers and artisans rebelled against the wealthy bourgeoisie while peasants mounted an insurrection against those they deemed oppressors. Rising prices driven by the economic crisis in France set the cycle of conflict in motion. Food shortages escalated it and spread suspicion through French society. Thomas Jefferson observed that every man seemed either a hammer or anvil, either a sheep or a wolf.[12] The larger problem involved failed governance. Unable to resolve a fiscal crisis when the state could no longer finance its debts, French ministers lost political control once the Estates General assembled. Disorder highlighted a power vacuum ambitious men struggled to fill. Only in retrospect did witnesses to events discern trends within the chaos.

Jenkinson sharply chided Canning for neglecting the chance to observe "one of the most extraordinary revolutions that ever has happened." When his friend asked for news, Jenkinson tartly replied that "he who has not the curiosity or courage to be present does not deserve to be informed of what passes."[13] The priggish tone recurred throughout Jenkinson's youth alongside praise from elders he sought to impress. Despite an appreciable thinning in the number of polite salons taking place as those who frequented them fled, Jenkinson pursued social and educational opportunities. Sightseeing taught enough about the fine arts to spark a lifelong interest fueled by later travel in Italy. Socializing improved his spoken French. It also immersed Jenkinson in the polite culture of the *ancien régime* and forged sympathies toward the French nobility and administrative elite. Boutin found his guest easygoing, receptive to advice, and of good appearance. Though lacking social polish, he thought Jenkinson had sense and wisdom beyond his years. The only faults charged against him were not keeping company with young Englishmen in Paris and spending his mornings in studies. The royalist Abbé Barthelemy found Jenkinson's modest and simple manner an interesting contrast with his firm character.[14] Little had yet passed to test him. William Eden, who met Jenkinson in Paris, told Hawkesbury that his son was "in every respect what a father would wish [and] what very few fathers enjoy."[15]

Returning to England in November, Jenkinson continued his studies at his father's London house in Hertford Street before his last term at Oxford. He received his degree by March 1790. An honorary M.A. degree followed the next month before a further tour through the Low Countries, France, and Italy that completed his education. Jenkinson crossed the Channel and landed in The Hague in July 1790 after spending the night in a post chaise on deck for lack of better accommodation. The journey continued through Amsterdam and Utrecht. Along with Bolingbroke's *Letters on History*, he read Louis-Pierre Anquetil's *Esprit de la Ligue* on France's struggles during the sixteenth- century wars of religion, which became increasingly timely as violence there grew. Another history of that conflict by Enrico Caterino Davila, which Jenkinson later read in Rome, gave the American John Adams a way to frame his thoughts on the French Revolution.[16] Davila's use of Tacitus as a model to distill political insight from history had led Clarendon to treat him as a guide to the revolt against Charles I in the 1640s.[17] Jenkinson would have read the link between political machinations by ambitious men and the violence of crowds as a parallel informing the present.

Political observations in letters home blended with remarks on what Jenkinson read and saw. Many young Englishmen had a tutor, often known as a "bear-leader," to guide and supervise, but Jenkinson journeyed with only a servant. Besides lacking a disposition to vice, he often stayed with officials and diplomats his father knew. Traveling through France in December gave him another encounter with the Revolution. From Paris, he wrote that nearly 500 families had left the city since a mob had pillaged the Duc de Castries' house in November. Others followed every day. Scarcely an evening passed without rioting in the theater. Two tragedies, entitled *La morte de Caesar* and *Brutus* struck audiences as particularly applicable to present-day France. Republican virtues highlighted in a revived classicism served as propaganda for the revolution. Jenkinson also reported a French translation of Burke's *Reflections on the Revolution in France* drew a warm response among those he met. Many of them thought the work might in time produce some good effect.[18] The rapid pace of events, however, offered little chance for the French public to feel it. Unrest had spread since the previous year.

Manufacturing in Lyon, along with the historic city itself, offered much to see. It was the kingdom's second largest city, dating to Roman times as a trade center linking Northern France with the Rhone valley and Mediterranean. The population were great democrats with the local bourgeois very confident that in a short time France would become the envy of Europe. A counter-revolutionary plot had brought a police crackdown in Lyon, with guards waking Jenkinson at night to demand a passport. Order and tranquility in French theaters had given way to confusion and riot. He described language used in galleries and the pit as lower than anything his father could conceive. He attributed it to widespread irreligion, noting that the lower ranks of the people spoke of religion's decay with utter indifference.[19] Concern over the moral danger irreligion posed became an important theme later in his career. Jenkinson reported an attempted counter-revolution at Aix-en-Provence had produced great disturbances with three noblemen decapitated there. People in Marseilles shared the democratic tendencies he had seen in Lyons. The region seemed very much to dread counter-revolution. While talk of repudiating the commercial treaty with Britain circulated, Jenkinson doubted the National Assembly would venture upon so bold an act.[20]

Hawkesbury saw much of Europe along with France in 1790 as living "in a state of anarchy or in dread of it owing to distress in their finances or to a sort of political phrenzy that now prevails." His son was among the observers trying to make sense of developments.[21] Gibbon thought years would elapse before France regained its station among European powers, especially with "no symptom of a great man, a Richelieu or a Cromwell arising either to restore the monarchy or lead the Commonwealth."[22] Burke's *Reflections* appeared in November 1790 before Louis XVI's execution or the Jacobin terror. The controversy it provoked reconciled Burke with Hawkesbury as friends to French émigrés. Whether hostile or sympathetic, foreign observers thought internal disruptions precluded an active French role abroad. Hawkesbury's sense that Britain had no reason to apprehend war anticipated Pitt's declaration in February 1792 that the country might "reasonably expect fifteen years of peace."[23] Even the perceptive Jenkinson did not foresee the deluge ahead.

After journeying through Nice and Genoa, Jenkinson reached Florence where the French minister Comte de Durfort introduced him to society. Florence's artistic treasures impressed him with a week hardly enough to give them due attention. Study balanced sightseeing. Jenkinson had brought a collection of books that included Shakespeare and Blackstone's *Commentaries on the Laws of England*. Virgil was "a constant companion." Classical learning guided his exploration. Jenkinson told his father of having travelled with Aeneas through the grotto of the Sybil and other sights including the house of Cicero. Like earlier English travelers, he saw Italy through the writings of Roman poets and historians. Jenkinson also continued among French society in Italy, including royalists who had fled France for safety. Rome, the young traveler concluded, stood behind only London and Paris, as a center for elite sociability.[24]

Other observations were less sympathetic, often disdainful. Italy had fine roads – better than those he encountered in France or elsewhere – but inns "were infamous" for the service and facilities with traveling nearly as expensive as in England.[25] Jenkinson described Italians in general, particularly Neapolitans, as the most indolent people. Naples had 30,000 indigents living from hand to mouth. Nearly 3,000 murders made assassination, as he phrased it, commonplace. Corrupt judges whose poverty left them open to bribes did little to help. Women, the censorious Jenkinson continued, were gallant without being the least bit amiable or pleasing. Others were more tempted. It took "an extraordinary degree of prudence," as John Hinchcliffe, the master of Trinity College, Cambridge had remarked, for a young man "to return home with as few vices & follies as he set out." Jenkinson's sincere interest in study and sightseeing matched his propriety to minimize any tendency to dissipation. Most curiosities around Naples were at a distance from the town, so Jenkinson found the stop gave less time for private study.[26]

Jenkinson took every occasion to interact with Italian notables and other foreigners of rank. The British envoy to the Kingdom of Naples, Sir William Hamilton, found Jenkinson one of the most promising young men he had seen, especially alongside other travelers with "more foppery and less solid knowledge" who lived as they would in London without taking advantage of their surroundings.[27] His English servant's illness kept Jenkinson in Rome, where he noted the number of French refugees, longer than planned. In March, he watched an eruption of Vesuvius which, with the reflection of the fire on the sky, presented "the most sublime and beautiful picture ever beheld."[28] From Naples, he began his return journey taking a different route through Bologna and Padua to Switzerland where at Lausanne he met Gibbon, who showed him "every attention." Jenkinson intended to see Boutin once more on the way home through France, but revealingly thought it unwise to communicate the plans of French émigrés in a letter.[29]

Politics at home never drifted far from Jenkinson's mind. A general election in 1790 enabled Hawkesbury to secure his son's return to the Commons for Sir James Lowther's nomination borough of Appleby. Though Hawkesbury appreciated the favor, he remained wary of his quondam patron, and the government controlled borough of Rye offered a more appealing option. Both elected Jenkinson before he came of age to take the oaths. Hawkesbury deftly squared the irascible Lowther for his son to sit for Rye without giving offense.[30] Representing a town within the remit of the historic Cinque Ports from the medieval wool trade with France and the Low Countries brought Jenkinson into regular contact with Pitt after the prime minister became Lord Warden of the Cinque Ports in 1792. A member for a borough controlled by the government anyway would draw the prime minister's notice.

Relations between Hawkesbury and Pitt deteriorated when the latter brought his cousin William Wyndham Grenville into the government as home secretary in 1789 with a peerage and responsibility as leader in the Lords the next year. Hawkesbury had been the government's leading peer, particularly given the Duke of Leeds' chronic indolence. As Jenkinson would later know all too well, a prime minister often struggled to manage business and debates in the house where he did not sit. Whatever Pitt's motive, Grenville's promotion lowered Hawkesbury's importance. When Leeds resigned in April 1791, the balance within the government shifted further. Most general business fell to a triumvirate of Pitt, Grenville, and Dundas. Thinking Grenville's advancement a scheme at his father's expense, Jenkinson wrote that "however agreeable the profits of office may be, they never are to be sought at the price of reputation & honor."[31] Indignity meant more than a blow to self-esteem. Tolerating a slight diminished the personal authority that enabled public men to serve effectively. Grenville had shrewdly asked Hawkesbury to introduce him as a new peer, but commercial policy set them at odds.[32]

Such differences lay ahead. Jenkinson's return to England brought what he described to Canning rather stiltedly "as the most important period of my life."[33] Taking his seat in the Commons at the session's close, he voted on Sheridan's resolution on revenue. Canning doubtless found it tedious when Jenkinson reminded him of the knowledge on finance he had gained through application to "a subject [that] has puzzled some of the ablest and most experienced men of the day."[34] Travel had made Jenkinson more self-assured which gave new acquaintances a bad first impression and provided Canning ample material to mock his friend. Friends of his own age found the lofty, over-educated manner less pleasing than did the older men he had impressed abroad. Noting a change when Jenkinson visited Christ Church, Leveson-Gower thought "his excessive importance (unless one is prejudiced in his favor) becomes very disgusting."[35] The shadow of his father's reputation fell upon Jenkinson, but politics and society provided their own corrective to youthful conceit and checked his tendencies to self-importance. A sometimes priggish manner still built a hurdle he took a long time to surmount.

The 1792 parliamentary session marked Jenkinson's real entry into public life with a maiden speech defending Pitt's policy toward Russia during the Ochakov crisis. Pitt had worked to restore Britain's international position from its nadir after losing America. His efforts had secured a largely favorable balance in Europe. Cooperation with Prussia had kept France from controlling the Dutch Republic and restored the authority of the pro-British hereditary stadtholder in 1787. Britain thereby inflicted a major political defeat on the French as fiscal overstretch left them vulnerable. Spain yielded to Britain in a 1790 dispute over Nootka Sound, partly because it could not rely on France. Pitt had less success in compelling Russia to return the fortress at Ochakov to the Ottomans. Forced to back down, Pitt faced parliamentary criticism as the Whig opposition sought to embarrass him. Ministers defended the principle behind the stand while conceding it lacked public support.

Jenkinson opened the government's defense against Samuel Whitbread's February 29 motion condemning Pitt's policy as "gross misconduct" that incurred unnecessary expense and diminished British influence.[36] Leading the defense in a maiden speech shows considerable trust from ministers who had known Jenkinson as a schoolboy. Clearly well-briefed, he set out the reasoning behind Pitt's foreign policy. Earlier success in the Netherlands justified choosing Prussia as an ally, while Austria's connection with France made it logical to back Turkey to promote a general balance of power that favored British interests. France's internal unrest did not alter the need for a counterweight as Britain's rival "wanted but a well constituted and well regulated government" to recover and "again prove the terror of her neighbors." Russian ambitions also posed a threat, but Jenkinson argued that its dependence on British trade gave it a weaker position than critics saw that made concession likely. Rather than saving Britain from war, the clamor against Pitt had kept negotiations from succeeding. While recognizing public opinion's claim on ministers, Jenkinson warned that it sometimes occasioned mischief. Pitt's actions were justified by the duty to watch jealously over European affairs and maintain the balance of power.[37]

In the debate that followed, Charles Grey and Sheridan both complimented Jenkinson's speech from the opposition side.[38] *The Times* reported it as "able and learned; cloathed in the best language and delivered with all the powers and graces of oratory." Hawkesbury's old friend Robinson wrote that Jenkinson had given "one of the best Speeches ever delivered by any Man on his first Effort, and as good a Speech almost as was *ever* delivered by any Man in that House."[39] Burke also congratulated Hawkesbury on his son's effort. Jane Long, wife of the other MP for Rye, wrote in friendly hyperbole that it was better than Pitt's own maiden speech. Pitt, who had told the king that Jenkinson's defense of the government excited general admiration, sent Hawkesbury a joint congratulation with Dundas.[40]

The prime minister doubtless welcomed a strong speaker on the government side. He included Jenkinson in a meeting of ministers at Downing Street eight days after the speech and drew the younger man into his own circle. The government carefully planned key debates, with Pitt lining up speakers to answer opposition figures and clarifying points to be made. Regular meetings at Downing Street briefed government speakers and settled on strategy. Pitt deliberately cultivated parliamentary talent. The diarist Wraxall described him "surrounded by a chosen phalanx of young men who participated in his triumph, pressed near him on a day of suspected debate, and constituted the resource of his leisure hours." Personal loyalties Pitt built among his protégés, along with their experience working together in parliament and administration, united them as a party. Jenkinson stood out among several rising politicians the premier worked to promote, including George Canning, whom Jenkinson introduced to Pitt.[41]

Jenkinson spoke twice more that session. His remarks in a March 7 debate on William Wilberforce's motion to abolish the slave trade ranged him against leading men on both sides of the Commons, along with later generations that viewed slavery as an abomination. Pitt backed his friend Wilberforce when he first raised the question in May 1789. Grenville, Fox, and Burke also supported abolition. Within the cabinet Dundas and Hawkesbury opposed abolishing the slave trade. Leeds, who shared their view, had acknowledged the position's unpopularity by readily giving his undersecretary James Bland Burgess leave to support Wilberforce with his opinion as well as his vote.[42] Opponents of slave trade abolition, including George III, viewed the question in commercial and imperial rather than moral terms. Much as it appalls posterity, which sees it as a stain on their reputation, many were convinced Christians who set questions of property rights and prudence before sentiment.[43] Colonial opinion saw abolition as a threat to established interests that underpinned British prosperity. The city of Liverpool's corporation voted Hawkesbury their official thanks in 1788 for speaking against it. If West Indian resistance to anti-slavery campaigns sprang from what David Lambert aptly called "the Counter-Revolutionary Atlantic," it also brought out tensions between Britain and colonists which had contributed to the American Revolution and thereafter made ministers cautious.[44] Hawkesbury thought Pitt "hardly in his senses on the matter" and warned privately that backing abolition offended the commercial part of the kingdom.[45]

Jenkinson took a more apologetic tone in debate that points to the awkwardness of defending what many Britons at best reluctantly thought an unpalatable necessity while public sentiment turned against it. He acknowledged that he spoke against a popular measure backed "by a greater combination of abilities" than ever united on a subject where disagreement could reasonably exist. Denying that those opposed to abolition set policy above humanity, he argued it would simply throw the trade into other hands with less concern for the Africans themselves. British merchants would suffer for no gain. Better to improve conditions in the West Indies and thereby encourage slaves to reproduce so a reduced demand for imports would curtail the slave trade naturally. Jenkinson rather weakly insisted disagreement only involved the means of ending the slave trade not the larger aim.[46]

Sir Gilbert Elliot, a Whig friend of Burke, dismissed Jenkinson's speech as a set piece "composed and delivered in mimicry rather than imitation of Pitt," showing "all the confidence, arrogance and conceit that could belong to a veteran." Interestingly, Elliot came to like him after a split over the French Revolution brought conservative Whigs closer to the government.[47] A few points in the speech point to Jenkinson's emerging political outlook, not least his claim that "in the most perfect system some weaknesses, some defects must necessarily exist." He thought it misleading to prejudice the whole by drawing inferences from extraordinary instances. Rather than abstractly weighing right and wrong, Jenkinson believed statesmen must consider the specific disadvantages likely to ensue from abolishing an evil against the consequences of its continuing.[48] Practical results outweigh noble intentions. Jenkinson's argument for amelioration as an alternative to immediate abolition of the slave trade illustrated his broader outlook on governance.

Growing concerns about unrest seemed to confirm Jenkinson's caution. The Birmingham Riots of July 1791, when a loyalist mob provoked by a banquet celebrating the French Revolution targeted Protestant dissenters, including the scientist Joseph Priestly, and burned their houses and chapels, prompted Whitbread to call for a parliamentary inquiry the following May. Methodists broke with fellow dissenters by supporting established authority. Whitbread linked the violence

Illus. 2. Robert Banks Jenkinson by Sir Thomas Lawrence (1793–6). Young Jenkinson as he wanted to be seen at the start of his career: an orator and political man of action. The pose channels his nervous intensity into direct engagement with the viewer.

to Pitt's government and growing public criticism of British admirers of France. Jenkinson passed over the event's particulars to reject a parliamentary inquiry "when the ordinary mode of appealing to the laws would provide every redress necessary."[49] With a straightforward effort to parry the attack, he struck what would become a common theme: no grounds for sweeping reform or extraordinary measures could be argued where the existing law and institutions provided means to resolve problems.

A further round of European travel after the parliamentary session closed in June continued Jenkinson's apprenticeship. The journey brought him to the French émigré headquarters at Coblenz reporting on military and political developments to his father along the way. France had declared war on Austria in April with the Habsburg Low Countries an obvious target. Prussia joined Austria in a coalition against France. French émigrés rallied to the army led by the Duke of Brunswick. Rumors circulated that Jenkinson went to Coblenz on a mission from Pitt, prompting a rebuttal in *The Times*. Leveson-Gower, who journeyed with him part way, thought his friend pleased by the attention. He also noted Jenkinson's fluency in French, acerbically likening it to the eloquence "for which he is so famous in the House of Commons."[50]

After landing in Ostend, Jenkinson reached Brussels on July 15. From there he reported efforts by French émigrés to draw support from foreign courts. Baron de Breteuil, who had succeeded Jacques Necker briefly as Louis XVI's minister before fleeing to exile, had declared that the king and queen only awaited the presence of a foreign army in France to declare their support for it. Émigrés urged Brunswick to march on France and requested the privilege of serving in the army's vanguard. Jenkinson reported the Austrian Netherlands contented after their earlier revolt against Joseph II's reforms with no prospect of being "infected with the Democratic madness." Even if the French and Flemish character were not so different, he wrote, recent violence in France would had filled observers with abhorrence and disgust.[51]

British opinion – and the government itself – lacked enthusiasm for intervening in France. European courts acted cautiously much to the émigrés' frustration. Outsiders viewed the problem as anarchy within France. During the journey to Coblenz with Leveson-Gower, Jenkinson sketched a plan to stabilize France under Louis XVI that amounted to a general reform of its government. He proposed reestablishing the king's authority and treating liberties given the people as a royal indulgence rather than a right. Louis XVI should send a lieutenant to each province with instructions to call a parliament of two houses – one of the commons and the other of the nobles and higher clergy – so all provinces would have a uniform constitution. In times of emergency, the king would summon two deputies from each province empowered to determine whether the nation would aid the king. Each provincial parliament would vote to impose its own taxes. Leveson-Gower thought the project good, but saw the potential for conflict among provinces and reflected that nobles accustomed to living in Paris might object to spending as much time in the country as the plan would require.[52] Shorn of its emphasis on royal authority, it amounted to what many early British admirers of the French Revolution in 1789 had sought; a Gallicized version of Britain's own parliamentary monarchy.

At Coblenz, Jenkinson saw the French émigré army along with Prussian and Austrian forces under Brunswick. Only 500 of the 16,000 French were ordinary soldiers. The rest were officers. Prussians of all ranks treated the French with "sovereign contempt."[53] Prussian discipline impressed Jenkinson, but he also realized that Prussia's limited population and resources afforded scant means to replace losses. A major defeat would leave Prussia a secondary power. Austria could stand a prolonged conflict, especially since its countryside provided a natural environment to form excellent soldiers. Brunswick welcomed Jenkinson, doubtless viewing him as conduit to the British cabinet, but he would not discuss Poland or other controversial matters. After speaking with the Prussian king and others at Coblenz, Jenkinson told his father that, because those living under an arbitrary government have no experience "with the variety of interests that must be consulted in a government like ours," they cannot grasp the reasoning to justify its behavior.[54] The gap he saw between Continental and British perspectives involved more than separate interests. Britain's political culture, not to mention parliament and other institutions, set a different context for decision-making that made cooperation or even understanding difficult as Jenkinson found through his career.

Impressed by the army Brunswick commanded, Jenkinson noted tensions within it. Prussians and Austrians hated the French, and also hated each other to a scarcely conceivable degree. Rather than marching against France, Jenkinson wrote that Prussians at home thought their king should have aided the Poles against Russia.[55] Informed earlier that Berlin had foresworn compensation for restoring Louis XVI, he now learned that Prussia expected reimbursement. If Austria's delay seemed a mystery, its determination to engage Prussia in the west to limit its ability to intervene in Poland answered the question.[56] Jenkinson's letters sketch a discerning view of the European scene. He understood the dynamics behind the war unfolding before him. Demands for compensation had destabilized international politics during the closing decades of the ancien régime. Competition for advantage in central and eastern Europe, particularly in Poland and the receding frontier of the Ottoman Empire, overshadowed concerns about France. Just as British opinion preoccupied with domestic or colonial affairs misread French events, so European courts took anarchy for weakness and directed their attention elsewhere. A newer, more brutal phase of international relations had begun in the 1770s that added ideology and popular politics to a zero-sum competition for advantage. As the historian Paul Schroeder argues, statesmen only changed their approach once the war with France forced them to realize that survival required placing general stability about the single-minded pursuit of particular interests.[57] That later shift, however, followed bitter experience of prolonged war and successive defeat.

Jenkinson's reports, circulated through his father, confirmed British doubts about intervening, though Burgess hoped Brunswick would soon get to Paris and make a striking example of punishment on the revolution.[58] Concerned figures in Britain warned against a false sense of security as keeping the "downfall of despotism in a neighboring kingdom" from exciting discontents at home became a fear. A proclamation in May alerted magistrates against seditious literature and corresponding societies.[59] Hopes for a quick end faded with news of Brunswick's retreat after a French army checked his force at Valmy on September 20. The French deposed Louis XVI and declared a republic the next day. Grenville thought it best for Britain and the Dutch to hold back, even if it gave the appearance of indifference and inactivity. French decrees offering to aid subjects who resisted their governments in the name of liberty and equality raised the stakes in November by encouraging subversion. An invasion of the Austrian Netherlands that threatened the Dutch Republic posed a clear threat, while the trial of Louis XVI horrified many British observers.

When parliament met in December, Jenkinson spoke on events during a debate on Fox's motion to send a British representative to France. Britain had withdrawn its ambassador, Lord Gower, the previous August. One of Gower's last acts had been to urge the National Assembly to respect the persons of the French royal family. Although Jenkinson opened by criticizing the motion itself as an encroachment on the executive prerogative of negotiating with other powers and making peace or war, he quickly turned to the central question of France. French ambitions were nothing new, but "when a whole people, and those powerful, were ambitious, as was now the case in France, the alarm grew serious." Recent success "rendered them less cautious to conceal their views of universal empire." Jenkinson detailed French aggression against neutral states along with flagrant interference in the internal affairs of other countries. Not "content with the ordinary mode of conquest," the French sought to overthrow governments and impose "principles subversive of order, morality and religion." He closed by urging the need to check French aggression at the earliest moment.[60]

Besides outlining the danger, Jenkinson noted the difficulty of conciliation "where there was no government." To what quarter should Britain apply, he asked "where persons and things were every day changing, where all rule belonged to robbers and assassins."[61] Jenkinson never considered it logically inconsistent that a nation "whose government now was all anarchy and confusion" posed a serious threat. Government supporters in the 1790s linked upheaval with French aggression. The *ancien régime*'s collapse had begun a cycle with anarchy bringing despotism familiar from classical antiquity. Like Alexis de Tocqueville much later, Jenkinson saw how revolution had swept away constraints on mobilizing resources behind an aggressive foreign policy. Burke too noted that revolution gave France "a complete unity in its direction" under a system "where nothing rules but the mind of desperate men" and later opposed any peace with "this new system of robbery."[62] Knowledge of France and connections with émigrés attuned Jenkinson to developments that others only gradually discerned.

While defending Pitt's measures in early 1793, Jenkinson often linked threats from France with the danger of discontent at home. What he had recently seen in France and his reading of history showed that unscrupulous men would use popular grievances to advance their own ambitions. Jenkinson's warnings about the effects of Thomas Paine's writing on those who lacked the education to see through its delusionary theories echoed his father's view of Rousseau in the 1770s. He argued that unreflective men might be led to believe that overturning the present system would better their situation rather than thinking it might instead create a greater evil. Those without property or stake in the country had nothing to "check their rage of experiment and innovation," which heightened the risk from subversive writings circulated by the French and their English allies. France sought to "kindle the flame of civil war in this country" by "a system to propagate principles and doctrines by the sword" that demanded a timely check.[63] Jenkinson was a government teller in the division on Fox's resolution against war with France on February 18. His speech in the debate set out three distinct *casus belli* justifying the conflict even before France declared war. *The Times* praised Jenkinson's remarks, which Pitt described to the king as of "uncommon ability and effect."[64]

When Charles Grey offered a motion for parliamentary reform on May 6, Jenkinson noted that it came as the constitution faced both subversion from within and being assailed from abroad by France. Since no complaint from the people had raised the question, Grey's effort showed only a group of gentlemen trying to stir grievances. "If they had succeeded in rousing the lion," Jenkinson continued, "could they have supposed they could have led it at their discretion?" France had shown that a people once excited could not easily be appeased. Under such circumstances, Grey and his fellow Whigs risked a conflagration by demanding reform.[65] French affairs had already divided Whigs far beyond the split between Burke and Fox. Elliot likened the issue to Aaron's rod in swallowing up all other concerns as "truly the just criterion of public conduct and connection."[66] Jenkinson's charge of recklessly stirring public opinion in wartime highlighted an image that kept Foxite Whigs on the political margin for a generation. It also cast Pitt's heirs as guardians of national independence and domestic order. Their claim to have saved the constitution from faction in 1783 and 1788–9 had put Fox on the wrong side of public sentiment twice already.

The question of reform itself led Jenkinson to sketch a broader view that tapped a family tradition. Accidental circumstances, often not perceptible, shaped the effects of government on the people far more than general principles. While plausible theories ought not to prevent reforms where real grievances exist, theory never justified reform when neither actual complaint nor practical advantage could be seen. Critics had not proven that the present system produced either improper attachments or unwarranted confidence in ministers. Insisting the alleged defects lay not in the system of representation, but in human nature itself, Jenkinson insisted "our eyes had better be turned to an improvement of that." As the British constitution balanced principles of democracy, aristocracy, and monarchy, pushing any of them beyond its proper sphere risked upsetting the whole. Noting that "speculative theories" build upon ideas of perfection that cannot be found in real experience, Jenkinson argued that "human institutions must be adapted not only to the virtues, but to the weaknesses and passions of mankind."[67]

Jenkinson's outlook differed from Pitt's stance as an independent Whig and reflected views Hawkesbury had expressed decades earlier. Warnings against speculative reform and cautions about flawed human nature echoed a strain of Tory sentiment that returned to public discourse from the 1770s. The French Revolution's role in sparking popular loyalism, along with the impact of Burke's *Reflections* on public debate and the political shift as Whigs broke with Fox over France, eclipses other important continuities.[68] Members of Hawkesbury's patronage network, notably including William Jones of Nayland, drew on Tory and high church arguments to provide intellectual underpinnings for loyalist opinion. The arguments resonated not only for the younger Jenkinson, but among a larger popular audience and publications pitched to them that shaped the revived Tory party that emerged among Pitt's protégés after his death.

John Reeves, a clerk for Hawkesbury at the Board of Trade who had tutored Jenkinson, founded the Association for Preserving Liberty and Property against Republicans and Levellers in November 1792. As a lawyer of forceful temperament who turned polemical and organizational skills to rally conservative sentiment, Reeves anticipated in a minor way John Wilson Croker's later career.[69] The group proved amazingly successful, established over 2,000 branches that tapped a deep vein of public sentiment. Hawkesbury and his son shared those prejudices in a way Pitt – who never showed Reeves any mark of civility – did not. Foxite Whigs instigated charges of seditious libel against Reeves for a 1795 pamphlet entitled *Thoughts on the English Government* that called monarchy the tree of which Lords and Commons were merely branches. Its arguments drew on a Tory perspective from Clarendon and Sacheverell, but Pitt disowned Reeves to stifle controversy.[70] The Jenkinson connection with Reeves underlined the links with an older Toryism. Interestingly, Hawkesbury was the only minister who donated to the subscription for French refugees in 1792. Jenkinson himself served on the Wilmot committee to aid French clergy who had fled persecution. Hawkesbury, with his son, stood alongside Burke and William Windham as the main British friend to the émigrés.[71]

Besides drawing notice as a capable speaker for the government in debates and acting as a teller for divisions, Jenkinson also gained other experience during his early years in the Commons. The house elected him on May 28, along with Burke, William Wilberforce, Lord Mornington, and Pitt to a select committee assigned to examine the progress of Warren Hastings' impeachment.[72] Pitt named Jenkinson to the India Board, the government department overseeing East India Company affairs, on July 3, 1793. Besides handling trade with India and other parts of Asia, including China, the company governed British possessions in India. The position with a £1,500 salary drew Jenkinson closer to Pitt, who attended many of the board's meetings, and Henry Dundas, who chaired them. It also trained him in an important branch of public business that involved commercial, financial, and political matters beyond the company's administration. He attended roughly three-quarters of the sixty-four meetings held between November 1793 and May 1796, a proportion only Dundas exceeded as chairman.[73]

Joining the India Board marked Jenkinson as an insider. Sheridan charged him with presumption during a May 1794 debate for speaking on the purposes of the war beyond what Pitt and Dundas themselves had intimated; Jenkinson's tone suggested he knew the secrets of ministers enough to deliver their sentiments, "unless we were to suppose that he had an hereditary knowledge of politics, and that a deep insight into the secrets of cabinet ran in his blood."[74] Nobody could miss the allusion to Hawkesbury's reputation. Pitt replied that Jenkinson had not spoken out of turn and said he shared his views.[75] Having known Hawkesbury's son as a schoolboy, he welcomed an able speaker with a wide range of knowledge to the government benches. The fact that Jenkinson possessed many of his father's strengths without the liabilities, encouraged Pitt and Dundas to promote his early career. Indeed, his relationship with Pitt offered the premier an indirect avenue for communicating with the proud and often forbidding Hawkesbury.

The Christ Church set revived in London as its members moved from university to launch their careers and two of them reprised accustomed roles. Jenkinson and Canning remained inseparable. Contemporaries noted the fact. They would be pictured hanged together from a lamppost in Gillray's famous 1796 caricature of the *Promised Horrors of the French Invasion*.[76] Jenkinson introduced Canning to Pitt. Their first significant meeting was over dinner at Addiscombe, Hawkesbury's house. Despite his uncle's Whig ties and friendly overtures from Fox, Sheridan, and the Duchess of Devonshire, Canning resented the idea that certain families ought to be at the top of government with a "kind of hereditary ministry in the Russells and Cavendishes" that excluded talented outsiders like himself. Ambition originally drew Canning to Pitt because any man without wealth or connection had to start public life with an established party. Moreover, his view of the French Revolution brought him closer to the government as France turned to conquest and subversion.[77] Pitt's encouragement and help bringing Canning into parliament forged a close relationship. It also removed political differences that earlier had made Canning see Jenkinson as a likely rival.

Jenkinson helped Canning on his maiden speech with advice drawn from his two years of experience in the Commons. When heckling from some of the opposition, particularly Grey, threw Canning off stride, Jenkinson and Pitt raised a cheer sufficient to give a pause that allowed him to continue. Afterwards Jenkinson went with Canning and other friends for a celebratory dinner.[78] Besides breakfasting in each other's lodgings and reading through official papers together before debates, they attended salons held by Dundas and Lord Malmesbury. Sociability reinforced political ties. Dinners and other gatherings cultivated relationships while providing avenues to exchange information. Where to take meals preoccupied Canning, who took great trouble over what a later era would call networking. Being clubbable – a phrase Samuel Johnson earlier coined to describe a convivial personality that made friends easily – could remedy other defects to win loyalty. Sociable as he was during these years, Jenkinson lacked such easy manners and paid a price for it.[79]

Jenkinson and Canning had a back-and-forth relationship, with most of the pushing on Canning's part. Jenkinson teased Canning for "taking mightily to unpleasant people," an assessment that captured more of the sharp edge to Canning's wit than perhaps Jenkinson realized. Another time Canning described himself passing the time with friends during a dull session of the Commons by "quizzing the debate, and the several speakers in it."[80] Canning retained a hint of condescension for his duller, more serious friend, treating him as an object for teasing despite his loyalty. Such nicknames as Jinks and Jenky succeeded later by Hawsbury, Jinksbury, and Jawkes recur in Canning's correspondence. Insecurity and jealousy at Jenkinson's rapid advance underlay the raillery, along with irritation at his occasional pomposity. Canning's wit had an edge that cut against those who did not defer to him.[81]

A practical joke at Jenkinson's expense showed how deeply that wit could bite. Jenkinson shared the military enthusiasm Canning viewed with a sardonic eye, and secured a colonelcy in a regiment of fencible cavalry Pitt had raised as warden of the Cinque Ports. Despite Jenkinson's encouragement to join as captain of a troop under him, Canning found his own military disposition insufficient and "only bargained *not* to *laugh* at *him* about it."[82] A parody recruiting poster broke that bargain when Jenkinson received it at a dinner party hosted by Charles Ellis where all the guests save him were in the plot. Part of the joke involved the burlesque appeal for "Tight lads, who would wish for a fair opportunity / Of defying the Frenchmen with perfect impunity" when the exception from service abroad militia enjoyed gave recruiters a common selling point. The prank so mortified Jenkinson that he became tearfull. Neither Ellis nor Lady Malmesbury could help him regain composure.

He left the party denying anger towards anyone while feeling that from Canning it was so unkind. Jenkinson's dramatic reaction horrified Canning, who had been at another engagement, enough to put him close to tears. Canning's absence from the scene, where he might immediately have apologized, made what could have been a brief exchange into a prolonged spat when he concluded that Jenkinson was at fault for overreacting. Reconciliation took several weeks. It only came when Canning's preposterous claim that fault now lay with Jenkinson for not have accepted his original casual apology brought the latter to bemused laughter.[83] The story brought out Jenkinson's emotional vulnerability, good nature, and lack of vindictiveness against Canning's insouciance coupled with a genuine, but superficial kindness.

Jenkinson's military enthusiasm fit a wider trend of volunteering that included other politicians. Most volunteer regiments were cavalry organized and officered by gentlemen. Although members of the elite, particularly those like Jenkinson with government ties, acted partly to set an example, volunteering marked a stronger personal commitment than expressions of popular loyalism. Volunteer corps turned primarily to internal policing as food shortages heightened social tensions. The Gordon Riots in 1780 had shown that mounted troops like Jenkinson's cavalry dispersed rioters more effectively than infantry[84] Service in the Cinque Port Fencibles gave Jenkinson tangible advantages including further interaction with Pitt. Its proximity to his parliamentary seat at Rye made it a logical company to join. Dundas presented the new regiment's colors in a field outside Windsor Castle. By October 1795 it comprised six troops of eighty men including non-commissioned officers.

The adventure of it all doubtless appealed to an enthusiastic man in his mid-twenties. Jenkinson learned military routine, but more importantly he experienced violent unrest at first hand with an introduction to the army's domestic role keeping order. Encountering riots and the conditions that caused them later helped him as home secretary to assess reports from local authorities. It also had a sobering effect Canning noted, particularly when Jenkinson marched to Brighton in May 1795 to keep peace when two soldiers were shot for pulling down flour mills. Since the militia food allowance of five pence a day fell short as prices rose, some units themselves joined the disturbances. Volunteer troops often kept on the move to minimize fraternization that might arouse sympathy with the locals they had been sent to police.[85] Jenkinson's regiment deployed repeatedly to Scotland where it provided a guard for Robert Burns' funeral at Dumfries in 1796. His disapproval of the poet's politics made him decline earlier to make Burns' acquaintance. Though hospitably received in Scotland, Jenkinson found the style of living gross and complained about slovenly accommodation and the bottle circulating too quickly for his taste at dinner.[86]

Jenkinson preferred female company, albeit respectable, over the sometime hard-drinking male sociability of his age. His entanglement in 1793 with Louisa Hervey, youngest daughter of the Earl of Bristol, brought a dramatic crisis. The match joined very similar temperaments from strikingly different backgrounds. She was the pious and retiring daughter of an unorthodox family touched by scandal. Her parents separated in 1782 after thirty years of marriage for reasons that remained unclear; a servant reported that after something passed between them on a carriage ride the two never spoke again. Lady Bristol told her daughter Elizabeth the next January that she could no longer suffer her husband's contempt and sought only to provide for Lousia.[87] An admirer of Voltaire and Rousseau, the earl had inherited the title as a younger brother after becoming Bishop of Derry where he dabbled in Irish politics and then pursued his interest in foreign travel and the fine arts. His older daughters made disastrous marriages, with Elizabeth part of the notorious Devonshire ménage a trois as the duke's mistress after joining the household as confidante to his wife Georgiana. The family's eccentric reputation had provoked an oft-repeated quip by Lady Mary Wortley Montagu classifying mankind under the general appellation of men, women, and Herveys.

After her parents' separation, Louisa had a strict, confined upbringing that all but stamped out the early sparkle of her personality until her mother allowed some company her own age. Canning found Lady Bristol and her family charming when Jenkinson introduced them in early 1794.[88] Sharing her sisters' beauty, Louisa differed in joining a deeply sensitive personality with strong Christian piety and moral seriousness. Jenkinson confided at first in Canning alone, who later wrote that his friend's "passion grew, as most passions do, so imperceptibly that it had gotten entire possession of him almost before he was aware of it himself."[89] Indeed, the anxiety it brought contributed to Jenkinson's response to Canning's joke about his regiment and a low disposition others noted. Once he won Louisa's consent, Jenkinson had to persuade their families. Canning not unrealistically advised first approaching her father, whose absence in Italy and changeable moods made the outcome uncertain. Bristol's response "proved favorable beyond their warmest expectations." Indeed, he promised a £10,000 dowry. Jenkinson's conversation with his own father on December 17, however, brought devastating news. Hawkesbury not only raised numerous specific objections to what he considered an imprudent and ineligible match, but wished his son not to marry before the age of thirty unless he married a fortune. Aside from prudential considerations and the Hervey family's notoriety and Whig connections, Hawkesbury resented being left out of the secret and had dismissed talk of the relationship. Matters deteriorated when Hawkesbury stated his absolute opposition and told Jenkinson to drop the whole matter.[90]

Here the dutiful son exhibited a deep stubbornness along with utter dejection at his father's command. Far from giving up Louisa, Jenkinson determined to persist. But in doing so, his agitation matched a scene from a romantic novel. Highly strung to begin with, the whole affair drove him to nervous fits and he sharply upbraided Canning for trying to encourage his hopes. Jenkinson still conspired with friends to bring his father around. Sir Ralph Payne, a West India grandee known for mediating disputes and thought to be someone Hawkesbury would hear, tried to reconcile father and son. The intervention only made Hawkesbury more determined. Jenkinson threatened to withdraw from politics, hoping that his absence from the Commons would force a change by playing upon Hawkesbury's pride in his son's consequence. He also thought, as a relative suggested, time would enable his father to deliberate and make enquiries that would remove doubts about the match.[91] Unfortunately, parliamentary rules forced Jenkinson to attend when the Commons was called over in late January 1795.

Besides Canning and his future brother-in-law, Lord Frederick Hervey, Louisa's friend Lady Jane Dundas joined her husband and Pitt in helping the pair, as did Grenville.[92] George III, a strong proponent of marital happiness, eventually took up Jenkinson's cause without having been solicited directly. The story could not by then have been a secret. Hawkesbury relented in February 1795, protesting that his son had not dealt openly by making his wish and intentions clear. By March, he gave consent and provided a financial settlement for the couple that Canning took as a measure to atone for earlier harshness. Jenkinson and Louisa married on March 25, with the groom on the previous day "in such spirits and such fidgets that it was quite uncomfortable to sit near him."[93]

Marriage gave Jenkinson the domesticity he craved. Louisa became a pillar of support despite lacking the touch to preside as hostess over a political salon. She never really tried to make a mark as a political hostess despite participating in society and trying often to be useful to her husband. The couple lived modestly with no evidence of money troubles. While many found Louisa charming, the couple shared a social awkwardness observers noted. Neither cared much as they were so wrapped up with each other. The couple exchanged few letters as they spent little time apart. Though Lady Holland mocked Louisa's "prudery," which she thought "came with an odd and questionable aspect from a Hervey," the match provided a social tie with the Whig Cavendish family through her sister Elizabeth that Jenkinson welcomed.[94] Unlike his father, he enjoyed good personal relations with political opponents. Sometimes mocked for his manner and always challenged on policy, Jenkinson never aroused the personal animosity many politicians faced.

Marriage also marked a watershed in other ways. Giving up bachelor life changed his relationship with Canning. Since their Oxford days, Canning had devoted much effort to keeping their circle together, taking pains to mend differences, including those with Jenkinson. Marriage drew Jenkinson from what Lady Holland called Canning's "little senate." Canning himself thought his friend's house would become less welcoming than before.[95] Indeed, retiring to the domestic sphere created distance that made a man less accessible to his associates in a political environment that valued personal ties. It hindered cultivating the friendships required to build a following, though it also kept Jenkinson out of quarrels and other differences. Domesticity could make a man appear censorious, but no evidence suggests it of Jenkinson. A reputation for respectability without censoriousness probably helped him given the increasing attention to private character within the political world. [96] Once Hawkesbury accepted the match, father and son became closer than before. The dispute had tested Jenkinson's mettle to show a characteristic determination behind the nervousness. His father's promotion to an earldom in May 1796 as Lord Liverpool, a title that recognized his long involvement with commercial affairs and praise from the city for his efforts, brought Jenkinson the courtesy title of Viscount Hawkesbury.

Neither marriage nor politics stifled young Hawkesbury's military interests. He spent summers after the parliamentary session on active service. At one point in 1795, he queried Pitt about arranging to billet the regiment near London. Mornington later mocked him privately as the Drunken Colonel – Hawkesbury disliked carousing – and told Addington that "he will never rest until he has drilled his housekeeper & taught his kitchen maid the manual exercise. They say he has had the cruelty to picquet his housemaid and dairymaid each five times in one night."[97] Louisa accompanied him to Scotland on several occasions. Her letters recount Hawkesbury's part in suppressing riots near Dunbar after balloting for militia service among unwilling locals. Soldiers prevented violence in the town where she had remained, but her husband's men intervened nearby to stop a furious riot that left dead and wounded. Hawkesbury thought "there never was a more daring and ferocious mob." Colliers were among the most disaffected, and he brought prisoners – seven men and one woman – to Edinburgh for trial.[98] Though peace had been restored, preserving it would require a large military force. Scotland, he observed, had always been the most factious part of the island. He found it hard to say whether Scots distinguished themselves more in their zeal in opposing the Stuarts on the throne or fighting for them during the Jacobite era.[99]

Suppressing plebeian unrest increased a contempt for mob violence that Hawkesbury had learned in Paris. It also provided frontline experience securing public order. He saw at first hand what caused riots and what suppressing them required. A Scots clergyman he queried on the disposition among the lower orders replied that "they were too much employed to have time for mischief."[100] The idleness and want unemployment produced made a combustible social mix that subversion threatened to ignite. Grain shortages that raised prices between 1794 and 1796 imposed near famine conditions on plebeian wage earners who subsisted on what they bought from the market. Living costs generally had risen some 30 percent since 1790, doubling since 1793. Higher wages did not match the increase. Bread's place as dietary staple made wheat prices especially important. Seldom more than 50 shillings a quarter in the decade 1784–94, it afterward never fell below that amount until 1849. The rise from 52 shillings in 1794 to 75 and then 78 shillings two years later was an increase not seen over the past two centuries. Prolonged high prices fueled popular discontent and alarmed officials who saw in it the prospect of insurrection.[101] Pitt responded to the danger in

1795 with the Treasonable Practices Act and Seditious Meetings Act, the latter aimed directly at checking agitation likely to foment unrest amidst scarcity. Other measures followed in later periods of stress.

Later as home secretary and prime minister, Hawkesbury turned to these years for precedents in handling unrest. Direct experience with crowd violence in the 1790s gave him context to interpret reports from justices of the peace and local magistrates. Home Office correspondence and business added breadth to those early lessons with his regiment. Hawkesbury's ability to synthesize information, especially through reading, was an asset that helped form his judgment on an important problem. The French Revolution had sharpened growing concerns among the British elite about threats to public order that dated from the Gordon Riots in 1780. A deep sense existed of the fragile underpinnings of a civil society threatened by dangers at home and abroad. Many thought crushing the anarchical tyranny in France would ease strain at home by restoring tranquility to Europe.[102]

Hawkesbury had been ridiculed for an April 1794 speech urging a march on Paris to tear up the Jacobin system from its roots. Canning thought his friend's speech admirable at the time. The logic behind concentrating a superior force on a single object remained unanswered.[103] Knowledge of France's unsettled internal state from his own earlier observations gave Hawkesbury solid ground for his judgment. Not all French regions benefitted from changes revolution had brought. Peasants, especially in the West and Southwest, faced worsening conditions that fueled resistance apart from ideological backlash. Royalists in the Vendée had moved so quickly in spring 1793 and faced such little opposition that it seemed briefly plausible they might march on Paris from the Loire Valley. Napoleon Bonaparte later remarked that, with nothing to stop them, the royalist standard would have flown from Notre Dame before the armies of the Rhine could have rushed home to save their government.[104] Although Hawkesbury had more justification than his critics then or later appreciated, the timing of his observation invited attack. He made the point in a debate on the failure at Dunkirk and the evacuation of Toulon, which Britain had occupied at the invitation of French royalists. Hawkesbury thought allied forces on the Continent were less effective than at the start of the campaign. Two years later they had managed only "to make all France soldiers."[105]

Britain faced difficulty translating maritime power into success on land, and a rough parity between France and Austria precluded either from a decisive victory. Grenville had embraced the "old system" of uniting Britain, Austria, and the Netherlands to counter France. A strategy that had guided policy from 1689 through Austria's defection in 1756 seemed to fit the 1790s, but neither Britain nor Austria could sustain effective cooperation.[106] The allies would rebuild a coalition near collapse in 1795 for another round of war. Spectacular French victories then failed to end the conflict.[107] Stalemate pointed toward compromise, but raised questions in Britain of whether peace could be made with France. Canning thought "the *form* of the government there" mattered less than "its *power* and *will* to afford and maintain *security* to other countries." Others doubted whether a regime veering between anarchy and despotism could meet those criteria. Mornington saw peace in 1794 as "certain ruin" since "the French openly avow the purpose of exterminating the English name & therefore would not grant peace on any terms."[108] The British elite would oppose what Burke famously called "a regicide peace" even if Pitt found a partner willing to negotiate.

Hawkesbury followed the war closely with an informed understanding. Once early hopes for success by decisive action with support from French royalists had been dashed and the allies met repeated checks, he realized the Britain public might lose faith when heavy expenditure failed to bring commensurate results. A disposition to economize might then suggest a wish to compromise rather than fight.[109] "All advances toward negotiation on our part" Hawkesbury wrote Canning in early 1796, "will appear to the French government to arise from some fear at home & will only make them more anxious to continue the war." Such overtures would more delay peace than promote it. He instead suggested contracting the scale of the war in order to act vigorously.[110] Allied defeat had not come by Britain's fault. Command of the seas and global commerce left Hawkesbury no doubt of ultimate success, a point he reiterated in August 1796. Even Austrian defeat in Italy and the prospect of a French advance on Vienna did not make him despair for the ultimate result.[111]

Setbacks abroad, naval mutinies, and financial crisis that peaked in 1797 strengthened the case for at least a temporary peace. Even before Austria signed the Treaty of Campo Formio in October 1797, leaving Britain the only remaining belligerent of the first coalition against France, a mutiny that spread through Royal Navy squadrons during April and May sparked worries even though a combination of concessions and force soon quelled it. Tax revenue had stagnated as war expenses rose to prompt a financial storm as government stock fell fifty below par. Walter Boyd, the main government loan contractor, nearly went bankrupt. A drain on specie led parliament to suspend cash payments by the Bank of England which took sterling off the gold standard. While a flexible exchange rate invigorated trade, it also made raising new loans harder. Pitt raised taxes further, introducing the first income tax, to stabilize public finances so Britain could sustain its war effort.[112] He also pressed the cabinet over Grenville's objection to accept a French overture in June and send Malmesbury as an envoy to explore peace. Financial strain and the prospect of fighting alone brought Pitt to seek a respite.[113]

While Hawkesbury did not reject peace on fair and honorable terms that protected British interests, he doubted they could be obtained "while the present system continues in France." Grenville and Dundas, along with others associated with the government, agreed. Betraying anxiety on the subject of peace, he told his father, can only make "the terms less advantageous whenever the time for negotiation shall arise." Canning kept him apprised of Malmesbury's negotiations over the course of 1797. Hawkesbury concluded the French lacked any fixed plan beyond attempting "to humble & disgrace us."[114] Like others close to Pitt, he saw no prospect for negotiations until France had a stable government able to conclude agreements and meet their terms. The following autumn, Hawkesbury hoped ministers would "form a coalition which under *our* direction may be able to accomplish those objects, which had we been honestly supported might long ago have been attained."[115] Questioning the reliability of allies, he overestimated British leverage over governments that had their own agendas. Indeed, a diplomat already had likened Prussia to boatmen availing themselves of the perilous situation of shipwrecked travelers "to drive a most unconscionable bargain."[116]

Private doubts underlay Hawkesbury's public support for the government. The hardline Windham thought his opinions very right. A second coalition in 1798 and victories that included Nelson's naval action at the Nile raised hopes to the point where Hawkesbury wrote of Alexander Suvorov establishing winter quarters for the Russian army in Paris. Cooperation between Russia and Austria raised hopes of securing Italy and even Switzerland.[117] The coalition faltered as the two Continental powers drew apart. An ill-advised expedition to the Netherlands with British and Russian troops in 1799 failed. Hawkesbury saw that even success would have drawn Britain into an unsustainable position as the principal in a continental war it could not sustain alone.[118] The expedition only made sense with committed support from Prussia or Austria, rather than Russia which was too distant from Holland to defend any gains. Hawkesbury thought it "a strange infatuation" to aid every description of allies "except those who have shown what they can do for themselves & whose interests are so interwoven in the cause that they cannot act falsely by us." British policy, he told Canning, long had been "to give support & assistance to those Great Powers upon the continent whose interests were the same as our own, but we have always avoided acting as principals in a continental war."[119] His observation about Britain's proper role in a European war tapped a skepticism over entanglement in Continental affairs that Bute, North and George III had shown at various earlier periods.

Setbacks had brought a gloom over the country as early as the end of 1794 that involved a mixture of rage at French triumphs, mortification at British defeats, and indignation at the "infatuated turpitude" of some allied powers, along with a suspension between doubts about pursuing the war and doubts whether any step towards peace could be made.[120] The situation encouraged Pitt to recruit Portland and other dissident Whigs into a coalition that broadened his administration while further weakening Fox's opposition. When Portland Whigs started backing his measures during 1793, Pitt observed that "they see that their titles & possessions are in danger, & they think their best chance for preserving them is by supporting government & joining me." Simply as a process, drawing factions into an existing administration was a standard eighteenth-century tactic to blunt potential or actual opposition.[121] Portland became home secretary, a post Dundas vacated to direct

strategy as secretary of state for war. Finding offices for the newcomers, five of
whom joined the cabinet, hurt junior politicians like Hawkesbury and Canning
who naturally expected to step up as opportunity arose.[122] Subordinate offices and
posts outside the cabinet rewarded supporters, while giving them experience. But
not enough pasture existed for all the new sheep. Political management became an
increasing problem for Pitt. Broadening the government also made policy disputes
more likely, adding to existing differences that already set the Jenkinsons against
Grenville on trade and economic policy.

Pitt had consulted with Dundas and Liverpool, as President of the Board of
Trade, in January 1793 on restricting the grain trade during war and preventing
shipments to France even where it involved compulsory purchase by the British
government. Liverpool had told Pitt that the occasions and circumstances of war
governed the conduct of belligerents and neutrals during conflicts. A pragmatic
approach drawing upon precedent shaped his advice. He created an administrative system to govern captured Caribbean islands directly as crown colonies that
set an effective model for other territories.[123] Experience made Old Jenkinson
a natural advisor on trade and colonial policy, despite growing infirmity that
removed him from active politics by the decade's close. Ill equipped to breach
Pitt's own reserve or compete for attention from outside the premier's inner
circle, Liverpool held the awkward position of indispensable odd man out.[124]

He therefore stood at a disadvantage in clashing with Grenville over trade with
America. Eager to preserve British advantages, Liverpool mobilized mercantile
interests against opening trade in the West Indies to the United States. Illness,
and perhaps his unwillingness to face a direct rebuff, kept him from the cabinet
meeting on August 29, 1794 to discuss the treaty. Instead he sent a memorandum
arguing that concessions on the West Indian carrying trade would break the navigation system that secured Britain's present advantage.[125] Liverpool lost. Risking
war with the United States posed too great a danger for Pitt. American ships also
took British goods into markets France had closed, securing a valuable profit.
While Liverpool did not resign – indeed his promotion in the peerage came later
– and still spoke in the Lords, he became more diffident in offering advice. The
earldom Pitt pledged in 1795 may have been an effort to keep Liverpool's active
support. An unsigned note suggests his son made preliminary overtures.[126] Still,
Hawkesbury shared his father's views and thought a consistent opinion mattered
more than holding office, though he doubted Pitt would risk losing them both.[127]

Food policy also created tensions within Pitt's government that partly
reflected differences between doctrinaire political economy and pragmatic
responses to crisis. Portland had opposed price subsidies or increased imports
to alleviate shortages in 1795. Instead, he proposed adulterating bread to stretch
supplies. Liverpool, however, saw imports as a temporary response to a problem
that better harvests would solve. Between January and August 1795 the Board
of Trade devoted thirteen meetings to the shortage of wheat. Liverpool presided

over twelve of them. He and other interventionists won the battle and introduced bounties for imports in October 1795.[128]

Grenville later complained that Liverpool had lured Pitt into "the mazes of the old system" despite their shared commitment to Adam Smith's principles of political economy. Portland as home secretary, though less doctrinaire than Grenville, feared the unintended consequences of intervention.[129] Liverpool had also read Smith, who exempted food staples from free trade on grounds of national security. He thought distress and the threat posed to order justified temporary intervention where the market failed to provide bread at an affordable price. When grain prices again spiked, he warned that serious insurrections might occur with yeomanry cavalry possibly fighting each other. Taking 1701 as a baseline, the aggregate price of cereals increased from 148 of that amount in 1798 to 228 in 1801. Cost thereafter fell, to peak again between 237 and 243 in 1812–13. People in cities and great manufacturing towns averse to farmers would fight others in the countryside disposed to defend them. Civil peace required securing affordable bread to contain tensions between consumers and producers. Pragmatism drew Liverpool to a policy of guaranteeing food supplies that Grenville resisted on principle.[130]

Hawkesbury took an increasing part in the question, particularly when shortage recurred in 1799. He moved for a parliamentary committee on regulating bread production which he chaired. It proposed restricting production of starch from wheat and regulating the manufacture and price of bread, along with bounties on the import of wheat, flour, and rice. Hawkesbury also urged the use of potatoes as an alternative food to ease demand for wheat, oats, and barley. These steps broke with laissez-faire orthodoxy and faced opposition in debate, but they addressed the food shortage at a time when it threatened public order and the war effort. Far from the monopoly critics alleged, the proposed London Company for the Manufacture of Flour, Meal and Bread met less than a tenth of metropolitan demand by offering a product other millers refused to provide. It corrected evils "aggravated by artificial causes" and promoted competition while adding to the food supply.[131] The measure passed, but Hawkesbury felt himself badly used when others in the government resisted his proposals. He complained sharply to Pitt that not only had responsibility been thrown onto him personally for a measure the prime minister approved, but Spencer Perceval, one of Pitt's protégés who held junior office, joined the opposition to attack it and even served as a teller for votes against.[132] Hawkesbury had stepped easily into his father's role as commercial expert and manager as cracks within the government widened.

Hawkesbury spoke for Pitt's government in a range of debates from 1796 that included responding to opposition motions on the game laws and the state of the nation as well as foreign affairs. Involvement with administrative matters gave him a useful apprenticeship along with a growing reputation. Karl Anton Hickel's 1793 painting of Pitt addressing the Commons showed Jenkinson seated

beside Dundas on the Treasury Bench. Two years later Gillray cast him with
Burke and Dundas as mourners at Pitt's bedside in a caricature satirizing an
opposition fantasy of the premier dying in despair over the war. Showing Pitt
mistaking Hawkesbury for Alexander the Great mocked again the young politician's earlier call for a march on Paris.[133]

Thomas Lawrence's portrait in 1796 captured Hawkesbury's nervous intensity
even after marriage and his father's advancement to an earldom. The painter's
fascination with youthful masculinity on the brink of maturity found expression
in a portrait conceived around the ambitions of its subject. Hawkesbury fixes the
audience with an unusually direct stare while holding a stance that suggests him
taking the floor in a parliamentary debate. The desk with official papers serves a
backdrop to focus attention on the dramatic tension heightened by Hawkesbury's
lanky, shambling appearance. A bas-relief of Demosthenes looking up from the
base of a pillar to the twenty-six-year-old flattered his pretensions as an orator
while recognizing a now established reputation.[134] Politicians increasingly cultivated the image of orator and statesman. Appearing either at the dispatch box
to speak or with pen and paper suggested the burdens of office rather than its
perquisites or power. The emphasis reflected a different self-image among statesmen than that of the Walpole and Newcastle era.[135] Hawkesbury held Pitt's confidence and that of other ministers, along with access to privileged information.
Liverpool had largely withdrawn from active politics to advise his son.

Promotion came in March 1799 when Hawkesbury became Master of the
Mint. His father earlier had held the same post at the Irish mint as a sinecure and
had inspired the last recoinage of gold in Britain during the 1770s. Liverpool's
knowledge certainly helped Hawkesbury. The elder Jenkinson delved into research
on currency as a result of the 1797 restriction on cash payments and the problems it
caused. He framed the objectives of a privy council committee on coin whose eventual findings shaped policy after 1816, and in 1805 Liverpool published *A Treatise
on the Coins of the Realm in a Letter to the King*.[136] Canning promoted his friend's
move, largely so he could fill the vacancy it left at the India Board, but Hawkesbury
welcomed the opportunity. Rather than the sinecure it had long been considered,
the mint now involved business some of which related to financial matters where
he had already shown promise. Hawkesbury found the salary of £2,500 up to
a possible £3,000 higher than expected without any intervention on his part.[137]
Appointment to the privy council made him eligible for other responsible posts
and provided closer contact with the king. The suspension of cash payments in
1797 had made currency both a political and a policy issue.

In December 1800, Hawkesbury faced one of the opposition's periodic efforts
to catch ministers off guard when John Nichols moved for an inquiry into the
state of gold coin that challenged his oversight of the Mint. Nichols justified
a parliamentary inquiry on the ground that circulation of gold had dropped
over the previous two years. He flourished statistics going back over a decade to

support his case.[138] Hawkesbury replied extemporaneously with an analysis of the causes behind the drop in gold coins circulating that demolished the motion. Shifts in the balance of trade caused by food importation after successive poor harvests explained Nichol's figures. Exporting specie to buy foreign goods, along with subsidies to allied powers fighting against France, had reduced the coinage in Britain, but only temporarily. Government measures could not keep coin within the realm against the market, but a favorable balance of trade would naturally correct the situation. Moreover, Hawkesbury noted, the exchange rate worked as an effective bounty on exports that promoted British trade. Noting that Nichols had offered a similar motion before, he concluded that the market's return to its normal pattern would remove the grounds for alarm.[139] Hawkesbury again showed he could draw upon a wide body of information to analyze a subject and then discuss it concisely.

Concerns over food prices and their impact on social cohesion raised questions Hawkesbury grappled with later as prime minister. The 1815 Corn Law sprang from his desire to protect consumers by securing a stable and moderate price that would avoid shortage, price spikes, and consequent distress. Self-sufficiency based on a steady home supply offered an early solution from which ministers gradually retreated in the 1820s. Experience in the 1790s shaped the later responses to the fear of scarcity that dominated early nineteenth-century policy debates.[140] Other problems of Hawkesbury's first decade in public life, including currency and public finance along with dangers of plebeian unrest, set the agenda over the next quarter century or so. He not only enjoyed an insider perspective on how Pitt's administration grappled with them, but took a direct part himself by speaking in debates for the government and serving on pertinent boards. Work at the most direct levels of administration – and suppressing unrest as militia officer – shaped how he would lead the foreign and home departments. Those experiences, along with travel and reading, guided his assessment of reports and development of policy. Hawkesbury enjoyed an apprenticeship that served him well.

Roughly two years at the mint ended Hawkesbury's political apprenticeship and positioned him for advancement. His chance came abruptly with the collapse of Pitt's government in 1801 over a clash with George III over Catholic Emancipation that led Pitt to resign, handing power to Henry Addington, who had served as speaker in the House of Commons since 1791. Education and upbringing had introduced Hawkesbury to the political world with the advantage of his father's connections and the liability of his reputation. He took full advantage of traveling in Europe before entering public life to broaden his horizons. The confidence it brought showed in Hawkesbury's twenties as he built a reputation for diligence and ability. While recognizing his parliamentary talents, Glenbervie thought Hawkesbury "ambitious beyond his years, having been pushed on by his father."[141] Liverpool increasingly placed his hopes in Hawkesbury who found wider scope for his abilities over the coming years along with much turmoil.

CHAPTER 3

Politics and War

TAKING OFFICE AS Master of the Mint had marked Hawkesbury for advancement, but opportunities seemed limited as Pitt's government looked increasingly threadbare. Pitt and Dundas had held power for more than fifteen years. Divisions within the cabinet had taken their toll. The prospect of victory receded as domestic strains grew. A clash with George III over Catholic Emancipation shattered political alignments that had held since the mid-1780s. Pitt's resignation brought Hawkesbury to the Foreign Office in a new government formed by Henry Addington. Two decades of fairly intelligible politics gave way to a renewed factionalism where no one group could form a stable ministry. Leaders instead bid for support from rivals with whom they had ostentatiously disagreed. The change brought to mind Gibbon's observation on Pitt taking office in 1783 with "patriots whom I left ministers, ministers whom I left boys, the whole map of the country so totally altered that I sometimes imagine I have been ten years absent from England." It complicated politics by weakening successive governments while opposition cohesion also declined. Violent parliamentary debates, broken careers, and settling of scores among rivals marked a period when a brief peace gave way to renewed struggle with Hawkesbury at the center of events.[1]

Ministers had stumbled in their pursuit of an effective path to victory. The king remarked perceptively at an early stage that "the misfortune of our situation is that we have too many objects to attend to, and our force consequently must be too small at each place."[2] A poor war leader, Pitt eventually admitted distrusting his own ideas on military subjects and he relied heavily upon the judgment of cabinet colleagues who differed. Dundas had long warned that public opinion strongly distrusted Continental wars or directing the country's strength into any channel besides naval operations. Past conflicts which ended with colonial gains bartered for French concessions in Europe supported his view.[3] But overseas victories had little impact in Europe and the Caribbean became a graveyard for British soldiers. The Duchess of Gordon quipped that before the war's end George III would be in possession of every island in the world save Great Britain and Ireland. Burke's protégé Windham warned against "the danger of running after distant objects, while the great question lies still – of hunting the sheep till you have killed the dog." Popularity won by foreign conquests would be fleeting, especially since victory in France itself provided the quickest end to the war.[4] Britain, however, could not carry on a Continental war alone. Even Grenville, who thought a large independent force might spare the need to depend upon Russian faith or Austrian energy, admitted that once the Continental powers withdrew, Britain's only option was maintaining its maritime strength by consolidating foreign possessions and securing its commerce.[5]

Hawkesbury's view reflected his sense of British strengths and limitations. Although Jacobinism posed an ideological threat that precluded tranquillity "till the principle itself be attacked and subdued in its citadel at Paris," he realized that after two coalitions had failed Britain alone could not accomplish that aim. Napoleon Bonaparte opened interesting possibilities in late 1799 when he overthrew the French Directory that had rejected earlier British overtures. Hawkesbury thought that with an army behind him Bonaparte would end the republic. Experience had proven that France could not go on as a republic. The question would be whether Bonaparte would found a new monarchy of his own or restore the Bourbons. Bonaparte's fellow consul Emmanuel-Joseph Sieyès, might accept the Duke of Orleans as king, but as a regicide he could not look to the putative Louis XVIII. As "a soldier of fortune" who had seized opportunities revolution gave to promote his own fame, Bonaparte stood on different ground. Hawkesbury speculated he might follow the path of George Monck who had orchestrated Charles II's restoration. Bonaparte's propositions in 1800 came to him as no surprise. While seeing a chance for peace, Hawkesbury opposed an immediate naval armistice and hoped to gain Egypt before fighting ended.[6] Although George III believed peace with France could be nothing but a risky armed neutrality, Canning questioned whether the public would fight on merely for better terms. Edward Cooke, a friend of Castlereagh in the Irish administration, thought the nation would demand peace "upon every account."[7]

A very different issue, however, sparked a clash with George III that brought Pitt's resignation. Catholic Emancipation, which the government proposed to accompany Ireland's union with Great Britain, would allow Roman Catholics to sit in the new imperial parliament in London. Relations between Britain and Ireland had been problematic since the 1780s as legislative independence created friction with the Dublin parliament. By 1892, Pitt saw no ultimate solution to Irish affairs besides a union of the two countries, but he had private doubts that it might be achieved or even that it would be prudent to hint at it.[8] Ireland's parliament had already made some concessions on religion, including suffrage for Catholics who met other qualifications to vote. While Pitt and Dundas believed policy and justice alike demanded admitting Catholics by degrees to advantages held exclusively by Protestants, they realized sharply altering that monopoly would spark a sectarian backlash.[9] Deliberate caution obscured the aim of their policy. It seemed to some insiders that Pitt himself had not determined on any step until he brought forward a proposal in late 1800.[10] General consensus within the British government viewed economic development as the best way to assuage Irish discontent and cement the connection with Britain. The Irish Rebellion of 1798 and a French landing to support it forced the question of a legislative union along the lines of the 1707 union with Scotland.

Hawkesbury backed plans for a union as the fragility of social and political order in Ireland made Pitt's measure the only way to address specific problems. Echoing Burke's view that "it is not about Popes, but about potatoes, that the minds of these unhappy people are agitated," he thought tithes the greatest practical grievance. Irish peasants resented being called to pay a fourteen shilling tithe to a clergyman of a different church than their own for his acre of potatoes after paying three pounds rent to a landlord.[11] Hawkesbury's entire agreement with what Pitt had outlined included "giv[ing] the catholics (if possible) the little that remains to be given them" as well as equality of trade with England and other economic concessions.[12] Though not advocating Catholic relief – and Cooke, working with Lord Cornwallis to pass the union, thought him overly cautious – Hawkesbury stood open to it. He even stated that union would permit the Catholic question to be decided without endangering Britain's stability. Liverpool told a confidant his son thought Catholic Emancipation "might be right under certain modifications and to a degree."[13] Hawkesbury never displayed theological aversion to Catholicism. The high church milieu in which he had been raised took a moderately respectful view of Catholicism. Tory publications expounded pro-Catholic sentiments in the 1790s that reached into the political elites backing Pitt.[14] Until George III blocked Pitt's measure, it seemed possible Catholic Emancipation might pass as part of the Irish union without controversy.

The king believed the Church of England's constitutional position rested upon fundamental parliamentary legislation. Altering the law threatened to undermine safeguards that went beyond Ireland. Fundamental maxims of Britain's constitution required those employed to serve the state be members of the Established Church that formed part of its fabric. Besides citing his coronation oath to uphold the Established Church, he offered a prudential argument that giving equal rights to all Christian churches would revive political discord over religion. George III had already expressed his dislike of civil relief for Irish who worshiped outside the Church of Ireland in 1798. Earlier in 1795 he ruled out a decision on the Catholic question by the cabinet alone.[15] Hawkesbury's language suggested that Pitt had downplayed the centrality of Catholic relief to his policy, particularly with those colleagues he thought might differ. During ongoing discussions, Pitt had avoided taking a vote of the cabinet and sought to deter opposition.[16] Although he had brought the king around before on other matters when they differed, circumstances had changed. Hawkesbury had heard George III say that the Irish union removed any pretext for admitting Catholics to further privileges. The king told Dundas at a levee on January 28, 1801 that he would consider every man who supported Castlereagh's proposal for Catholic Emancipation to be his personal enemy. When the formidable Scot expressed regret, the king replied sharply that Dundas had always known he saw matters in that light and his minister acknowledged the fact.[17] The exchange paralleled the king's earlier challenge that had brought down the Fox–North coalition in 1783. Miscalculation now left Pitt no alternative but to resign or submit.

Liverpool disparaged the idea that Pitt had resigned over the Catholic question. Having found it impracticable to continue a stalemated war, he thought Pitt simply preferred others to make peace with France.[18] While Catholic Emancipation was the catalyst for a break, other dynamics shaped it. Indeed, Pitt's attempt to press George III into a policy he opposed may have been partly an effort to regain the upper hand in their relationship. The king no longer needed Pitt to keep out Fox. A change in ministry would not alter the government's political complexion. George III now had more flexibility than at any other time during the previous sixteen years and greater irritation at what he deemed the overbearing and neglectful attitude of ministers. Pitt and Dundas both seemed exhausted. Dundas had sought to retire on several occasions, especially as the war effort faltered in 1798. He only stayed on at Pitt's insistence. Pitt too showed the strain of office – and hard drinking – which raised doubts about his capacity.[19] As his political dominance had faded, Pitt did well to influence his successors so much.

Henry Addington later observed that "Pitt told me, as early as 1797, that I must make up my mind to take the government." He had known Pitt since childhood as his father, Anthony Addington, was a fashionable physician whose patients included the elder Pitt and Charles Jenkinson. Critics mocked Addington as "the Doctor" for stepping above his station to become prime minister "with the indefinable air of a village apothecary inspecting the tongue of the state." Integrity and evenhandedness had earned him broad respect as Speaker of the Commons since 1789. The position had brought him closer to Pitt while avoiding policy disagreements that might have accompanied a cabinet post. Addington had sufficient influence to curb Pitt's heavy drinking, suggesting more personal authority than contemporaries granted.[20] George III regarded him highly, enabling Addington to act as an intermediary between Pitt and the king in early 1801. Both pressed him to form a government once Pitt's resignation became inevitable. Lady Malmesbury, however, thought it "impossible that Pitt's friend and creature should be his real successor, or more than a stop gap until matters are settled and he may come in again."[21] Addington seemed a placeholder guided from behind the scenes, though he soon showed a will of his own. When George III fell ill before arrangements were complete, Pitt briefly floated the idea of rescinding his resignation. Addington balked now that he had left the speakership. Pitt drew back.[22] Not until March 14 did the king recover sufficiently to accept the seals of office from Pitt and give them to Addington. With some of the new government sworn in and others who had resigned still in office, the halves of two administrations briefly operated in parallel with both included at one cabinet meeting.[23]

Short term continuities aside, the change marked an important shift with long-term consequences. It made the Catholic question a leading issue. Royal opposition emboldened those who might otherwise have compromised, while advocates became more entrenched in their stand. Splintering the coalition behind Pitt's government revived factionalism around leading personalities and made holding support in parliament and the country more difficult.[24] Although Pitt urged his friends to stay on in Addington's government, many insisted on resigning. Grenville, Dundas, and Lord Spencer at the Admiralty refused to serve under Addington, as did Canning, Leveson-Gower, and Castlereagh. Sheridan likened the result to a ship throwing its great guns overboard in preparation for battle instead of the lumber. Resignations "had literally knocked out the brains of the administration." He witheringly asked whether "this skeleton administration, was the phantom that was to overawe our enemies, and to command the confidence of the House and people."[25]

When Pitt broke the news privately on February 4, 1801, Hawkesbury first pressed him hard to reconsider and then decided to resign as well. Only after a second interview with Pitt at the brink of tears did Hawkesbury accept the inevitable. After consulting with friends, he agreed to serve under Addington. Louisa called the situation an "awful crisis, the event wholly unexpected." But her husband and others "finally agreed it was their duty to stand firm and brave the storm, and not forsake the King at such a crisis and drive him into the Hands of Opposition."[26] Hawkesbury announced the absence of Pitt and Addington to the Commons on February 9. Two days later he proposed Sir John Mitford to succeed Addington as speaker.[27]

Hawkesbury's place in the new government remained uncertain. Addington told a confidant that Dudley Ryder, Pitt's close friend who had served as a second in a duel with the opposition Whig George Tierney, had accepted the Foreign Office before reconsidering. George III reportedly considered Lord Malmesbury, but the retired diplomat's health precluded it. Pitt then approached Hawkesbury, who required considerable persuasion before he accepted.[28] The king welcomed the appointment of his old friend's son which strengthened the connection with a family that "had a hereditary hold on me." He told Hawkesbury when they met on February 20 that he had often given over the seals of office "but in no instance with such pleasure." Glenbervie thought the remark an honest compliment. Pitt paid his protégé a generous tribute in the Commons, challenging the opposition to name anyone among them besides Fox who matched Hawkesbury "in experience, information, or any of those qualities that marks a man for great affairs."[29]

Canning and his friends responded differently. Their private mockery of Hawkesbury underlined resentment toward Addington, whom they blamed for

Pitt's resignation. The change had created a kind of third party with Addington and Hawkesbury claiming Pitt's mantle while Canning's friends resented having sacrificed their interests to principle by resigning.[30] Leveson-Gower told his mother that their circle of friends from Oxford "cannot certainly look up to him with any great admiration." They believed Hawkesbury had been promoted above his merits. John Hookham Frere, the British minister at Lisbon, told Canning that other diplomats were "crystallized with agony" at the thought of Hawkesbury at the Foreign Office.[31] Gillray placed him prominently among the Lilliputian successors to Pitt and his colleagues with Hawkesbury unable to fill Grenville's breeches as Pitt's hat and coat smothered Addington.[32] While Grenville expressed pleasure at giving Hawkesbury "the difficult and arduous situation" he had held, he insisted "firmness alone" could extricate the country from its predicament. Grenville would remain "a sincere friend and cordial well-wisher" only so long as Hawkesbury followed the path he had marked in advance. [33] A government designed to preserve continuity – Pittite measures without Pitt and his cabinet – and the relative weight of its leading figures made Grenville expect influence over his successor that soon brought trouble.

Hawkesbury's constituents at Rye returned him without difficulty on February 23 – MPs had to stand for election upon taking a salaried office – and he spoke in debate for the first time as foreign secretary on March 27 to defend the previous government against French charges of breaking faith and pledged to lay before the Commons relevant official papers.[34] Besides relations with France, unfinished business remained with other European powers. The maritime strategy imposed by the fourth coalition's demise had only intensified resentment that weakened Britain's position against France. Friedrich von Gentz described jealousy of British power as the dominant political principle of Europe's political writers and theorists. European opinion believed Britain's wealth meant poverty for the Continent while its industrial and commercial preponderance amounted to a hateful monopoly.[35] The United States, despite naval clashes with France that amounted to an undeclared war, showed Britain no sympathy either. Gouverneur Morris, the American envoy, told Grenville that his countrymen thought Britain prolonged Europe's agony for its own advantage by setting unrealistic peace terms. European complaints thus found a transatlantic echo that underlined British isolation. Although war had enabled Britain to purge the Orient of all its European rivals and secure a near monopoly on overseas trade, those gains cast it in the invidious position of decrying French ambitions as its own riches grew.[36]

An incident in July 1800 when British warships fired on a Danish frigate that refused to permit the search of a convoy for contraband brought Russia and Sweden into a league of armed neutrality with Denmark. Britain treated maritime rights – the legal authority to impose a blockade in wartime – as a vital interest the Danes had challenged deliberately. Hawkesbury hoped Britain would not concede the point, especially since its position was much stronger than at

Illus. 3. James Gillray, "Lilliputian-Substitutes, Equiping [sic] for Public Service." Critics charged Pitt's successors, especially Hawkesbury, with lacking the stature to fill their predecessor's place. Early impressions proved hard to overcome.

the end of the American War of Independence when Catherine II of Russia led a similar neutral protest.[37] A diplomatic mission led by Lord Whitworth, formerly ambassador to Russia, brought the Danes to a compromise in August 1800. Tsar Paul revived the issue by declaring an embargo on British shipping and offering the Scandinavian powers help to form a new league. Russian overtures to France prompted more worries. Britain sent Denmark an ultimatum backed by a fleet in March 1801 before Russia or Sweden could act. It seemed by January as though Britain stood at the edge of war with the whole world and exclusion from European ports.[38]

Except for France, Europe's governments would lose heavily from a situation that gave Napoleon a free hand in Western Europe while paralyzing trade in the Baltic and distracting Britain during the early days of Addington's government.[39] Hawkesbury drew upon plans Grenville had developed, and Nicholas Vansittart arrived in Copenhagen to negotiate as Britain's plenipotentiary on March 9. The breakthrough came when Nelson's squadron destroyed the Danish fleet on April 2 and then gained an armistice that suspended the league of armed neutrality. A group of Russian nobles had assassinated Tsar Paul on March 23 ending the prospect of Franco-Russian cooperation along with support for the armed neutrality. Whitworth said he would "as long as I live, celebrate as a festival the day on which I learnt of the death of that arch-fiend Paul." Bonaparte, however, reportedly cried out in despair on hearing the news. Hawkesbury thought a letter from the courtier Count Peter Alexeyevich Pahlen announcing the event marked "the strongest disposition on the part of the new Russian government to renew their connection with this country."[40] The king approved Lord St. Helens' appointment in late April as ambassador to Tsar Alexander, a proposal Hawkesbury made after consulting Whitworth and the Russian diplomat Count Semyon Woronzow. The arrival of a Danish envoy to resolve the dispute with Britain enabled Hawkesbury to report on May 8 that the league of armed neutrality had been dissolved. [41]

Conciliating the Northern powers raised tensions with Grenville. While congratulating Hawkesbury on restoring Anglo-Russian friendship, he expressed unease at concessions or omissions that lessened restrictions on neutral trade. Grenville believed Hawkesbury gave up too much for rapprochement with Russia. Earlier he warned Addington not to restore Danish vessels seized during the embargo to give "a strong impression of the certain loss which Denmark incurs when she embarks in any such confederacy as the present."[42] Liverpool thought Grenville's comments varied between solid criticism and points that were either frivolous, capricious, or literal. Hawkesbury considered what he thought the serious points, while following Pitt's advice to throw the others "into the fire" and take no further notice of them since "it would be a fruitless endeavor to persuade Lord Grenville."[43] Grenville then decided that Addington's government – particularly Hawkesbury – lacked the nerve or skill to protect vital interests as he would have. Support that had only been conditional faded.

Hawkesbury also worked to resolve other questions. He instructed Arthur Paget, Britain's minister to Sicily, to urge peace with France, even authorizing him to state that Britain would accept its shipping's exclusion from Sicilian ports as an act of necessity. The point became part of the peace treaty signed with France that aligned Sicily against Britain.[44] Portugal had sought British aid as it faced Spanish invasion, but, lacking troops to send, the government urged its ally to make peace even on terms at odds with their prior engagements. If Portugal chose to fight, Hawkesbury still offered a subsidy and help negotiating a loan. Pitt and Dundas attended the cabinet meeting that submitted the policy to the king with their recommendation.[45] Grenville, however, warned Hawkesbury against giving any pretext for charges that Britain had abandoned Portugal, noting the country had "adhered to its system of connection and alliance with Great Britain, with so much steadiness as can ever be expected from a power so circumstanced." Although Hawkesbury asked parliament on May 18 to grant the Portuguese queen a promised subsidy, within a month Portugal had concluded a treaty with Spain that ended the war and closed its ports to Britain.[46]

Success in the Baltic, with developments in Portugal and Sicily, set the backdrop to negotiations with France. Liverpool believed that if Bonaparte seriously intended to make peace, Britain could secure "just and honorable terms, provided the government is firm, notwithstanding Bonaparte's puerile & impertinent menaces respecting Portugal."[47] Pitt had seen no grounds in 1799 for refusing to treat with Bonaparte so long as he offered advantageous terms and seemed likely to uphold a peace. Never committed to a Bourbon restoration, Pitt had sought a system in France that combined moderate behavior at home with ending revolutionary aggression beyond its borders. He saw nothing in the form of a stable, moderate government to make a treaty with it unsafe. The matter turned on the prospect of Bonaparte keeping the peace.[48] A cabinet minute dated March 19, 1801 recommended overtures to Paris. Despite his absence due to illness, Liverpool concurred in the decision. The king approved it the next day.[49] Hawkesbury accordingly contacted Louis-Guillaume Otto, the French agent for handing the exchange of prisoners. Born in Strasbourg with an America wife, Otto had started his career under the *ancien régime* and survived the terror despite Girondin ties. He had accompanied his friend Sieyès as an aide on a mission to Berlin in 1798 before coming to London two years later. Preliminary negotiations remained entirely with Hawkesbury, who preserved great secrecy in what observers took as discussions about prisoner exchange.[50]

Before opening talks, he sought his father's advice. Liverpool warned against making the previous government's opinions the foundation of their own conduct. As Britain had not been compelled by defeat to negotiate, it should not act now if it were. Proceeding with dignity was essential. French strength in Europe gave Britain a just claim to increase its power overseas. Viewing Addington's government pledged in a certain degree to secure peace, Bonaparte would strive to turn the situation to French advantage and British discomfort. West Indian islands aided British commerce more than the East Indies, so the latter might be returned to French allies for concessions elsewhere. Although the Cape of Good Hope was an expensive colony to retain, the threat it posed in French hands made Liverpool prefer it be held by Denmark, Sweden, or even the United States rather than the Netherlands under French control. Egypt brought no such risk. France gained nothing from holding it, but Liverpool wanted time for developments to unfold and make the relative advantage clearer.[51]

Hawkesbury, like his father and Pitt, saw that Britain lacked the means to challenge a French hegemony in Western Europe that upset the Continental balance of power. There was, he told Lord Minto in Vienna, not a single European power on which Britain could rely. Getting parliamentary support to finance an ally would be very difficult. Isolation meant accepting what now could not be changed.[52] Rather than abandoning a central principle of eighteenth-century British foreign policy – and Hawkesbury had spoken of upholding the balance of power in his maiden speech in the Commons – his position reflected a more nuanced view. He distinguished supporting powers able and willing to act effectively toward a common objective from Britain itself taking a principal role in a Continental war. Traditionally, as he had told Canning in 1799, Britain avoided the latter.[53] Hawkesbury's take on the balance of power also looked beyond Europe to encompass commercial and maritime factors. Economic strength – and the sea power it sustained – insulated Britain from European convulsions while the loss of wealth over the past decade's upheaval left France less powerful than critics of the eventual peace believed. Hawkesbury considered more than territory and population in calculating the balance of power, but he also reckoned with a stalemate that would be hard to shift unless circumstances changed.[54]

An early pattern emerged as Hawkesbury tried to pin down French terms. His stubbornness became a noteworthy asset as Otto worked to catch him off guard. Information presented as fact often proved incomplete or false. Hawkesbury patiently stuck to his terms and politely avoided efforts to deflect attention.[55] Britain required France to evacuate Egypt while pledging to return its own conquests overseas. French terms were more detailed and stipulated retaining Egypt while Britain kept Mysore in India. Other British acquisitions, including Minorca, Trinidad, Malta, and the Cape of Good Hope, would be returned to their previous owners along with French and Dutch trading stations in India. Relinquishing its claim to the Ionian Islands and pledging Spain to return Portuguese territory, France expected Britain to give up all West Indian conquests.[56] Those terms amounted to a victor's peace leaving Egypt to France while Britain gained nothing. Hawkesbury outlined territories Britain would restore to France and the Dutch, including Caribbean islands and outposts giving the French access to the Grand Banks fisheries. Britain would return the Cape, provided Cape Town remained a free port. France would relinquish Egypt to the Ottomans.[57]

Hawkesbury said nothing of what Britain intended to retain, including Malta and Ceylon which dominated vital sea-lanes. Malta would become a sticking point. News that events had turned against France strengthened Britain's position. Progress still remained elusive as Hawkesbury sought a clear statement of French terms. France, he implied, had yet to provide an intelligible reply from which to bargain.[58] The loss of Egypt turned attention to Malta. If Britain to ceded Minorca to Spain, the island would provide an alternative naval base to cover operations in the Eastern Mediterranean. Were French dominance in Europe to stand, Hawkesbury concluded, Britain would insist on keeping Malta.[59] Evacuating it depended on Malta's ability to maintain its neutrality by excluding other powers lest France occupy it and then prove difficult to dislodge. Russian patronage of the Knights of Malta under Paul complicated matters by drawing Russia into the question.

In June, Hawkesbury insisted that France declare which points of his proposal it opposed so he could respond. George III directed that no further concessions be made.[60] Otto's more detailed statement of French terms allowed negotiations to proceed. France agreed to evacuate Italian ports and return Egypt to the Ottomans while Britain restored other conquests, including those in the West Indies such as Martinique. Britain would return Malta, with its fortifications destroyed, to the Knights of St John and cede Minorca to Spain.[61] What Hawkesbury considered a favorable turn prompted him to request full powers to conclude peace. George III remained doubtful and reminded Hawkesbury to take as high a tone as comported "with perhaps the too tame language" held so far.[62] Bonaparte still delayed. Hawkesbury forced the question with an ultimatum that required France to make peace or accept continuing the war.[63] Although Otto acquiesced, another dispute arose. Hawkesbury then stated that Britain had reached the limits of its concessions. If the French should persist in any further demands, he warned, "there can no longer remain any prospect of the negotiation being brought to a happy conclusion."[64] Otto again gave way. The negotiators signed the preliminaries on the evening of Thursday, October 1.

Preliminary terms restored all British overseas conquests except Trinidad and Ceylon to France, Spain and the Dutch respectively, with Cape Town under Dutch rule a free port open to the shipping of all nations. Britain would also restore Malta to the Knights of St. John under the guarantee of a third power. France, in turn, would evacuate Egypt, Naples, and the Papal States, while guaranteeing Portugal's integrity. Otto and Hawkesbury agreed to send plenipotentiaries to settle the final terms in a meeting at the northern French town of Amiens. Critics charged Hawkesbury with conceding too much, but comparing the final document with terms in April shows that France not Britain had given way. Hawkesbury stuck by his early position despite tricks and provocation. Delay only made the French position worse as Britain resolved the problems it had faced in January.[65]

When Hawkesbury reported the preliminary terms to George III, the king declined to oppose peace, but urged a substantial military establishment be maintained. His claim months before that there is "no destruction of Jacobinism unless royalty is reestablished in that country" underlined visceral distrust of the regime in Paris.[66] Dundas opposed giving up the Cape and Malta, but, while refusing a vote of approbation, he also declined to press his view in a debate "which must tend immediately to weaken the king's government and ultimately end in a factious opposition to it." His words showed the dilemma facing many of Pitt's friends and former colleagues. While opposing the terms, they feared that enfeebling or overthrowing Addington's government would only bring to power Foxites "whose professed principles and uniformly rash conduct" risked accelerating the dangers Grenville saw as a distant consequence of peace.[67]

Pitt supported the treaty and devoted considerable effort to bringing recalcitrant friends behind it. Even peace for two years would be better than war, he told Canning. It offered the chance to avert another war or prepare to meet it. He thought the terms highly satisfactory. Authorities differed on the value of the Cape, which Pitt wished had been kept, but the great object had been ensuring that peace did not appear dictated in any way and guarding British possessions in the East and West Indies.[68] The agreement preserved national character while securing a breathing space from an inconclusive struggle. Grenville, however, complained about "a tone of unnecessary and degrading concession" with both Russia and France. Elsewhere he described the terms Hawkesbury secured as inadequate to any reasonable expectation. Departing from Grenville's earlier line seemed a breach of implicit faith. He told Pitt that "all confidence in the present government is completely and irretrievably destroyed." Pitt's warning that any public conduct tending to weaken Addington's government would bring consequences "which you of all men living would wish to avoid" had no effect. Grenville's opposition made restoring the shattered political alignments of the 1790s far less likely.[69]

Public opinion welcomed the prospective peace. A crowd drew the carriage of the French representative carrying the ratified articles past cheering spectators on October 12. News came as a surprise. An insider remarked that "no state secret was ever so well kept." Public funds rose eight percent on the announcement.[70] Lord Cornwallis, the general and Irish viceroy Hawkesbury selected to conclude the final peace at Amiens, shrewdly noted even before terms were announced that ministers would face little trouble over the preliminaries. Pitt had committed himself too far in support of them. Country gentlemen would back Addington, partly because his administration was more open to peace than its predecessor and partly from "dread of the democratic principles of the [Foxite] opposition."[71] The test came when parliament opened in late October with the king's speech announcing the outcome of negotiations during the previous few months in a deliberately neutral tone. Sheridan borrowed a phrase from Philip Francis to

Illus. 4. James Gillray, "Preliminaries of Peace – or – John Bull and his Little Friends 'Marching to Paris.'" Criticism of Hawkesbury's peace talks revived jibes by insiders at his earlier call for a march on Paris to end the French Revolution, but British public opinion in 1801 welcomed the experimental peace with Napoleon.

describe Hawkesbury's work as "a peace which every man ought to be glad of, but no man can be proud of." It involved "a degradation of the national dignity, which no truly English heart can feel with indifference," but, he concluded "the peace is perhaps as good as any man could make under the circumstances."[72]

Hawkesbury made his case a few days later, rejecting Leveson-Gower's unfavorable comparison with Malmesbury's earlier abortive negotiations. Although Leveson-Gower described Britain's position as far stronger than before and the concessions now made to France far greater, he still declined to vote against the peace or peremptorily assert better terms could have been made.[73] Rising to speak earlier in the debate than he had intended, Hawkesbury pointed out that his predecessor would have been glad to have taken less than he had demanded from the outset for peace with France. Solemnly disclaiming the plea of necessity – that Britain had been compelled to accept terms – he asked what continuing the war would accomplish. Britain had gone to war, not to destroy republicanism and halt the course of revolution, but to check French aggression. Hawkesbury pointed out that Britain at least had diverted France into "a channel less dangerous to the general happiness and interests of the world." Without a new coalition what object could war serve as neither France nor Britain could strike a fatal blow?[74]

Hawkesbury's defense of the preliminary articles focused on the negotiation's timing and tone, along with the terms. Delay offered little prospect of better circumstances. Britain had negotiated from strength. The tone had been one of dignity and independence, while the terms served Britain's interests and met obligations to its allies. Hawkesbury denied that acquisitions brought an increase in power, a point which guided British policy since the disillusionments brought by the American war. Wealth and commerce brought real power, as his father had noted in the 1770s. Hawkesbury cited figures that showed British trade increasing as French trade fell. If war returned, Britain would renew it under more advantageous circumstances. Territories ceded held little value and could easily be regained, while those kept, such as Ceylon and Trinidad, strengthened Britain's position. Hawkesbury pointed out that he and Addington had taken office "when the country was involved in war with almost every power in Europe," but extricated Britain "with honor and advantage." Firmness and moderation would provide a counterpoise to every threat while dangers remained.[75]

Glenbervie called the speech "a very able opening and apology, for it certainly was an apology."[76] Even those siding with ministers expressed apprehensions. The peace amounted to a bet on Napoleon's good will. And Hawkesbury faced sustained challenges. Henry Lascelles voted for the preliminaries, but admitted that "he could not rejoice at the peace without a mixture of anxiety and apprehension." Pitt defended Hawkesbury, reiterating his unhappiness at differing with longstanding friends and insisting the dissolution of the coalition against France made eventual peace a matter of terms. He saw nothing that might have been obtained to justify protracting the war.[77] The Commons approved the preliminaries without a division. Thomas Grenville and William Windham made the strongest opposition. Grenville forced a division in the Lords, but opinion there overwhelmingly favored the government. Critics argued that the peace conceded too much and relied excessively on French good will, but they offered no alternative. Gillray depicted Hawkesbury with a sulky youthful profile inscribing "peace" on Britannia's death warrant as Pitt stood behind him guiding Hawkesbury's hand with a finger to his own lips silencing doubt. The print illustrated Windham's strident attack on the terms as a death warrant that left Britain a conquered people.[78]

Criticism set Hawkesbury's public image as he struggled to make peace work. He defended the convention with Russia which Grey thought had just left matters as they were without resolving the underlying dispute. Lord Temple, Grenville's nephew, listed the five points in question with the neutral powers before concluding that, despite Dudley Ryder's "ingenious speech" proposing a *resolution* of thanks, none of them had been settled.[79] Denying the charges, Hawkesbury argued that conflict with the Northern powers had sprung from their efforts "to dictate a new code of maritime law to Europe." Britain sought no more than "to preserve our ancient and incontestable rights," and had done so by shattering the incipient league of armed neutrality and negotiating terms with Russia, its leading member. Hawkesbury discussed the terms with Russia in detail, pointing out that they secured British interests. While some "saw no policy but in violence," Hawkesbury, provided he received justice, would not only let off an enemy without blows, but also help him escape. Magnanimity aided a settlement that showed Britain would neither give up its rights nor exercise them beyond the bounds of reason.[80] The reply showed Hawkesbury's pragmatism, but its apologetic tone made him seem weak.

Amidst debate over the preliminaries, planning continued for the final negotiations at Amiens. Hawkesbury proposed Cornwallis as plenipotentiary, noting the advantages his military reputation and character provided. George III agreed nobody could be more proper in a situation where "uprighteousness is to be the only defense against the want of it."[81] Now well past sixty, Cornwallis had surrendered at Yorktown in October 1781. Later service in India earned a reputation as a soldier–statesman and a marquisate in 1792. As Lord Lieutenant of Ireland, Cornwallis had brought order after the 1798 rising and then oversaw passage of union with Great Britain. Old, tough, vastly experienced, and deeply conservative, he had the qualities to withstand French tactics. Anthony Merry, a professional diplomat who had been in Paris since the summer, would join Cornwallis and two military secretaries to handle negotiations.[82] Joseph Bonaparte, Napoleon's brother, led the French delegation, but the foreign minister, Talleyrand, sought to work around him as did Napoleon. Though Hawkesbury authorized Cornwallis to hear Talleyrand's views and enter into any explanation, he urged "more than usual caution and circumspection."[83] Cornwallis quickly encountered the same obfuscation and delays Hawkesbury had faced before.

Hawkesbury instructed Cornwallis to press for the adoption of the preliminary agreement with only three points open for amendment: the costs of supporting French prisoners, Newfoundland fisheries, and the final settlement on Malta. Cornwallis should propose France cede Tobago in return for Britain relinquishing part of its claim for prisoner expenses, but let the French initiate a proposal on the fisheries. A separate letter noted the importance of securing Hanover to its legitimate sovereign – a point mooted by Prussia's withdrawal – and told Cornwallis to reiterate Britain's determination to secure compensation for the Prince of Orange. Restoring Sardinia's king would also be desirable, but not at the expense of a general peace.[84] Hawkesbury aimed to settle the treaty quickly. Most remaining questions had been deferred simply to end the preliminaries. Malta's strategic position in the Mediterranean and Russian involvement complicated resolving its status. Hawkesbury proposed restoring the Order of St John of Jerusalem as civil governors of Malta independent from Britain and France. Maltese natives would be admissible to the order, while the King of Naples would retain suzerainty with forts under his command. France and Britain would pay the expense of defending Malta while Russia's Tsar would guarantee the arrangement.[85]

Besides indicating difficulties to come, early weeks of Cornwallis' mission offered insight on the French regime itself. Colonel Edward Baker Littlehales wrote that he "never saw a country possessing more of the semblance of liberty than France at present, and less of the reality." A session of the Corps Legislative looked more like "a military procession than a legislative body" having sentries with fixed bayonets at various posts. Cornwallis described France as a military despotism "wisely, but not mildly administered" under which "people of all ranks seem to look on quiet as the *summum bonum* – *ce grand homme nous a tranquilisé*."[86] The desire for peace might have raised hopes, but Cornwallis found it at odds with Napoleon's unwillingness to surrender any point unless more could be gained by the concession. During a private interview, Napoleon offered assurances to gratify British concerns about indemnifying the Prince of Orange but skipped details on how it would be done. Cornwallis thought it prudent to leave without comment Napoleon's questions about opponents of his regime sheltering in Britain.[87] Already weary of Talleyrand's "spirit of chicanery and intrigue," he sought to open talks at Amiens with Napoleon's brother Joseph "who has the character of being a well-meaning, altho' not very able man." Hawkesbury warned against reopening points settled in the preliminary articles.

Cornwallis faced delays in the arrival and credentialing of the Dutch and Spanish envoys whose consent a general treaty required. French tactics slowed matters further. "In no instance," Cornwallis lamented, "is there any show of candor in the negotiation."[88] The decision came in March. Hawkesbury concluded in late February that ending talks offered the only way to conclude matters. A break had to be managed to throw blame upon Napoleon. Liverpool concurred, and advised Hawkesbury to compose a paper highlighting French conduct through the negotiations. Financial pressures also mattered since Addington needed peace to secure a government loan.[89] Cornwallis had made some progress in early March before receiving Hawkesbury's instruction to give the French eight days to agree on the final treaty or leave Amiens. George III had approved the ultimatum to end French "chicanery."[90] Cornwallis, however, held back, which Hawkesbury later acknowledged as judicious, and concluded a final treaty on March 21.

Hawkesbury had secured an object that eluded Grenville and Pitt. Even if the terms fell short of his expectations and left problematic matters unresolved, Napoleon had failed to gain further significant concessions. The whole process had set audacity against stubbornness to give Britain the respite it sought. By disrupting the prospective league of armed neutrality, restoring ties with Russia, and ending an inconclusive war with France, Hawkesbury had resolved the country's most pressing threats within eight months. Relations with the United States also remained positive, especially as Hawkesbury responded promptly to complaints about seized American shipping in the Caribbean. Later efforts resolved a boundary dispute with Maine and settled claims by British creditors at Philadelphia, prompting Americans to remark on the friendly disposition they found.[91] Hawkesbury met Windham's harsh criticism of the Amiens peace, complimenting his opponent's speech and saying he would concur had the terms been as Windham described. Taken as a whole, however, they met British objectives. Hawkesbury pointed out that the public "sighed for the termination of a struggle that had lasted nine years, and which they were reluctant to continue without any definite object." With interests and honor secure, reluctance to continue a costly, inconclusive war had become conclusive.[92]

Critics had gained little ground since last autumn. Hawkesbury showed a better grasp of public sentiment. Despite his private doubts, Lord Eldon had told Addington that reactions to the preliminaries taught him that "we ought to be hanged, and that Parliament had so forewarned us, if we rejected such a peace as we had made." Another correspondent described critics as men who "would save their country if they could, but d – n if another should."[93] Addington's reputation as a fair-minded Speaker of the Commons won allegiance among country gentlemen and backbenchers who already sympathized with the case he and Hawkesbury had made. Windham's strident tone and reputation as a hardliner made him easy to deflect. The haughty Grenville's lack of charisma or personal warmth left him an unlikely rallying point. Pitt backed the treaty, as did the Foxite Whigs, albeit on different grounds. Many skeptics remained silent. Even though it remained an experimental peace, general consensus accepted it, if only for a respite.[94] The treaty also prompted most French émigrés, including moderate royalists and constitutional monarchists, to return home in 1802. Only hardline adherents of Louis XVIII, disdained by many other émigrés, and those who had become British subjects remained. The rest largely accommodated themselves to Napoleon's regime or retired to private life in France.[95]

Addington now held a strong position. Pitt continued backing the government despite pressure from Canning and a brief fit of pique in February over what he took be a slight in Addington's response to a Foxite attack during a debate on finance.[96] His ties with Addington and Hawkesbury – indeed the perception in some quarters that he remained effectively in charge – limited Pitt's flexibility. Castlereagh, one of Pitt's protégés, joined the government in July 1802 as President of the Board of Control for India. Peace not only helped Addington secure a loan, it also facilitated a broader program of financial restructuring. An income tax of a shilling in the pound deducted at the source raised £4.76 million in the first year compared with the £5.6 million Pitt's had netted over three years at twice the rate. Continuing the suspension of cash payments may have brought inflation and a disadvantageous rate of exchange that raised import costs, but it also prevented a contraction of the money supply that would have stifled trade. Commerce revived as European markets opened. Another good harvest in 1802 lowered domestic food prices while ending the scarcity that had prompted alarm during Pitt's last year in office. Other reforms expanded the militia and raised volunteers for home service while easing the manpower crisis that had strained the army under Pitt. Addington had shown, as Canning ruefully admitted, that "Pitt at the head of the Treasury is no longer essential to the salvation of the country."[97]

Parliament's dissolution on June 29, 1802 made the elections over the next two months a test of confidence. It also deferred political discussions until autumn. Hawkesbury thought the new House of Commons with an additional hundred Irish members more likely to support the government than its predecessor. His own election passed uneventfully, but the corporation at Rye transferred expenses of its own to Hawkesbury's election bill for an unanticipated £2,596 charge that his father covered to avoid making difficulties in the borough. Around this time, Hawkesbury and his wife bought a country house near Kingston upon Thames in Surrey, which they made their main home. Despite a two-hour journey from London, Coombe Wood's relatively secluded location made it a refuge from the capital. Louisa described an occasion in 1803 when she persuaded her husband to leave the Commons early for a short visit that gave "a feel of comfort not to be expressed." The next morning they enjoyed "above an hour's walk and potter in the midst of workmen, pigs, and Turkeys" before returning to interviews and engagements in London that comprised Hawkesbury's day. Renovations took years – Louisa still complained in 1808 of the inconvenience – but they occupied the house by August 1802.[98] Domesticity provided a welcome escape from politics.

Settling points related to the Amiens treaty gave Hawkesbury considerable trouble. Arrangements for Malta were especially difficult because restoring authority to the Order of St John involved preconditions over which Hawkesbury had little control. The order, which did not include native Maltese, had lost much of its property. Many of its knights had taken shelter under Tsar Paul's protection after Napoleon had occupied Malta in 1798. Britain's capture of the island had not brought them back. Besides securing 2,000 Neapolitan troops as a garrison, the order needed to elect a new grand master and the six powers named as guarantors had to accept their role. The Neapolitan garrison could only be sent after the election of a grand master and confirmation of the guarantee by Russia, Austria, and Prussia. Pope Pius VII appointed Barthelémy de Ruspoli grand master, but Russia prevaricated on the guarantee while Austria and Prussia held back pending its decision. Hawkesbury pressed British envoys to secure the powers' accession without success. By October 1802, Britain suspended plans to evacuate Malta and even supplemented its garrison with troops from Egypt.[99]

Hawkesbury also faced damaging criticism in Britain behind the scenes. Rufus King, the American minister who had worked well with Grenville, complained of delays without considering the demands of business with France and Russia.[100] An early dispute with the Russian diplomat Semyon Woronzow – Tsar Paul had broken with the quondam favorite in 1800 and Hawkesbury declined to handle business except through an accredited Russian representative – sparked a personal animosity that his opposition to peace with France only amplified. Woronzow described Hawkesbury in 1803 as "absolutely incapable of transacting common business." He complained further of "an actual imbecility in his Lordship, which no man can have a comprehension of who has heard him speak in Parliament." The already disdainful Grenville provided a ready audience for charges of undue bias toward France which Wornozow shared more widely.[101] Jibes from Canning and his friends shaped the environment in which malice against the foreign secretary circulated, not least through Canning's ties to newspaper writers and caricaturists like Gillray to whom he often suggested topics and provided information.[102] Hawkesbury's nervous temperament had become a staple for caricaturists. His manner which combined formality with awkwardness worked badly with foreign representatives. George III later described the animosity and contempt towards him among diplomats as decidedly unanimous.[103]

Was the king's remark in 1804 simply malicious gossip? Or had Hawkesbury antagonized diplomats and mishandled business? Dealing directly with people had never been a strength, and he faced a steep learning curve in taking over a major department of state. Foreign statesmen and the department itself had been used to Grenville, which made Hawkesbury's challenge all the greater as he put his own stamp on its work. Hostility amplified occasional slips in management and he lacked the grace to smooth over difficulties. A diplomat's successes, Lord Salisbury later argued in defending Castlereagh, involve microscopic advantages won by a judicious suggestion here, an opportune civility there, and "sleepless tact, immovable calmness and patience that no folly, no provocation, no blunders can shake."[104] Hawkesbury lacked the personal attributes that later made Castlereagh a diplomatic success. Indeed, his sometime inability to pick up social cues put him at a severe disadvantage. Conciliating diplomats and countering private malice proved beyond Hawkesbury's reach.

Evidence still fails to uphold the charge of incompetence. No major errors blot Hawkesbury's record. Indeed, he directed the resolution of several problems and played a difficult hand with France as well as anyone might have expected.[105] Others handled most negotiations aside from the preliminaries with Otto which mainly called for a persistent, firm line rather than conciliation. Hawkesbury showed knowledge and strategic grasp from the start. His management of business improved. The real problem was a deteriorating situation beyond his control for which he took the blame and a corresponding failure to read how the consequences played in political circles and among diplomats. Critical talk from Woronzow and others damaged Hawkesbury's reputation more than he ever realized. It reinforced early impressions that he lacked the weight a foreign secretary required and denied him the benefit of the doubt when problems arose. An impression once made became hard to change. Hawkesbury's political standing eroded as diplomacy gave way to crisis management.

Difficulties began soon after the final treaty when Talleyrand prevaricated over naming a representative, whom he insisted be accredited an ambassador rather than an envoy. Napoleon's plans to change the French constitution by becoming emperor seemed calculated to insult European monarchs. Hawkesbury instructed the British representative in Paris to press Talleyrand hard on restoring British property and opening ports as the treaty required.[106] French agents in Austria opened the dispatches of Britain's ambassador to Vienna, who reported in June that Napoleon had told the Habsburg foreign minister Ludwig von Cobenzel hostilities were likely to resume soon.[107] Hawkesbury still urged British diplomats over the summer to continue their efforts to draw other governments into a general settlement with France. Trade disputes further soured relations. Although Liverpool observed that the French had more to lose from commercial warfare than Britain, Napoleon took a different view, using tariffs to secure Continental markets for French manufacturers and supplant Britain there.[108]

Articles in the British press sparked difficulty in August when official complaints submitted to Hawkesbury coincided with a scathing attack against the British government in the *Moniteur* that Napoleon reportedly penned himself. Émigré newspapers had long stung Napoleon's considerable pride, but the tone of British newspapers inflicted further offense despite the fact that they treated everyone with disdain. Hawkesbury at first pointed out that the government had no means of preventing such articles. It could only prosecute libels after the fact with doubtful chances of success.[109] As with other disputes, he took a conciliatory line to avoid a break. Liverpool warned that "those who were most disposed to censure the administration [for the peace], will censure them with greater justice if they do not take every proper measure to secure the continuance of it." He drew upon long experience to sketch points for a reply, noting that extensive political discussion in the English press only dated from the publication of parliamentary debates. Broad circulation of English papers in France had only begun since the revolution. Realizing the danger of French language publications, especially given the zeal of émigrés who had lost so much, Liverpool observed that foreign governments had rarely complained before of items in the British press and then only of personal aspersions against a sovereign.[110]

French complaints thus broke with precedent. After further pressure from Otto, Hawkesbury replied the British government neither could nor would grant foreign powers any concession which might even to the smallest degree infringe "the liberty of the press as secured by the constitution of this country." While acknowledging the objectionable tone in articles, he noted that British papers, unlike the *Moniteur*, operated beyond government control. British law prohibited libel. Its courts would resolve complaints under due process of law. Since Britain did not interfere with French laws, Hawkesbury insisted the French act likewise and extended the point to demands for the expulsion of French émigrés. Those who did not violate British law would be permitted to remain, just as France had allowed the presence of Jacobites decades before. Hawkesbury set out a detailed justification of Britain's position that explained the limits to what the government could do and challenged France to meet its obligations of mutual forbearance.[111] George III praised the firmness of Hawkesbury's reply to what he considered a weak and improper note that reinforced the king's view of the French as a faithless people.[112]

Developments in Switzerland, which sought to resist French influence by seeking the great powers to guarantee its independence, brought further tension. Napoleon had warned in early October that continued unrest between pro-and anti-French parties would bring intervention, but Addington's cabinet supported the Swiss and encouraged Austria and Russia to lend aid. Since Austria had already conceded Switzerland to Napoleon, Britain alone supported the Swiss, even though it lacked the means to act effectively. Addington posed as the defender of an oppressed people. Hawkesbury warned Otto that the British nation, and consequently its ministry, would regard "the march of your troops" as a hostile act. French troops still marched. Resistance ended by October despite scattered fighting. Britain had accomplished nothing for the Swiss, but it delayed evacuating territories, including Malta, it was to relinquish.[113]

Hawkesbury discerned "the most unbounded views of ambition" in Napoleon's encroachments, but complaints only brought the retort that Britain should confine itself to the terms made at Amiens and not interfere with Europe. Such actions justified demands in return or at least holding securities for French behavior. Renewed war seemed merely a question of time, but he understood that favorable timing and circumstances also mattered.[114] Pitt concurred on withholding restitutions to France, but urged a conciliatory tone while making naval and military preparations and securing allies.[115] Hawkesbury told Whitworth, who had arrived as Britain's ambassador to France in November, that war under the present circumstances would be "impossible even if it were prudent." Consequently, Addington's cabinet adopted a lower and more pacific tone than they originally intended. Hawkesbury noted the need to discreetly lay the groundwork for a defensive system with Austria and Russia. Liverpool called the government's approach "firmness clothed with moderation, and consequently large establishments, but great temperance in language."[116]

Whitworth and Hawkesbury still bore the weight of an increasingly uphill effort to sustain the failing cold peace with France. An ambitious soldier turned diplomat who had earlier served as ambassador to the Russian court and then Denmark, Whitworth had married the Duchess of Dorset, whose first husband had been ambassador to France as the revolution unfolded. She was also the daughter of Hawkesbury's stepmother from her earlier marriage to Sir Charles Cope. The relationship cemented a personal tie shown by Whitworth's private correspondence. Whitworth reported that advisors urged the first consul to focus on Europe rather than the Caribbean, where Napoleon sought to regain Haiti. Such French efforts in neighboring states were "what we have to fear." Circumstances, may still force Britain to abandon conciliation and stand its ground to the point of a rupture.[117] Whitworth faced the same repeated complaints and provocations on minor points. The situation exposed Hawkesbury to renewed charges of weakness and excessive concession.

Windham had described Bonaparte perceptively as "a player, who, if the game is going against him, will be apt to pick a quarrel and ask us if we can draw our swords."[118] Malta provided the test. The French anticipated renewed expeditions to the east. Publication of a report by Colonel Horace Sébastiani claiming Egypt could be recaptured quickly without large forces created a European sensation.[119] Hawkesbury called it an avowal of Napoleon's intentions that demanded explanation, but he told Whitworth to test whether the French might now consent to Britain retaining Malta even if it required "a moderate *douceur*" of £10,000 or £20,000.[120] Napoleon insisted on the Amiens terms as both sides maneuvered to ensure that blame for war fell upon the other. He and Talleyrand renewed old complaints, while Napoleon himself dismissed British grievances as bagatelles. Hawkesbury refused to give ground, though to avoid a rupture he proposed a six- or seven-year British occupation of Malta. He later offered Elba and other political concessions in Italy to enable Napoleon to save his honor completely if he saw Malta as more a question of honor than possession.[121]

Despite trying to keep the peace, Hawkesbury thought it "impossible to suffer the present state of things to continue long & the conclusion *must* be that in addition to some point of solid security there must be some treaty or convention by which the differences of the two countries will be settled or there will be *war*."[122] Too much remained unresolved and tensions were unsustainable. Whitworth understood that peace now depended less upon fulfilling the Amiens terms than keeping in British hands territories whose reoccupation by France would force "a war under every disadvantage."[123] Since Napoleon refused a settlement that gave Britain security, the value of peace rapidly diminished. Hawkesbury told Whitworth on April 4 that discussions must be brought to an issue and instructed him to ascertain whether the French government would come to terms. If so, Hawkesbury provided a project to open talks. Otherwise, Whitworth should declare amicable relations impossible and announce his intention to leave Paris. When the final discussion came with Talleyrand, the French minister prevaricated and insisted that some in England would agree with him France had played a fair part since Amiens. Whitworth merely replied that he stood at a loss to guess who such persons were.[124]

Much as they wished to postpone war, Hawkesbury and Addington did not hesitate finally drawing the sword. Their attempt at peace showed Britain could have neither compromise nor coexistence with France under its present system. Napoleon negotiated in a spirit of "what's mine is mine and what's yours is negotiable" that only became clearer over time. Agreements with Britain and Austria offered the chance of a standard eighteenth-century peace lasting a decade or more by recognizing spheres of influence and separating them. Napoleon, with his rage and frustration at Britain, refused to make the terms work. Having consolidated his power in France, Napoleon's larger ambitions required victory and the rewards it brought.[125] Robert Liston, a seasoned British diplomat, who looked upon "this would be Caesar" as threatening to establish a new Roman Empire and subject Britain to the fate of Carthage, invoked an old analogy for Anglo-French rivalry that returned from the 1790s. Congratulating Whitworth on "being delivered from an embassy which must for some time have been very unpleasant to you," Liverpool captured the mood in describing Napoleon as "nothing better than a captain of bandits" with "neither the sentiments, the language, nor the manners of a gentleman."[126] The English public shared Liverpool's view of the "great Lilliputian," as they called Napoleon. Contempt for a usurper incapable of moderation or fair dealing guided future policy. Hawkesbury and his colleagues had a sharp lesson from trying peace. They never trusted Napoleon again.

Addington's government still held an apparently strong position, but factionalism shaped a dynamic that undermined it. Support for Pitt and Fox had given politics some coherence, but "now that the main armies are broke down into independent corps, and each has its own discipline, we know not how to handle our votes, shoulder our consciences, or where to look for the word of command."[127]

Illus. 5. James Gillray, "Bat-Catching." Sidmouth and Hawkesbury hunted for support as opposition to the government grew and soon included the formerly supportive Pitt. Broadening government support would be a recurring challenge over Hawkesbury's career

When Pitt stayed away from the 1802 parliamentary session to recuperate his health, he also ceased publicly backing the government and coolly rebuffed Hawkesbury's request for advice on dispatches. A disagreement with Pitt over the summer had set Hawkesbury "on a more independent footing."[128] Support for peace by Fox and Sheridan had limited the scope for opposition to Addington, but their forbearance could not be expected as relations with France deteriorated. Windham and the Grenvilles formed the main opposition in December, and Liverpool noted the latter family's unpopularity despite Lord Grenville's abilities. Canning sniped ineffectively and tried to set Pitt against the government. Tierney thought Addington benefitted from the violence of their hostility, while Hawkesbury reported the government had a stronger hold on public opinion in January 1803 than before. Pitt's absence strengthened its position.[129] Addington still tried to win support, eventually gaining Tierney, who joined the ministry in May as Treasurer of the Navy with a seat on the Privy Council.[130] But he sought a more substantial acquisition as renewed war loomed on the horizon.

Addington invited his predecessor to a meeting on January 5, 1803, where he cautiously broached the subject of Pitt returning to office. Nothing definite followed, especially since Pitt had already decided to oppose the government's financial policies. Their conversation ended on the need to ascertain the king's views. Misreading the situation, Addington made further overtures through Dundas, now raised to the peerage as Viscount Melville, proposing to serve with Pitt as secretaries of state under a mutually acceptable third party. It offered a plausible arrangement with accepted precedents – not least Fox and North's coalition under the Duke of Portland – but Pitt rejected anything besides the acknowledged lead. He remarked "with a sly severity" to Wilberforce that "I had not the curiosity to ask what I was to be." Melville reported that Pitt insisted on "an avowed and real minister possessing the chief weight in the council and the principal place in the confidence of the king." Authority "must rest with the person generally called first minister" who "ought to be at the head of the finances." Pitt firmly believed the First Lord of the Treasury must lead in fact as well as name while thinking any lesser post would diminish his public character.[131]

Despite the rebuff, Addington persisted and tried to mend growing differences in further exchanges that each man misunderstood. Pitt made clear that he would only return if the current government resigned and the king called upon him to form a new ministry which might include his earlier colleagues along with men now in office. Addington brought the proposal to his cabinet, including Hawkesbury and Castlereagh, which rejected it, well aware Pitt might choose to replace them with their fiercest critics. A step barely short of admitting incapacity threatened their own public standing. When Addington laid the matter before the king, George III sarcastically observed that Pitt wished "to put the Crown in commission" and "carried his plan of *removals* so far it might reach *him*." Later the king dismissed the exchange as "a foolish business from one end to the other, which was begun ill, conducted ill, and terminated ill."[132] Hawkesbury's position became more difficult as war resumed.

Hawkesbury put the government's case before the Commons on May 18 in a debate which drew so many spectators that reporters could not find space in the visitor's gallery. Only "a very imperfect sketch" remains. Hawkesbury's argument justifying the war contrasted Britain's "open, liberal, and friendly" approach with the "restless spirit of ambition and domination" that drove the French to injurious and extravagant pretensions.[133] The real clash came on June 3, when a backbencher, Peter Patten, moved to censure ministers. Pitt urged a middle course between censure and approbation before moving the orders of the day to close discussion without a vote. Hawkesbury then demanded a vote on Patten's censure as "the compromise offered between a direct censure and a total acquittal" would betray the duty he and his colleagues owed themselves. Moving the previous question could not dispose properly with a direct charge. Declaring that "never before had he risen with such feelings as those that now oppressed him," Hawkesbury challenged Pitt to offer his criticisms directly so ministers could meet them. Rather than "acquiesce in the discredit of a suspended censure," Hawkesbury would prefer to resign and entreat the king to appoint a more worthy successor.[134]

The challenge could not have been clearer. Hawkesbury did "extraordinary well shewing [sic] both a proper spirit of resistance and a proper feeling at being compelled to make it against an old friend," according to Fox who declared the passionate impromptu reply "the best speech he ever made." Canning stated his unwillingness to end the debate without a division, noting in pained tones that it was the first time he differed from Pitt. The Commons overwhelmingly rejected Pitt's motion by 56 to 333. Patton's original censure then failed. George III congratulated Addington on a result he took as support for ministers against faction.[135] Hawkesbury wondered if Pitt's mind were not completely unhinged by personal friends opposed to Addington's ministry. Liverpool believed the incident significantly damaged the former premier's reputation.[136] Although Pitt had mishandled the situation, the public break showed Addington needed to shore up the government.

Part of that strengthening involved moving Hawkesbury to the Lords to manage business where the premier could not take a direct lead. Liverpool and Grenville had served that role under Pitt. As prime minister, he later grappled with the lack of debating talent on the Treasury bench in the Commons. Rumors had circulated in January that Hawkesbury would go to the Lords. Even before then, Addington had sought to have Castlereagh recognized as his primary lieutenant in the Commons. Liverpool's declining health made Hawkesbury's accession likely at any time. Rheumatism had crippled him so much that a secretary wrote his correspondence. Lord Pelham's inadequacy as leader in the upper house and estrangement from the rest of the cabinet over foreign policy forced a decision

Addington made in May 1803 as part of a wider reshuffle.[137] Liverpool opposed the move as dangerous to his son's prospects. Ill health cast doubt on Pitt's political future. The old peer believed the former premier's old friends, along with many Foxites, would serve under his son. Leading from the Commons would make it more likely for Hawkesbury to continue as prime minister when he moved to the Lords on his own death. Addington may have been "a worthy and good man, with a certain degree of talents," but Liverpool considered his merits insufficient against "the aristocratic feelings of mankind." Hawkesbury's prominence made Addington "little more than an instrument supported by" his son who should not risk future prospects to prop up a weak government.[138]

Hawkesbury nonetheless acquiesced and went to the Lords in November under a writ of acceleration with his father's subsidiary title Baron Hawkesbury. Liverpool told Hawkesbury's grandmother in India that the move spared him the burdens of late night sittings in the Commons, while his character made him "very popular and a favorite with everyone." Lord Hobart thought Hawkesbury displayed "a readiness and confidence about him that will be very useful" to put business on an advantageous footing. But Addington's loss of control over the Commons after Hawkesbury's departure marked a key step in the government's decline.[139] Whatever authority he gained by managing business in the Lords, Hawkesbury lost his prominence as the most able government speaker in the Commons. Castlereagh, Canning, and Spencer Perceval, another of Pitt's protégés, would compete there without him. Being sidelined, however, kept Hawkesbury out of their rivalries. It helped him build a reputation as a political broker that eventually strengthened his own hand. Agreeing to the move despite his father's qualms also showed him willing to set aside his claims for the government he served.

While shoring up the political position at home, Hawkesbury worked assiduously to build a coalition against France. He supported the old policy of securing a Continental sword by aiding great powers that shared Britain's interest while avoiding "acting as *principal* in a Continental war" where it could not land a decisive blow alone.[140] Invoking the principle was easier than applying it, particularly as subsidies alone would not persuade allies to accept British leadership. When Grenville had looked to Austria as a counter to France, Hawkesbury thought Russia a more likely foundation. Even before the Amiens settlement failed, he worked to resolve differences that kept Britain and Russia apart, but Russia, like Austria, set internal matters and recovery from the last war over an assertive foreign policy.[141] Rivalries among the main European powers limited the scope for cooperation. Prussia resisted ties with Austria, partly to avoid drawing Napoleon's wrath, and sought security instead by appeasing France. Austria had no desire for a war in which it would bear the primary burden. Hawkesbury complained in July that "the court of Vienna appears to be very feeble, that of Petersburg very flat & that of Berlin very false."[142] French encroachments did more than British enticements to lead European powers to a renewed coalition. Only in spring 1804 did Hawkesbury's effort start bearing fruit.

By then, however, Addington's government had fallen. The country faced a threat of invasion that lasted until Nelson's victory at Trafalgar in 1805 assured British control over the seas. Preparations to resist attack included contingency plans for a small privy council to remain in London with Hawkesbury, Eldon, and St Vincent to issue necessary acts and orders while Addington joined the king at an advanced headquarters. Confidence in Addington fell as danger grew. Malmesbury reported that from January debates grew longer and more contested. No government measure passed unnoticed or unopposed. George III's illness, which Louisa likened to the 1788 episode that had brought on the Regency Crisis, resumed from February through May, creating further uncertainly.[143] Despite their past differences, Grenville and Fox joined against Addington in a coalition Cornwallis thought "full as profligate as that of Fox and Lord North without holding out a prospect of the same benefit to the country." Pitt also stepped up his efforts to turn out the government he had done so much to form. Addington's situation became untenable by late April. Observers took Hawkesbury's request to postpone a motion in the Lords on April 30 as a sign. Pitt met with George III on May 7 to start discussing a new government.[144]

Hawkesbury's career had advanced, but the country still faced a renewed war against France without a clear strategy. Anticipating a prolonged struggle, the government hoped for a French internal and financial collapse while expecting Napoleon's aggression to prompt a new European coalition against him. Hawkesbury's diplomatic overtures aside, it meant little more than waiting on events.[145] Difficulties with peacemaking and coalition building had taught Hawkesbury that Napoleon would neither compromise nor coexist with Britain. The experimental peace had still allowed the country to recover. Many of Addington's fiscal policies, not least changes in the income tax, brought advantages over the long term. Hawkesbury laid the foundation for Pitt's cooperation with Russia. However dismaying he found criticism of his tenure at the Foreign Office, the experience shaped his later approach to war and diplomacy. Foreign affairs also had delayed the impact of fallout from Pitt's resignation. The eventual split between Pitt, Addington, and Grenville reinforced factionalism. Addington now felt wronged by Pitt and Grenville, neither of whom gained from breaking with him. More importantly, he could not return intact the political structure Pitt had bequeathed. Rivalries and the problems they created shaped Hawkesbury's future.

CHAPTER 4

Political Broker

Hawkesbury's tenure as foreign secretary, despite its frustrations, staked his claim to prominence. As colleagues resigned, they gave him their seals of office for safekeeping as the only secretary of state to continue in Pitt's new government. The small detail points to the role he quietly acquired over the coming years.[1] Moving to the Lords, as his father predicted, took Hawkesbury from the contest in the Commons among Pitt's followers for the lead. It eventually cast him as the mediator among the eventual claimants to Elijah's mantle. Hawkesbury also stepped into his father's role as George III's confidant, a position strengthened by handling quarrels between the Prince of Wales and the king. His most challenging negotiations, however, involved Pitt and Addington, whom he eventually brought together in a short-lived reconciliation. Exchanging the Foreign Office for the home department at Pitt's insistence sparked unwelcome controversy of its own from an early stage.

Pitt no longer dominated politics as the infant Hercules resting upon Chatham's shield or the giant factotum who towered over the Commons and amused himself with the globe. His speed filling leading offices in May 1804 belied the fact that he now operated within a more limited scope. By refusing to admit Fox to the cabinet, George III dashed plans for a comprehensive administration with leading men from all parliamentary factions. Pitt argued that Napoleon's conduct had superseded differences over the French Revolution. A broad government free of opposition would facilitate a new military coalition against France. It also would remove anxiety that agitation of the Catholic question would revive by precluding support from any faction.[2] After rejecting the original plan, the king later agreed on the value of an extended administration. He even waived objections to certain figures holding particular offices, but persisted in rejecting Fox, whom he saw as the most dangerous of politicians, without, however, denying him a post abroad.[3] Refusing to accept office without Fox, Grenville condemned any principle of exclusion. His stance, which prevented an inclusive government, irritated Pitt and reinforced factionalism. Pitt indignantly declared he would teach that proud man how with the king's confidence he could do without him.[4]

Doing without Grenville and the Foxites narrowed Pitt's options, but he had overcome similar constraints in his first government. His problem now involved the lack of weight in parliament rather than filling offices. Too many leading men either stood with the opposition or would soon join it, which set a premium on colleagues who could hold their own in debate. Pitt had to balance the liability of Hawkesbury's record at the Foreign Office against personal feelings and need for his talents. Grenvillites blamed Hawkesbury no less than Addington for the "criminal annihilation of the internal and external political strength of the country." Pitt's early cabinet plan excluded him.[5] But needing help with managing business in the Lords, Pitt persuaded Hawkesbury to take the home department. The Foreign Office could then be used to recruit Lord Moira and thereby secure backing from the faction associated with the Prince of Wales. When Moira declined, Pitt sought the post for his friend Lord Harrowby, whose health and talents he claimed were unsuited to a more demanding office. Hawkesbury again waived his objections.[6] Liverpool thought the move harmed his son's reputation, especially when it meant accommodating Harrowby rather than Moira. With political squabbles far from done only Hawkesbury's "acknowledged talents and the excellence of his temper" would overcome difficulties ahead.[7]

The first problems came in June when Canning vented his resentment in a public attack that drew attention to Hawkesbury's move from the Foreign Office. Holding junior office as Treasurer of the Navy – considered a plum for its salary and perquisites – stung his pride while Hawkesbury and Castlereagh sat with Pitt in the cabinet. Canning privately described his rival as "kicked from the foreign to the home department with as little ceremony (indeed less than) I used in making Brown under butler again after he had officiated as butler."[8] A June 18 debate prompted him to attack the previous ministry in the guise of defending his personal consistency:

> ...he had objected to the administration of foreign affairs, and that had been changed, he had objected to the naval administration, and that had been changed; he had objected to the military administration, and that had been changed; he had also objected to the general superintendence of the whole, and that had been changed.[9]

Hawkesbury alone among those Canning indicted remained in the cabinet. Nobody missed the implication that Canning had demanded the change. Addington's brother-in-law, Charles Bragge Bathurst, landed a telling blow by noting that Canning owed his introduction to public life and present office to Hawkesbury's early friendship. Pointing out Canning's ingratitude failed to answer the charge of incompetence. Sheridan questioned Pitt's judgment in having once ranked Hawkesbury with Fox only to replace him with the untested Harrowby.[10] Weakly defending the "noble friend whom I have always loved and esteemed," Pitt dismissed the whole discussion. Fox ardently disagreed that the move involved no degradation of Hawkesbury, but acknowledged Pitt could "form his own judgment on such a humiliation."

Unwilling to act hastily, Hawkesbury took a day before sending Pitt his resignation. He had agreed to move against his own preference to accommodate Pitt. Duty made him set aside concerns about the impression it gave, but he could not honorably continue in office when a colleague supposed to hold Pitt's confidence marked the transfer as a censure. The imputation now made publicly, he noted, had circulated privately for some time past.[11] Pitt faced a serious problem. Castlereagh might also leave if Hawkesbury resigned, along with other veterans of Addington's cabinet.[12] Liverpool thought Pitt would be in "high wrath" with Canning for bringing on the whole situation. Having "at least concealed the truth, if he did not in effect tell a falsehood," Pitt "acted in a manner unbecoming a man of honor." Hawkesbury held a strong position. Beside the king's personal esteem, Liverpool thought Pitt "will not know what to do in the management of the House of Lords if you should quit the administration" since Melville could not lead English peers.[13] Avowing the real ground for moving him – that his tenure as foreign secretary had been too controversial – would have been a rebuke, but Pitt could not openly deny it. Canning's malice had brought a crisis.

When they met, Pitt sought to dissuade Hawkesbury from resigning. He even offered Canning's resignation. Although Canning had stated that he, if anyone, should resign, being offered as a sacrifice to propitiate Hawkesbury's wrath would damage his reputation. Luckily for him, Hawkesbury thought it discreditable to force Canning from office. Liverpool observed Canning now owed his son not only an introduction to public life but continuance in his present office.[14] Hawkesbury still wished Pitt to make clear publicly that no blame attached to his conduct as foreign secretary. Explanations to date had not resolved the point. Carefully avoiding his unwillingness to keep Hawkesbury at the Foreign Office, Pitt declared he would readily testify that nobody would ascribe the move to anything besides personal accommodation. Whether "any other consideration of expediency weighed in my mind," however, could never be a subject for public discussion.

Although Pitt hoped it closed the dispute, Canning revived controversy in early January by complaining to Hawkesbury that "persons calling themselves friends of yours & professing to speak *from authority*, go about asserting" that he had "*asked your pardon*" for his expressions respecting the change of office. More seriously, they reported Pitt had declared, if Hawkesbury insisted, "*it was his determination that I should go out.*" Pitt had denied this when Canning approached him, saying he had merely repeated Canning's own offer to resign. While not believing that Hawkesbury thought Canning suspected him of misstating the facts, he considered "a distinct assurance" as nothing more than due to them both.[15] Hawkesbury stood his ground and presented Pitt's stand in very different terms. However painful he might have found Canning's resignation, Pitt thought himself bound to accept if Hawkesbury insisted. He instead had refused that anyone be sacrificed on his account. Regretting as much as anyone that "it should have been unavoidable to say anything respecting" the matter, Hawkesbury bluntly stated he had not created the necessity.[16] Having tried to press Hawkesbury into an admission, Canning found Pitt had prevaricated with them both and dropped the matter.[17]

What seemed an echo of teasing and quarrels from Christ Church days anticipated Canning's famous duel with Castlereagh in 1809. Hawkesbury took a firm line, but held back from damaging a man he still considered a friend. Canning resented Pitt's willingness to make him "a propitiatory sacrifice." The refusal of his offer to fill Harrowby's place temporarily – without title, salary, or place in cabinet – while the foreign secretary recuperated from a serious injury embittered him further. Hawkesbury took a more conciliatory line when Pitt appointed Mulgrave to succeed Harrowby. Canning still disparaged his rival to Pitt, remarking with a backhanded compliment that Hawkesbury "speaks as much above his talents, as he talks (in common conversation) below them…he is not either a Ninny – or a great and able man." Pitt replied that he "could not do without him in the House of Lords and though I do not say he is the man to whose decision singly I would commit a great question of policy, yet with his information – that I hardly think you put high enough – and the habits of reflection which he has acquired, he is by no means a contemptible advisor."[18] While Pitt ranked Hawkesbury as a pillar of state rather than a potential capstone of its edifice, the exchange suggests why Hawkesbury was the tortoise to Canning's hare in the race for preferment.

George III welcomed Hawkesbury's appointment as home secretary with responsibility for reporting to him on parliamentary business. The king's health remained a concern for an administration that needed his firm support. While "perfectly good" in the company of those he respected, he behaved erratically among "the female part of his family" or servants. Want of discrimination in conversation presented more difficulty than any incoherence.[19] Hawkesbury thought a relapse unlikely so long as the king remained calm, but noted "those who see him at unguarded moments" believed he had not recovered as far could be wished.[20] Conflicts within the royal family risked a relapse. The Prince of Wales put his parliamentary following against Pitt's administration. Indeed, having told Canning in early May that his father remained "as mad as ever," the prince urged allies not to trust reports of physicians alone, but to raise the matter in parliament. Concerns from the Regency Crisis of 1788–9 returned. Many feared pressure from opposition groups might overset the king's mind to force a regency that would bring Fox and Grenville to power.[21] Queen Charlotte and the Duke of York had sought Pitt's return partly because they doubted Addington could back them effectively against the prince. The royal family had split with the

Duke of Kent "acting a doubtful part between them."[22] Faction upset the court just as Pitt needed help shoring up his government and Napoleon threatened invasion.

Pitt's desire to neutralize the prince by bringing Moira into the government led him to promote a reconciliation between father and son that agitated George III. The prince had declared himself open to a rapprochement, a step his political advisors urged, but he reacted badly on learning the king had received his estranged wife, Caroline of Brunswick, with their daughter present. An ill-conceived marriage had brought together fundamentally incompatible personalities. Mutual dislike curdled into resentment that made otherwise routine matters contentious. The prince's uncompromising stand on anything involving Caroline stirred trouble with ministers and his family. He only conceded that George III could supervise his granddaughter's education if Caroline had no part in it. A new row followed when the king incensed his son by showing Caroline favor when he met her. The prince's disrespectful tone in a note cancelling a planned interview with the king made Eldon refuse to forward it. He instead told the king that an indisposition kept the prince away. Rather than reconciling George III with his wayward son, the incident provoked him to abuse the prince in the presence of his other sons and postpone their meeting until after a seaside holiday at Weymouth.[23]

Hawkesbury accompanied George III to Weymouth, partly to handle administrative business requiring the king's attention but also to deflect problems likely to agitate him. Managing the king became part of his brief. As a courtier, Hawkesbury sought to uphold the king's personal dignity while helping him fulfill his public duties. Monarch and minister shared opinions along with a sense of moral purposefulness that strengthened their relationship. The court's importance for brokering and staging politics made Hawkesbury's role important. Liverpool told his son the king should always have around him somebody in whom he could confide and, if necessary, remove members of his family who might disturb him.[24] Hawkesbury took care to avoid the appearance of "a settled plan" to watch over the king lest it upset him. Calm in late August gave way to renewed excitability in September and early October. Outbursts of rage and suggestive remarks to ladies sparked uneasy laughter. George III also pestered Lady Pembroke with love letters, though Lady Bessborough later remarked that "in favor his taste, she is the handsomest woman of seventy I ever saw." He was also politically indiscreet with occasional diatribes against Catholics, reformers, and Pitt. [25] The king still improved from his time at Weymouth where Hawkesbury kept from him the news of talks between ministers and the Prince of Wales. Although George III met the prince on November 12 without unpleasant consequences, nothing substantive passed between them.[26]

Hopes of reconciliation foundered over their inability to agree on Princess Charlotte's education. Discussion of the matter had resumed in October, but the king did not realize his plan for the princess had antagonized his son. Moreover, some of the prince's allies sought to dissuade him from drawing closer to Pitt. Hawkesbury concluded that the point could not easily be settled and nothing political would arise from a meeting between the king and his heir.[27] At the same time, Hawkesbury faced an unexpected revival of Catholic agitation in Ireland, encouraged by English politicians, including the Grenvilles. Besides stirring Irish discontent and raising an awkward question in parliament, he thought agitation would drive Whigs further from the king to make overtures harder. While Pitt would be forced to resist concessions, others who might support Catholic Emancipation would take a position against it they would find hard to drop later. Pressing the issue would be "little short of insanity for the Catholics" as the timing risked embarrassing ministers without much chance of success.[28] At this point, the politics of the Catholic question outweighed its substance for Hawkesbury. Combined with the failure of overtures to the Prince of Wales, it pointed to the advantage of reconciling Pitt and Addington whose differences were more personal than involving policy or principle.

Rapprochement between them served Hawkesbury better than Pitt's hopes of support from Grenville or Fox. Brokering it became an important challenge. Liverpool noted that men of Addington's character "will always recover the good opinion of the public when they are out of office, though they are neither praised nor sufficiently respected so long as they retain their power." Addington had gained credit by declining an earldom and pension when he resigned. Liverpool saw him a likely successor if illness forced Pitt to resign, but the king's incapacity would bring Fox and Moira to power under the Prince of Wales as regent.[29] Addington retained some bitterness towards "those of the new government who were recently my colleagues & who still call themselves my friends." Visits with Liverpool kept him informed and rebuilt relations with Hawkesbury whose conduct in the dispute with Canning had impressed him.[30]

Loyalty to the crown made Pitt and Addington subordinate their own personal feelings and interests. Addington intended "to remain quiet and aloof," unless duty compelled him to state a position. Otherwise, he sought to "avoid the reality, and as far as possible, even the appearance of cabal," and refused to be "the stalking-horse of opposition."[31] When failure of talks with the prince forced Pitt to seek other support, Hawkesbury believed he and Addington could be brought together so long as the resentment of his friends did not lead the latter astray.[32] The prospect of agitation on the Catholic question made him a more solid partner than Grenville. A dinner with the Hawkesburys, their first friendly meeting since the previous government resigned, updated Addington on political news and provided an opening for further discussion. Addington showed little disposition to take office. Finding a suitable place for his friend, the former secretary for war and colonies, Lord Buckinghamshire, presented difficulties. Hawkesbury convinced Addington by pressing the need to consolidate the king's government. The overture came at his own initiative. Only after broaching the subject of a rapprochement with Addington did Hawkesbury receive the authority to negotiate.[33]

When they met on December 12, Hawkesbury found Addington's "personal feelings everything that can be wished." Concurring in Hawkesbury and Pitt's general view of public affairs, Addington thought full advantage of their agreement required a formal union. While he still resisted a peerage from concerns his own fortune would not support the dignity, he also saw it would be awkward to stay in the Commons while holding office under Pitt. Hawkesbury thought further reflection would remove the difficulty. Despite preferring one of the secretaryships of state, Addington would be satisfied with the presidency of the council. The main difficulty involved finding a suitable office with cabinet rank for Buckinghamshire, but Hawkesbury trusted they could resolve the issue.[34] Talks faltered since Pitt had nothing presently available for Buckinghamshire. Hawkesbury emphasized how the proposed reconciliation would help the king's health. Besides impressing upon Pitt the need to bring Addington into office, he also sounded out George III, whose favorable response enabled Hawkesbury to note the king's gratification at a reconciliation likely to counteract "the many & cruel vexations to which he is unfortunately exposed."[35] The friends turned rivals met at Combe Wood on the afternoon of Sunday, December 23 for a three-hour interview. Hawkesbury left the room as Pitt entered and told Addington "I rejoice to take you by the hand again."[36]

Hawkesbury's sister-in-law, Lady Elizabeth Foster, thought the news so strange as to be only a rumor until she saw it declared openly. Friendship among public men who had violently opposed each other was far from novel, but "to forgive cold unpitying scorn and contempt has been hitherto unheard of and the *Morning Chronicle* will not let it be forgot that Pitt applied the most contemptuous terms to Addington and his administration."[37] Despite favorable newspaper reports and encouraging congratulations from friends the new arrangement seemed fragile. Even as Addington met Pitt, Hawkesbury had warned "the Devil will be at work to separate you as *he* was before, nine times *he* will fail, but the tenth *he may* succeed."[38] Hawkesbury alluded to Canning, whose continuance in office Addington twice declined to contest when the point arose. Partisans of both leaders had fed animosities with jibes and witticisms that stung more than straight criticism. They remembered slights their leaders preferred to forget. Sir William Scott also thought the number of their adherents made any adjustment impossible as "there was not pasture enough for them all." Bathurst, despite his friendship with Addington, considered the terms higher than reasonable, not least because he thought Hawkesbury's partiality and good humor precluded hard bargaining.[39]

Pitt took charge once he met Addington at Hawkesbury's house. The three settled arrangements over the following weeks. Addington became Lord President of the Council as Viscount Sidmouth. Hawkesbury magnanimously offered him the lead in the Lords, but he declined. Buckinghamshire became Chancellor of the Duchy of Lancaster, a post Mulgrave vacated to succeed Harrowby as foreign secretary.[40] Despite not only brokering the reconciliation, but pressing it upon both Pitt and Addington, Hawkesbury kept in the background. Fox at first thought it Pitt's own work, but later concluded the initiative lay with George III who had a fine triumph that humiliated Pitt by forcing him to seek aid from a former ally he had come to disparage. *The Times* also credited the king, whose scheme Hawkesbury merely facilitated.[41] As during the earlier negotiations with France, he seemed an instrument rather than an actor. The impression suited him, however, and reflected his preference for operating behind the scenes. Canning cut a brighter figure, but the blazing flame of his uncontrolled personality, as Croker later wrote, "had no use but to raise the wonder of distant spectators and to warm the very narrow circle that immediately surrounds it."[42] Hawkesbury's discretion helped provide the staying power his rival lacked.

Although Hawkesbury thought Harrowby's departure from the Foreign Office might return him to a post whose business particularly interested him, neither Pitt nor the king welcomed it. Mulgrave was a loyal and sufficiently capable alternative who made no waves and might step aside without objection if Pitt needed the post to win further support. The publicist William Cobbett thought Pitt's choice of Mulgrave enraged Liverpool and Hawkesbury. He revived the earlier quarrel with Canning by reporting the offer Pitt had made at his protégé's expense. But Hawkesbury increasingly preferred his new position over the Foreign Office where he had faced constant attacks. Experience as a political lightning rod left him wary. Reuniting Pitt and Addington raised his standing with George III, who praised "the judiciousness and fairness of his conduct."[43]

Leading the Home Office brought Hawkesbury closer to the king while drawing him into the wide range of government business internal affairs involved. Threats of a French invasion which peaked in August 1804 dominated his early months. Reporting Napoleon's preparations in ports from Ostend to Cherbourg to his father, he issued an August circular to lords lieutenant on arrangements to preserve order and prevent alarm in case of invasion.[44] Routine business included submitting warrants for the king's signature and reporting to him parliamentary debates. Largely formal replies to petitions and addresses highlighted the department's role as conduit for communication between king and subjects. Maintaining public order was a more serious task. Local magistrates, sheriffs, and justices of the peace exercised direct authority in partnership with a central government which lacked the means to act directly on its own. Hawkesbury handled requests for pardons which went to the king. The Home Office corresponded with local authorities on social conditions, along with the riots and disorders they caused. Reading these reports over his long tenure gave Hawkesbury insight on local concerns and a strong feeling for sentiment among country gentlemen and clergy whose backing ministers needed. Irish business also fell within Hawkesbury's brief. By touching a whole range of domestic issues the Home Office trained him both in those matters and the internal governance of the realm.[45]

A combination among boot and shoemakers in London to press for higher wages and the exclusion of journeymen adopted the model of the radical corresponding societies during the early 1790s, prompting employers to petition for their prosecution. The petition raised concerns about trade unions which would become increasingly prominent. Hawkesbury took a cautious approach and referred the matter to the Attorney General, Spencer Perceval. Perceval's response separated the legal question of whether those involved were liable to prosecution – he concluded their combination was illegal – from the political wisdom of pursuing the case. Prosecution would set a precedent. Given "similar combinations in almost every trade in the kingdom," other employers would demand the government act in their cases as well. Blaming the conspiracy on the timidity of the employers responsible for prosecuting in their own interest, Perceval noted that complaints always exist on both sides of such cases. If journeymen sought a prosecution of employers for a conspiracy against their men, government risked "testing its impartiality."[46] Hawkesbury declined to initiate a prosecution and the matter dropped. Concerns about law and order in London led him to propose a horse patrol to secure the three principal roads into the city. Having been robbed by a highwayman during his schooldays, he appreciated the benefits of reassuring travelers. A toll would eventually cover the expense. Improved security would bring savings when the gradual extension of horse patrols cut the number of foot patrols. The Treasury Board approved the plan. George III praised Hawkesbury for steadily improving the means to police "the overgrown metropolis as well as […] the rest of the kingdom."[47]

Eagerness to impress Pitt embarrassed Hawkesbury in an incident that showed how he could occasionally strike a ridiculous pose. When Pitt asked the cabinet for suggestions on the insignia of an order of merit he decided to establish in 1805, Hawkesbury arranged a color scheme and design. Lady Hester Stanhope, Pitt's acerbic niece, told the story that he arrived in her uncle's absence and presented his work to the company. Hawkesbury proudly declared he "had endeavored to combine such colors as would flatter the national vanity. Here is red for the English flag, blue for liberty, and white to denote the purity of motive." Some of the group expressed admiration in toadying words. Lady Hester pronounced the colors charming, having seen them very often. When Hawkesbury nervously asked where she had seen them, she blandly replied "in the French soldiers' cockades." He then quailed at his error in ordering five hundred yards of ribbon. Poor Hawkesbury, "who was a good sort of man, but who had been putting himself forward in the thing he was not fit for, had stupidly overlooked the tri-colored flag, and was thunderstruck." Lady Hester told him the ribbon would serve well "to tie up your breeches; for you know, you always have such a load of papers in your breeches pockets, that I quite fear to see them some day fall down." [48] Zeal, and a woman's sharp wit, had the better of him.

Irish affairs fell to the Home Office. Revived agitation for Catholic Emancipation presented Hawkesbury a more serious challenge that risked upsetting Ireland's internal tranquility while France remained a threat. Hawkesbury told Lord Hardwicke, Lord Lieutenant of Ireland, in November that, since Pitt could only resist demands for Catholic Emancipation to the utmost, it was

> little short of insanity for the Catholics to think of presenting their claims at present, for the consequence will infallibly be that many persons will be committed against them who under other circumstances might come to a different conclusion, but who having taken this line upon the question, may be disposed afterwards to adhere to it.

Hawkesbury reasoned presciently as later events would show. Since "removal of the existing disabilities would not *practically* benefit ten persons in the whole country," renewed agitation must aim either to embarrass ministers or bring further demands likely to alarm those "attached to the existing constitution in Church and state."[49] The frustration behind those words had led him to broker the reunion with Addington.

Hawkesbury worked with Hardwicke into the winter to persuade Catholic spokesmen to postpone their demands or at least present them in respectful terms and without expecting government support. Again in January he called pushing the question unintelligible because it could never be resisted with such strength. While believing it best to avoid any agitation, he privately wished the matter be debated and decided rather to have the Irish "kept in a feverish state." The point underlined Hawkesbury's concern with maintaining order. Opposition encouragement stirred activity in Ireland, and he thought they would be "severely disappointed" if the question did not arise in the current parliamentary session.[50] A renewed suspension of habeas corpus would be necessary given the danger France would invade a disaffected Ireland, but he also held out the possibility it might be avoided if that threat diminished. Although he later hoped the Catholic Deputies would not put their petition in the hands of opposition leaders after Pitt had seen them, Hawkesbury feared nothing could be done to prevent controversy.[51]

Other matters intervened before the opposition brought the question forward. A letter from Napoleon with a peace overture reached the Foreign Office on January 7, 1805. Pitt forwarded it to George III suggesting a reply pointing out that Britain sought a peace which provided for not only its own interests but also those of Europe. Consequently, it would not open talks before communication with other interested powers.[52] Renewed efforts to build a coalition against France paralleled the breakdown of relations with Spain, which Napoleon squeezed for money and resources. Hawkesbury insisted during the debate on the announcement of war with Spain that ministers had no disposition to do anything rash or precipitous. Grenville declared he could "not hear it made the source of self-congratulation and panegyric, that we have been near two years at war, and have not yet been invaded...that is no great cause of triumph."[53] Ministers now faced a united opposition of Foxite Whigs and Grenville's friends when parliament opened.

Pitt's familiar indolence and reluctance in what Camden had called those little attentions needed to recruit and hold parliamentary support became a serious problem.[54] Hawkesbury's role in managing business, rallying support, and leading debates in the Lords became all the more vital. A motion on February 15 to repeal the additional forces bill enabled Grenville to criticize ministers broadly, especially for acquiescing to the king's veto on Fox. Mulgrave warned that sacrificing principle "for an ill-timed spleen or caprice" marked a dangerous expedient. Hawkesbury pointed out that Grenvillites and Foxites profoundly disagreed on constitutional principles and both foreign and domestic politics. "Such a coalition," he insisted, "marked it the object of universal astonishment, if not of indignation."[55] Divided on principle and policy, Hawkesbury implied, their only bond could be a self-interested desire for office. Rumblings among the government's followers nevertheless hinted at difficulties between Pitt and Sidmouth.

Charges of malfeasance against Melville in the tenth report of the Commissioners of Naval Inquiry published on February 13 made the spark that ignited conflict. Melville had appointed as paymaster to the navy Alexander Trotter, a Scots protégé of Minto, rather than Melville himself, who Pitt had recommended. Trotter had speculated illegally with public money, misusing some £1,000,000 in 1795. Although Melville had not acted illegally himself – and the report noted that the treasurer did not perform his official duties in person, but rather devolved "the whole charge and conduct of his office by a general power of attorney" – he stood culpable for having shielded Trotter, borrowing money from him, and occasionally diverting funds from the navy to other public business. His carelessness had allowed the private diversion of public funds. Pitt saw the danger.[56] Enemies made over a long career left Melville vulnerable. General knowledge that George III disliked him did not help. Many shared Windham's view that none could regret "the termination of power raised by such means as his and employed in such a way." Taking the Admiralty from hands "that would soon have given us a Scotch navy" offered "a separate piece of good fortune." Sidmouth, backed strongly by Hawkesbury, urged that Melville either face an independent enquiry or resign to forestall a hostile parliamentary motion. Pitt, who originally preferred confronting any challenge à outrance, reluctantly agreed.[57]

Samuel Whitbread, one of the more radical Foxites, moved a censure that alleged illegal use of public funds and charged Melville with conniving at Trotter's peculation. The debate on April 8, 1805, which Malmesbury thought exceeded others in "savage feeling," ended with a 216 vote tie. Thirty-two of Sidmouth's friends voted with Whitbread. "White as a sheet," Charles Abbott, speaker of the house and a staunch critic of administrative irregularity, departed from the usual practice of giving time for further reflection and cast the deciding vote for Whitbread's motion. "Huzzas and shouts" then arose, with Sir Thomas Mostyn crying from the opposition benches "we have killed the Fox." A celebrated account written years later described a tearful, stunned Pitt led from the chamber.[58] Pressure diminished after Melville resigned the next day, though Pitt had to concede his dismissal from the Privy Council. George III declared the virulence against him "unbecoming the character of Englishmen." Melville's impeachment taught politicians the public would tolerate neither scandal nor careless management. Behavior shifted accordingly.[59] It also cost Pitt a valued ally and close friend while forcing the awkward question of replacing Melville at the Admiralty.

Hawkesbury expressed private misgivings about taking the job, even before Pitt raised the possibility. Under the present circumstances, however, he did not think it creditable to decline. Rumor circulated. Cobbett told Windham that Hawkesbury had declined as the change was "a *degradation*" that made him appear "a man to be used; a mere bolt to be shoved backwards & forward."[60] Liverpool warned his son's reputation would suffer as it had by the earlier move and cost the credit he had recovered by his conduct in Lords. News that Hawkesbury declined gratified the suspicious Liverpool. When Pitt directly raised the question, Hawkesbury argued that relinquishing leadership in the Lords would weaken the government at a dangerous time. He privately thought political tensions among naval officers made the Admiralty a particularly thankless post likely to draw criticism. The choice instead fell between the elderly Sir Charles Middleton, a naval officer with long administrative experience, and Sidmouth's ally Buckinghamshire.[61] Middleton's appointment opened a quarrel with Sidmouth, who thought it weakened the government. He told Pitt that staying in office would be "neither useful to the public nor honorable to myself," a sentiment he repeated several days later. Hawkesbury again negotiated between Pitt and Sidmouth, who complained Pitt had used him for political convenience.[62] Although Buckinghamshire resigned on April 23, Pitt kept Sidmouth from an immediate break without mending their quarrel.

The Catholic question eclipsed other differences when Grenville forced the debate Hawkesbury had sought to avoid. After Grenville gave notice of his motion for May 10, 1805 and had the petition read in the Lords on March 25, Hawkesbury acknowledged the right of petitioning as a sacred privilege. Nothing could exempt the house from receiving petitions unless the matter were beyond their lordships jurisdiction or somehow disrespectful in form or language. Since neither condition applied to the Catholic petition he did not object to its being laid on the table, but withheld further comment.[63] Grenville closed a long speech on May 10 by moving to consider the petition. Hawkesbury charged that his intemperate tone in suggesting the question must inevitably be carried held out "something like a menace to the house." Grenville sharply called Hawkesbury to order for grossly misrepresenting a phrase which "only meant that sooner or later truth and reason must triumph over the prejudice of any party." The home secretary coolly replied that he stood "equally ready to meet him upon that ground."[64]

Hawkesbury approached the Catholic question from the perspective of public order in Ireland and the constitutional position of an Established Church. Hitherto, he had carefully avoided public comment. The concern he privately expressed that the present agitation would push opponents into a harder line than they might otherwise choose perhaps applied to himself. He certainly saw Grenville pressing the question as factious opposition. Hawkesbury consulted John Ireland, his father's chaplain and private secretary, who had published an 1801 pamphlet against ending disabilities against Roman Catholics and an earlier work in 1797 that likened puritan opponents of Charles I to French Jacobins. Ireland's views highlight a harsher tone against Catholicism that emerged among High Churchmen after 1800. He complimented Hawkesbury's speech after the debate and advised on revising it for publication.[65] Hawkesbury told the peers that Grenville's motion went beyond the petition to the full extent of repealing all religious tests in every part of the empire, a step he opposed at any time and under any circumstances. Stating that his opinion sprang from long reflection and inquiry, Hawkesbury argued that political power – and the constitution bequeathed by 1688 – rather than toleration was at stake.[66]

"Every class of religious persons" Hawkesbury insisted, "deserves the support, the toleration, and protection of a rational state." He had always believed "toleration should be extended to all classes of religionists, and to all sectaries." The French Revolution had shown beyond doubt that "men who possess any religion, be what it may, are to be preferred both as men and as subjects from those who have none." Catholics had proven on many occasions "most loyal and excellent subjects even to a Protestant sovereign." But access to political power differed from civil liberty – and Hawkesbury insisted that while no man should be denied civil liberty, the extension of political power should operate according to the opposite principle. That the king should be Protestant and hold communion with the Church of England was a fundamental principle derived from the evils of a king hostile to the religion established by the state. Hawkesbury argued that what applied to the crown should also cover its immediate advisors and officers of the crown acting by its authority. Otherwise those outside the Church – and who viewed it as heretical or idolatrous – would exercise authority over it. Bitter experience in the seventeenth century showed the dangers. Catholics, unlike Protestant dissenters, also acknowledged a foreign jurisdiction in the pope. Should they be granted "political power of every description at the time when they refuse to accept the authority of the state?"[67]

Irish circumstances sharpened the question of extending Catholics' political power. Giving them the vote there had produced "something approaching very near to universal suffrage." It brought little inconvenience now as they could only vote for Protestant candidates. With Protestants holding most land, tenants by the natural order of society generally followed their landlords. Opening parliament to Catholics, Hawkesbury warned, would bring priests to exert influence in favor of Catholic candidates. The influence of property and religion would then operate against each other to produce "internal disorder and confusion." Pressure would fall most injuriously on the lower orders as competing interests targeted them. Ending the religious test, Hawkesbury insisted, would "afford no advantage whatsoever to the great mass of the Catholic population of Ireland." Abolishing tithes concerned them far more than political office. Catholics already enjoyed admission to all but thirty-eight higher offices of state and the houses of parliament. The concession Grenville demanded only changed the ground of the political contest by yielding the outer defense of a church establishment fundamental to the balanced constitution. Appealing to Whig veneration for the bill of rights and Tory support for the monarchy and Established Church, Hawkesbury urged his listeners to "cherish the laws under which you have lived and prospered" and "not despise the wisdom of our ancestors, nor forget the dangers which they averted."[68]

His thought-out defense of the Church establishment echoed arguments his father had made earlier in an English context during the 1770s. Hawkesbury's points regarding Ireland would seem prescient from the standpoint of the 1820s when Daniel O'Connell organized Catholics into a mass organization. The king had made similar ones privately to Pitt when he rejected Catholic Emancipation. Irish circumstances differed both in the proportion of the population outside the Established Church and developments from the 1791 Catholic Relief Act that granted Catholics in Ireland the franchise through the 1798 rising, and the Act of Union. Hawkesbury's speech committed him much further than any earlier statement. Its argument precluded settling the Catholic question through a concordat with Rome protecting the Established Church and the Protestant interests in Ireland while drawing Catholics closer to the British state. Others government speakers, including Shute Barrington, the Bishop of Durham, shared Hawkesbury's view that the petition demanded power rather than toleration. Lord Redesdale spoke from his experience in Ireland by describing the clergy's influence there as "almost unbounded" since they "assumed an authority much greater than belonged to the catholic clergy in any other country whatsoever."[69] Debate adjourned around 3 a.m. The division went against Grenville's motion by 178 to 51.

It had been a pivotal debate whose larger implications were only felt much later. George III expressed satisfaction as "the question of toleration will now stand on its true legs and not pretend to mean more than any wise government can possibly admit."[70] Defeat of the petition inflicted a major setback on the opposition while highlighting Hawkesbury's leading role. A burlesque print drawing on *Paradise Lost* showed him just below Pitt – and well above Sidmouth – giving a blast of wind that overwhelmed Grenville presenting the Catholic petition in bishop's garb. Other petitioners, including Sheridan holding a monstrance featuring a crowned N for Napoleon, were also swept aside. The outcome underlined popular suspicions that the opposition wore English ways very lightly even where not actually clothed in foreign ones. Renewed suspicions of Catholicism joined distrust of Foxite policy towards the French Revolution and the present war against Napoleon to taint the opposition.[71]

Further trouble came from the Melville affair as the independent line Sidmouth's friends took angered Pitt. Hiley Addington and Nathaniel Bond not only voted for a harsher penalty, they also made provocative speeches criticizing Melville. "Unprejudiced persons," as Hawkesbury phrased it, thought the Addingtonians had taken an unnecessary line that hurt the government.[72] Matters deteriorated rapidly. Hawkesbury told his father Pitt's friends were in a rage with Sidmouth. Even if they once more avoided a break, he feared grave inconvenience. Besides Pitt's objections, the king refused the appointment for Bond that Sidmouth demanded as the price of staying on. Hawkesbury's relations with Sidmouth, who had made no confidential communication to him for two months, withered as he fell "wholly into the hands of others."[73] When Sidmouth gave up the dispatch box key upon resigning, he told a very uncomfortable king that he was no longer on speaking terms with Hawkesbury. To Bathurst he complained that Hawkesbury's coldness and neglect had lost opportunities to cement the union with Pitt.[74] Thinking the resignation "ill-judged, unnecessary, and at this moment cruel to the king," Hawkesbury thought Sidmouth sacrificed every other consideration to remain "head of a party."[75]

Although the break further weakened the government, Pitt had already returned to his earlier idea of an inclusive ministry and authorized discreet overtures to Grenville. Thomas Grenville believed Hawkesbury's relationship with both the king and Pitt himself would make his remaining in office a likely condition, a sticking point given Lord Grenville's views. Their brother Buckingham noted that since Pitt and Fox could only act together on a ground of equality, another person would need to take the nominal lead which meant "the real push will be to place Ld Hawkesbury at the treasury." Although Grenville had earlier dismissed the notion, Buckingham pointed out that Pitt would not accept a Foxite and the post must go to someone agreeable to both sides.[76] Hawkesbury's standing with George III made him a plausible candidate. Liverpool, however, feared it might be a trick to discredit his son and thought Pitt capable of any measure that would serve his aims.[77] The discussion marked Hawkesbury's place as a star in the political firmament, though one described as shining with a borrowed, albeit brilliant, light and taking a course "liable to continual aberrations."[78]

When parliament rose on July 12, pressure faded. Foreign concerns, particularly building a coalition against France on an earlier agreement with Russia, took most of Pitt's attention. Diminishing eyesight forced George III to abandon plans for a tour through the midlands before his customary holiday at Weymouth, but the king visited Hawkesbury twice at Coombe Wood in June. Louisa told her father-in-law that both visits went well. Besides his vision, the king seemed in good health. Hawkesbury noted the king had "almost wholly lost the power of distinguishing persons, though he can see light."[79] Renewed conflict with the Prince of Wales over Princess Charlotte's education and the death of George III's favorite brother, the Duke of Gloucester, drew Hawkesbury again into the royal family's affairs. George Rose noted his higher standing that summer as the king increasingly relied on him. When Pitt again raised the idea of a broad government, Hawkesbury resisted from a strong position and even suggested renewing ties with Sidmouth to avoid overtures to Grenville.[80]

Hawkesbury determined to have no part in a coalition with Fox and Grenville he thought fatal to the government's reputation and injurious to the country. Bringing together men who had disagreed on almost every substantive issue, he had said publicly in February, would make it "the object of universal astonishment, if not of indignation." Such arrangements – and the Fox–North coalition of 1783 cannot have been far from mind – sacrificed public character to keep office. Liverpool shared his son's view of any union as a coalition of "discordant principles." Public disapproval would only enhance Hawkesbury's stature for having opposed it.[81] Beside the question of principle, Hawkesbury also saw danger in upsetting the just distribution of power and influence the constitution required. "A confederacy of powerful men to dictate the administration" he warned the House of Lords, "would, in effect, annihilate king, Lords, and Commons, and constitute an aristocratic usurpation."[82] Earlier critics of Walpole and the Old Corps Whigs had seen their ascendancy as such a usurpation, though Hawkesbury never drew the parallel. Beside his concern for upholding an inclusive, though still elite-dominated, political order, Hawkesbury's views reflected family loyalty to the king and distrust of those who sought to bend the monarch to their will. George III's preference for "fighting it out as we are" scotched Pitt's hopes that an overture to the opposition might preempt the difficulties anticipated in the next parliamentary session. The coalition never came to pass.[83]

News from Europe seemed promising with an alliance of Britain, Austria, and Russia against France that drew Napoleon's army from its encampment at Boulogne to face its Continental rivals. Nelson had spent the preceding months hunting the French fleet through the Mediterranean and Atlantic to prevent a juncture with Spanish ships that would threaten British control of the sea. Victory over the combined Franco-Spanish fleets at Trafalgar on October 2, 1805 ended the danger at the price of Nelson's death. Ominous reports that an Austrian army had surrendered to Napoleon at Ulm followed in early November. Canning presciently remarked that Pitt's fate hung upon that of the Austrian emperor.[84] Napoleon won as decisive a victory on December 2 over Austria and

Russia at Austerlitz as Nelson had won at sea. It left Pitt's hopes for the war as broken as his health. Since plans for countering the opposition in January rested upon success against Napoleon, Pitt faced rough prospects as 1805 closed.

Organizing Nelson's funeral arrangements fell to Hawkesbury as home secretary. The task distracted him from political worries. Describing Nelson's death as worthy of his life, he noted the admiral survived long enough to know the battle's outcome.[85] Hawkesbury proposed to the king a general thanksgiving for the victory and commissioned a monument by the sculptor John Flaxman for St Paul's Cathedral. A hailstorm punctuated the funeral on January 7. Lady Hawkesbury described the lying-in-state at the Admiralty to her sister:

> You can easily imagine our feelings as we looked at that little coffin and thought of what it contained. The dead silence too of the room – hung with Black – the funeral Torches – the melancholy chaplain in his mourning cloak at the head of the bier – altogether spoke more directly to the heart than all the pageantry of the morning.

Checking final details kept Hawkesbury up until 4:30 a.m.. He detailed two Bow Street Runners to accompany Louisa as she watched the funeral procession to St. Paul's. The ceremony lasted the entire day with the final part of the service conducted by torchlight.[86] Its melancholy air resonated as implications of defeat in Europe and a deteriorating political balance at home loomed.

Pitt had gone to restore his health at Bath in December with the meeting of parliament deferred a fortnight. Hawkesbury and Castlereagh managed business in Pitt's absence. Along with other colleagues and political friends, they joined the prime minister in Bath. Hawkesbury, in his last letter to Pitt, urged him "to come directly to Coombe; you will be there not only in good air, but you will find a particularly warm house."[87] Instead Pitt left Bath for Bowling Green House, which he had rented on Putney Heath, near an earlier home. A meeting with Hawkesbury and others to concert plans for the opening session exhausted Pitt, who felt "cut in two." Parliament delayed substantive discussions by general consent in deference to Pitt's indisposition. A melancholy group of friends gathered at Hawkesbury's house in St. James Square to await news.[88] Pitt died at a quarter past four on the morning of January 23. Hawkesbury told his father the last sad chapter had closed, but deferred further report until meetings over the course of the day which included a long, distressing audience with the king. The country, he later declared in moving a vote of thanks to the navy, faced the misfortune to lose within months two of the most distinguished characters that ever graced its annals.[89]

Hawkesbury's office and personal relationship with the king made him the cabinet's intermediary. Rumors circulated he would succeed Pitt with Castlereagh at the exchequer.[90] The king had sought advice when Hawkesbury told him the news. Little disagreement arose when the cabinet met. Discussion focused upon two questions: first, whether the present ministers could remain in office without Pitt, and, secondly, whether there might "be any considerably addition of strength within reach" to form a new government. Ministers present, including Castlereagh, Eldon, and Mulgrave gave to both questions a negative. Portland and Pitt's brother Lord Chatham later concurred.[91] Hawkesbury told the king, who clearly hoped to form a new administration from Pitt's cabinet. When pressed to take over, Hawkesbury briefly wavered. He later told his sister-in-law that he had been minister for two hours but lacked the courage to go on. Rather than proceed in a forlorn hope against which his colleagues advised, he eventually counseled George III to send for Grenville and waive the exclusion of Fox for the public good. When Grenville said he could do nothing without consulting Fox, the king replied "I suppose so." He then stated he had no objection to Fox and urged settling the business promptly.[92] A dispute arose when Grenville proposed bringing the office of commander in chief of the army, held by the Duke of York, under cabinet authority. Dreading his son's censure or dismissal, George III demurred. Hawkesbury again met the king. The final arrangement gave the cabinet authority over the duke who would act with a council.[93]

A government uniting the nation's political talents – save those of the outgoing ministry – had its own divisions. Forty offices, including all held by MPs, changed hands to meet demands on patronage. The new appointments made a sweep through senior administrative personnel.[94] Had they not broken, Grenville's stature and experience made him Pitt's natural successor. Some Pittites even saw him as such for a time. Now he had joined with Fox and Sidmouth rather than Pitt's heirs. Lady Holland believed Grenville turned to them mainly from the belief he could trust them in case of a quarrel with the king while Hawkesbury and Castlereagh would not be reliable.[95] Besides the union with Grenville, Fox had managed a rapprochement with many Whigs who had differed with him over the French Revolution. Catholic Emancipation and abolishing the slave trade provided the main points of agreement beyond their earlier opposition to Pitt. Sidmouth and his friends shared few principles with their new colleagues. Their presence served mainly to satisfy the king. Lord Rous likened Sidmouth, with Lord Ellenborough at his side, to "a faithful old steward with his mastiff, watching new servants lest they should have some evil designs against the old family mansion." Sidmouth brought a following along with his own voice in the Lords. Likening him to "the smallpox and measles, everyone must have him *once*," Canning archly captured the balancing role of such factions.[96] Addington showed the many backbenchers who respected him and their counterparts among country gentlemen beyond parliament that the government was a safe choice.[97] Like Pitt, Grenville and Fox had to guard the cohesion of their supporters while angling for new adherents.

Hawkesbury received a controversial parting gift when the king made him Warden of the Cinque Ports. North and Pitt had held the office as a personal favor. George III now insisted Hawkesbury accept the remunerative sinecure which included the use of Walmer Castle on the Kentish coast. Louisa told her sister that

> Thanks to the Dear King's Gift and Lord Liverpool's liberality, we shall be perfectly well off in circumstances. Our income will remain precisely the same. The Cinque Ports are £3,000 and Lord Liverpool is to give Lord Hawkesbury £4,000, these two make just the amount of the Secretary of State office and Lord Liverpool's present allowance of £1,000.[98]

Resignation cut their income since Hawkesbury had long held office. The news aroused criticism. Lady Foster noted that some blamed Hawkesbury for taking a post Fox would have given to Lord Chatham, Pitt's elder brother, as a mark of esteem to the family. Holland, Fox's nephew, wanted the prize for himself.[99] Liverpool considered it an impressive mark of royal favor given Hawkesbury's age and the general circumstances. Lord Sheffield's angry observation that "the Jenkinson craving disposition will revolt the whole country" raised an old charge of leveraging court ties for personal gain. It never marred Hawkesbury's reputation, however, bringing out an important difference between the public's view of father and son.[100] Rather than grasping avarice, the appointment reflected the hereditary loyalty George III saw in Hawkesbury.

Loyalty raised difficult questions for the new opposition. Political groupings organized around a single figure typically lack means to find a new leader. George III's unwillingness to part with Pitt had helped ensure the lack of a clear successor. Lord Carrington, one of Pitt's friends, saw no obligation "to abide with a party which had lost its leader, and with its leader everything." Canning thought they had buried their allegiance in Pitt's grave.[101] The old cabinet still held together to give the king an alternative. Rose assumed Hawkesbury, Castlereagh, and Camden would take the lead. Canning originally kept his distance, but drew closer as talks with Grenville failed to bear fruit.[102] Pitt's heirs muted their criticism until the king showed ministers had lost his confidence. Disdain for factious opposition strengthened Hawkesbury's natural caution. Where Charles Jenkinson had worked actively to drive out the Fox–North coalition, his son let the Talents stand or fall on their own. Hawkesbury thus avoided the charge of conspiracy or illegitimate influence that had damaged his father's reputation. Instead, he enhanced a reputation for fair-mindedness and disinterested attention to the public interest.

Hawkesbury's brother-in-law, Lord Bristol, brought the first clash by criticizing the inclusion of Ellenborough in the cabinet as lord chief justice for wrongly combining judicial and executive functions. Despite the charge he raised the question to damage the new administration, Bristol entreated the Lords not to consider it a party issue. Hawkesbury did not object to Ellenborough being in the cabinet, but only his sitting in it as a chief justice. Citing Montesquieu and Blackstone, he argued that no union could be "more dangerous than that of a judge and a minister of state." Others noted the conflict of interest. Hawkesbury called it a constitutional innovation likely to diminish the character of a judge. "Whatever might be the decision," the country's general feeling opposed the appointment.[103] Bristol's censure failed without a division, which the opposition had agreed not to press. The debate recorded an objection more than it offered a challenge.[104] When Grenville presented a message on April 23 regarding the Prussian occupation of Hanover, Hawkesbury twice stated his "entire approbation." Mulgrave, Pitt's foreign secretary, concurred.[105] Unless a question raised a particular difference, the new opposition held back. Where disputes arose, Hawkesbury and his friends largely vindicated their position while laying down markers for the future.

Hawkesbury's opposition to unrestricted American trade with the West Indies paralleled his father's earlier dispute with Grenville, who privately refused to sacrifice commerce to navigation, the principle to the accessory. Sheffield cited Liverpool's 1784 and 1791 reports on trade in a May 12 debate. When the American Intercourse Bill eventually passed, Hawkesbury consoled himself that it would render ministers very unpopular.[106] Several times he had urged delay to consult interests affected. Ironically, Grenville opposed Hawkesbury's motion to question general officers on the merits of extending the length of enlistments with an argument Hawkesbury might have made against setting a precedent.[107] Hawkesbury emphasized consequences and argued effects rather than principles. The question of recalling Sir George Barlow from India, for example, involved not the government's right to act, but "whether it has been soundly or unsoundly exercised." Elsewhere, he accepted that necessity might dictate an exception where the general system remains sound and worth retaining.[108]

Renewed measures against the slave trade brought out Hawkesbury's emphasis on consequences. Grenville bluntly stated that "no consideration relative to our commerce or navigation could induce him to think that the slave trade ought to be continued." He thought it "a cruel and unjust traffic which ought to be abolished."[109] Admitting that there could be no difference of opinion where interest and humanity stood opposed, Hawkesbury argued that others would take over the slave trade and abolition would injure British property. Later in June, he called slavery and the slave trade "undoubtedly an evil," but warned that sudden change might bring a greater evil. In the final debate, Hawkesbury weakly asked if British withdrawal from the trade would really end it.[110] Why lend his voice to a losing and morally dubious cause? Pragmatism would certainly justify a silent vote, if not abstention or dropping a position others had abandoned. Hawkesbury's objection to brushing aside the concerns of so large an interest as West Indian merchants and planters set him against public opinion and posterity. It also shows his concern about balancing interests, especially those closely involving trade, within an equilibrium that upheld property rights.

The slave trade ranged Sidmouth, who shared Hawkesbury's position, against his colleagues. Other factors also weakened the Talents. Fox's health rapidly declined. Upon hearing that four gallons of fluid had been drawn from Fox, Liverpool acidly wished "the same operation could draw out of him all the iniquity of which in the course of his life he has been guilty & for which he is answerable."[111] Grenville realized he needed new support, but overtures to Perceval and Canning failed. Considering the animosity Charles Grey, now Lord Howick, and Sidmouth both held toward Canning, Grenville would have gained little. Attempting a juncture eroded tenuous bonds with Sidmouth, but Canning reported Grenville's desire to bring Pitt's followers, excepting Hawkesbury and Eldon, into the government.[112] Further overtures to individuals also failed. Hardwicke thought Fox's death would shatter the current ministry just as Pitt's had ended the last. Neither party could survive without an acknowledged leader, but who that might be remained unclear. While Hawkesbury had the qualifications to act as minister in the Lords, he could not fill the gap in the Commons.[113]

Relations between the Prince and Princess of Wales sparked an incident that summer with dangerous future implications. An inquiry into charges that Princess Caroline had delivered an illegitimate child made their quarrel a public scandal in August 1806. The inquiry comprised Erskine, as Lord Chancellor, and Grenville, Spencer, and Ellenborough with Sir Samuel Romilly advising them as solicitor general. Perceval represented Caroline in what became known as the Delicate Investigation. He also wrote a formal defense of her conduct.[114] The prince's longstanding relationship with Fox and Sheridan – not to mention Whig hopes of royal favor in a new reign – complicated the government's position. Hawkesbury, who counseled Perceval, believed the prince entirely at fault. Liverpool agreed and encouraged his son's involvement with Caroline's defense. Her "oppressed virtue closeted with some imperfections in manner" contrasted sharply with the prince's "avowed profligacy, publicly practiced and endeavored to be made fashionable, contrary to the general disposition of the people." Liverpool advised a published defense of Caroline fully presenting "the illegalities, injustice, & hardship" heaped upon her as the public will set them "against any levities" charged in her private life.[115] Political fortunes would sharply reverse the sides when as prime minister Liverpool struggled to secure George IV a separation from his estranged wife now backed by the Whigs. The fuse lit in 1806 fourteen years later detonated the great crisis of Liverpool's administration.

For the moment, however, Hawkesbury and his wife spent much of the year after the parliamentary session enjoying Walmer Castle. Louisa wrote enthusiastically of how the house and grounds exceeded their expectations when they arrived in August.[116] The wardenship carried a few duties and some local patronage. When Grenville persuaded the king to dissolve parliament in hopes of strengthening his government in the Commons, elections brought controversy. Hawkesbury thought the results by no means favored ministers. He joined his cousin, Charles Jenkinson, in canvassing successfully at Dover, where his influence as warden helped counter government backing for an opponent.[117] Tierney and Holland complained ministers had left too many seats without candidates and generally mismanaged elections. Rose thought ministers gained eighteen to twenty seats in England and Wales.[118] Perceval believed the opposition too passive. Nothing, he told Melville, "can fling ministers on their backs in this country, unless there are others forward on their legs shewing themselves willing and able and ready and in a body of apparent sufficiency to supply their places."[119]

The government fell when it clashed with the king on a proposal to open army commissions to Roman Catholics. Besides antagonizing Sidmouth – and thus dividing the cabinet – it made George III believe his ministers sought more than they originally said. When he demanded a written pledge they would not raise the plan again, ministers declined. The king again insisted on a positive assurance. Bathurst privately urged Grenville to avoid a struggle that would cost the country more than ministers could possibly gain. Embarrassed by the situation, Grenville insisted the king had been fully informed and acquiesced. Meeting the king's new demand, he believed, would cast doubt on his own integrity.[120] Instead of resigning or trying to force the point, the cabinet simply left George III to determine his next step. "His decision," Grenville reported, "has been to look for other ministers."[121]

On receiving the cabinet's answer, the king reflected alone at Windsor before dictating letters to Hawkesbury and Eldon.[122] Hawkesbury had not been in contact with him for some months. He told colleagues that he and Eldon had been summoned to an audience on March 19, 1807. Canning expressed surprise. Privately he thought "nothing could be more delicately & judiciously done" than sending for the opposition leaders two at a time. Over a two-and-a-half hour conversation, the king set before Hawkesbury and Eldon his correspondence with ministers and offered Hawkesbury the premiership. When Hawkesbury urged a neutral figure to head the government, George III pressed him to return as home secretary and leader of the Lords.[123] The previous year, Hawkesbury had agreed with Castlereagh, Canning, and Melville that if they were called back to office Perceval should be Chancellor of the Exchequer with management of the Commons.[124] Perceval had spoken well in debates as solicitor general. Although Pitt had marked him for preferment, he had been a lawyer rather than a politician seeking office. Giving Perceval management of general business avoided placing Canning or Castlereagh over the other. The same considerations made the elderly Portland an obvious choice to lead the government as in 1783. None of the younger men could feel their ambitions thwarted.

Hawkesbury brokered the government's formation, telling his father that at the audience he never saw the king so well in health or more composed.

Illus. 6.   James Gillray, "A Kick at the Broad Bottoms! – ie Emancipation of all the Talents." George III's resistance to Catholic Emancipation drove from office the Whig-dominated Talents administration and brought Hawkesbury back with Pitt's other protégés. The issue, however, became a double-edged sword.

George III facilitated matters by stating directly that he "had no restrictions; no exceptions to lay on the Duke of Portland; no engagements or promises; he may dispose of *everything*." Hawkesbury and Eldon conveyed the news to Portland, who accepted with the caveat that the king would release him whenever he found a suitable alternative. Willing to preside over forming a government, the ailing sixty-nine-year-old could do little more. After further inquiries, Hawkesbury told George III arrangements could be completed "with as few difficulties as can be expected."[125] A group including Perceval, Canning, and Castlereagh discussed arrangements that evening. Portland's absence due to ill health marked a portent, but he outlined the prospective cabinet in a March 23 letter to the king. Besides Hawkesbury at the Home Office and Perceval at the exchequer, Castlereagh would take the war department, Canning the Admiralty, and Wellesley the Foreign Office. Eldon returned as Chancellor with Camden as president of the council and Westmorland Lord Privy Seal.[126] George III approved, but Wellesley declined the Foreign Office which Canning took instead with Mulgrave at the Admiralty.

The change of administration sparked debate in parliament before many outgoing ministers had surrendered their seals of office. When Hawkesbury moved that the Lords adjourn on March 26, Grenville gave a three-hour defense of his conduct on the Catholic relief measure. As silence made it possible to misrepresent the former ministers' motives when the administration changed by royal prerogative rather than resignation, he felt compelled to provide a full explanation. The late ministry had made preventing the revival of the Catholic question one of its first objects. While Grenville's views on the point remained unchanged, he also believed Catholics had injured their cause by pushing it forward at this moment. The proposed relief measure sought merely to reconcile British law with an earlier Irish measure that opened army rank to Catholics. Royal opposition led ministers to withdraw their proposal, but then they learned the king had "thought fit to appoint a new administration." Grenville demanded his ministry not be charged with "obtaining from any man, by fraudulent means, his consent to a measure when he disapproved."[127]

Hawkesbury, in reply, complimented Grenville for holding to his principles, but thought it rather extraordinary that, having "given up their half-measure," he and his colleagues reserved power to bring forward the whole question. The king had authorized Hawkesbury to state that the measure brought forward differed widely from the original proposal his majesty had sanctioned. He declared himself ignorant of the whole transaction until summoned with Eldon to an audience. Once called to serve, Hawkesbury felt it his duty to obey. His words preempted charges of conspiracy. Later Hawkesbury denied any pledge limiting him or his colleagues in advising the crown.[128] He told George III the debate made as favorable an impression as possible and nothing unpleasant to the king had passed. On April 8, Sidmouth asked the king's leave, if debate resumed, to give particulars

explaining the matter. Deprecating the discussion for setting an unwelcome precedent, the king authorized him to state what he thought proper.[129]

The Marquis of Stafford revived debate on April 13 by moving that any
pledge, implied or expressed, restraining ministers from advising the king on any
subject violated their duty. Lord Aberdeen thought it calculated to justify the
late ministers and "insinuate blame" elsewhere. Harrowby lamented the debate's
indecorous character" with its "direct effect of censuring our sovereign." Calling
the motion "a kind of surprise on the house," Boringdon noted more than an
insinuation that secret advisors had brought about the change. He then moved
an adjournment to end debate.[130] Sidmouth went further in rejecting supposi-
tion of a wrong done and the intervention of a secret advisor, charges so unsup-
ported by evidence as to be manifestly unjust. Besides insisting such a motion
"ought not to be entertained under any circumstance," he challenged accounts
from Grenville and others in the cabinet. Mulgrave called the late government so
"puffed up by silly and idle flattery" that they possessed all the country's talents as
to "think they could dictate to the crown."[131]

The motion amounted to a censure of the king and his present ministry. It
showed the Whig nobility viewed themselves as an essential check on the crown
and believed advice given privately by men not responsible for it to parliament a
threat to constitutional liberty. Mulgrave's insistence that present ministers "had
never entered into any captious opposition" highlighted a contrast in outlook
between them and the new opposition.[132] Grenville called the present ministry's principles unconstitutional. Challenging both their doctrines and abilities,
he denied that Pitt uniformly approved of them and singled out Hawkesbury's
tenure at the Foreign Office as a particular target. Hawkesbury called the whole
of Grenville's statement, along with the debate itself, "proceedings altogether
irrelevant and unparliamentary." The previous ministry sought to cloak themselves by arraigning the king's personal conduct. Far from shirking responsibility,
Hawkesbury declared again he had taken office from duty and would hold fast
to that obligation.[133]

The motion failed by eighty-one votes, a greater majority than ministers had
expected. George III expressed surprise that Stafford's motion had been more
strongly worded than its counterpart in the Commons and pressed to such a
length. Perceval told the king that the Commons had turned decidedly in favor
of the new government.[134] Portland asked the king to dissolve parliament so that
government could appeal to the public. An immediate election was indispensable
as they could not go on with a sure majority of only twenty-three.[135] Hawkesbury
noted the danger in allowing a public current running so strongly in their favor
to subside while Buckingham anticipated "the cry of Church and King" would
aid them. Ministers cast the election as a choice between the king's stand on
Catholic relief and a "cabinet junta" attempting to force the issue.[136] As during
the Fox–North coalition and Regency Crisis, they claimed to be defending the

constitution from faction. Hawkesbury worked closely with Sir Arthur Wellesley, the new Irish chief secretary and brother of Lord Wellesley, to manage elections in Ireland. Indeed, he had offered the younger Wellesley the post and their relationship became increasingly close.[137] Besides encouraging reports from Ireland and Scotland, Hawkesbury told his father elections in England had gone well. Majorities in both houses beyond expectations gratified the king. Liverpool still predicted a violent session as "all the king's old antagonists" who resisted him from the start of his reign had now got a leader in Grenville, who will teach them every violence and extravagance.[138] With a stronger position in the Commons and the king's backing, Portland's government stood well placed to resist. Its dangers lay elsewhere.

CHAPTER 5

Pillar of State

HAWKESBURY'S ROLE MANAGING relations with the king and business in the House of Lords made him a key figure in Portland's government. Cabinet rivalries, however, threatened its cohesion. Since Pitt left no obvious successor, his more ambitious followers refused to subordinate their own claims. Only a neutral figure like Portland, who never intended an active role, could mute jealousies by taking the nominal lead. With so many ministers of equal or near equal pretensions, as Perceval noted, the Portland administration inevitably became a "government of departments" vulnerable to a split.[1] Poor coordination and differences on managing the war heightened tensions. Responsible for defending measures his colleagues initiated and directed, Hawkesbury gained stature by prudent counsel and loyalty. Besides yielding his own claims to facilitate arrangements, he managed to keep out of quarrels that split the cabinet. When the break came, Hawkesbury helped forge a new government from the wreckage. Taking over the War Department then gave him responsibility for managing the war at a critical stage.

What Louisa called their year of holiday ended in 1807. The hurry, bustle, anxiety, and worry brought by high office sharply contrasted with the tranquil *séjour* they had enjoyed. Although she did not rejoice at the change, Louisa hoped that Hawkesbury had not been spoiled by his brief escape from a minister's hectic life.[2] It was Hawkesbury's only time out of office since his twenties, a fact that underlines how politics dominated his life. Liverpool's age and growing infirmity drew Hawkesbury into closer involvement with family matters, including arrangements for his half-sister Charlotte's betrothal to Lord Grimston's son James Walter Grimston. Negotiations over a settlement broke down, much to the young couple's dismay, when the elder Grimston insisted upon a more generous dowry. Since additional money for Charlotte would come from Hawkesbury's inheritance, Liverpool refused. He became more adamant on learning Grimston had more wealth than he had admitted.[3] The story echoed Hawkesbury's earlier romance with Louisa. It ended with Charlotte taking her inheritance early so long as Grimston gave his son an additional £500. The arrangement went through despite Liverpool's grumbling and the couple married in August. Liverpool even gave Charlotte £500 for wedding clothes, telling Hawkesbury "you see that in all respects I am sufficiently liberal."[4]

The Hawkesburys welcomed the new couple to Walmer on several occasions. His influence as Warden of the Cinque Ports helped secure the elections of both his cousin and younger brother. Cecil Jenkinson became MP for Sandwich and an under-secretary at the Home Office despite his indifference to politics. Family loyalty never outweighed Cecil's lack of ambition, though he voted and spoke on the government's side. Hawkesbury's brother-in-law Grimston kept his seat for St. Albans even though observers expected he would fare badly.[5] Only father and son among the Jenkinson family were active politicians competing for office. Liverpool, despite his physical frailty, kept up an informed correspondence with his son. Having drawn up his will in late April, he wrote to Hawkesbury on May 7, 1807 that "they tell me I have this day completed my 78th year." So long as his health lasted, Liverpool pledged to pray daily for his son's success and "endeavor to make you richer, & if possible, happier than you are at present."[6] Family and public life remained intertwined for Hawkesbury.

Troubles within the royal family, including unfinished business from the "Delicate Investigation" the previous year into the Princess of Wales's conduct, fell to Hawkesbury. When the inquiry cleared her of wrongdoing, he gave George III the cabinet's opinion, shared by their predecessors, that Caroline be admitted to his presence and received at court in a manner due her rank and station. He then conveyed the monarch's decision to the estranged couple. The prince distrusted Hawkesbury, whom he described to his mother as "one of the worst of the whole crew," and determined to restrict Caroline's access to their daughter. Pressure from both parties agitated the king. The final arrangement did not spare him deep regret at their failure to reconcile.[7] Although it solved the immediate problem, the king's own marriage felt the strain. Queen Charlotte sympathized with her son. The king's sometimes erratic behavior brought relations with his wife to a separation by late October.[8] Hawkesbury took great care lest alarm or stress upset his health to bring a crisis with larger implications.

A deteriorating situation in Europe isolated Britain as Napoleon imposed peace on his own terms. The Treaty of Tilsit in July 1807 made Russia a French ally and excluded British trade from Tsar Alexander's domains. Napoleon had gained control over North Germany and subjugated Prussia the previous year. Since British maritime supremacy locked France into Europe, he sought to leverage hegemony there through economic warfare. Imposing trade restrictions known as the Continental System pressured Britain and neutral powers alike.[9] Hawkesbury's colleagues feared Denmark might side with France and give Napoleon a fleet to replace losses at Trafalgar. They endorsed the armed diplomacy Canning proposed to coerce the Danes into surrendering their navy. Hawkesbury's contribution focused on the consequences for British trade in the Baltic, but he also secured Sir Arthur Wellesley's appointment to a military command in the expedition. Wellesley sent the home secretary frequent news and commentary as diplomacy gave way to force with the bombardment of Copenhagen.[10]

George III approved preparations, but also urged "proceeding with temper & caution" in any step towards Denmark, which may appear unprovoked. Concerned not to drive the Danes into alliance with France or provoke a renewed neutral league against Britain, he questioned the propriety of coercion. Canning noted the king thought seizing Denmark's fleet "a very immoral act…so immoral that I won't ask who originated it." George III himself told the diplomat who submitted the ultimatum that the Danish king had just cause to kick him down the stairs for such an impertinent demand.[11] Ministers, however, stressed the need to deny Napoleon ships that could threaten Britain. Hawkesbury thought the expedition ended the risk of a French landing in Ireland, telling Richmond "our left flank is now completely at liberty."[12] Bombarding Copenhagen still cast a wave of horror across Europe and beyond. Thomas Jefferson cited it with Napoleon's aggressions as proof of an epoch marked "by the total extinction of national morality."[13]

Jefferson's reaction showed the wider repercussions of British policy. Hawkesbury saw the potential for a clash with the United States, particularly when the Royal Navy's forcible seizure of British deserters from the USS Chesapeake closed America ports to British warships pending an explanation. Complaining that Pitt had made too many concessions to the United States, Liverpool thought the business must be brought to a decision, probably through war. Excluding the ships of one belligerent while permitting those of another violated neutrality. Hawkesbury thought an American war "certainly an evil" amidst other difficulties, but one avoidable if by "unbecoming concessions." The admiral commanding in Nova Scotia warned that without showing force ministers could expect Americans "to think you are afraid of them."[14] Deteriorating relations with the United States complicated Britain's strategic position as it faced Napoleon's blockade.

Perceval proposed a plan to license neutral trade. French "prohibitions contrary to the usages and practice of war" justified retaliation, but a complete ban on trade between neutrals and France would hurt Britain. It might drive the United States into war. Limited commerce would convey British goods through neutral ships and give America enough trade to have some access rather than a total restriction.[15] Hawkesbury observed that while a complete ban would only raise the price of colonial goods in France, a licensed neutral trade would destroy all remaining French commerce while denying its farmers access to export markets. A focus on France and Holland rather than all of Europe offered a better chance of success.[16] Orders in Council issued on November 11, 1807 required ships entering French or French occupied ports to pass first through Britain. Hawkesbury noted plans for duties on foreign colonial goods to help British plantations and "compel our enemies to pay toward the expense of the war." [17] Napoleon declared a blockade of the British Isles on December 17 that subjected to seizure any vessels sailing to Britain's ports or submitting to its regulations. The United States responded with an embargo codified by legislation that built on an earlier non-importation act excluding certain British manufactures. All trade effectively became smuggling with economic consequences that affected Britain's internal stability. [18]

Irish affairs, which fell to Hawkesbury at the Home Office, showed how economic strain affected political conditions. Indeed, Ireland provided vital experience for addressing unrest in Britain after 1815. Although he thought it "scarcely possible that Bonaparte should have thought of sending out an expedition," Hawkesbury sought Wellesley's take on Irish security. [19] Arguing it "must be considered as an enemy's country," Wellesley urged constructing fortified places across Ireland as rallying points. Dublin's "peculiarly disaffected temper" required particular attention. Since political measures could not alter the general disaffection, "we have no strength here but our army." Antipathy operated among "even the middling classes of shopkeepers and tradesmen," some of whom speculated whether England's defeat by the loss of trade and increased taxes might bring Irish independence. [20] Sharing Wellesley's assessment, Hawkesbury worked with Castlereagh at the War Office and Lord Chatham at the Ordnance to improve Ireland's defense. Chatham's deliberate, if not dilatory, manner delayed progress. Related plans for a depot in Cork where troops could be assembled strengthened internal security while enabling the government to send expeditions overseas more easily than from English ports. Hawkesbury further urged Wellesley to adapt his police system for London and its surroundings to Dublin and other large Irish towns. [21]

At the same time, Hawkesbury sought to conciliate public opinion and ameliorate grievances. Having considered tithes a longstanding problem that burdened the poor while feeding resentment toward an Established Church to which few Irishmen belonged, Hawkesbury worked to commute them without denying the clergy income. Wellesley thought rents and low wages a more serious cause of discontent than the exclusion of Catholics from parliament and public office. While other concerns delayed action on tithes, he reported that unrest sprang more from the people's restlessness and some oppression by landlords than religious differences. Government support to educate priests at St Patrick's College at Maynooth drew Sir Arthur Wellesley, Hawkesbury, and Perceval into further discussions in 1808, with Perceval more critical than either colleague. [22] The Irish born Wellesley supported Protestant authority on political rather than theological grounds, while Hawkesbury held a deeper commitment to the Established Church's constitutional position on its own terms. Neither shared Perceval's hostility to Catholicism itself. Their differences showed the range of opinion within the government even among those who opposed Catholic Emancipation and the difficulty of resisting Irish demands. Hawkesbury and Wellesley lacked the means to solve underlying economic problems they rightly saw as the real danger. The task required nothing short of wholesale social transformation akin to the Highland clearances in Scotland or the French Revolution, but such a sweeping change would upset the relative tranquillity they tried to maintain during wartime.[23]

Hawkesbury also dealt with the unexpected and potentially embarrassing arrival of Louis XVIII, exiled Bourbon claimant to the French throne. After receiving what Hawkesbury called "a very foolish and improper letter," George III suggested his guest reside in Scotland and offered Holyrood Palace. Louis XVIII, however, refused. Hawkesbury thought he instead wished to be near London.[24] He predicted trouble from the French king and his attendants partly from quarrels among émigrés. Most émigrés in Britain had returned home in 1802, leaving the hardline supporters of absolutism and the Bourbon dynasty who before were a minority among those who had fled revolution. Louis XVIII's arrival helped recreate habits of the 1780s among exiles and a Francophile set among British aristocrats.[25] Hawkesbury feared popular sentiment might turn against the war if it became seen merely as a struggle to restore the Bourbons. Indeed, Louis XVIII tried repeatedly to persuade his "brother monarch" to aid his restoration. Hawkesbury deflected successive requests until the French king accepted his terms and took up residence at Hartwell, which the Marquis of Buckingham placed at his disposal. While firm – and careful to ensure Canning and other colleagues took the same line – Hawkesbury sympathized with Louis XVIII's situation and showed a generosity that brought the exiled monarch's acquiescence.[26]

When serious illness kept Castlereagh at Brighton into the autumn, Hawkesbury took over his duties at the War Office.[27] Aiding Portugal, caught between France and Britain, fell to him. The situation remained fluid during the summer of 1807 as the Portuguese explored options. Rather than bow to Napoleon, the royal family, along with much of the government, nobility, and Lisbon's wealthier inhabitants, sailed for Brazil on November 29 under British protection.[28] Hawkesbury already had planned either to cover the royal family's retreat or seize Madeira if the Portuguese bought peace by closing their ports. He predicted France and Spain would soon find cause to repent their aggression. Napoleon's occupation of Portugal escalated the economic war and began a struggle in Iberia that became Britain's primary focus.[29]

The parliamentary session in January 1808 faced Hawkesbury with responsibility for defending government measures. Portland's inability to take an active role prompted abortive efforts to replace him with Pitt's brother, Chatham. The now weary Hawkesbury again declined the lead. He struck an uncharacteristically pessimistic note in describing Britain standing alone against Europe and probably America with an ineffectual war policy.[30] Hawkesbury proposed bringing Melville and Harrowby into the cabinet and giving the former's son

Robert Dundas office either at home or in India. Melville's refusal blocked the plan. The ministry needed support in the Lords, as Hawkesbury told Canning. Glenbervie attributed such talk to the idea that Hawkesbury alone could not face both Grenville and Grey.[31]

Ministers expected criticism over Copenhagen. Grenville denounced the expedition, asking what Europe could think on seeing parliament approve the attack without evidence to justify it. He rejected separating the issue from relations with the United States because they both involved retaliation on neutrals for Napoleon's blockade that produced more conflict.[32] Hawkesbury, acknowledging his share in advising the measure, denied it abandoned "every principle of morality and justice." Lord Wellesley sketched the context of Napoleon's plan to coerce Portugal as well as Denmark into turning their navies on Britain. Hawkesbury elaborated while declaring self-preservation the first and strongest principle of international law. Seizing the Danish fleet removed a threat and the need to guard against it. Europe felt more dread of France than outrage toward Britain since "nothing prevented France from acquiring universal dominion but the naval power of Great Britain."[33]

When Hawkesbury presented the Orders in Council, Auckland likened them to persons trying to starve each other and thereby insuring their own inevitable starvation.[34] Grenville warned that with all Europe against Britain, "we should not be too eager to add America to the long and formidable catalogue of our enemies." Acknowledging the value of good relations with the United States, Hawkesbury refused to buy amity by sacrificing the maritime rights "upon which our very existence might be said to depend."[35] Grenville had declared already that he would never compromise on maritime rights. Indeed, the Earl of Galloway revealingly contended that ministers might draw their justification "from the speeches of noble lords on the opposite side of the house." The point gave ministers a welcome advantage. Hawkesbury framed the choice as submitting to burdens Napoleon threw upon British commerce or taking some measure of retaliation.[36]

The United States had already retaliated with an Embargo Act passed by Congress in late December and supplementary legislation in early 1808. Its policy reflected Jefferson's belief from experience with non-importation campaigns in the 1760s and 70s that economic reprisal offered an effective political weapon. Holland described America as the most prominent, if not the only nation against which the Orders in Council operated since the measure forced a choice of confiscation by France in Europe or Britain on the high seas.[37] Grenville charged ministers with complete indifference toward relations with America, a point Hawkesbury found hard to refute. The argument that America should hold Napoleon responsible carried little weight, though Hawkesbury thought war unlikely given the general tenor of American newspapers.[38] Liverpool could not understand why the American government pressed an embargo depriving its citizens of their whole trade. He viewed it as a hostile act. Telling his son that "we should do no more than they have in effect done to themselves," he urged strictly enforcing the Orders in Council and excluding American trade from the East and West Indies.[39] Parliamentary criticism, however, pointed to more serious trouble at home if British trade suffered enough to give Whigs a foothold with popular opinion.

Hawkesbury fell short of his usual fluency in debate as accumulated fatigue took its toll. Besides departmental responsibilities, he carried much of Portland's burden and had filled Castlereagh's place at the War Office over the autumn. Sporadic attendance by government supporters and the lack of able colleagues in the Lords increased the strain. Hawkesbury's health declined in early March, prompting him to take a day off before returning as the lead speaker in debate the next day. The period marked an especially low point for Hawkesbury. A January 1808 letter describing Britain as fighting all of Europe, and possibly the United States, alone showed uncharacteristic pessimism.[40] Fearing the Spanish uprising would be directionless given the decline of their nobility, Liverpool echoed his son. He lamented that "the ancient nobility across Europe are in reality extinct," and decried how they had lost their old sprit and with it their influence. "Bonaparte and his myrmidons owe all their success," Liverpool believed, to the failure of leadership among Europe's aristocracy. Besides pointing to the Jenkinsons' roots in the old, pre-revolutionary world, their laments showed the strain on ministers.[41]

Resistance to Napoleon's coup seizing the Spanish throne for his brother Joseph brought the first good news in a year. Reports of provincial revolts against the French-backed regime followed news of a brutally suppressed popular uprising in Madrid on May 2, 1808 that Francisco Goya's paintings immortalized. Aid to Spain and Portugal, Liverpool pointed out, gave "some prospect at least of a serious resistance." Hawkesbury said the news "excites hopes in which we have been very unwilling to indulge for some years." Ministers immediately suspended hostilities with Spain and ended the blockade of ports outside French control while preparing 10,000 men to serve abroad.[42] Enthusiasm spread when representatives from the provincial assembly of Asturias arrived on June 8 seeking aid. The idea of a popular rising against Napoleon appealed to Whig and radical newspapers. Sheridan, though drunk to the point of incoherence, gave a June 15 speech in parliament supporting Spain. Canning replied that the government wished to afford every practicable aid. By declaring any nation determined to oppose "Europe's common enemy" a British ally, he set an important principle. Canning may also have suggested the design for a satire of the Spanish bull throwing Napoleon and trampling Joseph after breaking its chain. That image of the Corsican matador in danger with Europe's rulers cheering captured a new enthusiasm.[43]

The government sent Wellington with considerable discretion on an expedition to liberate Portugal. Reports of early successes at Roliça and Vimero sparked public jubilation. Sidmouth called Wellesley "the Nelson of the army." Hawkesbury anticipated more good news from unofficial accounts that the Spanish had cleared the way to Madrid.[44] But when two senior generals, Sir Hew Dalrymple and Sir Harry Burrard, superseded Wellesley, they turned his success into a stalemate resolved through negotiation. The Convention of Cintra secured French withdrawal from Portugal at the price of returning them home with equipment and personal property, much of which had been looted from the Portuguese. Nothing kept their troops from returning to active service. By signing an agreement in which he took no part, Wellesley bound himself to its terms.[45] Newspapers condemned it as a disgrace to Britain and a betrayal of its allies. Lord Erskine archly suggested that henceforth humiliation be spelled "Hewmiliation" after the responsible general.[46]

The embarrassment raised serious questions about how the cabinet managed the war. Differences among generals prompted the *Morning Chronicle* to ask why the best person had not been appointed to command from the start.[47] An official inquiry gave Wellesley a professional near-death experience. Canning sought to repudiate the terms, even though he treated Wellesley more sympathetically than often claimed. Ministers tried salvaging what they could, including Wellesley's future service. Hawkesbury found the treaty especially painful as "it tarnishes the reputation and glory of those whom we should most wish to uphold."[48] Originally hesitant to question commanders on the spot, he concluded everything offensive to public feeling might have been avoided by pressing the French harder. Nothing could be done now besides holding out until the storm passed in "the muffled whimper of an official inquiry."[49]

Cintra weakened an administration where cooperation among ministers was already difficult. Hawkesbury described cabinet government as

> necessarily a government *inter pares*, in which every man must expect to have his opinion and dispatches canvassed; and this previous friendly canvass of opinion and dispatches appears to be absolutely necessary under a constitution where the public acts of government will be ultimately hostilely debated in parliament.[50]

The system required forbearance among colleagues and an authoritative minister to coordinate while keeping differences in check. Defending measures to keep parliamentary and public support demanded cooperation which had become hard to maintain. Problems from a weak lead seen under North and Pitt afflicted Portland's administration even more. Hawkesbury complained that nearly all business required long cabinet meetings. The lack of understanding between Canning and Perceval, as well as Castlereagh and Chatham whose responsibilities for the war overlapped, impeded efforts.[51] When the cabinet decided its position on Cintra that summer in Canning's absence, he gave the king a dissenting opinion and further lost confidence in colleagues. Friction grew and pressure to restructure the cabinet brought crisis the next year.[52]

Hawkesbury increasingly discussed foreign policy with Portland and Canning, offering suggestions on revising dispatches. He again managed the War Office when Castlereagh fell ill during October.[53] Napoleon and Tsar Alexander made a joint peace overture to Britain, while stipulating France's retention of Spain. Hawkesbury saw an opportunity to tighten the connection with Spain while establishing firm public grounds for pursuing the war by proposing Britain negotiate for both itself and its allies with the prior recognition of Spanish and Portuguese independence and Ferdinand VII's restoration as Spain's king. The terms, if talks brought peace, would have justified risking negotiations, but compromise on the Spanish question proved impossible.[54] Sir John Moore, who had taken command of British forces, advanced into Spain to aid the insurrection. Napoleon personally led an army into Spain that forced a British retreat ending with Moore's death and the army's evacuation. Widespread disappointment gave ministers another frustrating setback as news reached London during the parliamentary session.

Family matters also preoccupied Hawkesbury through December. Lady Liverpool suffered a horrific accident when her clothes, including a veil covering her head, caught fire. Servants extinguished the flames, which burned her neck, back, and hair, although sparing injury to her face. Liverpool described it with deep concern as a miraculous escape from a worse situation than he had apprehended, noting that she did know the whole of the physician's report. Recovery "will be a long business, not without some risque."[55] Liverpool's reserve kept him from expressing how upset his wife's predicament had made him. She became enraged and concluded he no longer cared for her. The domestic drama escalated as the invalid Liverpool's own health broke down with a violent bowel complaint. Pride kept him from either asking his wife's forgiveness or explaining himself. After his strength failed on December 15, family arrived at Liverpool's side and the aged politician died in the early morning two days later.[56]

The new Earl of Liverpool had an exceptionally strong relationship with his father, comparable only with his marriage to Louisa. The two men conferred regularly. Charles Arbuthnot, who worked closely with him for years on political business, remarked in 1822 about "how Liverpool always quotes his father."[57] They only quarreled over his marriage. Resolving that difference made their relationship stronger. Although Pitt brought him to office and helped his early career, his father trained Liverpool to become a statesman and remained a guide. Their relationship grounded Liverpool in an older Tory tradition while providing him with valuable knowledge and experience drawn from his father's long career. Cecil praised his brother's attendance on their dying father as "everything I could have expected from the best of sons & the kindest of brothers." Liverpool further showed filial piety when he buried his father beside Amelia Jenkinson on

December 30. The dowager countess of Liverpool, despite having not forgiven her late husband, received his promise she would not suffer financially.[58] Reporting his father's death to George III, Liverpool noted the many favors he and his family had received from the king who replied that the first earl's integrity and fidelity made him deeply regret the loss.[59]

A few weeks after the funeral, the new Earl of Liverpool took his place in the Lords expecting a more aggressive opposition than last year. Perceval reported a general "disapprobation and dissatisfaction" among government supporters. The Speaker of the Commons thought the very mention of Cintra would throw a firebrand into that house.[60] It had the same effect in the Lords. St. Vincent called the campaign in Portugal "the greatest disgrace that had befallen Great Britain since before the days of the Revolution." The aged and irascible naval hero seized upon the question of command, asking why one of the royal princes or even the experienced Moira had not been employed. He denounced the resort to councils of war among commanders as a cloak for cowardice that had thrown away victory. Ministers should have known better. Inexcusable ignorance made them unfit for office. St. Vincent then called for the cabinet's dismissal before stalking dramatically from the chamber.[61]

Grenville spoke in more measured tones with a wider critique of the government's war policy. Sending a British army into Spain to meet the whole disposable force of France without any great powers as an auxiliary matched in wildness and absurdity Liverpool's "far famed march to Paris." Grenville never mentioned his antagonist's name, but the jibe's target would have been clear. He warned against wasting resources "where failure is pregnant with calamity."[62] Liverpool coolly replied that "those who inferred that the cause was desperate" from disasters past "reasoned upon a most contracted and imperfect view" of the contest. It would be difficult to conceive any situation warranting better hopes of ultimate success than Spain. Its people stood unanimous. Their resistance marked "the only instance since the French revolution in which a whole people had taken up arms in their own defense." Geography, including the fact that Spain's territory matched that of France within its ancient limits, favored the defense. Liverpool insisted that the Spanish cause, "most interesting to the best feeling of the human mind," offered Europe's last chance against Napoleon.[63]

Liberation seemed distant as news of Moore's retreat fueled more criticism. Erskine claimed the army might have been better "shot upon the parade of St. James Park" than sent "to endure insufferable, ignoble, and useless misery" rendered pointless by Napoleon's advance with 100,000 men. Lord Westmorland replied, however, that "the noble lords opposite" did not accept when they held office that all blame for unfavorable military events rested with ministers.[64] Liverpool stoutly defended the government, deflecting calls for papers and other harrying motions. When Grey condemned the cabinet's policy in Spain and Portugal, the home secretary observed with a touch of irony that while "each individual who censured their plan had a plan of his own," none of their alternatives shared a single point. From there, he justified in detail plans and steps taken to execute them before noting Britain's success aiding Spain. Napoleon held no more territory than he had the year before. Spain had not lost confidence in Britain. Liverpool pledged to persevere while the chance for even a fragment of success remained. He showed a command of detail equal to Pitt at his best, though the number of peers opposing the government on a question involving the war surprised the king.[65]

Lord Grosvenor struck a telling blow by charging that Portland "was not the efficient and responsible minister." He demanded that the administration have a minister responsible for its acts.[66] Only recorded as attending the Lords fifteen times as premier, Portland never spoke in debate. Liverpool carried much of the burden there while Treasury business fell to Perceval. The cabinet lacked direction even before Portland's health failed entirely.[67] A scandal involving the Duke of York's mistress – unbeknownst to him, she had taken bribes from officers seeking promotion – forced him to resign as the army commander-in-chief. Ministers were themselves tarnished. Perceval responded with legislation in 1809 that criminalized soliciting money for procuring offices.[68] Other measures, including efforts to curtail bribery in elections followed. Scandal offered a clear narrative to frame charges of corruption and malfeasance. Only economic strain caused ministers greater trouble. Corruption also now encompassed what before 1780 had been considered legitimate patronage. Politicians and officials had to adapt. Although his father's reputation might have made the focus on corruption damaging, it now began playing to Liverpool's advantage. Propriety guided his conduct. When French princes again sought to draw him into their disputes, Liverpool warned them against prejudicing the cause of royalty itself by irritating public opinion.[69] Their exchange came weeks before Canning's first overtures to Portland about removing Castlereagh from the war department.

Subsequent maneuverings involve an oft-told tale that ended with the famous duel between Castlereagh and Canning.[70] When Liverpool heard of the matter from Canning on July 9, 1809, he complained to the king about Portland's failure to consult on a matter that concerned ministers individually no less than as a cabinet. Liverpool further observed that without any prejudice towards individuals he thought Canning more essential to the government. Any decision between the two colleagues on public grounds must favor him. Liverpool, however, dissented from Canning's objection to Castlereagh's management of the War Office. Since removing him without some alternative to reconcile his feelings to so harsh a measure was a "manifest cruelty and injustice," Liverpool offered to resign so Castlereagh could take over the Home Office with a peerage and leadership of the Lords. Moving Lord Wellesley to the War Office could keep the government afloat. Liverpool sought no office for himself and pledged to back the ministry as if he remained in it.[71] George III made no reply, but Canning rejected the idea. While complimenting Liverpool's "fair and manly tone," he realized the government would face trouble without him. Jealousy had softened into a more favorable view of his old friend. Canning described "poor Hawky" as the colleague he "should least like to lose" and "one of the most useful, if not the most so." [72] But he ruled out replacing Portland with Liverpool by insisting the prime minister sit in the Commons, and refused to serve under Perceval who would not yield to Canning.

Delays and the king's insistence on secrecy until plans were settled ensured a clash when the matter became public. Allowing Castlereagh to initiate an expedition to seize the mouth of the Scheldt to Austria's renewed war against Napoleon while they worked to replace him provided another grievance especially when the landings at Walchern failed embarrassingly. The government collapsed when Portland and Canning resigned. Castlereagh followed and challenged his rival to a duel they fought at Putney on the morning of September 21. When the first exchange passed without injury, Castlereagh insisted upon a second shot that wounded Canning's leg. Canning later quipped that for anyone minded to try the experiment of being shot through the thigh he would "recommend Lord Castlereagh as the operator," but the bravado did not hide the damage to his standing. Castlereagh too suffered from exacting what Wilberforce later called "a cold blooded measure of deliberate revenge." [73] The duel put them both out of consideration as former colleagues built a government from the wreckage. It also underlined the importance of reputation, making political consistency, personal integrity, and claims to precedence all the more central. Sacrificing them could sideline a career.

George III reportedly told Liverpool "you are my eyes, and I know I can trust to you that I shall not be imposed upon." Observers saw him with Eldon as leader among the king's friends. Liverpool wrote that having taken office to protect the king, he felt ministers were bound not to desert him now. The obligation made it all the more disheartening to see "a government which had nothing serious to apprehend from its enemies brought to the point of dissolution by its friends' divisions." Wellington believed "inordinate ambition, want of judgment, and vanity" had thrown the king and his government into the opposition's hands. [74] Ministers realized that losing three leading figures demanded new support. A minute to the king urged an overture to Grenville and Grey. George III clearly disliked the prospect and took time to consider before authorizing Perceval and Liverpool to send a communication as joint negotiators. [75]

Tierney had predicted an overture, but thought it simply a maneuver to stay in office or at least show that ministers resigned from the impossibility of continuing rather than from fearing to try. Grenville saw no way "to treat with these people as an existing government" since their cabinet was "broken to pieces." He came to London mainly to avoid reproach for refusing the king's command. Grey, who never left his Northumberland estate, would only discuss matters at the king's personal command.[76] Liverpool thought the offer worth a fair trial and was even willing to give up the Home Office. Grenville privately wished the two ministers had left him alone as he wanted neither a part in "their intrigues" nor "the consequence of all the mischief they had done."[77] He believed the terms spared them criticism while ruining their prospective new colleagues by implicating them in policies they had long attacked. Later overtures foundered on the same shoals.

Reporting that "Grenville will have nothing to do with us," Perceval saw "no option but to surrender the king or go on." Grenville's refusal had relieved the king, who named Perceval to succeed Portland on October 2, 1809. He concurred entirely with the recommendation that the prime minister sit in the Commons.[78] Filling other offices presented a greater challenge. Liverpool offered Lord Wellesley the Foreign Office on October 5, but his absence on a diplomatic mission in Spain delayed a response. Talk that Wellesley had left letters with Canning authorizing his recall should the latter resign made the overture seem extraordinary, but Wellesley had ability and prestige to bolster the government. Liverpool wished to remain at the Home Office, whose duties fit his role as leader in the Lords. Interestingly, he now rejected Perceval's suggestion he take over the Foreign Office temporarily "on account of the run made at him when he held the situation before." While still deeply interested in foreign policy, Liverpool preferred leaving direct responsibility to a colleague. Ill health precluded Harrowby from even a brief return. Bathurst took the post until Wellesley returned.[79]

Replacing Castlereagh at the War Office raised difficulties. Liverpool managed the department temporarily, and Perceval thought Melville's son, Robert Dundas, would fill the post. Melville refused, and compelled his son to reject any other office under the present administration. Charles Philip Yorke also declined as his brother, Lord Hardwicke, opposed it. Perceval then decided that nothing remained but prevailing upon Liverpool to lead the department and replace him at the Home Office with Richard Ryder.[80] Despite his own preference and George III's suggestion Ryder take the War Office, Liverpool agreed and persuaded the king. Ryder's health would not let him combine the heavy business at the War Office with regular parliamentary attendance. Perceval also wanted at least two ministers with him in the Commons to speak for the government. After Liverpool's appeal, the king declared he could not delay sanctioning the plan.[81]

Few expected the government to last. Liverpool thought loyalty obliged ministers to go on as best they could and, if defeated, provide a rallying point as during the Talents administration.[82] While Keith Feiling described Perceval's administration as the first wholly Tory government, its guiding outlook blended the assumptions of Court Whigs with varying Tory strains and personal ties forged serving together under Pitt. Long cooperation had fostered an executive ethos that bound men who shared principles together for common ends. Liverpool's repeated willingness to set aside his own claims and preferences to serve reflected a governing sensibility that served purposes Burke attributed to party. Indeed, Pitt's heirs under Perceval and then Liverpool operated as a party ranged against a Foxite dominated opposition. Cohesion among ministers and their allies provided a useful counterpoint to a growing public sense that public men were ineffectual and corrupt. Events since 1802 that discredited ministers and opposition alike had fueled calls for systemic reform that found expression in borough and country meetings along with a strident tone in the press.[83] Loyalty provided an anchor during a tense period.

Grenville's election as Chancellor of Oxford University marked an early setback and a personal disappointment for Liverpool. The chancellorship offered an alluring prize for an alumnus whose career had fulfilled the early promise of his academic success. Portland's rapidly declining health made a vacancy a matter of time. Grenville had already begun canvassing. Thomas Grenville thought the government's difficulty finding support at Oxford favored his brother. Sydney Smith's quip likening the Whig canvass for Grenville to "the trustees of the Magdalen applying to place a reclaimed prostitute at a bawdy house" made no difference.[84] The heads of several colleges approached Liverpool. Perceptive observers thought him the strongest opponent to Grenville. Clergy, a dominant force within Oxford, opposed Grenville on Catholic Emancipation and generally sided with ministers. Liverpool realized, however, that defeating him would gain little while losing would bolster opposition. Risk outweighed reward. Liverpool set aside his claim for the Duke of Beaufort, whose eagerness made him certain to stand anyway, so government friends could rally behind a single alternative. Beaufort wavered. Eldon then allowed himself to be nominated with Liverpool's support only for Beaufort to stand as well.[85] The split opposition Liverpool had sacrificed his own pretensions to avoid cost Eldon the chancellorship by thirteen votes even though he and Beaufort had above 700 between them.[86]

Liverpool entered the War Office with formidable advantages. No longer a shy and awkward youth whose private manner fell short of his public speaking, he increasingly showed a maturity and confidence bolstered by considerable administrative experience. Substituting for Castlereagh had familiarized him with the War Office. He and Wellington had already worked closely together on Irish business.[87] Having a strong sense of what both political insiders and public opinion would accept enabled Liverpool to anticipate their concerns. Confidence and cooperation from colleagues also minimized friction that had plagued his predecessors. Informed reflection on Britain's conduct of the war since the 1790s along with a sure grasp of geopolitics and strategy guided Liverpool's approach. Recognizing the distinction between aims set unilaterally by policy and the operations to achieve them by overcoming enemy resistance, he knew to give commanders in the field with the freshest information discretion to act as circumstances demanded. Like politics, war involved reacting to opposition and deflecting an adversary rather than unilaterally implementing a plan. Liverpool had shown determination under pressure. He also had a knack for piecing together impressions quickly to capture "a truth the mind would ordinarily miss or perceive only after long study and reflection."[88]

British operations, Liverpool believed, should focus on Portugal so long the army did not face undue risk as it offered the best prospect for effective action. Steps he took even before permanently accepting the War Office guided his course. Assuming French efforts would focus on Spain following Austria's defeat, Liverpool queried Wellington on the likely consequences. What chance would the French have of subjugating Spain, even with some partial exceptions? Would they be likely to attack Portugal in force before securing Spain north of the Sierra Morena, dividing Andalucia from the rest of the country? What then were the chances of successful resistance? If opposition risked the British army without prospect of success, Wellington must consider the danger in delaying withdrawal until the French entered Portugal in force. Abandoning Portugal until "absolutely necessary" was "neither just nor politic," but Liverpool warned against sacrificing the greater part of Britain's disposable force "for want of timely precaution."[89] The decision involved balancing risks that could only be understood with further information. Wellington gave an encouraging reply. The French had neither the means nor the intention of invading Portugal. If they tried, he expected to resist successfully. An attack would be likely before the French subdued Northern Spain – they already held Old Castile in the center of the country as terrain gave the stronger army, especially in cavalry, a decisive advantage – but it would not come for several months. While the British could embark in the unlikely case of defeat, the French would need very large reinforcements to control Spain.[90] Liverpool had already determined to remain in Portugal and promised Wellington "to do my best for you, though I cannot promise I shall always succeed." Indeed, Liverpool thought he might be more useful to Wellington than any other person directing the War Office.[91]

Managing the war effort involved coordinating a complex structure partly outside Liverpool's direct authority. He controlled policy and strategic plan-ning – along with colonial administration – but not transport, artillery, or the commissariat operated respectively by the Admiralty, ordnance department, and Treasury. Administering the War Office also fell to a separate junior official. The army's commander-in-chief, a professional soldier directly responsible to the king, oversaw army discipline, promotions, and postings. Wellington had to work with at least five separate departments. A simple request for reinforcements involved correspondence with no fewer than six ministers plus the commander-in-chief.[92] On many points, Liverpool could be no more than an intermediary with his office a sorting box for Wellington's requests. His relations with colleagues, espe-cially Perceval, who oversaw both the exchequer and the overall government, helped contain inevitable friction. Liverpool's military undersecretary, Lieutenant Colonel Sir Henry Bunbury, an officer with field experience and previous service as quartermaster general, worked loyally and raised the department's efficiency.

Few among the officials purged by Grenville had returned. Many of those who had returned later retired to make way for younger men. The change in personnel brought renewed vigor and efficiency as demands increased from 1810.[93]

Finance posed a key problem that worsened in 1809. Beyond the difficulty providing what the army and navy needed for overseas service, the heavy cost of underwriting both allied and British efforts had strained public finances as Portland's administration collapsed. William Huskisson, a protégé of Pitt and Dundas who had become a leading expert as secretary to the Treasury, warned in August that Britain could not sustain the present level of expense. Political concerns about the level of taxation parliament would accept underlined the difficulty securing enough revenue to meet rising costs. Unless ministers reduced spending to 1805 levels by sweeping cuts, the country risked either a convulsion or peace with France on humiliating terms. Huskisson resigned with Canning in September, but repeated his insistence that without serious economy, national independence stood at risk. George III endorsed the concern, and Wellesley accepted that plans had to match the means of pursuing them.[94] Similar fears about public finances during the closing stages of the Seven Years War had led Bute and George III to seek peace, but the country now faced a different situation. Perceval avoided the crisis Huskinsson predicted, benefitting from an upsurge in trade lasting into late 1810, along with much tighter budgeting and management. Increased exports and import substitution amidst volatile trade cycles brought direct revenue to sustain the war and capital that floated government loans.[95] The situation, however, underlay Grenville's deep pessimism about the war and Liverpool's sometimes difficult relations with Wellington.

Liverpool officially took over as the financial crisis became acute, but it had influenced his earlier questions on prospects in Portugal. A December 15, 1809 dispatch told Wellington that Britain would provide £980,000 to Portugal; £600,000 for Portuguese troops already in Wellington's pay, £130,000 to increase officers' pay, and £250,000 for an additional 10,000 men. A £600,000 gap remained since Portuguese revenue had fallen short by Wellington's account. Liverpool stated that the government could do no more, warning privately "that if the war is to continue, we must look to economy." Never before had Britain made such an effort. While hoping Wellington found the arrangement satisfactory, he added the unfortunate phrase that "we are naturally anxious to know, with some certainty, we have our money's worth."[96] Pressure to economize angered Wellington, who feared more than anything else the failure of financial provision. Neither personally a spendthrift nor dismissive of financial concerns, he believed that he had done more than anyone to minimize expenses. Lack of specie had delayed operations in 1809 as Wellington needed coin for transport and provisions while paying his troops.[97] He failed to see why the government could not do the same as individuals who bought and exported specie, especially since it would save twenty percent on the transaction. He bluntly asked in June

1810 whether they fought for Britain's independent existence and if it were not then "advisable to maintain the contest as long as possible at a distance from home? If so, government must incur expense."[98]

Instead of rebuking Wellington for his acerbic dispatches, Liverpool exercised great patience and scrambled to meet the army's needs. Their relations tested his ability to manage a difficult subordinate who feared being sacrificed for political considerations at home. Working by letter rather than face to face helped avoid a clash with the volatile Wellington. Tensions between commanders who believe themselves unfairly denied resources and civilian officials pressed with demands beyond their means recur in civil–military relations. Liverpool handled them well. He eventually pointed out that war on a large scale could not be conducted without some difficulties, pecuniary shortages being the most trying. Britain still paid suppliers and troops better than the French. Doing so precluded resort to the enemy's financial shifts and expedients. Resources, Liverpool insisted, would be focused on the war in Portugal and Spain rather than dissipated elsewhere.[99]

Wellington insisted Portugal could be defended. Indeed, he argued the French took a greater risk in exposing their whole fabric in Spain by concentrating forces for an invasion. Rather than fighting desperate battles, he had kept to a defensive plan of wearing them down and maintaining Britain's position. Aware of both the dangers and responsibility, Wellington now asked only to be "left to the exercise of my own judgment" and given "fair confidence."[100] Liverpool provided that trust, though Wellington only slowly appreciated it. He thought ministers feared he would "get them and myself into a scrape" from anxieties their parliamentary difficulties reinforced. The prickly general later griped "that Govt. & Country are going to the Devil as fast as possible" and he expected "every day to hear that the Mob of London are masters of the Country." Complaints about vague instructions – with official dispatches authorizing "a fair and manly line" balanced by "private hints which direct one that would disgrace us forever" – matched his worries that political weakness drove vacillation.[101]

Liverpool understood the stakes better than Wellington appreciated. His very real problems aside, Wellington inferred suspicions where none existed. Liverpool sought information to allay concerns, not least to satisfy the king and his colleagues, while pressing the general to clarify his plans. He appreciated distinctions between policy, strategy, and operations that politicians often blur or misunderstand, and readily deferred to Wellington's judgment and better local information. Liverpool also provided better support than the general credited. To do so he and Wellesley had to convince Perceval and their colleagues. Wellington had urged further aid to Portugal, and parliament doubled the subsidy from £1 to £2 million. British rank and file under Wellington's command increased from 42,000 in January to a peak of 57,000 in October 1810, though illness lowered the number of effective troops. Liverpool's measure that allowed up to 10,000 militia annually to volunteer for the regular army brought recruits to sustain higher deployments. Specie remained a problem. Liverpool urged Wellington to use bills of exchange drawn on London where possible. Despite the general's skepticism, those bills covered £8½ million of the £9 million spent in 1811.[102] Resources came in spurts like water through a leaky pipe rather than as a continuous stream, but the system operated well enough to meet the army's needs. Liverpool provided the political cover and administrative support to make it work.

Grenville warned in January 1810 that ministers soon would have to account for the treasure and lives "they have sacrificed in useless and unprofitable expeditions."[103] Castlereagh backed an inquiry into the Walchern expedition to vindicate his own conduct in office. Canning thought the government could stand, albeit with little credit, but Perceval warned the king of the impression when ministers were in a minority on any major question.[104] Liverpool had a stronger case defending Wellington's campaigns, along with Wellesley's help in debate. He carefully separated the conduct of the army and its commanding officer from the campaign's general management to move a vote of thanks for the victory at Talavera. Wellington's march into Spain had been "well considered, wisely planned, and deliberately executed." Liverpool praised the success won "against such an immense disparity of numbers."[105] Grey replied that Wellington's dispatches gave a totally different meaning from Liverpool's words. Failure to disperse the French army and subsequent retreat made Talavera anything but a victory, while lack of support from Spanish authorities left British forces ill-supplied, almost starved in a friendly country. Wellesley refuted Grey point by point. Grenville hesitated challenging Wellesley directly, but turned back to an attack on government policy over the past two years. The motion passed without a division, though Grey pressed Liverpool a few days later to name the military advisors on whose responsibility general orders had been issued. Ministers also deflected calls to open the whole correspondence relating to the late campaign.[106]

Grenville opposed further operations in the peninsula in a debate on the convention with Portugal. Lamenting the "thankless task" of repeating predictions "despised and rejected" while too fatally fulfilled, he insisted that he did it to avoid similar future calamities. Wellington's army could not defend Portugal. Support from allies had never matched the expectations ministers had raised. Expecting "effectual cooperation with a Portuguese army" ignored recent lessons including the need to husband British resources and the present ministers' incapacity.[107] Liverpool framed Grenville's argument as a motion to remove the cabinet that would abandon Portugal. His reply defended leveraging popular opposition to France in Iberia to Britain's advantage. Spain offered "hope of the support of a whole armed population" while Lisbon provided a secure base. Nothing had been spared to animate the allies, and Portugal had raised a substantial army. If those troops lacked experience, "every army must have a beginning." Ministers had won the Spanish and Portuguese people's confidence by decisively supporting them. Liverpool asked whether "a cold, cautious, and phlegmatic system of policy" as Grenville urged could have prevailed. If he truly opposed further operations, Grenville should immediately move to withdraw the army from Portugal. Harrowby echoed that point by asking why, if the opposition wanted ministers dismissed, they did not call for it, "rather than attempt to tie up their hands while in office."[108]

Liverpool and his colleagues cast the opposition effectively as a self-interested faction quicker to criticize than propose a constructive alternative. No matter how much that impression played to public suspicions of the Whigs, it did not strengthen the government or assuage popular fears. Grenville used a March 2 debate to "deprecate that system of double government which puts forward one set of men as the ostensible administration, but invests another set of men concealed from public view with all the effective powers of government."[109] Chatham's correspondence with the king on Walcheren prompted the complaint, but Grenville aimed it at Liverpool given his father's reputation. Grey charged ministers with subsisting "shifts and expedients calculated only to meet the passing events of the hour." They vainly hoped to face "all the perils of the storm without chart or compass or rudder to direct them."[110] He sought to claim a middle ground between a failed administration and the wild opposition seen in the recent Burdett riots. Liverpool shrewdly parried by arguing if he had made a similar challenge during the Talents ministry "what disgraces, calamities, failures and disasters could he not have crowded into it."[111] The censure failed. Liverpool now showed far more confidence than at the low point of early 1808.

The government sought to expand its basis. Wellesley urged overtures to Canning, Castlereagh, and Sidmouth to bring the remainder of Pitt's friends together as no strong government could be formed without them. A general change would clear objections to recruiting either Sidmouth or Canning alone, but Sidmouth declined to serve with Canning.[112] Yorke replaced Mulgrave at the Admiralty, freeing the latter for the Ordnance's less demanding responsibilities. Robert Dundas again refused the Admiralty unless the government won outside strength. Wellesley continued to urge a joint overture to Canning and Castlereagh, and even suggested approaching Canning alone.[113] Liverpool's colleagues firmly refused his offer to make the War Office available. They preferred to offer them the Admiralty and Home Office. Castlereagh declined, stating the proposal would neither raise public confidence nor inspire the nation that the government stood united. Talks between Canning and Perceval reinforced the prime minister's suspicions and confirmed Eldon's view of Canning as "vanity in human form." Mulgrave expressed the cabinet's sentiment that they "must make the best battle we can & if necessary die in the last ditch."[114]

Besides fighting that battle, Liverpool struggled to convince Wellington that the government backed him. Castlereagh's brother, Charles Stewart, who served under Wellington discerned an element of *aut Caesar aut nihil* in a commander "disinclined to everything he does not originate." Interestingly for a soldier with his political experience, Wellington showed no sense of the wider problems facing Liverpool and the cabinet. He complained of having no assistance from either ministers or "the worst British army that was ever sent from England." Genuinely frustrated with his political superiors, Wellington was particularly alienated from Liverpool and Perceval.[115] Liverpool took great pains to conciliate him. Besides patiently explaining the reasons behind decisions, he shared personal news of Wellington's sons and conveyed the king's approbation. Insisting "that every person with whom I have had an opportunity of communicating" did the general ample justice, he stood at a loss to see why Wellington supposed ministers lacked confidence in his steps to defend Portugal. Liverpool had from "*private sentiments*" never seen a question where the cabinet differed less.[116] Smoothing tensions and building a relationship with Wellington took time, effort, and patience. It mattered as much to the war as Liverpool's other responsibilities. Only after the successful defense of Portugal did Wellington's view of ministers gradually improve.

The return of George III's illness cast a shadow as fortunes seemed to improve. Liverpool reported his anxiety and distress over Princess Amelia's illness. Her rapid decline overthrew the king's equilibrium, particularly after she silently gave him from her sickbed a lock of her hair with a ring inscribed "remember me."[117] She died on November 1, but Liverpool had already warned Bathurst of the king's increasingly disturbed behavior. The presence of physicians at the king's request forced ministers to consider the matter. As symptoms might subside, it seemed expedient to keep things quiet while updating colleagues so they could return to London.[118] The cabinet called in specialists who had treated the king before, despite the royal family's opposition; Queen Charlotte had pledged her husband that the mad doctors would never be forced upon him again. Although ministers sought delay, they could not postpone the parliamentary session without a commission the king could not give. A thinly attended parliament adjourned for a fortnight on November 1 with hopes of better news. Eldon and Perceval secured a further adjournment until November 29, but the question could not be avoided much longer.[119]

Ministers faced the same danger that had threatened Pitt during the 1788 Regency Crisis. Unless the king recovered soon, their tenure in office would rely upon a Prince of Wales who had been politically and socially linked with the Whig opposition since his youth. Ward reported the prince wished to dismiss none of the ministers, but merely introduce some of his own friends to the cabinet "to watch the rogues his father had chosen."[120] Policy differences made that difficult, as earlier overtures had shown. Liverpool feared the repercussions for the war effort, particularly given attacks by Grenville and Grey. The war made an important difference from 1788. So did the fact that only Grenville and Sheridan remained of the leading politicians then. Grenville now stood with Fox's political heirs rather than Pitt's. Ministers had the advantage of unity, while Grenville and Grey distrusted the debauched Sheridan who stood higher in the prince's confidence. Uncertainty how the present illness would develop forced caution. Indeed, Liverpool thought a regency would hinder the king's recovery by agitating him when he needed calm.[121]

Laying a report of the king's health before the Lords on November 29, Liverpool echoed Grenville's earlier point that any decision would only be making a choice among difficulties and moved an adjournment until December 13. The motion brought a short debate in which Harrowby said it was only natural "to wish for every possible delay before they should proceed to set aside the monarch." His words sparked uproar. Grenville denounced "so monstrous a proposition" amidst calls to order. Harrowby stood his ground, but discussion went further than Liverpool would have liked.[122] He thought Grenville's conduct "beyond anything we could have conceived to be possible." Liverpool also reported that, while Sidmouth and Castlereagh backed ministers, Canning remained absent and his friends did not vote.[123] Having delayed as long as possible, Liverpool moved on December 13 for a committee of twenty-one peers chosen by ballot to take evidence from the king's physicians. The measure, he noted, followed the precedent from 1788. It passed without dissent.[124] With the cabinet's backing, Perceval told the prince on December 19 that, despite the delicacy involved, "the defect in the personal exercise of the royal authority" must be resolved. Ministers therefore proposed a bill empowering the prince to exercise royal authority is his father's name during the illness, albeit with restrictions.[125]

Prince and ministers differed over the restrictions, with the future regent referring Perceval back to his views during the earlier crisis in 1788. He also assembled the royal princes at Carleton House to hear the correspondence read, prompting his brothers to make a formal protest to Perceval.[126] Perceval and the cabinet stood their ground. On Thursday, December 27, 1810, Liverpool introduced three resolutions already passed by the Commons that opened the way for a regency bill. A key point involved the right of the Lords and Commons to enact lawful measures without the royal assent given the king's indisposition. Liverpool sketched the constitutional principles behind the precedent, which included parliamentary limits on a regent's powers. When Stanhope objected to his assertion that no legal challenge could be made to a bill passed under the great seal, Liverpool quoted at length Lord Camden's opinion in 1788 justifying the claim and followed with an historical precedent from the sixteenth century.[127] The Duke of York opposed the proceedings as derogatory to the crown's dignity and subversive of its rights. Besides giving authority to pass statutes without royal assent, the plan would restrict the regent in a fashion "not less dangerous in principle than in precedent." Moira cast the restrictions as slight on the prince that would produce a weak government at "a most awful period of difficulty and danger." Grenville could not abandon his earlier position without seeming opportunistic, but he still charged ministers with assuming the exercise of regal authority in a manner not seen since Cromwell.[128] Perceval faced worse in the Commons where opposition worked to drive home the wedge set between ministers and the soon-to-be prince regent. Wellington had questioned following the 1788 precedent too closely. He told Wellesley-Pole that limiting the prince's authority would democratize the government with permanent consequences and induce him to raise a party against ministers that would make their situation still more difficult.[129]

Indeed, the prince consulted with Grenville and Grey, who provided a draft reply to the address from parliament with resolutions outlining terms for the regency on January 8, 1811. He had told Moira that only those two peers could form a strong government. Talks on apportioning offices began among the opposition.[130] Trouble came, however, when the prince submitted the draft to Moira and Sheridan, and preferred the latter's version, which took a stronger line on the restrictions. Grenville and Grey then insisted that taking Sheridan's advice showed a want of confidence that precluded them taking office. Holland told Sheridan directly that the prince must be considered as withdrawing his confidence if he took another's advice, but Grey and Grenville won their point at the cost of antagonizing the gossipy Sheridan and annoying the prince. Sheridan's goodwill, Holland believed, would have been useful and won cheaply had they not treated him with disdain. It also seemed unlikely the prince "would bear to be flogged like a schoolboy by his two masters." If Perceval, as he quipped, "had a monstrous deal of antipathy to overcome before he could even get the length of being endured," Grenville bore the same burden.[131]

Perceval had shown his mettle through the whole controversy. Even opponents complimented his determination in playing a weak hand during debates in the Commons. Although Liverpool held better ground in the Lords and suffered fewer defeats – his difficulty involved absent peers rather than outright deserters – he won credit for handling a delicate problem with care. Ministers had "no share whatever" of the prince's confidence, he wrote, though backed by "a considerable majority of the well-disposed and respectable part of the community."[132] Changing the government after the bill passed would have required both more initiative than the prince regent could summon and a stronger foundation for a new ministry than the Whigs could provide. A rally by George III, who expressed approval of what had passed to date, made the prince hesitate in any step that might upset the king's recovery. Liverpool still expected to lose office as late as February 1, 1811, but the prince announced three days later that he would not remove the present ministers from power.[133]

The reprieve saved Wellington's plans from the Whigs. Napoleon had appointed Marshal André Masséna in April 1810 to command an invasion of Portugal after having earlier prepared 100,000 reinforcements for Spain. Wellington doubted the campaign would produce anything very brilliant, but he determined to hold until withdrawal became necessary and then carry it off without disgrace.[134]

Extensive defensive positions known as the Lines of Torres Vedras made evacuation unnecessary. Wellington kept the full preparations from ministers, which partly explained Liverpool's apprehensions, lest newspapers convey information to the French.[135] Masséna captured Ciudad Rodrigo and Almeida in the summer of 1810 before Wellington checked him at Bussaco on September 25. The victory satisfied British opinion and enabled an orderly withdrawal. Masséna had neither supplies to sustain his forces nor the artillery and manpower to break lines garrisoned by militia with British and Portuguese regulars behind them. Having largely stripped the countryside, Wellington left the French to suffer through the winter despite Masséna's attempt to draw him out by a calculated withdrawal. Starvation then forced a retreat. Invading Portugal cost Masséna some 25,000 killed and captured and inflicted the greatest and most obvious defeat upon French arms since Napoleon had established the empire seven years before.[136]

Brighter prospects in the peninsula raised confidence in Wellington as offensive measures became possible. They overcame doubts to provide more resources. Liverpool thought the French retreat formed "a new era in the war." He sought Wellington's advice on future proceedings. Hints of a renewed conflict in Northern Europe kept unaltered the determination not to be diverted from the peninsula. "If we can strike a blow," Liverpool wrote, "we will strike it there."[137] Wellington agreed Napoleon's position in Spain would become difficult and thought British persistence could bring the struggle there to an adequate close.[138] Discussion turned to where further efforts might be most effectively concentrated. Britain moved beyond a limited commitment to defend Portugal into an active role against France. Liverpool had other responsibilities beyond supporting Wellington, including a force in Sicily, but the peninsula remained his priority. New orders in late May giving Wellington full discretion set the terms for his conduct of the rest of the war. His distrust of Liverpool only ended later, but the minister's commitment provided a foundation for ultimate success.[139] Britain had a clear strategy for the first time since 1793. Effective partnership between Wellington, Liverpool, and Perceval ensured the focus to pursue it consistently.

Cautious escalation followed over the next year. So long as the French remained willing to send troops over the Pyrenees to replace losses and reinforce their armies, they could keep their hold on Spain.[140] Still, with Liverpool's support, Wellington prepared to exploit French vulnerability as he saw the chance. Political cover in Britain was key to that support, particularly with the opposition doubtful at best over the chance of defeating Napoleon. Liverpool played a vital role coordinating support for Wellington and keeping strategy focused on the peninsula. Correspondence shows Liverpool's attention to detail. Wellington had complained about leaks since 1809. Security prompted him to withhold information on defensive plans from dispatches the next year.[141] Liverpool's inquiries about the source revealed that information mostly came from letters officers sent home. An order prohibiting such news with the mail to be stopped entirely upon further leaks seemed the only recourse. Liverpool wrote that Moore had taken that step earlier. Wellington replied tartly that a commander could not prevent officers corresponding with their friends.[142] Liverpool also realized public interest had to be satisfied lest silence produce an unfavorable impression. He proposed Wellington write dispatches so they could be published safely and keep confidential observations for private letters. If that caused too much trouble, the general could mark sections for publication and Liverpool would see his wishes were followed. Security had to be balanced with demands of public opinion and politics. Wellington recognized as much, crafting his dispatches and revising those of subordinates to cast news in a favorable light, though he distrusted the press through his career.[143]

Letters and information from officers with opposition ties gave critics ammunition. They remained an irritant that tried Wellington's limited patience. Liverpool did much to assure Wellington of the cabinet's backing and favorable circumstances at home, pointing out that Perceval stood higher than any minister since Pitt.[144] Ministers could not rely wholly on a prince who showed them only grudging favor, especially as limitations on the regency expired in February 1812. George III's health deteriorated in July, dashing hopes that he would recover. The king did not however die as many expected. Since the prince regent had withheld major changes in hopes of his father's recovery, the prospect of George III's death or permanent incapacity reopened political questions. Every conversation by autumn revolved around the question of what the prince would do when he had full authority. Besides changing the government, how would he act on the Catholic question with a new petition coming before parliament? The prince had never taken his father's hard line against Catholic Emancipation. He now stood as the potential arbiter between two parliamentary groups.[145]

The role fit neither the prince regent's talents nor his inclinations. He sought to avoid a choice by delaying it as far as possible. Eldon remarked on how the prince "had totally altered his opinion of the men whom he had hated," including the chancellor himself. More importantly, ministers had distinguished themselves in their support of the war. The prince regent, who shared their commitment to overthrowing Napoleon, determined not to depart from the present system at a critical moment. While open to including "some of those persons with whom the early habits of my public life were formed" in a government "on the most liberal basis," the prince's wish to pursue the current policy with vigor made their support unlikely. Although his letter written for Grenville and Grey never mentioned Perceval by name, it effectively confirmed his cabinet in office.[146] The only alternative might be a new government on a broader foundation, but still pledged to the war. Wellesley saw himself as the logical head of such an arrangement. Disillusioned with his colleagues and their failure to extend the government, he had intended resigning until the king's illness stayed his hand, even though he became steadily more alienated.

Wellesley threatened resignation in a communication with Bathurst before proposing himself to the prince regent as the only figure who could form a government including both Canning and Castlereagh. He and Canning had decided Liverpool could manage daily business in the Lords, with Castlereagh joining him there as home secretary.[147] The proposal only made the cabinet call Wellesley's bluff. A joint stand made his plan impossible and left the prince a choice between the present ministers and the Whigs. Wellesley's failure to appreciate the highly personal nature of politics and the collaboration cabinet government demanded sidelined his career. Lacking the tact to work easily with colleagues or the humility to realize when to mute criticism, Wellesley kept aloof from the give and take that brought ministers to an agreement they could defend in parliament. Vanity spoiled Wellesley, ending his chance to stay in high office until Liverpool appointed him Lord Lieutenant of Ireland in 1821. An observer noted "how foolish is that once great man" who squandered his laurels from India and "failed in an endeavor of intrigue rather than ambition so spiritless as to be even ridiculous."[148]

Wellesley's departure and the prince regent's decision to back Perceval facilitated the juncture with Castlereagh and Sidmouth ministers had long sought. Liverpool managed the Foreign Office until arrangements could be settled.[149] He made clear, however, he would not remain there to let Castlereagh resume his old post. Castlereagh seemed to consider taking the War Office a point of honor that would vindicate him, which also applied to Liverpool at the Foreign Office. Political difficulties with that logic aside, Liverpool did not want the Foreign Office. Mulgrave also thought him too good a war secretary to be spared. Liverpool outlined the objections in a letter Perceval could use to persuade Castlereagh, who accepted the Foreign Office where he soon made his name. Sidmouth became Lord President of the Council, with offices for several friends. Robert Dundas, Viscount Melville after his father's death in May 1811, replaced Yorke at the Admiralty.[150] The appointments formed a strong, cohesive ministry committed to the war and sure of backing from prince regent and the public.

If Perceval dominated the new government, Liverpool remained its essential pillar. Besides his own departmental responsibilities, he filled in for absent colleagues and showed a sure grasp of general administration. Internal tensions had underlined character's importance to public standing. Liverpool's candid and fair-minded conduct had won respect from colleagues and the wider political elite that raised his reputation from the low point of his stint as foreign secretary. Sitting in the Lords had kept him out of quarrels among those struggling for Pitt's mantle as he showed his willingness to facilitate arrangements by waiving personal claims. Liverpool's standing among the cabinet then helped make him an effective war minister. His political style behind the scenes further contributed to his success. Salisbury later pointed out that "a war minister must find his reward in his conscience or his salary" rather than aspire to fame. The "pale and reflected glory" from Wellington's victories satisfied Liverpool, who helped make them possible.[151] Improving prospects in the peninsular, along with Napoleon's war against Russia, strengthened the government's hand in early 1812. Economic difficulties pointed to challenges in the upcoming parliamentary session, but Liverpool and his colleagues stood well placed to withstand them.

CHAPTER 6

Prime Minister and Peacemaking

Sllightly after five o'clock on May 11, 1812, John Bellingham shot Spencer Perceval in the lobby of the House of Commons. As Perceval staggered forward with a single cry and fell dead, Bellingham seemed to have thrown politics back into confusion. *The Times* believed "the firm is entirely broken up by the death of the chief partner."[1] Appearances mislead. Perceval's cabinet united behind Liverpool, who saw the prospects as "doubtful, but not desperate."[2] After grasping for alternatives, the prince regent appointed Liverpool prime minister. Cabinet making and domestic politics soon afterwards led into the complexities of peacemaking abroad.

Perceval's assassination shocked a political elite focused on economic trouble and an acrimonious debate over the Orders in Council. Bellingham, a failed merchant driven to insanity by a grievance over his imprisonment in Russia, shot Perceval as a target of opportunity. Henry Brougham had finished examining a witness before the Commons when the shot was heard. Business continued as those present outside took Perceval's body to the speaker's apartments. Bellingham admitted his guilt. Isaac Gascoyne, a Liverpool MP, identified him and the speaker ordered the murderer taken into custody.[3] As news reached the Lords with a cry "Mr. Perceval is shot," peers crowded into the chamber. Eldon, who had passed Bellingham earlier on a stairwell, called them to order as witnesses confirmed the report. Tears overcame both Eldon and Castlereagh the next day when they conveyed the prince regent's wish that provision be made for Perceval's family.[4] Not since the Duke of Buckingham's murder in 1627 had an English minister been assassinated. Plebeian crowds celebrated in Nottingham and Leicester while others at Wolverhampton exclaimed that "now the great Man in the Parliament House is dead, we shall have a big Loaf" seemed an alarming portent. Amidst elite unease over such talk of revolution, Canning noted the difficulty loyalists had in seeing the murder as an entirely apolitical act. Bellingham's trial and execution still passed quickly without event.[5]

Since the government stood largely on Perceval's authority, his loss raised difficult questions. Eldon told the prince regent that the cabinet believed it their duty to continue under any present minister he chose. Their preference for Liverpool became clear as he handled overtures to Canning and Wellesley after Perceval's funeral. At least an attempt to gain support from Pitt's two protégés or the Whigs seemed essential, but it would be on the cabinet's terms.[6] Liverpool met them separately to propose continuing the administration on its present basis with their support. Castlereagh would keep the Foreign Office and his lead in the Commons, while the ministry would include Canning's – and Wellesley's – friends with Liverpool as premier. Canning, who took a précis of the conversation, wished to speak with friends before making any reply beyond asking if sentiments on the Catholic question remained unchanged. Liverpool said that they did, although he included Castlereagh, who shared Canning's view.[7]

Liverpool took Wellesley the same terms. Defending the cabinet's policy against his past criticism, he also said that Sidmouth and his friends would remain and realized Wellesley would not join unless Canning received a fair offer. Wellesley agreed, but noted he and Canning were free to act separately.[8] After conferring, both declined. Canning said that pledging to set aside the Catholic question would sacrifice his "personal & public character." Wellesley gave the same public reason. Liverpool replied that he had never absolutely refused to alter the present laws and believed circumstances might render some change advisable. But he opposed an inquiry that would only stir controversy. Since Wellesley knew ministers differed on Catholic Emancipation his insistence suggests it was merely a pretext.[9] A statement in *The Times* on May 20, published without his authorization but never contradicted, gave his reasons for resigning before attacking Perceval and the remaining ministers. Besides scandalizing the queen, it antagonized ministers who now refused to work with him. Wellesley then determined to oppose a government formed without him.[10]

Matters could have ended with the refusal of what the cabinet thought a fair offer. On May 22, however, James Stuart-Wortley moved that the Commons urge the prince regent to appoint "a strong and effective administration." A change of mind on the Catholic question prompted the step. While he told Liverpool beforehand, a question of confidence posed by the husband of his wife's niece could only embarrass. Interestingly, Stuart-Wortley had not asked anyone to second the motion and did not know if it would draw support. That Lord Milton, eldest son of a leading Whig peer – Lord Fitzwilliam who had broken with Fox over the French Revolution, but later returned to opposition – seconded it amplified the effect. Louisa promptly cancelled an engagement to avoid meeting her niece. After the resolution passed by four votes, Stuart-Worley and Milton presented it to the prince regent. Liverpool never again took support in the Commons for granted. He and his colleagues recommended steps to form an effective ministry while promising to carry on in the meantime.[11]

The prince regent asked Wellesley if he could form a ministry. Wellesley grounded his plans on concessions to Roman Catholics and rigorous prosecution of the war, but exceeded his brief by opening discussions with leading figures of all parties. Holland and Lansdowne referred him to Grey and Grenville.[12] Canning, at Wellesley's request, approached Liverpool and Melville who both declined. Liverpool said his colleagues did not consider it worth discussing as they would not serve under Wellesley, whose behavior had made joining him incompatible with their honor and character.[13] The prince urged Liverpool to reconsider with such "heat and intemperance" that the premier feared for the prince's mental balance. Resolved "to see him no more," he instead sent a cabinet minute saying no benefit could arise from joining Canning and Wellesley. The prince regent then sought written statements of each minister's reasoning.[14]

Liverpool replied that differences over Catholic demands – the conduct ministers should adopt toward those claims as much as the question itself – made cooperation with Wellesley and Canning impossible. However desirable their support might be, a junction would cost strength elsewhere. Liverpool tactfully forbore naming Castlereagh and Sidmouth.[15] Sidmouth pointed out that Canning's "splendid talents" alone would not compensate for losing Perceval and Castlereagh. Eldon expressed himself willing to consider, though he did not say grant, the Catholic petition, which went further than Liverpool. He agreed, however, that Canning and Wellesley would not accept any proposition the cabinet would be likely to back.[16] Distrust made a junction impossible. Liverpool preferred to be out of office, even if he supported a new ministry. Wellesley then approached Grey and Grenville. If Catholic Emancipation impeded cooperating with ministers, aggressively prosecuting the war did the same with the opposition. The two Whig peers would not back policies they opposed. Settling offices with four or five posts at their disposal in a cabinet with Canning held little appeal. They sought power, not a partial share under Wellesley.[17]

The prince regent had a rapprochement of his own with Moira, who had been estranged since February 1812. His tears punctuated a meeting Grenville described as a *scène larmoyante* with the prince lamenting past errors and Moira recounting the country's terrible state. Although nothing distinct passed about politics or arrangements – Moira suggested the prince might wish to regain his composure before entering into details – the prince regent now had a figure more likely to recruit some of Perceval's friends into a government with Grenville and Grey.[18] Moira thought the prospect "dreadfully difficult, the ground being so soiled." Protagonists now held positions they would not have taken before. Whig leaders showed an "unhandsome impatience at not having everything at their own disposal" and focused "upon petty distractions and little captious forms." Moira saw nothing could be settled with them.[19] Liverpool offered support, but would not hold office. His leading colleagues agreed, which left Moira only Canning and some of the less prominent of Pitt's protégés. By June 8 his effort had failed. The prince regent named Liverpool prime minister with full authority to complete arrangements.

Negotiations had tested the idea of a broad administration to destruction. Liverpool was now the only figure able to lead a government committed to the war and secure public confidence. More than anyone save the tactless Wellesley, he had taken a firm and consistent line on prosecuting the war to the limit of British means. Holland saw in him little appetite for office, much less avarice or ambition. Liverpool, he believed, did nothing to obstruct formation of a new government or preserve the old one, but let matters take their course. Thomas Grenville had anyway doubted the prince's intentions, suspecting he intended "to collect as many difficulties from all public men" which he could then plead to holding with Liverpool. Ministers could now expect support from the prince's friends and even some who had voted for Stuart-Wortley's motion. Aberdeen quipped that the opposition had given Liverpool his job again, along with parliamentary strength to keep it.[20]

Liverpool first settled cabinet appointments. On returning from the prince regent, he told Sidmouth "*You* must take the Home Department…it will be everything to me." Besides having the seniority to win over the former premier, the post suited his diligence and integrity given the acute social tension. Respect he held among backbenchers and conservative-minded gentlemen beyond parliament helped the government. Sidmouth's views on the Catholic question gave cover on Irish affairs and patronage. Appointing Vansittart to the exchequer tied Sidmouth's friends more closely with the government though Liverpool himself set financial policy.[21] Bathurst went to the War Office, where his easy manner and administrative skill made him a great success. Like Liverpool, he sprang from an old Tory family whose fortunes had revived after languishing under the first two Hanoverians. A self-effacing personality underlay his gregarious wit and reserved decorum. Bathurst joined Liverpool and Castlereagh in directing foreign and military policy, with the premier exercising authority behind the scenes. That colleagues never challenged them showed the confidence they enjoyed and the smooth working of Liverpool's cabinet.[22]

Perhaps surprisingly, Liverpool tried again to recruit Canning. Personal regard, along with respect for Canning's abilities and hopes of his followers' support, brought a step that suggests Liverpool had a far greater claim to being a saint than Wilberforce. The government needed support in the Commons. Castlereagh raised no objections and even offered the Foreign Office as an enticement. Bathurst made his own post available. The problem was whether Canning or Castlereagh would lead the Commons. Raising Castlereagh to an English peerage would solve it, but, despite six weeks of effort, the prince regent failed to persuade him.[23] Canning, while ready to act cordially "on a footing of equality," would not serve *under* Castlereagh. Pained, Liverpool declined comment until they could meet, while noting objections to placing in abeyance the management of general business in the Commons. Canning then proposed leaving general business to Vansittart, a notoriously poor speaker, rather than either secretary of state.[24]

Talks broke down. Liverpool thought Canning's alternative unworkable and likely to generate trouble. Indeed, he had proposed Castlereagh take the exchequer with the lead partly because two-thirds of business naturally fell to that office and Canning's acceptance of the Foreign Office would provide compensating prestige.[25] Discussion itself raised difficulties, particularly when Castlereagh refused anything that implied his own subordination and Canning asked how regularly he would be expected to attend debates.[26] They drew back into irreconcilable stands. Canning finally determined not to serve under Castlereagh with the exhausted Liverpool expressing regret.[27] The prince regent blamed Canning, whom he described as taking "as much courting as a woman." Had Canning joined Perceval after Portland's departure, as Wilberforce noted "he would now have been the acknowledged head and supported as such."[28] Instead, his hopes for office faded.

Castlereagh's limitations as a speaker posed a serious problem. Governments had to explain and defend their policies. Silence broken only by the tramp of feet into the lobby to provide majorities encouraged the impression that their power derived from something other than parliamentary confidence. Only an effective presence in both houses could enable ministers to cut opposition down to size, justify themselves in debate, and demonstrate capacity before the legislature.[29] Having failed to recruit Canning, Liverpool brought forward promising younger men, including Croker, Henry Goulburn, and Sir Robert Peel. At a dinner party in 1822, he surprised Princess Lieven by predicting that Peel would be prime minister within a decade, but that later assessment provided no help in 1812.[30] "I should be most happy," he told Wellington with a surprising degree of self-effacement, "if I could see a second Pitt amongst them, and would most willingly resign the government into his hands, for I am fully aware of the importance of the minister being, if possible, in the House of Commons."[31] Since that was not possible, Liverpool and his colleagues had to manage as best they could. Wellington saw the magnitude of the challenge, but rightly pointed out "there is nothing like trying."[32]

Controversies could not await cabinet arrangements. Well before parliament met, Henry Brougham had directed provincial discontent into an effective campaign against the Orders in Council. Meetings to draft petitions captured attention usually given to debates. Introducing each petition sparked parliamentary discussion newspapers reported, and the resulting publicity fed the cycle of petition and debate.[33] The inquiry Castlereagh conceded in April 1812 as "merely a concession to the wishes of the country" allowed Brougham to escalate pressure. Perceval's death brought a short delay, but Brougham braved "the censure of enemies and shocked the more timid and more gentle of his friends" by resolutely arguing his case. Holland believed Perceval "had too much spirit to be intimidated and too much bigotry to be convinced." Castlereagh stood on weaker ground.[34] Liverpool ended controversy by withdrawing the Orders, which Castlereagh announced in debate. Brougham's campaign pointed to future trouble on issues where Whigs could use provincial opinion for leverage in parliament. It showed the weight manufacturers and merchants, especially in the north and midlands, could put behind demands for attention to their interests.

Liverpool further blunted possible opposition in June 1812 with what became known as the Little Toleration Act. While the Toleration Act of 1689 suspended penalties on dissenters who subscribed to thirty-six of the Established Church's Thirty-Nine Articles of belief and secured licenses for their meeting houses from magistrates, earlier penal laws still remained in force. Unsympathetic magistrates could deny licenses for meetings or preachers. Fears of subversion during the 1790s led many to do so. Dissenting opinion turned away from Pitt after the outbreak of war in 1793. Cooperation among sects as the ranks of nonconformity grew brought influence that largely aided the Whig opposition while demanding peace and political reform. Wesleyan Methodists, however, largely sided with established authority. As a dynamic revivalist movement outside elite control that simultaneously taught respectability, obedience, and sobriety, Methodism was conservative even as it challenged the status quo. Many of its leaders preached against subversion. The Methodist Conference had pledged in 1798 its opposition to anything that would "molest the quiet of the best of kings" or derange the happiest of all civil constitutions.[35] A fault line opened among dissenters Liverpool could exploit.

Sidmouth's attempt to regularize the status of dissenting clergy in 1811 catalyzed Liverpool's initiative. Concerns about subversion underlined complaints that the 1689 Toleration Act could not manage "modern sectaries assembled in barns, in the rooms of private houses, or in other buildings of the most improper kind to hear wild effusions of a mechanic or ploughboy, perhaps not more than fifteen years of age." Inquiry showed a rapid growth in the number of licenses issued while confirming suspicions about the qualifications of preachers receiving them. Sidmouth proposed restricting licenses to ordained ministers of proven respectability and excluding lay preachers entirely. Dissenters quickly united against his measure to produce 799 petitions at short notice. Nearly 30,000 people signed 250 Methodist petitions alone.[36] The response matched Brougham's mobilization of provincial opinion against the Orders in Council while significantly overlapping with it.

Although Sidmouth's measure failed, magistrates in 1812 followed its guidelines by refusing licenses. Perceval and then Liverpool met complaints with a conciliatory tone aimed to draw Methodist support. On the day Castlereagh announced the Orders in Council's withdrawal, Liverpool assured a delegation his cabinet would not resist ending the licensing requirement for dissenting ministers and congregations. He met weekly through June and July with

Thomas Allan, a Methodist solicitor, to frame a revised Toleration Act that removed all restrictions on Trinitarian dissent and required magistrates to impose the mandated oaths.[37] Only the much evaded Test and Corporation Acts, which made office holders take communion according to the Anglican rite, remained as a burden on dissenters. "An enlarged and liberal toleration," Liverpool argued for the measure, gave "the best security to the established church" whose strength rested not upon exclusion, but in teaching and ministry grounded upon scripture.[38] He distinguished truth from error by framing toleration as part of the process of inquiry by which the Church recovered those seduced by false teaching. The measure extended toleration on substantially the same terms as Roman Catholics to Trinitarian dissenters whom Liverpool viewed as loyal and respectable. (Anglican churchmen saw Rational or Unitarian dissenters, who rejected any human authority in religion and the larger principle of subordination along with Trinitarian Christianity, very differently.) [39]

Liverpool deftly used the most generous measure of toleration since the Glorious Revolution to break the old Whig monopoly as "friends of dissent." By not specifying dissenting groups by name, he appealed deliberately to Methodists, whose ambiguous relationship with the Established Church joined occasional conformity and assent to doctrines with separate meetings.[40] Suspicious of radicals since the 1790s, the Wesleyan Conference sent its local societies a circular after the Toleration Act passed urging them to "Fear the Lord and King, and meddle not with them that are given to change." Preachers in manufacturing districts fought a prolonged campaign against Luddites and pressure from popular radicalism tested Wesleyan discipline. Methodist leaders, despite tensions within congregations, gave Liverpool's government considerable support.[41] The Little Toleration Act of 1812 retreated from stifling dissent without ending qualifications for office set by the Test and Corporation Act. Liverpool used it effectively to reduce political opposition from Nonconformists. Churchmen and dissenters alike favored revising the East India Company charter in 1813 to allow missionary activity where the company exercised control. Later concessions that absolved Unitarians from the crime of blasphemy marked the kind of judicious toleration Liverpool thought an intelligent way to defend the Church of England.[42] His approach worked to broaden support for the established order and peel away from opposition such groups as could be won.

The end of the parliamentary session relieved ministers who had done the business needed to finance the war. Liverpool saw news from northern Europe as a sign Napoleon's invasion of Russia faced major problems.[43] Wellington's victory at Salamanca on July 22 came on the heels of debate over the cabinet's refusal to discuss terms with Napoleon short of complete withdrawal from Spain. Liverpool remarked that he "had never saw an army so beaten." Salamanca enabled the allies to advance on Madrid and raise the siege of Cadiz. Louisa shared a report by semaphore telegraph of 1,700 prisoners and 1,800 pieces of cannon taken at Madrid with her sister Elizabeth who noted the firing of guns at the Tower of London in celebration.[44] By September, Liverpool thought the prospects "never so brilliant" and expected the French would soon be driven across the Ebro. Other news suggested a favorable turn elsewhere. Treaties with Russia and Sweden broke Napoleon's Continental System and foreign markets opened. The harvest looked promising after a year of scarcity.[45] Liverpool seized the moment by persuading the prince regent to dissolve parliament for a general election.

Rumors had circulated through summer, and canvassing began weeks before any official announcement. Liverpool sent government supporters a confidential circular in late September warning them to expect a dissolution. Changes since the last election that included two prime ministers, the king's final incapacity, and Stuart-Wortley's motion justified appealing to public sentiment. Canning anticipated the step, but thought the prince regent would put himself forever in the present cabinet's power by agreeing to it.[46] Liverpool took a leading, if discreet, part in government electioneering. Most elections tested the strength of local interests rather than embryonic national parties. Infrastructure had not yet developed to operate national campaigns. Electioneering at that level mainly involved matching candidates with seats and deploying a diminishing amount of patronage to aid government supporters. Curwen's Act of 1809, which Liverpool had backed despite Perceval's opposition, prohibited the buying and selling of parliamentary seats. Croker, not without reason, complained such reforms "throw the boroughs into the hands of mere adventurers, who will stick at nothing to get in, to the exclusion of those who have any scruples at all." Regardless of what Liverpool recognized as "considerable difficulties," he insisted the government not enter any transactions contrary to law, though its agents could recommend candidates to patrons of close boroughs.[47]

Results came gradually. Constituencies polled on different dates and a contested election could take days. News travelled no faster than mail coaches. Only divisions when the new parliament met would show the real balance. Despite a few notable contests, including Liverpool where Canning faced Brougham with backing from rival local interests, the election lacked polarizing issues. Liverpool told Peel on November 1 that English elections provided a gain of between thirty and forty, with Whigs losing Brougham and other leading speakers. Canning lost seven, while Wellesley gained nearly as many. His attention to their numbers hints at the danger these factions posed, especially as Canning sought to bend ministers to his will by standing "upon the isthmus between the two parties."[48] Liverpool saw the threat from Canning and Wellesley "who will represent themselves as holding the same opinions as we do on all popular topics, who will say that they have as much right to be considered the successors of Mr. Pitt's party as ourselves, and whose object will consequently be to detach as many of our friends as possible." Who will be the "*True Demetriuses*" as he phrased it – the real heirs to Pitt – was the question upon which his government's fate stood.[49]

The test came when parliament met in late November. Wellington's autumn retreat to the Portuguese frontier gave Wellesley a pretext to charge ministers with denying him the means to exploit his victories.[50] Ironically, Bathurst and Liverpool had drastically expanded the funds sent to Wellington since August 1812. Rather than making that point, however, Liverpool shrewdly argued that "the exertions of a country must depend upon the means which that country possessed." Would it be consistent with duty, he asked, to "hazard the main power, the heart's blood of a country, merely to make a flourish – to risk perpetual strength for the peculiar triumph of one year?"[51] Liverpool here played to Wellesley's reputation for imprudence while acknowledging the need for careful finance. Opposition leaders skeptical of the war could hardly object. Wellington began returning the confidence Liverpool had long shown him which further protected the government from his brother's attacks. A renewed effort in March 1813 by Wellesley and peers associated with Canning failed by seventy-six.[52]

Wellesley also raised the Catholic question, prompting Liverpool to repeat his opposition to discussing it without a measure likely to satisfy Catholic demands. Although the government stood neutral, Liverpool worked quietly to block concessions. He privately stated his fears to Charles Abbot, speaker of the Commons, who made Liverpool's case in a speech on May 24 against opening parliament to Catholics. Despite strong backing from Castlereagh and Canning, it lost by four votes in one of the largest recorded divisions.[53] Besides showing how Liverpool managed controversial issues, the incident also dented further Canning's fading optimism. Partnership with Wellesley had grown threadbare. Canning decided in July to set his parliamentary friends at liberty.[54] Having failed to take the tide at the flood in 1812, he lamented that "no possible combination of circumstance can place me again where I stood in July last year."[55] Wellesley's fortunes had waned even more.

Liverpool had outlasted rivals and critics to land the prize for which his father had trained him. Confidence, along with the solidity of emerging middle age, had replaced the nervous tension Lawrence had captured in 1796. Satirists found more useful the image of Liverpool as a careworn, melancholy figure whose tall frame bent under the burdens of state. Lacking Castlereagh's aloof elegance, Liverpool presented a plain, ungraceful figure with a heavy, thoughtful expression when not lit occasionally by a pleasant smile. Harriet Arbuthnot later noted his "*untidy* look & slouching way of standing" along with "the profound & penetrating expression of countenance."[56] Although Liverpool's personal quirks remained on display, they drew more amusement than friction with those around him. Defending the government in the Lords since 1803 had taken a toll, but by 1812 Liverpool displayed unpretentious confidence. Calm had replaced the nervous agitation of his early years. The ability to speak "in cool and measured tones, clearly and logically, with every argument in its place and all fitting neatly together," as he did in the April 1813 debate on the Catholic question, won

respect, if not always agreement.[57] Holland noted both Liverpool's personal courtesy and his disinterested approach to office. Indeed, Liverpool privately spoke of
his "indifference to office unless I can hold it creditably." Willingness to subordinate his own interests to the government's wider needs had earned colleagues'
trust. Their backing had staked a claim to Pitt's mantle that Liverpool asserted
in 1813 and held thereafter without serious challenge.[58] He had closed the split
opened in 1801 when Pitt resigned in Addington's favor.

Experience had shaped Liverpool's understanding of governance. He knew a
prime minister had to exercise a coordinating and supervisory influence to avoid
a government of departments where colleagues went their own ways. Under
North and Portland that pattern had diminished effectiveness, heightened internal differences, and made defending measures harder.[59] Liverpool knew business across the whole range well enough to coordinate and direct departments
while defending measures. He also took care to minimize disagreement. Since
ministers shared responsibility, he believed "every man must expect to have his
opinion and his dispatches canvassed." Such discussion *inter pares* tested opinions in friendly exchange to clarify positions and forge a shared consensus they
could defend publically.[60] That said, Liverpool separated policy from the cabinet's political role. Working with Bathurst and Castlereagh to manage strategy
and peacemaking, he also used advisors outside the cabinet on economic and
financial questions. Besides reducing contention among ministers and enhancing
Liverpool's influence, it later helped take the sting from controversial measures by
implicating others beyond the government in adopting them.[61] Liverpool quietly
guided policy even as colleagues implemented it and handled their department's
business. His political arts balanced preserving consensus, or at least comity, with
effective management and ensuring control.

Besides managing the overlapping spheres of politics and administration,
Liverpool also faced matters pertaining to the royal family. The Jenkinson family's
"hereditary loyalty" to George III and Liverpool's responsibilities as home secretary had put him on the wrong side of differences between the king and prince.
Castlereagh had a better personal relationship with the prince regent through his
ties with Lord and Lady Hertford. The old king's resentment over his support for
Catholic Emancipation as part of the Irish union cannot have hurt. Nonetheless,
the prince regent cared little for the evangelical Perceval or even at the time
Sidmouth. Indeed, he had complained to the Archbishop of York in February
that "he has now only Lord Liverpool."[62] Their relations warmed. Averting difficulties with the prince's estranged wife, which threatened public controversy in
early 1813, helped. So did Liverpool's support for the prince in difficulties with
his daughter, Princess Charlotte, who disliked both Liverpool and his wife. Court
occasions occasionally revealed a different side of Liverpool. At a dinner party in
1813, Princess Charlotte complained all the men at one table were dead drunk
and none of the ministers could speak; Lord Liverpool "confessed he had *but just*

recollection enough to know where and with whom he was."[63] Even the staid Liverpool occasionally joined in Regency England's robust male sociability.

Politics had such a central role for Liverpool as to almost eclipse his personal life, but domestic life set the tone. Contemporaries remarked how close he and Louisa were. The few letters between them show how rarely they were apart. Louisa enjoyed the excitement her husband's role brought and took pleasure in being useful. Her correspondence reveals more than a little self-importance, along with maternal care for her busy husband. It also had a moralizing strain that resonated in the age of Wilberforce and Hannah More balanced by sincere concern for others. While some found Louisa's manner grating, Liverpool relied heavily on her support.[64] The lack of children brought them closer. Liverpool chose not to occupy Downing Street, but remained at Fife House in Whitehall where he and Louisa had moved in early 1810. Although he held property in Gloucestershire, the couple moved between Fife House, Coombe, and Walmer Castle. All were fairly close, enabling Liverpool to escape the city while keeping up with events. Only the Admiralty and War Office required ministers to stay after parliament ended. Others scattered to their country seats or resorts like Bath.[65] Liverpool and his wife had plenty of space to entertain, including children of their extended family and the dowager Duchess of Devonshire. It made for a livelier household than their temperaments might suggest. Louisa was the pillar of her husband's success.[66]

A key part of that success had begun under Perceval as the war began to shift. The French lost the strategic initiative in the peninsula, partly because Napoleon withdrew some 27,000 of his best troops to invade Russia and stopped replacement drafts, while Britain gave it the highest priority.[67] Liverpool appreciated the wider geopolitical context. He kept Wellington abreast of developments even amidst his own political struggles. Noting how Napoleon had shifted French attention across Europe, he expressed great confidence if Alexander "really determined upon a *guerre à morte*" rather than concluded a dishonorable peace. War in Russia opened "a prospect to the allies in the Peninsula of which every practicable advantage should be taken."[68] Wellington had done just that with a string of victories, including Ciudad Rodrigo on February 19, Badajos on April 6, and then Salamanca on July 22. Salamanca prompted ministers to favor more aggressive efforts to destroy French armies or drive them from Spain.[69]

A shortage of specie in 1812 hampered operations and Wellington complained of the army's distress. "Our principle and great want is money," he told Bathurst," with which I'm afraid you cannot supply us sufficiently."[70] Disappointed by shipments from Asia, Liverpool took a gamble Perceval never would have made. Along with Vansittart at the exchequer, he supported Bathurst's demands on the Bank of England to release foreign coin and gold bars. Bathurst had hundreds of thousands of pounds shipped in early autumn. Liverpool applied further pressure on the bank while seeking additional specie from the East Indies.[71] When shipments exceeded available reserves of foreign coin, Bathurst filled the gap by using a rule that permitted disbursing guineas to pay British troops. By not directing that money's use, he freed Wellington to spend it as needed, but that omission went beyond the law. Bathurst cheerfully joked with Harrowby that "for this I shall have my head off, if we should not succeed." His friend replied that "you and all of us should deserve to lose it, if we refrained from using a vigor beyond the law to enable Lord W. to pursue his successes and it is fortunate that you have a good legal cloak for so good a deed."[72]

The gamble worked. Trade revived after an early 1812 slump and markets for British goods opened as the Continental System unraveled. Bathurst and Liverpool had acted with their colleagues' support, which itself reflected a growing commitment to the war effort. Liverpool confirmed Wellington's assessment that Napoleon would struggle if Alexander showed prudence and his men fought, adding that "Bonaparte has not been able to conceal his difficulties even in his bulletins." Avoiding a general action until the French had exhausted themselves would "answer the most sanguine expectations."[73] Liverpool took a brighter view of Russia, particularly as he saw reports from Lord Cathcart, sent as ambassador to Tsar Alexander. Russia had the example of Spain, plus the advantages of geography.[74] Ministers began considering the wider strategic situation. While noting the fluid situation in Russia – and Napoleon's knack of extricating himself from danger – Liverpool favored operations in Southern France rather than a descent on Italy or the Low Countries, a view Bathurst shared.[75] Describing "the most formidable army ever collected by Bonaparte" as "substantially destroyed," he told Wellington the last twenty years had not seen such a change of fortune. Napoleon, who had alienated Russia from France and united it with Britain, now faced a choice between abandoning Spain and losing Germany. If Austria and Prussia would take advantage of Russian successes, Liverpool hoped to deliver Europe, but at present he expected only neutrality from Vienna.[76]

Bright prospects for 1813 did not hide problems. Drawing prospective allies into effective strategic cooperation would take effort. Britain could do little in Central Europe where the pivotal campaigns would be fought. The United States had become Napoleon's *de facto*, if not *de jure*, ally by declaring war against Britain. Its main threat, Liverpool appreciated from experience, lay in disrupting European negotiations as the continent stood poised between a new coalition against Napoleon and a compromise at Britain's expense. Liverpool understood how jealousy of British power resonated among Europeans and the diplomatic isolation it brought. Russia's foreign minister, Count Nikolai Rumiantsev, had viewed Napoleon and the United States for a time after 1807 as possible checks on Britain. A few of the Tsar's entourage now thought Napoleon no longer presented enough threat to justify a Russian advance into Germany. Metternich sought peace with an equilibrium that would secure Austrian interests, which meant not being squeezed by Russia or Britain as well as France.[77] Forging an effective coalition involved bridging conflicting interests and divergent perspectives, a challenge scarce information and delayed communications made harder. Even in mid-February 1813, Liverpool eagerly awaited the Gothenburg mail for some clue of Austrian and Swedish intentions.[78]

Liverpool took a defensive line as Britain lacked either a clear view of its potential allies' intentions or an authoritative voice in their councils. An effective coalition against Napoleon remained elusive, particularly when an armistice signed on June 2 gave Metternich an opportunity to negotiate between Napoleon and Russian and Prussia. Castlereagh doubted Austria would face "the risks of a more protracted struggle." Echoing language Liverpool had used since 1808, he also feared extended negotiations might dampen efforts by changing a war for national independence into a struggle for terms.[79] Events, however, took a different course. The Reichenbach Convention signed on June 27 that pledged Russia and Prussia to accept Austrian mediation if Napoleon agreed to specific terms, but also bound Austria to join the war if he refused.[80] Delay allowed Russia to rebuild its army, and French intransigence led Austria to declare war on August 12. A treaty signed at Töplitz on September 9 bound Austria, Russia, and Prussia to fight jointly until they secured a durable peace based upon a just balance in Europe. Britain now had the long sought coalition against Napoleon.

Castlereagh saw it "as the union of nearly the whole of Europe against the unbounded and faithless ambition of an individual." Again, he echoed Liverpool in calling what had been a contest of sovereigns a struggle now dictated by public feeling and necessity. Realization that isolated compromises with Napoleon had not bought its members safety gave the coalition a strong foundation. Castlereagh sought to extend it with a draft agreement to which Spain, Portugal, and Sicily might accede.[81] The depth of union remained uncertain. Russia and Austria had competing interests in Central Europe. None of the Continental powers fully embraced Britain's position on the danger Napoleon posed. They saw Britain more as paymaster to the coalition than full partner. Britain lacked influence. Its representatives never spoke with a single voice and could not go beyond their instructions. Defeat at Leipzig in mid-October shattered Napoleon's position in Germany, but also gave Metternich a chance for another effort at peacemaking that divided both allied leaders and the British envoys themselves. The allies consequently requested that Liverpool's government appoint a senior official with full powers to act for Britain.[82]

Other news had already turned attention to war aims. The first allied troops entered France under Wellington a fortnight before Leipzig when they crossed the Bidassoa from Spain. After Vittoria, Liverpool thought Britain's task had turned from ejecting the French from Spain to keeping a defeated enemy from trying to return. Even though he canvassed Wellington's thoughts on defending Spain, he emphasized the value of operations in Southern France.[83] Terrain, weather, and logistical difficulties held Wellington back from crossing into France until

October, but the expanding allied foothold raised questions about the future French government. The émigré Duc de Berry sought to join Wellington with a royalist detachment and claimed the French people would rise in favor of a restored Bourbon monarchy. Bathurst warned against imposing a government on France. Napoleon's downfall should grow out of French reactions to his defeat rather than outside intervention.[84] Liverpool recognized the need for caution and backed Castlereagh's suggestion that Wellington issue a declaration explicitly "disclaiming all idea of dismembering France" to take away the only pretense for reviving national enthusiasm.[85] Although he preferred a Bourbon restoration, Liverpool awaited a clearer sense of French opinion.

Liverpool sketched his public view when parliament met on November 4. He sought funds and other means to keep the army at strength before adjourning till March to minimize political distractions at home. Welcoming Grenville's declared support for all possible exertions to secure peace, Liverpool argued that events had reached a point at which "the balance of power might, without fear of ridicule, be talked of as the foundation of a just and lasting peace." The day had come from a "feeling of national independence" seen first in the peninsula and then across Europe, a formulation obliquely giving Britain credit for resistance when other powers had submitted to Napoleon. Liverpool contrasted past wars of governments with the present war between nations, and insisted that a successful end could only come by vigorously continuing present efforts. Policy must take "political justice and moderation" as a guide. Liverpool closed by stating to applause that "we should not ask from our enemies such terms, as in their situation we should not think reasonable to concede."[86] Avoiding specifics, he stressed moderation and justice to keep critics at bay as he reassured public opinion and coalition partners.

The cabinet met on December 20 to discuss sending the allies a representative empowered to treat with Napoleon. While Metternich and other allied ministers may have expected Canning or Wellesley – an assumption showing their ignorance of British realities – the cabinet briefly considered Harrowby who had taken a similar assignment in 1806. Harrowby, however, insisted on Castlereagh. The cabinet agreed. Liverpool informed allied ministers in London at a dinner party the next day, emphasizing that Castlereagh knew the cabinet's views and enjoyed its full confidence.[87] Besides accompanying the monarch on official business, no precedent existed for a secretary of state to go abroad for an extended period. It proved a wise decision. Castlereagh had the temperament and authority for the job. Bathurst managed Foreign Office business in his absence, while Liverpool handled foreign representatives and guided the prince regent's language as questions arose.[88] Having set general policy with his colleagues, Liverpool left negotiation to Castlereagh much as he had given Wellington discretion over military operations. He provided guidance, advice, and information from London, while retaining authority over larger decisions. Ceding the foreground while making his views felt behind the scenes fit Liverpool's indirect political style, but it also led historians wrongly to present him as a supporting figure rather than the force directing foreign policy.

Castlereagh's instructions, which he drafted for approval by the cabinet and prince regent, indicated likely peace terms. Britain stood ready to return overseas conquests, but specific concessions would depend upon the European settlement. Along with existing treaty obligations, the government insisted on an independent Netherlands under the House of Orange and France's exclusion from a naval establishment on the Scheldt River. The instructions briefly mentioned Italy, with arrangements to be negotiated, and offered British mediation on the internal affairs of Germany. They also expressed willingness to end hostilities with the United States, "in a general peace on the status quo ante bellum without involving in the treaty any decision on the points in dispute at the commencement of hostilities." But the offer was not to be made unless others raised the point. Finally, the alliance would continue in case France broke the peace. An attached memorandum outlined views on a maritime balance of power that included Spain and Holland's independence as maritime powers.[89] British terms focused on containing France in Western Europe. Amicable understanding between the allies would secure other points of a Continental peace. Castlereagh only realized how elusive agreement would be when he reached Basel on January 18, 1814, after an epic journey through one of the harshest winters in recent memory. He quickly saw that forging a durable equilibrium required Britain to take a leading part in problems it hoped to leave for others.

Liverpool, in the meantime, faced growing demands from French royalists who used Wellington's victories to advance their cause. The Netherlands offered a precedent when an uprising to restore the Prince of Orange gave British troops an opening as the French withdrew. Wellington reported in late November an "earnest desire" among the French to get rid of Napoleon "from a conviction that as long as he governs, they will have no peace." He also wrote that were he a Bourbon prince, nothing would stop him from coming forward in the field.[90] The prince regent strongly backed a Bourbon restoration. The cabinet thought it the best prospect for a stable post-Napoleonic France. Liverpool, though he agreed, believed it would require popular support in France that outsiders could not create. He also had to balance domestic opinion with Castlereagh's perspective from negotiations in Europe. Castlereagh warned against siding with the Bourbons, even in appearance, "whilst we are embarked in discussions for peace and ignorant how our allies would relish such a step." He thought the émigrés acted too soon and asked "what can a Bourbon without arms, money, or the avowed support of the allies hope to effect by his personal presence in a country hating their government, but still dreading its resentment."[91] Unfortunately, Castlereagh's principle of neither impeding nor encouraging any attempt by the exiled Bourbons offered no guide if a prince arrived at Wellington's headquarters.

Refusing to receive a Bourbon would be a rejection while anything else could be read as an endorsement.[92] Liverpool therefore pressed the exiled Bourbons to delay. The Comte de Artois replied that an uprising would be unlikely before a prince arrived in France to lead it, but Liverpool insisted vehemently. Effectively forbidding his departure, he said with a half-bow "Monseigneur, I am grieved to speak to you like this." Grieved or not, Liverpool secured the delay, while cautiously promoting an eventual restoration.[93]

Aberdeen's remark on his own arrival at headquarters that "the heroes we read of at a distance with respect dwindle into minor figures at a near approach" captures the scene Castlereagh encountered. Early conversations brought clarity, and a different view of relations among the allies. Castlereagh found that Austria would not oppose – and Metternich himself privately favored – a Bourbon restoration, not least to block Alexander's idea of placing Bernadotte on the French throne. Austrian interests converged with Britain's desire for a balance of power on the Continent, while the commitment to defeating Napoleon that Alexander shared mattered less as the war drew toward its end.[94] Castlereagh saw danger behind the tsar's "chevalresque [sic] tone" and feelings about Paris that involved more than just political or military concerns. A touch of radical chic inherited from Catherine the Great and confidence from his victories made Alexander an increasingly difficult partner. Stewart, Castlereagh's brother, had seen the Russian army in the field, prompting him to reflect on the need to limit Russia's formidable and encroaching power.[95] A stable balance required more than curbing Napoleon's ambitions. British policy would have to shift accordingly.

Ironically, Britain wished no more to negotiate with Napoleon than Alexander did. Liverpool pressed Castlereagh on the point, though he admitted that if France continued to support Napoleon "we must make peace with him" and avoid seeking his downfall by means that risked splitting the allies. The premier reluctantly set alliance cohesion before overthrowing Napoleon. He and Bathurst nonetheless kept open the possibility of continuing the war alongside Portugal, Spain, and French Royalists if the Continental powers insisted on peace with Napoleon.[96] Even when deferring to Castlereagh on negotiations, Liverpool pursued his larger aim. Alexander tried to embarrass Castlereagh with a letter from Prince Lieven in London stating that Liverpool and the prince regent wished to replace Napoleon with a Bourbon king. The report, which the tsar had shared with other allied ministers, threatened Castlereagh's authority by implying that he did not express his government's true views. But Alexander had mistaken preferences for policy. Liverpool soon wrote Castlereagh that the desire for Napoleon's downfall had no bearing upon negotiating with him at present. The foreign secretary alone spoke for the British government which would have instructed him if policy had changed. Alexander only raised suspicion of his own motives as Castlereagh made clear "that our views have been consistently and essentially coincident throughout." He mended relations with the tsar despite "painful discussions."[97]

Castlereagh took a pivotal step by securing a treaty at Chaumont that offered Napoleon a final ultimatum. If he refused, the allies pledged to fight together until his defeat. Britain would contribute 150,000 men and £5 million in subsidies to aid the allies. As the treaty was signed on a whist table, those present joked the stakes were never so high at any former gathering.[98] Napoleon's refusal won Britain a leading voice in the united coalition. It also removed constraints on supporting the Bourbons. Bordeaux declared for Louis XVIII when British troops arrived on March 12, though Wellington took care to avoid committing Britain too far until the tide swelled. Reporting similar displays at Pau and in Brittany and the Vendée, Liverpool observed that the rising had been sanctioned by civil authorities and the upper orders of the people. Castlereagh thought the declaration at Bordeaux "a providential feature in the question." When Alexander led his army into Paris on March 31, Talleyrand brought him around to accept the restoration. Napoleon abdicated unconditionally on April 6, 1814.[99]

The war ended none too soon. It had taken Liverpool "every effort of which I am possessed to keep anything like steadiness in our councils." Not only had talk of peace with Napoleon inflamed public sentiment, "but persons of weight, character, sense and respectability" shared the enthusiasm so much that he "found it difficult even to make them hear reason."[100] He played a vital role in giving Castlereagh cover at home as talks unfolded. The challenge of balancing foreign and domestic politics continued. Liverpool now focused on deflecting controversy so that France could be quickly settled. As he later argued in November, a conflict once Europe had returned to stability, although an evil, need not be different in character and effect from wars before the French Revolution. Renewed war now, however, risked a revolutionary struggle with all the upheaval that implied.[101] A secure peace would also allow the government to cut expenditure, strengthen public finances, and focus on long-postponed domestic concerns.

Peace terms with France started with the 1792 frontiers agreed by the allies at Chatillon. Britain would restore French colonies with a few exceptions that a generous financial settlement would make palatable.[102] Castlereagh urged "a liberal line on subordinate questions, having secured the Continent, the ancient family, and the leading features of our own peace." [103] The allies deferred questions beyond French matters to a congress at which France would be admitted, but British politics made one point unavoidable. Wilberforce had long pressed to include abolishing the slave trade in any peace settlement. Liverpool could not ignore the question without risking public clamor.[104] The man who once opposed abolition now pressed it effectively. Castlereagh, however, faced resistance in Paris. Abolition as a condition for returning colonies was degrading to French honor, according to Talleyrand, who said commercial opinion thought it would render those colonies unprofitable. Aiding Louis XVIII with a favorable peace clashed with British domestic pressure for abolition. Castlereagh compromised by giving France five years to abolish the trade, but a public outcry in Britain made abolition an important goal for later negotiation.[105] The treaty signed on May 30 gave France generous terms and secured its agreement to Holland annexing the Low Countries, enlarging Piedmont as a barrier to the south and granting Austria Lombardy and Venice.

Liverpool had joined the crowd that greeted Louis XVIII in London when the prince regent accompanied him to the capital from exile at Hartwell. On April 20, the prince regent invested the French king with the Order of the Garter, buckling it himself around Louis XVIII's enormous leg – which he likened to "fastening a sash around a young man's waist" – before the obese king continued to France. Louis XVIII attributed his restoration to the prince regent and Britain, "after the will of Providence." Alexander had sent Pozzo di Borgo to accompany the French royal party and advise Louis XVIII, but the Bourbons viewed Britain and Austria more favorably.[106] Peace celebrations in London to which Alexander had been invited created the chance to include the rulers of Austria and Prussia lest he gain popularity against Britain's interest. While Francis declined, leaving Metternich to represent Austria, Frederick William III happily accepted.[107] Their impending departure helped draw negotiations in Paris to a close.

Liverpool faced another political drama before the June celebrations when Princess Charlotte quarreled with her father. The Privy Council in 1812 had confirmed restrictions on Princess Caroline's access to her daughter Charlotte. Liverpool and Castlereagh managed to deflect parliamentary discussion when Caroline demanded a full inquiry to judge her guilty or innocent.[108] Princess Charlotte revived the Hanoverian tradition of conflict between monarch and heir by siding with the Whigs her father had spurned. Opposition politicians had long cultivated the heir at the current government's expense in hopes of future preferment. While resolving to keep private her growing sympathy towards Grey and Brougham, she refused to be won over by her father's cabinet. Liverpool, whom she called despicably mean, did his best to contain tension between father and daughter.[109]

Charlotte now sparked controversy by rejecting a marriage to the Prince of Orange she had accepted hesitantly in December. The marriage would cement Anglo-Dutch relations and bolster an expanded kingdom intended as a more solid barrier to France than the Austrian Netherlands and Dutch Republic had been. By placing Charlotte under a husband's control, it also checked a "spirit of restlessness & premeditated systematic kind of dissatisfaction" the prince regent associated with her mother.[110] Noting the deference owed to her father and urging she avoid the appearance of a public opposition, Grey still advised Charlotte to delay marriage, particularly against her own inclination.[111] She rejected the match on learning that she would be expected to reside in Holland much of the year. Despite the assumption that Tsar Alexander's sister Catherine, who deliberately cultivated Charlotte, had turned her against the marriage, the real cause was a secret infatuation with Prince Frederick of Prussia.[112] The prince regent treated her more strictly after she broke the engagement. Charlotte then fled to her mother at Connaught Place in London. A dramatic scene, ending with her return to Carlton House escorted by the Duke of York sparked public scandal. Her uncle, the Duke of Sussex, raised the matter in the Lords, but Liverpool stopped further discussion. Eldon supported him, noting that the prince regent "had the exclusive right to direct the education of his child and that no man had the right to interpose."[113] Although the quarrel did little beyond ending hopes of the Dutch marriage, it marked a dangerous political fault line.

The family drama played out against the backdrop of celebrations. Castlereagh drew an ovation in the House of Commons on June 6 when he arrived with the Treaty of Paris. Allied statesmen and rulers landed at Dover that evening to reach London the next day. Alexander deliberately avoided the crowds waiting to greet the party and rejected the prince regent's offer of accommodation at St James's Palace. His tactless behavior alienated a sympathetic public while antagonizing the regent and ministers. Liverpool managed to dissuade him from visiting the Princess of Wales, which probably would have sparked the prince's hatred, but the tsar and his sister Catherine still squandered British goodwill. Metternich's tact, and the government's appreciation of geopolitical realities, made Austria the beneficiary.[114] British manners, customs, and fashions had diverged from those on the Continent over the prolonged separation of war to leave a cultural gap to match differing geopolitical perspectives. Metternich told his wife in Vienna that London was more alien than Peking.[115] The prince regent invested Liverpool and Castlereagh, along with the King of Prussia, as Knights of the Garter a few days after the party arrived. A charge for fees and insignia followed the honor. The prime minister and Louisa entertained the tsar – whom the regent likened to a weathercock in that "one never knows what he will do" – at Coombe Wood after a celebration.[116] Nieces and nephews joined the party in the drawing room afterward. Although at the center of affairs, Liverpool tended to step back and leave the limelight to others.

The Princess of Wales, however, ceded attention to nobody. Pique over her exclusion from celebrations at St Paul's Cathedral prompted a decision to go abroad that she communicated through Liverpool. Never had the prince regent been more sincere than in commanding Liverpool to assure her that "he did not wish to throw any impediment in the way."[117] Caroline soon found a barrier herself in the fear a divorce would enable the prince to marry again, have a son, and thereby displace her daughter from the succession. She asked Canning to warn that if newspapers featured such hints neither the prince nor his ministers could be surprised at her immediate return. Doubtless bemused, Liverpool directed Canning to convey the fact that the prince regent, even if he wished, could not divorce her except by parliamentary authority. Parliament could not act without proof of adultery. He could not then see how she was any less safe abroad than in England.[118] Liverpool and the cabinet resisted later pressure from the prince regent to seek a divorce largely to avoid dangerous scandal, but they encouraged her to stay abroad where they assumed her profligate ways caused the least harm. Caroline lacked official standing and British diplomats would not receive her publicly. They were to provide reasonable assistance, however, as Liverpool thought it prudent "to make foreign countries agreeable to her" so she had no inducements to return.[119]

As celebrations in England gave way to negotiations at Vienna, Britain slipped into the awkward role of mediator. Liverpool saw no point to carry beyond consolidating the peace concluded at Paris.[120] Settling other European differences, however, drew Britain into controversies he disliked and made it a party to quarrels among the allies. National independence, like abolition, struck a popular chord. Parliamentary critics played to it by attacking the transfer of territories without their inhabitants consent. Responses to Sweden's acquisition of Norway offered an early sign. Liverpool privately recognized that since legal authorities including Vattel and Grotius granted a ceded province the right to refuse a new ruler, he would have to defend Britain's part on circumstances rather than principle. Grey denied Britain had guaranteed Sweden "peaceful posses-sion" of Norway or that Denmark could alienate sovereignty over it. Despite past transfers of territories or colonies, no precedent existed to exchange "an integrally independent state without the consent of its people." Grenville made a broader point in denouncing "the newfangled doctrines of utility" as "the tyrant's plea" on which all usurpations rested.[121] As he sought to deflect harassing opposition, Liverpool saw Norway's union with Sweden as the most awkward and embarrass-ing controversy Britain faced.[122]

Talks to end the conflict with the United States that paralleled Castlereagh's efforts at Vienna had implications for British influence in Europe histori-ans until recently downplayed. Sending able, but lower ranking men led by Goulburn to meet the Americans rather than prominent figures who might exceed their instructions allowed Liverpool to control negotiations more closely. Ghent's proximity to London facilitated his supervision.[123] Possible gains in America during the summer of 1814 raised the hope of negotiating better terms, but Liverpool sought to end the war assuming it could be done honorably and on reasonable terms. If British negotiators did not "feel the inconvenience of continuing the war," he called the financial strain "nothing now compared with what it might be a twelvemonth hence." Domestic complaints about taxes and the diversion of British resources from Europe where they might reinforce Castlereagh's diplomacy were both important concerns. Advice in September from Wellington, now British ambassador to France, that geography precluded a decisive blow allowing Britain to dictate terms or gain significant advantage confirmed Liverpool's view.[124]

Liverpool closely guided negotiations behind the scenes through the autumn, at times overruling the British delegation. He hoped the capture of Washington might soften American intransigence, but worried desperation might prompt them to fight on even after going bankrupt. Frustration grew. Liverpool compared their negotiating stance – "they will always be ready to keep what they acquire, but never to give up what they lose" – with what he had encountered before with Napoleon as foreign secretary.[125] That Britain's European allies would favor the United States to counter British maritime supremacy worried him. Wellington had to assure the French after the burning of Washington that Britain had no intention to dismantle the United States.[126] Liverpool still worked for an acceptable peace without pushing the Americans to extremity or staking positions which might cause future trouble. He also expected a difficult parliamentary session in 1815 with debates on taxes placing ministers at a disadvantage.[127]

Intermittent reports from Vienna raised other worries. Castlereagh realized that holding together the alliance and forging a stable peace required him to take a greater part in settling matters than Liverpool and other colleagues liked. Alexander's plan to establish Poland as a kingdom dependent upon Russia weakened Austria and Prussia while dashing Polish hopes of regaining independence. Compensating Prussia with Saxony – a German kingdom allied to Napoleon – upset the balance of power in Germany at Austria's expense and tied Prussia to the tsar. Castlereagh tried to block Alexander's plan, but Liverpool and the cabinet objected. Despite thinking Castlereagh right on the question's substance, Liverpool regretted involving Britain where it lacked either an immediate stake or much leverage. Popular sympathy in Britain for Polish independence and the odious nature of any partition meant it would only bring discredit.[128] Adam Czartoryski, the Polish statesman advising Alexander, had lobbied British figures in London during the summer celebrations. He also sent General Josef Sierakowski on an autumn speaking tour of England and Scotland to rally support for their cause. Brougham stirred discussion in the press to shape parliament's eventual response.[129] Liverpool backed his own view with the cabinet's opinion that enough had been done on Poland. Vansittart warned Britain risked being charged abroad with jealousy towards Russia and at home with instigating a system of partition. The question held no great importance to Britain. Bathurst later conveyed the prince regent's approbation of Castlereagh's firm manner, while noting the impossibility of going to war for any of the points discussed at Vienna.[130] Castlereagh shared their determination "to prevent disunion, and, still more, war" among the allies, and argued that his efforts had been to that end. He urged Liverpool in December to consider whether in case of war Britain should step forward at once as a party, interpose as an armed mediator, or wait until threats to a vital interest made intervention unavoidable.[131]

Liverpool backed Castlereagh's defensive alliance with Austria and France that kept Prussia from annexing Saxony. Besides rehabilitating Bourbon France as a leading power, it secured the Netherlands by further binding the French to terms agreed at Paris. While noting the case against the King of Saxony for aiding

Napoleon, Liverpool opposed the entire kingdom being lost. He disliked "the annihilation of ancient independent states" on principle and Prussia's annexing Saxony would have the worst moral effects throughout Europe.[132] Affairs had changed since Castlereagh had left for Vienna. Russia and Prussia had joined together, with France now a weight that could throw the balance either way. Liverpool thought Louis XVIII the only sovereign Britain could trust. Alexander was "profligate from vanity and self-sufficiency, if not principle." Prussia followed his lead. Metternich – "who considers all policy as consisting in *finesse* and trick" – had brought himself and Austria into difficulties a course of plain dealing would have avoided.[133] A compromise over Saxony moved negotiations forward using the treaty for leverage. The agreement remained secret, prompting a complaint from Mulgrave who thought it ought to have been either avoided or avowed since a secret treaty imposed a commitment that lacked deterrent effect. Liverpool, however, endorsed it without formal cabinet agreement. Doing otherwise, he told Bathurst, would break up the government, but Liverpool also saw it as a positive accomplishment.[134]

Liverpool's partnership with Castlereagh combined wide latitude and political backing with informed guidance and steady reports that drew on the prime minister's long experience in foreign affairs. Castlereagh, for his part, credited the success at Vienna partly to peace with the United States. The agreement signed at Ghent on December 24, 1814 recognized the stalemate by essentially confirming the status quo ante bellum. Liverpool understood the global stakes more than anyone else, and he moderated British terms to get a settlement. Although infuriated that Liverpool let the Americans off so lightly, Goulburn signed as instructed.[135] Suspicious enough to contemplate offering New England a separate peace "if Madison endeavours to play some trick in the ratification," Liverpool insisted that hostilities would only cease with the formal exchange of ratifications at Washington.[136] News came like a shot at Vienna. Talleyrand called it *"la paix sterling."* It strengthened Castlereagh's hand by allowing Britain to focus resources on Europe. Russian finances stood on precarious ground. Opinion at Vienna believed Alexander would be foiled by the French alliance and American peace.[137] An agreement on February 6, 1815 resolved the most contentious points, including Poland and Saxony, and secured British interests in Western Europe with a strong Kingdom of the Netherlands and an expanded Piedmont as barriers to France. Only the details and minor issues remained.

Even before the positive turn, Liverpool had pressed Castlereagh to return and take up his parliamentary responsibilities. Parliament could not be adjourned beyond the start of February at the very latest to secure taxes and provide time for debating other controversial financial measures. Castlereagh approached Wellington to take over so he might comply with his colleagues' wishes.[138] Growing opposition to the property tax particularly worried Liverpool. The short session before Christmas pointed to difficulties, including a weak performance by

ministers *"en première ligne* in the House of Commons." Castlereagh, despite his
flaws as a speaker, carried personal authority the government needed. Liverpool
wrote in January that "last year we could spare you; everything was quiet in
Parliament – everyone waiting for the result – and no symptom of party spirit
appeared." Peace had changed matters. Liverpool had never seen more party
animosity than in November 1814. Bathurst's son still thought it "a bad example
to shew an opposition that they can so bully you as to force home the man whom
they allowed to be the fittest negotiator."[139] Talk of the government's weakness
prompted rumors that Castlereagh would replace Liverpool, but the *Courier,* a
Tory newspaper, sharply rejoined that the opposition would find both men at
their posts when parliament met.[140]

Domestic questions dominated the agenda, though Liverpool deflected inquiries on foreign affairs as discussing them would be improper while talks remained
underway. Calls for papers, however, allowed the opposition to raise the awkward
questions he wished to avoid. With the country "peace-mad" and even government supporters thinking of nothing but reducing taxes and establishments
swollen during the war, Liverpool sought to blunt opposition by concessions.
Vansittart announced on February 9, 1815 that, unless the United States refused
to ratify the Treaty of Ghent, the government would abandon the property tax
and seek other measures to meet the consequent deficit. Liverpool refused to
drop other war taxes. He anticipated contending "for what will be a war expenditure in time of peace."[141] Holding political support from the landed interest and
the impact of falling agricultural prices – with dangers land would be withdrawn
from grain production to bring an eventual shortage as in the 1790s – prompted
a floor on prices. Liverpool founded the measure on the risk in relying on foreign
supplies, a position echoed by Huskisson and others who later pressed to lower
duties on grain. Ministers who knew the link between shortage or high prices
and social unrest stressed the need for self-sufficiency. Interestingly, parliamentary opposition to the original measure focused on details rather than its principle. The 1815 Corn Law passed with less difficulty than Liverpool anticipated,
but anything that raised bread prices sparked plebian outrage. A mob rioted on
March 7 attacking houses, including that of Frederick Robinson, who had introduced the bill in the Commons. They even threatened parliament itself.[142]

Events in France raised questions about the security of peace. Liverpool, a
perceptive judge, noted growing discontent. Despite a generous peace and British
financial support, Louis XVIII failed to build enough support for the restored
monarchy or stabilize politics. Wellington thought the country, and even Paris,
favored the Bourbons, but elite groups had their own grievances. The restoration
had disappointed those victims of the revolution who had looked to it as the end to
their sufferings. Napoleonic officers and civil servants saw "Bonaparte's system of
war and plunder" as the only remedy to their distress, but that step could never be
taken under the Bourbons.[143] Liverpool had urged precautions even before Louis

XVIII left England, including the presence of a Bourbon prince in Southern France where loyalty was strongest. He thought a convulsion at Paris likely. Conspirators who saw 1814 as a reflection upon the revolution looked first to the Duke of Orleans as "a king with a revolutionary title." Only later did the disaffected turn to Napoleon, who had become restive in his Lilliputian court at Elba.[144]

Napoleon's landing near Fréjus in Southern France on March 1, 1815 surprised the delegates at Vienna more than Liverpool. Castlereagh saw the key question as whether the Bourbons could get Frenchmen to fight for them against other Frenchmen. If so, Louis XVIII would have real partisans "instead of criers of 'Vive le Roi!' and doers of nothing."[145] On March 13, the allies declared Napoleon "an enemy and disturber of the tranquility of the world" who had cast aside the protection of law and rendered himself liable to public vengeance. They also pledged to maintain the 1814 Treaty of Paris. Three allied corps would deploy on France's border, with Wellington commanding in Flanders. Much as the British, especially Liverpool and Wellington, supported Louis XVIII, Castlereagh realized events might "leave us no cause to support except an undisguised dictation to France as to her monarch which we could not justify or regard as permanent even if we had power in a military sense to give it an existence."[146] Louis XVIII could not rely on his army to stop Napoleon. The French people remained observers as regiments went over to their old commander. Napoleon entered Paris on March 20, hours after Louis XVIII had fled. The allies signed a new coalition against him five days later.

Liverpool sought information on the rapidly changing situation. Typically, he warned against despair as Louis XVIII's position collapsed and noted the "incalculable mischief" of such language. The cabinet never doubted either opposing Napoleon or supporting another Bourbon restoration, but focused on how to act effectively. Harrowby joined Wellington in the Netherlands during early April to confer and report back. Liverpool drafted questions to elicit Wellington's views and provide guidance. He also outlined British options under likely contingencies, including allied defeat or a French withdrawal beyond the Loire. Both documents looked beyond the immediate crisis to Europe's future security. Liverpool stressed the need to prevent an escape which would enable Napoleon to bring on another crisis.[147] Wellington, who had engineered military solutions to political problems throughout his career, understood that defeating Napoleon's army would shatter his fragile position entirely. Unfortunately, the veteran British army he had commanded before, including its experienced staff, had been dispersed since last year. Providing an effective force took months as the government sent regiments from Britain and Ireland.[148]

Political dynamics at home favored Liverpool. A message from the prince regent brought an April 7 debate in which he acknowledged that "Bonaparte wielding the power of France" presented a just cause for war, while urging delay in pledging to any policy beyond armed preparation and concert with allies.[149]

Critics at first skirted the core question of war or peace by challenging ministers on where blame lay for Napoleon's escape or other points related to his earlier abdication. Liverpool disclaimed "any intention of imposing a government on the people of France." Britain might desire "to restore the legitimate monarchy of France" and work for that end, but the cabinet did not consider it "a *sine qua non*."[150] Ill-disguised sympathy for Napoleon had long set Foxite Whigs out of step with both public opinion and other parts of the opposition. Debates exposed the rift from an early stage, but Grey held back to avoid public disagreement with Grenville. Wellesley tried to score points by arguing that Britain had no right to attack Napoleon so long as he remained at peace and abided by treaties. The obvious inconsistency with his earlier line only lowered his standing further and perplexed Liverpool.[151] Castlereagh faced stronger criticism in the Commons, but public sentiment opposed Napoleon.

Liverpool argued for active measures on May 23. Emphasizing the seriousness of choosing between war and peace – a decision "more peculiarly important and awful" at the present moment – he acknowledged the disadvantages of entering into a war. But could Britain remain at peace and enjoy the advantages of peace so long as Napoleon controlled France? Without mentioning his own experience, Liverpool noted that no treaty with Napoleon had lasted "a moment longer than had suited his convenience." Only the French army and a few discontented persons backed him, largely because Louis XVIII would not gratify their "thirst for glory and plunder." The monarchy offered the best chance to "place the sword in its proper station," while Napoleon's return had established a government inconsistent with Europe's peace and tranquillity. Liverpool therefore urged immediate action while the allies stood mobilized to strike. Delay would only strengthen Napoleon. Recognizing the widespread concern with expense, Liverpool shrewdly presented the costly alternative as "peace with a war establishment."[152] Grey asked if every danger that by remote possibility could occur authorized Britain to intervene. Besides questioning Liverpool's claim that only the army supported Napoleon, he lamented the intemperate language against him and stressed the dangers of renewed war. Grenville, however, backed Liverpool entirely and called Napoleon "the common Enemy of Europe." Liverpool's motion passed by 112. More importantly, the debate highlighted general support. Critics, not ministers, stood on the defensive.[153]

Settling domestic politics gave the cabinet flexibility to handle contingencies abroad. Napoleon's hope lay in dividing the allies, either by defeating their armies in detail or eroding their unity by prolonging the war. Tension grew into early June. Liverpool told Canning that "during the twenty years we have passed in political life we have never witnessed a more awful moment than the present." While the military balance favored the allies, Liverpool saw the real problem as political: would Jacobins and Constitutionalists try to block the allies by overthrowing Napoleon and pitching a compromise? Could Louis XVIII maintain himself on the throne if the allies restored him there? Divisions within the

French royal family complicated the latter question, along with a tendency to view the Duke of Orleans as an alternative.[154] Napoleon brought on the crisis when he crossed into Belgium on June 15 to fight allied corps under Blücher and Wellington before they could join against him. Early defeats threw the allies onto the defensive, but Waterloo decided the campaign when Wellington shattered Napoleon's army with Prussian support. Wellington deftly took credit for a victory which gave Britain considerable prestige that soon translated into political leverage. It also checked tensions among the allies by ending the war before political questions or economic strain divided them.[155]

News reached London on June 20 when Major Henry Percy arrived with Wellington's official dispatch and two captured French eagles. Having stopped first at Downing Street to see Bathurst, Percy burst into a cabinet dinner at Harrowby's house on Grosvenor Square crying that Bonaparte had been beaten. Harrowby gave the news to a crowd in the square while Liverpool took Percy to the prince regent. One account describes the officer pushing through a crowded ballroom to kneel before him with the words "Victory, sir, Victory." The prince wrote Wellington two days later "of my joy and admiration at the unparalleled triumph of your last and greatest achievement."[156] Napoleon abdicated a second time on June 22. Paris capitulated to Wellington on July 3 after he pressed commissioners from a provisional government to make terms the allies would accept. A day after British and Prussian troops occupied the city, Louis XVIII returned. Bathurst had already reported the strong feeling in Britain of the need for security against further attempts to disturb Europe, "especially if Bonaparte survives." He told Wellington the cabinet wished to see the allies in a military position to facilitate a satisfactory peace. Castlereagh again journeyed to headquarters, urging that operations continue so the work would not be left "imperfect for a second time."[157]

Napoleon's surrender to Captain Frederick Lewis Maitland aboard HMS *Bellerophon* on July 15 brought some clarity. Blücher had favored a summary execution if Prussian troops captured Napoleon. Wellington discouraged "so foul a transaction" as unworthy and refused any part in putting him to death.[158] Liverpool took a sterner view, wishing Louis XVIII "would hang or shoot Bonaparte as the best termination of the business." Instead, he accepted the alternative of exile at St. Helena under British control. Napoleon could not be kept in Britain — early attempts to secure his release when he reached British waters pointed to the danger — but at St. Helena "all intrigues would be impossible; and being withdrawn so far from the European world, he would very soon be forgotten."[159] The measure worked. Napoleon had thrown himself on the British people's mercy with a grandiloquent letter to the prince regent likening himself to the Athenian Themistocles who had sought refuge from the Persian ruler whom he had earlier fought. Croker laughed, describing the letter as a base flattery Napoleon should rather have died than written. The only proper response would have been to send Napoleon one of his own newspapers accusing England

Illus. 7. George Cruikshank, "Buonaparre on the 17th of June – Buonaparre on the 17th of July." Napoleon's fall after Waterloo marked a turning point for Britain – and Liverpool's career – as solving one problem gave way to the emergence of others.

of assassination and every other horror.[160] A tragedy whose protagonist had been felled by his own hubris seemed to end in farce. Napoleon left for exile on August 8 as diplomats worked to settle arrangements.

Even with Louis XVIII again on the throne, Liverpool believed the allies needed securities. That meant taking France's fortresses on the frontier, including Lille on the route to the Netherlands, if only for Napoleon's lifetime or a set number of years. Liverpool insisted that Louis XVIII make an example of commanding officers who had gone over to Napoleon by subjecting them to penalties of high treason. The king must also "allay the fears of the purchasers of national property" seized in the 1790s by publicly assuring "the security of property" regardless how it had been acquired.[161] Liverpool hoped to put France's government on a stronger footing while reducing the danger in case the regime fell. His caution sprang from recent experience. Louis XVIII had told Harrowby that besides an "inert disposition" among royalists he had been forced to rely on an army and administration whose allegiance lay elsewhere. The king had employed men he could not trust "because none he could trust were fit to be employed." He could not see how he could have done otherwise.[162] Liverpool remained cautious even with Napoleon's fate settled. Indeed, he thought the king would never be "secure upon his throne till he has dared to spill traitors' blood." The general repugnance to executions Liverpool observed in France after decades of upheaval arose not out of mercy but from fear. Even a few examples of traitors held to account would demonstrate strength the monarchy needed to stand on its own.[163]

Castlereagh focused on the restored king's authority and downplayed the question of securities. He warned Liverpool from Paris that it took much circumspection "to combine what we may owe ourselves with what is due to the king whose authority will not be respected by the nation if we degrade it."[164] Wellington also urged the need to restrain the allies. He had already kept Prussian troops from destroying the Pont de Jena in Paris which Napoleon had built to celebrate a victory that still rankled. The two statesmen gradually brought Liverpool to their view on a moderate peace that would not antagonize the French population while providing a case to sway a skeptical cabinet and wider British public.[165] Liverpool still insisted that France return captured artwork to its original owners. Although willing to waive the point if France made other substantial concessions on dismantling fortresses or ceding territory, the prime minister returned to it when the allies moderated their demands. Liverpool took no regard of French sentiments on "the plunder they have taken from other countries." He considered the feeling "altogether one of vanity and of the worst description." Complaints that "storming the Louvre" had effaced the glory won at Waterloo bothered Liverpool not at all.[166] Besides reflecting his longstanding patronage of the arts, overruling Wellington and Castlereagh on the point showed his determination that France feel the consequences of supporting Napoleon's return albeit on a point of pride rather than substance.

A broader controversy arose when Alexander proposed a union of Christian rulers known as the Holy Alliance to which Austria and Prussia reluctantly acceded. Although, like Metternich, Castlereagh had tried deflecting the tsar from "this piece of sublime mysticism and nonsense," he proposed that the prince regent accede through an autograph communication among sovereigns. It brought Liverpool close to a rebuke. The joking tone of Castlereagh's note with an allusion to Wilberforce's religious enthusiasm reflected unease, but he rightly saw the merits of checking rivalries that had upset earlier negotiations and threatened ongoing instability.[167] Liverpool replied sharply that it would be impossible for the prince regent to sign a document so "inconsistent with all the forms and principles of our government." No king or regent could be party to an act of state "except through the instrumentality of others who are responsible for it." Tartly forbearing to discuss "the question of how it might have been more advisable, on every account, to prevent such a proceeding altogether," Liverpool met Castlereagh's aim with a letter sanctioning the wider aspirations of the agreement without formal accession.[168] Liverpool's more pragmatic, cautious approach kept in view domestic politics and overseas interests. It sometimes made him a brake on the foreign secretary.

Differences, however, sprang largely from their respective vantage points. Liverpool recognized the difficulty Castlereagh and Wellington faced in reconciling securities against France with upholding the restored monarchy. Their views converged. Liverpool accepted temporary rather than permanent cessions and waived the demolition of fortresses. An occupation during a set period combined with an indemnity laid the foundation for the eventual peace agreement Liverpool described to Bathurst in October "as *severe upon France* as would in any way be consistent with maintaining Louis XVIII upon the throne." He shrewdly urged that the negotiation be concluded with the present ministers so high royalists would be "saved all the odium of it" if the king brought them to office.[169] Britain held a stronger position in 1815 than two years before. The prestige from Waterloo brought influence that strengthened British diplomacy for a generation, as did security from any rival power controlling the Low Countries or Atlantic ports that might threaten Britain. Russia cooperated in securing a moderate peace with France. The broader settlement combined with a general sense of exhaustion laid the foundation for a general stability. The final treaty almost seemed anti-climactic. Liverpool kept Louisa apprised as he awaited the document in London after leaving her at Walmer, but his anxious tone expressed more about the warmth of their relationship than any concern over the peace. He informed the prince regent on November 23, 1815 that the treaties had arrived and doubtless would be considered satisfactory by the nation.[170] While the conflict that set the backdrop to Liverpool's career had ended, the problems of peace lay ahead.

CHAPTER 7

The Challenges of Peace

PEACE CAME AS a relief after more than two decades of war. Instead of drawing political dividends from the victory, however, Liverpool faced a hostility that limited his options. While most governments undergo the most strain at their start or end, his administration faced its greatest challenge in its middle years when public discontent and parliamentary opposition kept ministers on their heels.[1] Its strengths as a wartime government, as Liverpool had recognized earlier, dissipated or became liabilities in peace. Country gentlemen and others who backed ministers during the struggle now blamed them for economic distress or court profligacy. Loyalism became a rapidly depreciating asset while the charge of sympathizing with a foreign enemy no longer checked parliamentary opposition. The scale of wartime dislocation also made postwar economic adjustment more painful. While a younger generation accepted wartime patterns as the new normal, those who remembered conditions before 1793 sought a return to what they considered normalcy. Ministers thus faced competing pressures. Any decision aroused complaint which newspapers amplified.[2] Sharp downturns in the economic cycle and political agitation catalyzed unrest. Thrown on the defensive, Liverpool struggled to respond amidst successive crises.

The war had imposed a heavy financial burden. Taxes normally between 8 and 10 percent during the eighteenth century peaked between 1793 and 1815 at 20 percent of England's national income. Revenue not only paid current expenses, but also covered interest on loans and a sinking fund to repay debt.[3] Peace brought demands for retrenchment. Renewed concerns about taxes reinforced much older rhetoric attacking the supposedly parasitical system known as "old corruption" that enabled the elite to feed its appetite for money and power at public expense. War had expanded the size of civilian administration since the 1790s, along with the armed forces and national debt. William Cobbett, a loyalist turned radical, joined in attacking government pensions, church preferment, and contracts funded by burdensome taxation, along with financial policies that benefitted vested interests in agriculture, shipping, and finance at the expense of consumers. An 1829 satire that showed commerce and manufacturing breaking under the strain imposed by "the great tax eater Church and State" expressed a

Illus. 8.   R. Seymour, "State of the Nation." Charges of elite parasitism fueled plebeian radicalism along with middle-class demands for political reform. It cast both the Established Church and the British state as a drain on society's productive members with a narrative Liverpool struggled to overcome.

widespread critique. Dissenters linked their opposition to the Established Church with a larger attack on monopolies in politics and commerce along with religion that resonated widely.[4] Liverpool had to address the challenge in a context where political discontent often followed cyclical economic downturns which made the postwar transition harder. High food prices combined with unemployment or lower earnings brought peak cycles of social tension that sparked plebian unrest.[5] A parallel scissors effect hit the middling classes when merchants, manufacturers, and agriculturalists faced high fixed costs and falling earnings with the peace-time slump. Government policies, especially taxes, provided a natural focus for discontent which made the language of private interests acting at the expense of the public resonate.

Liverpool saw the danger well before the storm broke in 1816. Besides urging Castlereagh in late 1814 to return from Vienna for what he expected to be a difficult parliamentary session, Liverpool worked to forestall opposition. Meetings on the property tax, he noted, made it impossible to keep for another year without pledging to drop it after the war ended.[6] The levy, which Pitt first introduced and Addington later modified, taxed income earned on property or individual enterprise. Called either a property tax or income tax – though critics pressed the latter term – it was an important revenue source which spared the poorer classes. Taxes on property owners in large measure financed what had been partly a war for the defense of property. Especially from 1808, the property tax was vital to an exceptionally costly struggle. The burden it placed on the articulate classes, however, made it unpopular with those who had political leverage to make their views felt. Eighteenth-century governments had faced powerful and sustained resistance to direct taxation. Only the threat from Revolutionary France and the probable collapse of public credit had enabled Pitt to justify a property tax that still had significant loopholes.[7]

Conversations with provincial businessmen, including John Gladstone of Liverpool, had indicated the strength of opposition even among those who generally supported ministers. Canning failed to grasp public sentiment when he asked whether a clear line on the tax might have kept supporters from condoning or even backing local efforts against it. Although Liverpool wanted the property tax to cover arrears from the war and the costs of demobilization, he had to weigh political costs. Keeping the tax for three or four years might have been worth "a severe contest," but the prospect of a renewed struggle after only a year made him think abandoning it would render parliament more agreeable to alternatives. Other measures, including taxes assessed on carriages, horses, and servants would match the shortfall to defray the interest and sinking fund for loans through 1819. The way those assessed taxes worked as proxies for the wealth the property tax reached more effectively, however, showed its value.[8] Vansittart conceded the property tax in February 1815, while justifying it as a powerful resource in times of emergency. He also noted the unavoidable "winding up charges" at the end of a war. Canning accepted Liverpool's case given what "the temper of the times admitted." With current public feeling, he thought attempting to keep even a modified property tax "might have shaken the government to pieces."[9]

Victory at Waterloo did not change the temper of the times. Napoleon's return had enabled Vansittart to keep the property tax without opposition for a year from April 5, 1815 to cover the expenses of war or a defensive peace. He and Castlereagh, however, pointedly denied any intention to make the tax permanent.[10] Parliamentary discussion and public meetings still underlined the general impatience with taxation. Whigs seized upon the property tax to rally opposition in the country. Brougham had long seen it as a target for the tactics he had used successfully against the Orders in Council. Grey urged him in November to stir discussions before parliament met. Newspaper reports in January 1816 that the ministers planned to retain the property tax sparked a wave of provincial meetings to sign petitions.[11] Financial considerations had brought ministers to retain a modified version despite their earlier promise. Besides the costs of winding down military operations, servicing wartime debt was essential to keeping public finances stable if crisis demanded further loans. Liverpool warned Peel in January that finance and particularly the proposal to continue the property tax at 5 percent would bring trouble. The opposition, he noted, had already seized upon distress among farmers whose earnings had fallen with the drop in prices.[12]

When parliament met on February 1, Liverpool carefully framed the address to the prince regent's speech to avoid an immediate clash and give ministers time to justify their fiscal policy. He pledged they would present details on expenditure in departments with an "anxious desire to adopt every plan of restriction and economy" consistent with the public service.[13] Debates on treaties ending the late war postponed financial matters, but Vansittart's announcement that the government intended to retain the property tax at 5 percent set Brougham to call the country to make its view "of this most tormenting of all taxes" known. Tierney opposed voting supplies "piecemeal" until ministers had made the full amount known.[14] Economy gave opposition factions, including Grenvillites who had drifted away from the Whigs over the last two years, a popular cause to unite country gentlemen and independent radicals.[15] Grenville complained that the proposed military establishment far exceeded that of 1793, but Liverpool pointed out that half pay for officers and other allowances granted by parliament alone went beyond overall prewar costs. The comparison failed to account for wartime military reforms and the acquisition of new territories which required defense.[16]

Since the Commons initiated financial measures, Liverpool had to rely on colleagues there who responded less adeptly to opposition. Committee procedures allowed a thorough interrogation of ministers and voting on estimates by item which prolonged matters. Liverpool's relation by marriage Stuart-Wortley landed a blow by insisting Tierney had made a strong case and "that the time for

Illus. 9.   George Cruikshank, "The British Atlas, or John Bull supporting the Peace Establishment." Expenses justified in fighting Napoleon became an unpopular burden amidst demands for reduced taxes and economy in government that kept Liverpool's administration on the defensive.

economy was come." Illness briefly sidelined Castlereagh, but he told his brother the army estimates "had been fought for eleven successive nights inch by inch" with no less than twenty-five supporters joining the opposition.[17] Although the government never lost a division, diminishing majorities brought preemptive concession as ministers cut £340,000 before the final vote. Huskisson privately thought the further reduction "comes rather awkwardly" after earlier assurances of pursuing the utmost economy. Revising the estimates showed Liverpool and his colleagues' discomfort with the parliamentary situation.[18]

Liverpool knew ministers had to refute – or at least address – opposition criticism even when they had votes. Ignoring arguments fueled suspicions that support rested on patronage rather than persuasion and encouraged charges of illegitimate influence. Moreover, Whig leaders, including those Liverpool faced in the Lords where the government had a secure majority, spoke beyond the house to the wider public. London and provincial newspapers published full accounts of parliamentary debates which had a wide readership and shaped opinion felt at Westminster.[19] Writers and politicians now gave increasing attention to public opinion whose impact complicated governance as it linked provincial interests with metropolitan debates more directly than before. The lack of consensus rooted in a normative set of values shared by most privileged members of society over the years from the Jacobin scare of 1792 through the 1840s added to the challenge Liverpool faced. Politicians qualified the phrase "public opinion" as "respectable," "rational," and "intelligent" which made clear that they pitched their appeal not to the majority but those whose approval conveyed legitimacy.[20] Liverpool sought at least to engage, if not convince, that segment of the political nation at a time when the war's end had shifted public sentiment dramatically.

Petitions against the property tax made resistance clear. Even though opposition supporters initiated many of them, their efforts rode the current of popular sentiment. A petition "of an enormous size" from Clerkenwell gained 3,278 signatures in fourteen hours. Brougham said that its bulk made clear that it came against the tax. Mocking Castlereagh's ill-chosen reference to the public's "ignorant impatience with taxation," Tierney insisted petitions be read fully "so petitioners might be heard for themselves." When an old Perceval supporter questioned the exercise, Tierney insisted they could at least be heard, even if some chose not to listen.[21] He cast the Whigs as friends of a people suffering from a profligate ministry's indifference. Opponents also likened the assessment of earnings to "a lay inquisition" violating privacy. Brougham recounted the story of a man purchasing cheese wrapped in a neighbor's tax return. Old tax records had been sold as waste paper which allowed later consumers to devour their neighbors' financial details with the cheese. The next day a petition from Andover supporting the tax prompted Brougham to quip that the town be exempted from its repeal as the house cried "hear, hear."[22] Arguing for prudent finance did not counter the refrain. Satires depicted John Bull as a weary Atlas bent under an

excessive peace establishment and a victim bled gold coins by the "state physicians." The Foxite *Morning Chronicle* likened Vansittart to a leech bleeding the
taxpayer.[23] The imagery pressed a broader critique of government profligacy
draining wealth from the enterprising that kept ministers on a defensive.

Why then did Liverpool attempt to keep the property tax? Political difficulties
aside, he saw no other effective way to meet necessary expenses that included
debt service. If a new war occurred, he stood "at a loss to know where we are
to find taxes to defray the interest of our loans."[24] Strong public credit had long
been a tremendous wartime asset – Bute and Pitt both realized decades earlier
the danger of threatening it by straining the budget – but Liverpool also saw its
centrality to the peacetime economy. Those who complained took an unduly
"narrow view of their own interest" as he argued that restoring public credit,
which would raise the value of funded debt and consequently lower interest rates
for borrowers, would relieve distress more than any other possible measure.[25]
The whole debate showed much of the political class ignorant or indifferent to
economic considerations. Brougham himself entirely ignored how the government could service the national debt without the £14 million per year the tax
raised. He argued on entirely political grounds.[26] As Liverpool insisted after the
measure's defeat, the property tax offered not only the best plan of finance, but
the most effective aid for distress. It avoided, or at least minimized, loans to cover
expenditure thereby relieving public credit and promoting economic recovery.[27]
By shifting the tax burden to expanding sectors, notably commerce and manufacturing, whose growth would increase revenue even at a steady or lower rate,
it also reduced the pressure other levies placed on consumers and landowners.
Funds thereby secured would give ministers welcome flexibility to manage the
adjustment to peace after the dislocation of a prolonged war. Liverpool denied
any firm pledge to give up the tax as a solely wartime measure. That provision for
the income tax ceased at the end of the war did not preclude considering it as a
peacetime measure to reduce the public burden. He therefore urged the question
be judged on its merits when it came to the Lords.[28]

Liverpool thought his view had quietly gained ground. The Treasury predicted
a majority of forty for the measure on the morning of the final vote.[29] Optimism
aside, he refused on principle to give up a measure he and colleagues believed
correct. Liverpool insisted to a delegation that repealing the property tax "should
be the act of the House of Commons" with the government then having no
grounds to reproach itself. While accepting the still current view that "parliament existed to pronounce on the policy of the executive and regulate its particular acts," Liverpool also believed the cabinet had a duty to propose what they
believed served the public good. If the Commons differed, it must take the
responsibility. As a levy in part upon commercial and industrial property, the
property tax would have ensured that the most rapidly growing economic sectors
contributed revenue in proportion with their wealth. Recasting the tax system by

broadening its base would have relieved not only the landed interest, but also the poor who carried the heaviest burden from indirect taxes on consumption. But until crisis peaked in 1799, governments had faced insurmountable resistance to direct taxation of incomes and wealth.[30] Peace revived that opposition. What made sense in principle had to meet the test of political reality, though Liverpool insisted that the Whig opposition and other groups within the governing elite share responsibility for rejecting the policy.

The final decision on March 18 seemed anti-climactic, with the House of Commons so impatient it would hardly listen to further discussion. Debates had already taken place with successive petitions during the past weeks. But the presence of 400 members and a crowd outside awaiting a decision that came after midnight created dramatic tension. The majority of thirty-seven against the property tax sparked cheers. Brougham predictably took credit. A later print depicted him slaying the tax with petitions alongside John Bull as Liverpool and the prince regent fled the scene. Castlereagh informed the prince regent more soberly that the defeat left "but 12 millions of clear revenue to meet this year's expenditure of 30 millions." Even a peace establishment a third lower than planned created "a serious deficiency." Ministers could not have given up the property tax without a struggle, but Castlereagh thought it perhaps better to lose at once than having a small majority gradually chipped away.[31]

Although the property tax had not been a question of confidence where defeat would render the government's position untenable, if not compel its resignation, the vote indicated danger. Liverpool quickly gave up the malt tax as a preemptive concession to consumers and the landed interest. Castlereagh remarked that if the Commons "thought proper to relieve themselves" then ministers must take other steps to relieve the people.[32] He lamented that country gentlemen who had known and preferred them as war ministers now cared only for peace and retrenchment. As he told his brother, "I never found the House of Commons so weak to my voice."[33] Castlereagh denied in a March 20 debate "that he had ever denominated as clamor the fair and legitimate discussion of measures," but argued the opposition did try to "clamor down" the government by charging it opposed economy without hearing its intentions. Brougham inadvertently saved the day by attacking the prince regent for extravagance on favorites and surrounding himself with "an establishment of mercenaries."[34] Holland believed his words, which Samuel Romilly thought better framed to describe the Roman Emperor Tiberius, drove away men who had voted against the property tax.[35] Ministers could not rely on further mistakes. Despite a majority of twenty-nine, Liverpool called the prince regent to London for consultation at short notice. The government, he warned, "hangs by a thread" with the spirit of the Commons now as bad he could ever remember. Liverpool, the prince replied, "could depend upon my most resolute, firm, and persevering support...you shall find me now, as at all other times, true to the backbone."[36]

Liverpool's appeal could not have surprised him. A March 15 letter signed by Liverpool, Castlereagh, and Vansittart had warned that even supporters would desert them on any expenditures hinting at extravagance. Only by stating on the prince regent's authority or at his command that further work on Brighton or other buildings would be abandoned did they have any "prospect of weathering the impending storm."[37] Brougham's speech took a line of attack that others beyond parliament picked up, particularly Leigh Hunt who had famously denounced the prince regent in 1812 as "a man who has just closed half a century without one single claim to the gratitude of his country or the respect of posterity."[38] If such words antagonized respectable opinion, they also touched a sore point for the prince that risked conflict with Liverpool. A joint letter from ministers underlined the message while deflecting royal disapproval from any individual. Cabinet unity gave Liverpool welcome leverage against the prince regent's occasional recalcitrance, but it did not help in parliament. Needing more than royal support, Liverpool appealed to Lord Lonsdale and the Duke of Rutland, who together controlled fifteen seats in the Commons. He also held meetings at Fife House, one of which included the Duke of York, doubtless as army commander-in-chief. Besides appealing for attendance – and obviously support – at upcoming debates, the meetings gave an overview of military, naval, and civil estimates. Liverpool realized the need to show that he had the situation in hand with reductions underway and more planned.[39]

An important test came on March 25 with a debate over navy estimates where Tierney attempted a *coup de main* against the government's plans. He mounted an attack on Sir George Warrender, who introduced the navy estimates as the civilian Lord of the Admiralty, and his motion against proceeding into committee where Croker and other experts could answer critics threatened to inflict a possibly fatal defeat. Having once been Treasurer of the Navy, Tierney spoke with authority on the costs of its administration. He contrasted figures from war and peace in detail to show that the estimate for peacetime exceeded costs from 1814 by £20,000. Argument alone could not answer the charge of profligacy. Tierney declared that "facts, positive and clear facts alone could be brought against it."[40] Castlereagh asked Croker in alarm what answer could be made. Croker replied that Warrender had a memorandum with figures that he and Melville had prepared. Unfortunately, the memorandum had been left at the Admiralty. Warrender could only make a weak rejoinder noting that the estimates were not proposed as a permanent peace establishment.[41] A colleague, William Holmes, quickly fetched the box from the Admiralty. Croker then embarrassed Tierney in a devastating rebuttal. Figures on naval expenditure for the final year of war and first year of peace after every conflict since the 1697 Treaty of Ryswick showed a rise in the cost of the navy's civil administration as its work increased with the return of ships and sailors from duty at sea. Croker's statement "changed the face of the House in an instant." Now that Tierney had his facts the estimates went to committee without a vote.[42] The debate broke the momentum behind opposition. Liverpool's government recovered its footing over the remainder of the session.

Debates over military estimates also touched on concerns about the army's policing role Liverpool had to allay. Plans to form the United Services Club, which became "a very harmless association for enjoying over temperate repasts the society of old comrades," sparked talk of military enthusiasm jeopardizing public liberties.[43] Sir Thomas Graham, one of Wellington's subordinates and a lifelong Whig, had proposed the club in May 1815. Senior officers along with the Duke of York supported him. Anticipating danger even before the Whig opposition turned its sights on the army, Liverpool refused to lease the club crown land. "So far from being serviceable to the army," he perceptively warned "it will inevitably create a prejudice against that branch of our military establishment, and we shall feel the effects of it even in parliament." A petition against the club Thomas Foley, a Whig MP and militia colonel, brought before the Commons on March 4, 1816 proved Liverpool right.[44]

The army's wartime growth in size and prominence revived concerns about threats to public liberty that seem exaggerated in retrospect. Just short of half the members who sat in the Commons between 1790 and 1820 had served as militia or volunteer officers. An additional fifth were regular army officers.[45] Distrust of standing armies remained a public memory kept alive partly by the use of soldiers to enforce law and suppress rioting. Their role aiding magistrates often brought controversy even though officers and men alike remained subject to redress at common law for their actions.[46] Liverpool acknowledged "jealousy lest principles of the constitution be infringed," but asked whether fears of a 25,000-man army were reasonable. A nobleman's complaint of being stopped in Pall Mall by a soldier led Grenville to insist the military ought never to be used, even to preserve peace, unless civil power at the particular time and place were insufficient. Liverpool made no objection to what he took as a political truism. Sidmouth later agreed soldiers should only be called to act "at the requisition of the civil magistrate." [47] What seems in retrospect a tangential debate highlights concerns at the time about military threats to popular liberties. Sensitivity to complaints about deploying troops blocked any general policy of coercion while heightening caution about using the army even for local emergencies.

The 1816 parliamentary session showed the government lacked the reliable backing it had enjoyed in wartime. Unwilling to trust opposition Whigs, even when accepting their arguments for economy, the Commons still denied ministers its unqualified support. Its members saw their independent judgment as a check on a profligate executive. High taxes to service wartime debt seemed a transfer of wealth from the productive classes to well-connected fundholders. Debates had to be managed carefully to avoid compromising the government's authority and giving an opening for further challenges. Vansittart fared badly when illness kept

Castlereagh at home in February. The foreign secretary himself managed business more effectively than he spoke in debate. Thomas Moore cruelly mocked him as the "Malaprop Cicero" for his awkward rhetoric and idiosyncratic phrases. Lady Holland maliciously circulated the quip that "Lord Castlereagh likes all taxes, but *Syntax*." Brougham described Whigs passing the long hours of parliamentary business by tracking Castlereagh's mixed metaphors and grammatical errors. Castlereagh commanded respect for his fair-minded and businesslike approach, along with a cool detachment Croker likened to the "bright and polished frost" of Mont Blanc, but his difficulty in debates presented a problem.[48]

Securing Canning's debating talent would improve matters, especially since Castlereagh and Sidmouth had abandoned their personal objections. Liverpool had long sought to bring Canning into the government. The two maintained a friendly correspondence on public business even before Canning's 1814 appointment as ambassador to Portugal. Lord Buckinghamshire's unexpected death in February after falling from a horse opened the presidency of the Board of Control. Liverpool pitched the idea of appointing Canning to the prince regent who acquiesced providing that, as Liverpool believed, introducing him to the cabinet would not produce "disunion or any want of harmony" in a government he liked as it was.[49] With his colleagues' agreement, Liverpool made the offer, which Canning accepted. Although well below his pretensions in 1812, the offer itself left no grounds for complaint. News of the government's parliamentary difficulties rather confirmed his decision than prompted second thoughts.[50] When later challenged over accepting a post below his pretensions, Canning replied that "it is for the man to dignify the office, not the office to dignify the man." His return at the prime minister's initiative underlined Liverpool's quiet authority while promising welcome assistance in the Commons.

Relations with the prince regent brought their own troubles. A successful vote on the civil list toward the end of the parliamentary session deflected public controversy while avoiding a clash between the prince and ministers.[51] Liverpool and the prince regent had shared a commitment to defeating Napoleon that aided their wartime partnership. Peace, however, made the prime minister bearer of bad news to a prince who lacked his father's sense of duty and propriety. Like his father, Liverpool recognized a courtier's obligation to uphold the king in pursuing his duty. While a shared purposefulness had drawn Liverpool and George III together, the prince regent's self-indulgence made relations with the prime minister increasingly difficult. Public controversy over expenditure forced Liverpool to press economies on the court against the prince's wishes even when he accepted them. The scope for friction grew from 1816 with obvious risks.

Although the prince could deploy considerable charm when he chose, Liverpool combined acute personal sensitivity with a tendency to overlook the same feeling in others. Nervous irritability supplanted the calm that had characterized his manner since 1808 to render him less able to smooth over differences.

Stress during periods of acute crisis made him prickly. If the calm manner or personal equanimity to which later historians credited Liverpool's success had ever been that important, it swiftly faded.[52] Castlereagh, Eldon, and Sidmouth increasingly helped manage the prince regent. Cabinet unity strengthened their hand, and the sovereign was no longer a party leader as had been the case early in George III's reign. More cohesive ministries since Pitt's enjoyed greater independence. Although the turbulence of parliamentary and public opinion after 1815 made the cabinet more reliant on the crown, the difficulty the prince would face in replacing them on terms he would accept limited the danger ministers faced of a break with him. Pitt's hold on power had deteriorated in the late 1790s partly because George III – and the public which took his side in the early 1780s – had alternatives beyond Fox and his allies.[53] The same distrust that kept parliament from pressing ministers too far in 1816 constrained a prince regent who had only become further estranged from his former Whig friends. Managing occasionally tense relations at court still gave Liverpool another distraction.

Princess Charlotte's marriage to Leopold of Saxe-Coburg on May 2, 1816 mended relations with her father and sparked popular enthusiasm. The real danger that summer involved the prince regent's desire for a divorce that would free him from Princess Caroline whose absence had not diminished his loathing. Agents had been collecting evidence to substantiate allegations of Caroline's scandalous antics in Europe. Castlereagh's brother as ambassador to the Habsburg court at Vienna worked with Metternich and Austrian officials to facilitate inquiries. Rumors the prince regent would seek a divorce prompted Brougham, Caroline's lawyer, to authorize steps for preventing any proceedings against her.[54] The question of legal proceedings in Hanover to avoid the trouble could not be divested from considerations respecting the British constitution. Ernst Friedrich, Count Münster, a Hanoverian official based in London, told the prince regent "nobody can deny with candor that there is not a man in Great Britain who would not be divorced from his wife under such circumstances as are notorious respecting the Princess of Wales, yet they may not perhaps be thought sufficient to answer completely in your Royal Highness' case!" A separation decreed in Hanover would have little advantage without proceedings in England to the same end that demanded proof in a form required by law. By rendering adultery by the wife of the king or his heir high treason subject to capital punishment, English law made proving guilt more difficult.[55]

The political danger of scandal from a contested divorce overshadowed the legal questions, though Castlereagh noted considerable divergence of opinion when the prince regent instructed him to lay the matter before the Lord Chancellor and other lawyers.[56] Liverpool faced the delicate task of dissuading the prince from pursuing the case. A cabinet minute in August with copies of legal opinions urged the prince regent to abstain from further steps at present. Every option faced serious objections, particularly with the lack of reliable evidence and the certainty of delay and obstruction. They had no precedent for proceeding in the Ecclesiastical Courts or appealing directly to parliament in a judicial case which does not rest "upon the judgment of some regular & competent tribunal." Prudential considerations backed the cabinet's advice to delay unless fresh information or other circumstances made it expedient. Besides appealing to "the advantageous ground on which your royal highness now stands in the eyes of the country & of Europe upon the whole of this business," ministers warned of "the inconvenience & evil effects" from any measure that failed. Privately, they shared Charles Stewart's view that nobody could estimate the danger of pushing a circumstantial case "in these days of faction and a licentious press."[57] The prince regent set aside the matter without dropping it. Satirists lampooned a problem Liverpool could only postpone with either public scandal or a clash between prince and cabinet a real possibility. [58]

Private anxieties matched public concerns for Liverpool. Louisa's ill health forced her to travel by water for their usual autumn visit to Walmer. The prince regent expressed concern through his private secretary at Liverpool's account of ailments the fatigue of which she had long complained. Bad weather in 1816 cannot have helped her condition, though Louisa improved by October and began a slow recovery.[59] Weather devastated agriculture in Europe and North America during what became known as the "year without a summer." The April 1815 eruption of Mount Tambora in Southeast Asia, the largest ever recorded, was gradually felt across the globe. Torrential rain and hail punctuated a long succession of gray skies and drizzle in England over the following summer after a cold, backward spring with predictable consequences for the harvest. Low prices early in the year had pushed down wages, bringing riots to some rural counties during April and May. Higher prices from a lower yield simply changed the character of agricultural distress without diminishing its magnitude. A downturn in the trade cycle lowered commodity prices and manufacturing wages as food prices effectively doubled. Social tension brought protests and even riots that the army suppressed with some bloodshed.[60]

Liverpool took what might seem an unduly positive view of developments by welcoming higher prices with full employment of farm laborers as a boon to the landed interest. He thought the harvest in England's productive regions deficient more in quality than quantity, but recognized the toll bad weather had taken on northern counties and Ireland.[61] With the full impact on price and supply unclear, Liverpool looked to the recent agricultural depression's political impact. Landowners, whose opposition had been so troublesome, would benefit from the increasing availability of money at lower cost as government borrowing fell. The lagging indicators of revenue from internal taxation – the excise and assessed taxes – made Liverpool confident that prosperity had not diminished. Manufacturing districts, where distress and agitation brought severe unrest, presented a different outlook as Liverpool noted in October.[62] Welsh magistrates used troops to suppress what he termed an insurrection among miners in Merthyr Tydfil whose violent protest against wage cuts stopped work and extinguished furnaces at nearby ironworks. The incident marked a broader pattern which raised particular alarm. Only limited numbers of regular soldiers were available to aid civil authorities. When called upon those troops often had to march from some distance to the immediate crisis. Sidmouth, as home secretary, relied upon local magistrates to preserve order – a point Liverpool knew from his long tenure in that department – since authorities in London could only provide impulse and assistance to their efforts.[63] Ministers reacted to events without the capacity to direct them.

Financial questions and unrest pointed to "a stormy session" when parliament met in late January which would require deft management. Liverpool welcomed the fact that public finances relieved the government from the necessity of an earlier meeting. He had never known a case, he told Peel, where parliamentary discussions of internal distress had not done more harm than the benefit any measure of relief might afford. Although Sidmouth had originally agreed, he later urged an earlier session to secure additional powers and rally the loyal against unrest.[64] Liverpool's more cautious approach, however, prevailed. Tensions escalated with protests in London that began with a mass meeting at Spa Fields demanding political reform the radical orator Henry Hunt addressed on November 15. Conspirators used a second meeting in December as cover for a badly managed plot to seize the Bank of England and Tower of London that Sidmouth disrupted on December 2. The numbers participating in the meetings – upwards of 20,000 by reports – and rhetoric drawn from Thomas Spence's program for collective ownership of land raised more worries than the hapless conspiracy. Not all radicals backed Spencean Philanthropy, as it became known, but what amounted to overthrowing the political and social order alarmed the propertied classes. Earlier violent protest, even machine breaking and riot, had typically defended customary practices within a local consensus validated by license afforded by authorities and elites. The situation now involved wider aims that raised uneasy parallels with the French Revolution. Indeed, Liverpool told Peel that nothing he had seen as a member of the secret committee of 1794 during the panic over Jacobin conspiracies indicated nearly as much discontent and sedition.[65]

Either a bullet or stone pierced the prince regent's carriage window in a possible assassination attempt as he journeyed to open parliament on January 28, 1817. The incident gave weight to the government's call for measures against unrest, though Sidmouth pointed out that a February 3 message from the prince regent on dangerous meetings and combinations was neither founded upon nor connected with the attack. Liverpool proposed a secret committee to review evidence – a step also to be taken in the Commons – stressing that "we go into the inquiry with unbiased feelings." He sought to balance a strong disposition against infringing upon existing laws with taking the present situation seriously.[66] While parliamentary sentiment inclined to give ministers the benefit of the doubt, Liverpool sought to frame the issue for the wider public as it followed debates through newspapers. Doing so offered the chance to regain the initiative after resisting demands for rigid, unsparing economy for more than a year. Grey demanded prompt and effectual spending reductions in all departments from the session's opening. Sir Francis Burdett later struck a chord by describing ministers as "Expencians" whose measures threatened property far more than the villainous Spenceans.[67] Ministers had to avoid seeming more anxious to limit public liberties than attend to the distress critics charged to their own extravagance.

Liverpool expected the country gentlemen who typically backed the king's ministers to side with government on a question of order, but he also realized a case had to be made for stronger measures against unrest. Referring evidence to parliamentary committees enabled Liverpool to cast measures as their neutral recommendation rather than a government measure. Careful management in selecting those on the committee, which including opposition figures, particularly sympathetic ones, ensured the desired outcome and gave political cover. Indeed, Liverpool used the technique later with controversial economic policies like tariff reform and the resumption of cash payments. The secret committee in the Lords included Grenville, Fitzwilliam, and Bedford from the Whig side as well Harrowby, Sidmouth, Liverpool, and Eldon.[68] Fitzwilliam had been among the Burkean Whigs who had followed Portland into Pitt's government before a later rapprochement with Foxites including Bedford. Grenville remained titular leader of the opposition, but unrest divided those the financial questions had brought together during the 1816 session. Thomas Grenville had warned privately of "a systematic organization of the poor and hungry to draw from their distresses an ignorant clamor for reform of parliament" and refused to conciliate plebeian radicals by taking up reform. The Grenvillites viewed the proper scope for civil liberties more narrowly than their Foxite allies – Grenville shared Liverpool's view that conditions were more alarming now than in 1795 – making at least a gradual split inevitable.[69]

Harrowby presented the committee's report on Tuesday, February 18 with its conclusion that a traitorous conspiracy existed to overthrow the established government and conduct "a general plunder and division of property." Spencean Philanthropists represented the landholder "as a monster which must be hunted down…the fundholder as a still greater evil" casting both as "rapacious creatures, who take from the people fifteen pence out of every quarter loaf." Their efforts reached beyond London through societies and clubs, along with cheap publications "marked with a peculiar character of irreligion and blasphemy" which tended not only to overturn the existing political and social order, but "to root out those principles upon which alone any government or any society can be supported." Harrowby described "unremitting activity" to stir discontent, and the report's language – repeating such words as plunder – emphasized a threat to the moral and social order as well as to property.[70]

When Liverpool moved the report be considered on Friday, Lord Grosvenor urged that evidence upon which it had been founded be submitted for parliamentary investigation. Harrowby deftly appealed to the precedent of acting through a committee of secrecy so that greater trust might be reposed in its discretion.[71] When Holland and Grosvenor then moved to introduce a petition challenging a point in the report, Liverpool deemed the timing irregular as anticipating reports or measures violated parliamentary rules of order. Accepting it, Harrowby pointed out, would open the door to petitions by societies to which the report alluded and thereby embarrass proceedings in an unprecedented manner.[72] He sought to avoid repeating the government's experience from the campaign against the property tax, although Liverpool and his colleagues never questioned the right to petition according to parliamentary form. Indeed, Liverpool declared "the strongest disposition to treat every petition with the greatest indulgence." When the Lords accepted a revised version of the petition on February 24, 1817, Harrowby conceded that a grammatical error by the report's printer had wrongly linked the London Union Society with the Spencean Philanthropists. Grenville saw "nothing like any intention to deceive" and defended Harrowby's response.[73] The government's broader case largely stood.

Committees of both houses had made clear the threat of sedition and the inadequacy of existing law to contain it. Liverpool cautiously proposed suspending habeas corpus for a limited period and restricting seditious meetings. Those modest steps focused on an immediate threat from unrest stoked by agitators whom Sidmouth described as having "parliamentary reform in their mouths, but rebellion and revolution in their hearts." Every occasion of danger, Liverpool argued, did not prompt ministers to recommend such measures. But conspirators who showed "the determined and avowed design to sap all the foundations of morals and religion" presented a serious enough threat to justify temporary action to check their efforts. His tone and language stressed the temporary part. Describing habeas corpus "as a part of the ancient law and constitution," Liverpool called the power to suspend it "a most odious one…not to be confided to any man or any set of men, except in cases of the last necessity." But a society granting as much liberty to the subject as consistent with the safety of the state must have a power somewhere to suspend that liberty temporarily for its ultimate protection. "Domestic treason, indeed, might assume a character quite as desperate as foreign treason," especially since a country's internal state in wartime could afford a security unavailable in peace.[74] Liverpool outlined a reluctant, temporary response to clear dangers that sought to protect constitutional liberties rather than abridge them. Critics had a weak case amounting to little more than asking if existing law would not serve the purpose. Many of the opposition abstained while other registered a protest to measures that passed both houses without difficulty.

Aside from a proposal to license reading rooms along with political clubs that failed in committee, none of the measures affected the press. It might seem a surprise given complaints about danger from blasphemous and seditious publications. Critics deplored the corrosive social effects of attacks on men of character and rank along with a generally licentious tone among journalists. Respect for the press as offering free discussion on public matters balanced that feeling. Politicians largely accepted vituperation as an occupational hazard.[75] Liverpool, who years earlier had dismissed Napoleon's complaints about the British press and took its robust tone as a rooted aspect of public culture, never sought preemptive censorship. He defended the constitution as it stood with a much stronger feel for what public sentiment would accept than Tory publicists like Robert Southey, who urged limits on the press. Publishing libel, including blasphemous and seditious libel, remained a legal offense, but the case had to be proven before a jury. Magistrates risked legal action for wrongful arrest unless they had a previous judgment on the specific work to justify their charge. Sidmouth's circular letter of March 27 that offered the legal opinion that justices of the peace could issue a warrant for libel and compel the person charged to post bail achieved little beyond stirring complaints in parliament. Even the government hesitated to prosecute lest it cast them in an unwelcome authoritarian light. Criticism, however abusive or unsettling, had to be endured as abuses of the press could not be checked without curtailing its liberties in ways ministers themselves rejected.[76]

Support from parliament against unrest mattered to Liverpool as much as the measures themselves. Plebeian unrest rallied support in parliament and among the wider elite Liverpool had lacked during the 1816 session. The Whig opposition held a much stronger position in backing public demands for economy than debating the threat of sedition. Tierney, looking to an expected deficiency in the revenue from 1816, thought Liverpool's government vulnerable and claimed its junior supporters considered a change inevitable. His view in January misread parliamentary sentiment, while the idea that Whigs should place themselves at the head of moderate reformers "to gain the favor and confidence of people" – a position various Foxite Whigs had taken since 1812 – alarmed the Grenvilles.[77] Canning shrewdly attacked demands for retrenchment and reform as feeding discontent "to ripen it into disaffection." Rather than ending real abuses and limiting themselves to that narrower task, the Whig opposition "would pull down the edifice to obtain possession of the ruins."[78] The charge fit a familiar narrative reinforced by a Tory press that loudly denounced Whigs as the thin edge of a revolutionary wedge. Past sympathies remained a present liability when violent unrest drove the agenda.

While acting to counter subversion, Liverpool blunted criticism by showing the system could adapt and meet public concerns on its own terms. He and his colleagues understood the need to convince the country – particularly financiers in the city of London – that the government would not go deeper in debt. They reduced the army from 149,000 men to 123,000 and naval expenditure fell from £9,678,000 to £5,685,000. Such cuts alarmed professionals, but they showed the government's determination to economize.[79] Insisting that ministers had to do away with every post created since 1793, Liverpool reprimanded Palmerston sharply for not abolishing wartime offices in his department. The only position ministers could defend was returning to a military establishment "which had not been considered either as profusely extravagant or as dangerous to the constitution."[80]

Liverpool also consciously followed Pitt's example in the 1780s of personal indifference to emoluments and reduced the sources of patronage that had drawn protest. He recognized the cultural shift from his father's day which had taken the pursuit of wealth through politics for granted. Disinterested public service had supplanted openly avowing riches and power acquired through office.[81] If criticizing jobs and pensions involved more symbolism than substance, the symbols mattered. Old corruption had been an issue since Burke's 1780 campaign for economic reform with political influence as much concern as the cost to taxpayers. Opposition politicians had long complained how the civil list funding the court hid the king's discretionary spending along with the corrupting luxuriousness it subsidized.[82] The wartime expansion of government offices gave the issue a sharper edge. Perceptions underlined by Burdett's telling quip calling ministers "the sect of Expenceans" demanded a response.[83] Although Liverpool originally aimed for a compromise, reducing the number of offices to prewar numbers and keeping those with parliamentary duties, he soon realized a prolonged struggle to defend each post would antagonize country gentlemen. Conceding the whole question at a February 17, 1817 meeting at Fife House, he won their support and left critics stranded.[84]

Having "separated the question of economy from that of seditious reform," as Castlereagh boasted, Liverpool and his colleagues "became masters of both."[85] Measures against plebeian agitators, however cautiously deployed, drained the momentum from unrest. Even when prosecutions ended in acquittal, the ordeal and expense they involved deterred many printers or sellers of radical newspapers. Suspending habeas corpus scattered other radicals fearing arrest and broke up revolutionary cells.[86] Concessions on expenditure won backing from country gentlemen and other MPs, along with important segments of respectable opinion beyond parliament. High politics at Westminster offered a measure of a government's authority. Liverpool had seen at first hand in France from 1789 how control of events could slip from the government's control and initiate a cycle of confrontation and unrest ending in political collapse. Insurrection could be suppressed, by force if necessary, but regaining control once lost would be much harder especially if tensions escalated with demands for structural reforms.

Liverpool's colleagues feared weakness or mishap would unleash a dynamic they could not halt. They predicted a Whig government bidding for popular support would soon be displaced by radicals. The story of French advocates of constitutional monarchy like the Marquis de Lafayette and Comte de Lameth who had been pushed aside by extremists provided ready comparison with the Whig opposition that went beyond alarmist propaganda.[87] Croker's uses of that analogy through the next decade and into the reform crisis of the early 1830s expressed concerns his less articulate or historically inclined colleagues shared. Tory newspapers repeated the theme of feckless Whig patricians stirring tensions they could not control if they held the reins of power. Liverpool realized his government's public legitimacy rested upon a combination of demonstrated authority and answering criticism. Hence the care he took with presenting their case before parliament.

The abortive Pentridge rising marked the echo of a receding tide as unrest diminished. Curtailing political meetings without a license from a local magistrate disrupted agitation as the improving economy reduced the momentum behind public discontent. Fitzwilliam's charge, which Sidmouth rejected, that a government informant called William Oliver had instigated the Pentrige rising points to the changing dynamic. Oliver may have been reporting to the Home Office, but he neither fabricated nor incited the whole conspiracy alone. Indeed, his role points to how intelligence had improved even if upholding public order rested with local authorities rather than directly with ministers themselves.[88] The most distressing news in the autumn of 1817 came with Princess Charlotte's death on November 6 after delivering a stillborn child the previous day. Although the prince regent "had conceived a very unfavorable opinion of the case" and prepared for the worst, her death affected him deeply. Liverpool, on learning the news, left Walmer to attend the prince in London. Louisa, shocked herself at the princess' death, had never seen him more overwhelmed. Intense public interest from the announcement of Charlotte's pregnancy only magnified popular grief. As Brougham later wrote, "it really was as if every household throughout Great Britain had lost a favorite child."[89]

Charlotte's death had important political consequences. Whigs lost the prospect of a sympathetic future heir to the throne or of turning a generational split within the royal family to their advantage. Liverpool and his colleagues, however, also lost an important check on the prince regent's desire for a divorce. The cabinet strongly opposed it, as they had before, with "the public only waiting to see the prince take a part to take one against him."[90] Any step against Caroline would spark a new cycle of disruptive protest once it became known. Since the prince regent had no wish to remarry, the loss of George III's only legitimate grandchild made it imperative for his brothers to secure the succession. Even if apocryphal, the story that the prince regent assembled his unmarried brothers and told them to marry only for the Duke of Clarence to ask "but who would marry us?" captures an underlying truth.[91] None of the brothers had much to recommend them as husbands. Liverpool, who discussed the matter with the prince regent, described the government as "thrown quite out to sea" over the succession with "no expedient to which we can look with real satisfaction."[92]

The immediate trouble involved providing a financial settlement for the royal dukes without raising controversy. Expense itself mattered less than the deep unpopularity of George III's sons within the relatively small world of the political elite. Wellington described them as "the damnedest millstones about the necks of any government." Having "insulted – personally insulted – two thirds of the gentlemen of England" he thought the royal dukes must expect a justifiable revenge when parliament considered their case.[93] Liverpool tested the question in a meeting at Fife House with country gentlemen and government supporters after hearing early rumors of disapproval. Tierney thought that such meetings showed that ministers doubted they could carry measures without a previous rehearsal. Brougham criticized the informal canvass as "contrary to the spirit of the British constitution" in privately consulting a select group rather than openly bringing the plan before the Commons. George Holme Sumner defended Liverpool's meeting, but spoke for many country gentlemen by insisting that "the royal dukes, in common with every other description of persons in the country, must yield to the pressure of the times."[94] Only the Dukes of Cambridge and Kent received the halved amount ministers asked. Parliament refused Clarence an increased allowance and denied Cumberland, whose wife Queen Charlotte had refused to receive since 1815, any marital income. It marked the first defeat on a financial question since the income tax vote in 1816.[95] Resentment over expenditure simmered despite the relative calm. Indeed, country gentlemen and independent MPs who deferred to ministers in times of unrest or foreign war otherwise emphasized parliament's role as a check on the executive. It took careful political management to avoid defeats that might encourage further pressure on ministers.

Liverpool's proposal to support church building with a million pound grant might seem at odds with economy. It responded to the pressing need for parishes to serve a population that had outstripped the Church of England's parochial structure which dated, especially at the diocesan level, from before the Reformation. Not a tenth of worshippers in London and nearby Middlesex could be accommodated in existing chapels and churches. Growing towns like Birmingham faced the same problem. Establishing new parishes required an act of parliament until 1818, which made forming them a rare occurrence.[96] Liverpool's initiative sought to fix what he saw as an alarming problem. Holland's plea that the Established Church provide the funds from its own endowments fell flat when Liverpool and Grenville described it as likely to injure the Church while contributing "a mere mite" to the amount required. Holland acquiesced, albeit with a muted objection to superfluous expenditure on ornamenting churches.[97]

Although Vansittart introduced the financial measure in the Commons, Liverpool crafted the plan and worked with bishops to secure its passage. The measure reflected his view that the Established Church represented the nation in its spiritual aspect while playing to concerns about how agitation threatened public morality. If national prosperity rested upon the moral and religious habits of the people, their rulers had a responsibility to foster those habits through the Established Church. Population growth had created a deficiency in the number of places for public worship belonging to the Established Church, especially in manufacturing towns where much of that increase had taken place. Masses of people, Liverpool pointed out, could not be brought together without being exposed to vicious habits and corrupting influences dangerous to both public security and private morality. Providing churches by using parliamentary grants to supplement private subscription countered the threat while ensuring that those who benefitted from improved access to education "should not be obliged to resort to dissenting places of worship by finding the doors of the church shut against them."[98]

A considerable bloc of opinion beyond parliament shared Liverpool's view. He took care to avoid disparaging nonconformity or stirring controversy, but consistent support for the Church of England quietly bolstered his standing. Faithful churchmen, laity and clergy alike, gave Liverpool a foundation of political support beyond parliament. Whigs like Holland and Brougham suffered from a reputation for indifference, if not atheism. Castlereagh's sympathy for dissenters and Catholics also led partisans of the Established Church to question his commitment to it.[99] Liverpool's personal religious observance and public actions marked him in their eyes as faithful churchman. Historians including Gash and Hilton, who noted his abhorrence of Calvinism, have wrongly described him as an evangelical, partly because like many non-evangelicals he had attended sermons by fashionable preachers. Liverpool never showed the anxiety over his personal salvation or sought a conversion experience that defined evangelicalism. Nor did he share its particular emphasis on the Bible as a guide apart from tradition and reason. Instead he remained faithful to the High Church tradition with its liturgical worship and an outlook on political theology deeply rooted in eighteenth-century debates that reinforced currents in popular loyalism from the 1790s. With other High Churchmen, Liverpool equated Anglican orthodoxy with acceptance of social hierarchy and fealty to the crown. His conception of the Established Church as pillar of the temporal order involved more than an instrumental view of religion as a tool for social discipline. A sense of duty with paternalist implications shaped a faith Louisa's own piety reinforced.[100]

Holland might jibe at Liverpool considering building a few churches of such paramount importance, but the premier took great care over many church matters that included ecclesiastical appointments on which he clashed with colleagues and prince regent alike. Following his father's example on church patronage, he sought advice from the Hackney Phalanx, a High Church counterpart to the evangelical Clapham Sect. Whatever the world may say in other respects, Liverpool told Henry Hobhouse, they will at least credit him on the effort he took in selecting bishops.[101] Strengthening the Church was a priority, even when it meant forgoing patronage at a time where the means of influencing politics with salaried appointments had diminished precipitously. Support from influential laity helped the Established Church weather opposition during the early nineteenth century and renew itself from within. Liverpool's effort made key contributions a later generation would find hard to repeat.[102]

Lord Granville's remark that "at present nothing can equal the flat insipidity of politics" captured the scene as parliamentary elections loomed in June 1818. Besides the general political climate since 1816, the fact that the king's death would dissolve parliament had justified delay. A combination of economic growth and the degree to which unrest had thrown the Whigs onto the defensive gave Liverpool an opening in spring 1818. Nonetheless, the government had little enthusiasm on its own side. Noting that many respectable gentlemen chose to retire from parliament, Herries lamented "their absolute want of any attachment to the government, which they supported with warmth and even devotion through the times of Pitt and Perceval."[103] Such indifference among men who had backed ministers during the war now kept them on the defensive. Canning questioned whether delay might not have spared government friends trouble in contested elections and further calmed the public mind, but postponement would have been a risky bet.[104] The balance of loss and gain, which only became certain in divisions after the new parliament met, counted less than the general tone indicated by a higher number of contested elections than usual in counties and large boroughs. Although Canning held off a challenge at Liverpool, other high profile contests brought tumultuous setbacks even where overall numbers seemed to favor ministers. Huskisson complained that "the high popular party" would take victories in large urban constituencies as a mark of their strength and largely attributed the mischief to "the low periodical press." The Sussex yeomanry, he reported, might "despise the Whigs, but they are no longer what they were ten years ago in their attachment to the old Tory interests and principles which are prevalent in the nobility and gentry."[105] Uncertainty posed the greatest threat, especially with an opposition eager to test its strength.

Liverpool faced other issues before the new parliament met in January. Although British politics turned from foreign to domestic concerns in late 1815 fast enough to induce whiplash, important questions remained open. Allied troops under Wellington's command occupied France amidst periodic threats of unrest. Liverpool doubted the political judgment of French royalists and likened the Bourbons themselves to the Stuarts, but he realized that a continued occupation brought its own problems. Inevitable friction between occupiers and occupied led Wellington to urge withdrawing troops early lest sullen resentment turn to active opposition. Having considerably reduced the indemnity and cut reparations to less than a quarter of the original sum, the allies shortened the occupation to three years and withdrew a significant force in 1817 when the French paid an installment through an Anglo-Dutch loan.[106] Pressure to settle the entire indemnity grew as the occupation approached its end. Removing the army would leave the allies little recourse if France defaulted. Liverpool, who corresponded with Wellington in Paris, viewed the question from the perspective of finance as well as security. French loans carried over several years to settle the indemnity "would keep the money market in a fluctuating and uncertain state." That uncertainty complicated stabilizing British finance and the Bank of England's efforts to resume cash payments. Negotiation over the spring resolved the details, particularly when Russia and Austria rejected a British proposal to post an army of observation along the French border with the Netherlands.[107]

When Castlereagh represented Britain at the Congress of Aix-la-Chapelle in October 1818, Liverpool provided guidance while Bathurst handled Foreign Office business as before. Castlereagh reported such progress that his enthusiasm for congress meetings made him declare them "a new discovery...extinguishing the cobwebs with which diplomacy obscures the horizon...and giving to the counsels of the great powers the efficiency and almost the simplicity of a single state." More prosaically, he saw the value of regular, confidential talks among foreign ministers as a group for anticipating and removing causes of irritation. Political considerations at home gave the cabinet a very different view, though only Canning objected to periodic meetings on principle.[108] Liverpool thought the alliance a vital foundation of European peace, but warned that the meetings of its leading statesmen were so unpopular in Britain and elsewhere in Europe as to impose a significant cost. An invaluable resource for emergencies, they should be kept for dire necessity and otherwise avoided.[109] The personal relationships Castlereagh and Wellington had forged with European statesmen never influenced Liverpool. Overlapping commercial and geopolitical considerations along with political opinion at home weighed far more heavily in his calculations. Liverpool followed North and George III's earlier view in seeking stability across the channel without entangling commitments that risked expense or drawing Britain into disputes where it lacked direct interest. Circumstances now reduced the need for Continental allies to counter France or any other rival. Securing Antwerp and the Low Countries had given Britain an exceptional degree of security from external threats as Liverpool realized. The financial retrenchment peace enabled was also a welcome benefit given domestic pressures since 1816. Liverpool's caution over being drawn too closely into Continental affairs increasingly guided policy as the need for allied cooperation diminished.

Withdrawing the occupation army from France enabled Liverpool to recruit Wellington into his government as Master of the Ordnance. Mulgrave willingly stepped aside, although Liverpool had contemplated bringing Wellington into the cabinet without portfolio.[110] The victor of Waterloo and Vittoria whom kings and emperors treated as an equal brought prestige along with early administrative experience his military career had eclipsed. Liverpool regarded the cabinet as a political body the government could use to leverage the influence or authority of important figures, which made Wellington a valuable asset, rather than a forum to settle policy or draft legislation. Such business would be left to specialists like his father and himself who might well be outside the cabinet. The eighteenth-century assumptions behind that view also made Liverpool open to Wellington's criticism of "factious opposition to government" and his stipulation, if ministers left office, of remaining "at liberty to take any line I might at that time think proper." Allegiance to the crown outweighed a commitment to colleagues, especially in Wellington's case as a soldier, but his earlier civilian service had forged ties with Pitt's protégés even though relative standing among them had shifted greatly since 1808.[111] The change had little effect on Liverpool for whom Wellington never quite escaped a subordinate role compared with Castlereagh as the loyal – and essential – partner in governing or Canning the friend and former rival. Still, members of the government uneasy with Canning's influence welcomed Wellington as a counterweight.

Liverpool made other changes in 1818 that promoted men who played a key part in economic policy. Frederick Robinson entered the cabinet as President of the Board of Trade and Treasurer of the Navy. Though known for indolence, a nervous disposition, and occasional tears, he had proven himself in a junior capacity at the Board of Trade and worked successfully with both Canning and Castlereagh. The death of George Rose, an official and courtier whose career under Pitt resembled that of Liverpool's father, opened those two offices. Liverpool also advanced his protégé Thomas Wallace, a twenty-eight-year parliamentary veteran and commercial expert, to fill Robinson's place. Wallace and the premier had been together at Oxford.[112] Besides sharing Liverpool's commercial views, Robinson spoke effectively in parliament and had more popularity than the crusty Rose.

Other junior ministers outside the cabinet, however, resented the lack of advancement. Every promotion or bit of patronage left several nursing their disappointment with a premier who never had enough to satisfy all the claimants. Arbuthnot warned Liverpool about watching "our own people" given demands by Croker, William Vesey-Fitzgerald, and others in Peel's circle for his advancement with a view to their own benefit.[113] Peel himself sought a break from office after serving in Ireland since 1812 with a distinction that met Liverpool's high expectations. Later, accommodating his claim to office and deploying his needed talents without disrupting the balance within the government would pose a challenge. Canning, who had mended relations with rivals of his own generation, now found Peel at his back despite the fact that their only policy disagreement involved Catholic Emancipation. His ambition – along with Vansittart's less plausible hopes – to win the parliamentary seat for Oxford University vacated by Charles Abbott was dashed when Peel took the prize with backing from their old college Christ Church.[114] Possible tensions within the government balanced the advantage Liverpool won by strengthening its ranks.

The great test would come when the new parliament met in January. Grey argued for rigid and unsparing economy at a dinner in Newcastle on December 31, pushing a line that resonated among Whigs and country gentlemen alike. Whigs increasingly appealed to provincial interest groups by staking a middle ground between radicals and ministers. Tierney warned they needed a strong showing lest momentum from the election dissipate.[115] Liverpool saw the opposition's advantage in forcing issues – as he told Bathurst, "we cannot avoid a question if they choose to try their strength" – and feared a serious defeat early in the session might push the government into an uphill struggle, if not worse.[116] Accordingly, he had framed budget estimates over the summer of 1818 to preempt demands for economy. Most of the savings came from the army, where reducing manpower rather than full battalions made later augmentation easier, and the civil list. The navy had gone beyond any reasonable economy, but renovating the fleet was an expense parliament would be least disposed to resist. Liverpool also backed away from paying the invalid king's Windsor establishment from the privy purse when the prince regent and Duke of York strongly resisted. Abandoning an idea that broke with precedent anyway gave Liverpool leverage to cut the civil list.[117] Careful economy, along with the flourishing revenue and general prosperity, left Arbuthnot generally confident. Harrowby, however, anticipated "such abundance of work, that fighting Bonaparte was nothing to it."[118]

The 1819 parliamentary session reprised the struggle of 1816, particularly in the Commons. Whigs had more organization and esprit than before while ministers faced the old challenge of getting their friends to attend. Charles Wynn remarked after several votes that "the striking feature – to use a Castlereaghism – of the day is the unwillingness of most of the new members to be considered as belonging to government, to receive notes or answer whip."[119] Government majorities in February fell short of expectations while the Whigs bolstered their showing with support from independents. Castlereagh even remarked in passing to Tierney that "I should like to learn the secret of your association."[120] Minor financial points brought defeats or preemptive concessions. So far the session had echoed an old theme of conflict over finance. Whig measures on legal reform presented a greater danger because following a legislative agenda set by its opponents risked making the government appear to have lost its authority. Castlereagh's attempt on March 2, 1819 to block a proposal for a select committee on capital punishment embarrassingly failed by nineteen votes. Arbuthnot, who had not exerted himself so much since the controversy over the failed Walcheren expedition, stepped up efforts to secure votes in April with little to show beyond pulling junior officeholders into line. Defeat over a Scottish measure on May 6 which the opposition carried by five votes pressed ministers to force a vote of confidence.[121] The Commons then would have to back the government or deliberately choose to replace it.

Liverpool determined to propose £3,000,000 in new taxes, half raised by a version of the malt tax abandoned in 1816. Besides avoiding the controversial step of a large loan in peacetime, the plan served his larger goal of setting public finances on a stronger basis and returning sterling to a gold standard. As the prince regent warned, however, it also risked alienating country gentlemen with a tax on agriculture and raising plebeian opposition by increasing the cost of necessities.[122] Liverpool bet that forcing a choice upon independent MPs would strengthen the government's hand. He thought staying in office after repeated defeats "a positive evil" that disgraced ministers personally and weakened their ability to render positive service.[123] Holding power on the opposition's sufferance and only to pursue its agenda gave the appearance of clinging to office. Reputation mattered for maintaining parliamentary, let alone public, confidence. An informed observer expected Whigs to gain office, especially since they could rely upon supporters of the present administration to support them as a bulwark to plebeian radicals and agitators in the country.[124] Tierney preempted Liverpool when he forced the vote himself on May 18 by moving for a committee on the state of the nation. His attempt to separate the sheep from the goats drew a flock of record size – the total of 530 present, which, including speaker and tellers, was the biggest since the Irish union – and what Castlereagh called "a grand field day" to parade Whig troops ended with a government majority of 179. The vote decisively turned the political tide and left the Whigs stranded as independents made their choice for ministers. Not surprisingly, the financial measure Liverpool chose for a vote of confidence passed on June 7, 1819 by 320 to 132.[125]

Liverpool won a larger victory by returning the pound sterling to a gold standard abandoned from necessity during the war. Securing a £5 million surplus to redeem debt by increasing taxes enabled ministers to require the Bank of England to pay its notes first in bullion at market price from October 1820 and then in coin from May 1822. The gradual transition allowed the bank immediately to redeem notes it had issued. Ending the need for annual loans through debt reduction and settling the currency on a fixed basis brought a change Liverpool described later as the country "settling itself into a state of peace."[126] Those two steps marked a quiet, but important, turning point as Liverpool broke with the reactive posture of crisis management adopted since 1816. Rather than continuing to bridge deficits with annual loans and other expedients that had tied ministers to deeply unpopular London financiers, the government tackled the structural problem to set a trajectory for later economic growth. The commitment to a gold standard that resuming cash payments made also implied moving to a free trade policy aimed at pursuing wealth through access to foreign markets rather than a protected home market. Deregulation since 1815 had already taken steps along that path and the pace would quicken in the 1820s as conditions improved.[127] Liverpool's role illustrates both his economic outlook and a style of political management that served him well.

Resuming cash payments right after the war posed risks political and practical. Not only did ministers disagree among themselves on the means and timing, but commercial interests lobbied Liverpool on both sides of the question. Besides disrupting trade, returning to payment in gold without depreciating the currency to some extent meant sharp deflation. A critic in 1816 called deflation transferring wealth from landholders to financiers or, more provocatively, between those "who paid taxes to those who received them." The result would have made Liverpool's political difficulties far worse and put a sharper edge upon the attacks his government faced. On the other hand, as Grenville argued two years later, a paper currency meant "that no class of society, from the highest to the lowest could know what were their means, what their income, or their wages."[128] Price stability had its merits, especially in a period of widely fluctuating economic cycles. Liverpool, who shared his father's commitment to a metallic currency, largely concurred with Grenville on the benefit of resuming cash payments, but insisted the market had first to absorb the foreign loans France had used to pay its indemnity. Despite proposing a continued restriction in 1818, the government moved quietly that year to reduce unfunded debt and repay advances from the Bank of England as a step towards resumption. Liverpool's pragmatic approach differed sharply from both Huskisson's doctrinaire arguments and the moralizing criticisms of those who opposed it.[129]

A demand in January 1819 by the bank that cash payments be further postponed followed by Tierney's announcement of a motion for a parliamentary inquiry into public credit forced the question. However personally agitated Liverpool became – Huskinson described the situation as one of his grand fidgets—he played a deft hand. The government quickly substituted its own proposal for an inquiry with secret committees of both houses nominated to report on the question. Significantly, however, they were not charged to offer recommendations, but merely report evidence. Liverpool ensured that committees included "a large sprinkling of Opposition" along with talented men outside the government instead of the country gentlemen who typically provided ballast.[130] Peel, still outside the government, chaired the Commons inquiry. Its counterpart included bullionists Grenville and Lansdowne from the opposition even though Harrowby, a minister on record opposing resumption, chaired. Besides shifting attention from ministers to parliament, Liverpool took politics out of the question further by turning the inquiry's focus to technical points. He also brought the cabinet behind a gradual return to cash payments, either persuading or carefully marginalizing doubters within the government like Vansittart and Herries.[131]

The enabling legislation caught Grey and Holland by surprise, taking ground from under the opposition's feet. Liverpool not only defended the specific plans for returning to cash payments, but made a strong case for gold as a fixed standard of value. Allowing the Bank of England to issue notes without restriction gave it "the power of making money, without any other check or influence to direct them than their own notions of profit or interest." Paper, which had no value, only the promise of value, could not provide a lasting standard. The narrow gap between the market and mint price of gold—three percent—minimized the risk of sharp deflation, especially when the resumption would be gradual rather than a forced and precipitous contraction of circulation some had described. Separating the money supply from the price of gold, Liverpool admitted, may have some advantages in easing transaction and diminishing temporary suffering. Often, however, it encouraged speculation, unsound dealings, and accumulation of fictitious capital. Returning to a standard value would place transactions on a firm and honorable basis.[132]

Liverpool aimed much of the argument at leaders in finance and commerce, along with skeptics in his own administration. The opposition had already backed resumption in principle. Grey had agitated the question opportunistically, believing privately that the step would impose economic distress no government could survive. Once the consequent depression had passed, he anticipated the Whigs replacing a caretaker "middle administration" which would weather the immediate storm after the present government fell. Instead, Liverpool defeated the Whigs by securing a gradual return to cash payments backed by a clear revenue surplus. Doing so against overwhelming hostility from commercial and financial opinion also freed the government from its association with the unpopular monied interest.[133] Indeed, distancing the government from the fundholders, bankers, and other established groups seen as its social base helped deflect criticism and show ministers took a disinterested view of promoting the public welfare.

Seizing the initiative with a major shift in finance marked a quiet watershed for Liverpool's administration that checked parliamentary opposition. It also brought a much larger change over the longer term that reversed an eighteenth-century trend toward higher public spending. Victory in 1815 had provided Britain a security that ended need for a fiscal–military state and thereby made dismantling it possible. Beside a smaller, cheaper state, the country began moving towards a free-trade empire resting on a commercial foundation earlier policies had already laid by overcoming rivals and securing advantages.[134] Liverpool never lowered the number of salaried employees to the prewar level he had set as a goal to Palmerston, but the expense of central government shrank from its wartime peak. Public spending fell in real terms by twenty-five percent during the two decades after Waterloo and by seventy-five percent in per capita terms from 1801 to 1821. The British state took a lower proportion of gross national product than its nineteenth-century French counterpart. Liverpool's economic measures set a trajectory that made the laissez-faire state of nineteenth-century Britain a much lighter burden than its fiscal–military predecessor of the eighteenth century.[135] Postwar restructuring provided much of the financial precondition for his later work on commercial reform while reducing expenditure freed capital for investment and trade.

Parliamentary opposition backed by agitation in the country sharply limited Liverpool's flexibility in responding to the economic challenges of peace.

Economic cycles and their political impact set further constraints that increased the difficulty of managing postwar adjustment. Although the government had a stronger hold on office than its opponents presumed, the political contest at Westminster kept ministers largely on the defensive. The need to avert immediate parliamentary defeat overshadowed efforts to develop a coherent policy on key aspects of the transition from the war. Public pressure, including organized provincial interests, exerted more influence on parliament from 1816, though concerns about the danger from plebeian unrest worked to the government's advantage. Beyond crisis management, however, Liverpool moved to improve public finances and regain the trust of those who had backed his ministry through the final years of war. He began adopting measures whose effect in stimulating trade would further strengthen his position against critics. Before they took hold, a political storm broke as the crisis over a royal divorce nearly drove Liverpool from office. Agitation mobilized public sentiment against the government, which stood on the verge of losing both royal and parliamentary confidence. Navigating those dangerous crosscurrents presented the greatest test of Liverpool's career.

CHAPTER 8

Revolution Resisted

QUEEN CAROLINE UNLEASHED a crisis in 1820 that made it the hardest period of Liverpool's career. Having failed to secure terms from her, he faced the challenge of moving a bill to dissolve the royal marriage through a hostile parliament amidst popular outcry and a simmering quarrel with George IV. Scandal revived tensions from 1819 fueled by radical agitation amidst an economic downturn that had prompted the notorious Six Acts to check protest. Britain seemed at the edge of a revolutionary moment. Rather than the lurid imaginings of plebeian insurgency that satirists mocked as overwrought, the real threat involved the risk of a weak ministry being unable to hold authority amidst growing protest and a split within the elite. There lay the real parallel with France from 1789. Liverpool had seen for himself in Paris how failure to govern had thrown power to whoever dared seize it. Realizing that politics, like nature, abhors a vacuum, he saw the need to assert lawful authority, but doing so required a confidence from king and parliament that often seemed in doubt. Even once the immediate crisis passed, prospects remained uncertain while George IV was at odds with his ministers. Liverpool had to weather an exceptional storm and its aftermath.

A successful close to the 1819 parliamentary session had strengthened Liverpool's hand, but the prince regent again pressed the question of a divorce. His demands the previous year for an inquiry into Princess Caroline's scandalous behavior had led the cabinet to acquiesce reluctantly in what became known as the Milan Commission. Since material hitherto gathered gave insufficient proof of adultery, Sir John Leach, the prince regent's legal advisor named vice-chancellor in January 1818, proposed sending agents to secure direct evidence. The cabinet only consented on the understanding they pledged no further action regardless of what transpired.[1] Countenancing the step, Leach had told John Powell, the solicitor appointed to manage the inquiry, did not make it the cabinet's measure. He also made clear the aim to exclude Caroline from the throne and separate her from the prince.[2] Even with Liverpool's guarded consent, the plan went further than the cabinet liked. Unable to dissuade the prince regent they tried to downplay the proceeding's official character which amounted to a distinction without a difference.

The Milan Commission reached Italy in September 1818. Caroline, though never officially told, soon learned of its inquiries. Many former servants, including a favorite, Theodore Majocchi, gave statements. Rumors circulated that stories could be sold for a generous price. Caroline's relationship with Bartolomeo Bergami, her chamberlain and presumed lover, had drawn particular notice. Brougham had concerns from London and sent his brother James in March 1819 to Italy for a report. The younger Brougham thought the circumstances of her living effectively as man and wife with Bergami "would completely ruin her in the opinion of the people of England." The prince could get a divorce or at least prevent her becoming queen. Caroline feared the inquiry would make her position worse. James Brougham then suggested preempting any action with a negotiated settlement that would keep her out of England. His brother then pursued the idea.[3]

The problem Liverpool had postponed returned as the prince regent took a more determined line on a divorce. Brougham approached Lord Hutchinson, one of the prince's personal friends, suggesting a formal separation "to be ratified by act of parliament, if such a proceeding can be accomplished." Caroline would renounce the right to be crowned, taking some other title, along with the jointure to which she was entitled if she survived her husband, and receive her present annuity for life. While insisting she had nothing to dread from any proceeding, Brougham observed that a settlement would avoid "the manifold evils" of public inquiry into delicate matters involving the royal family.[4] He left unstated, but hardly unnoted, that Caroline's friends in parliament could either facilitate a settlement or force a confrontation. Forwarding Liverpool the communication, the prince regent suggested "the ultimate purpose of divorce" could be "effected rather by arrangement than by adverse proceedings."[5]

Liverpool promptly replied with a cabinet minute outlining impediments to a divorce. Not to be deterred, the prince regent claimed he had been misunderstood. Brougham must have known that evidence now available sufficiently proved Caroline's guilt. The lawyer therefore believed "the offense to public decency and public morals" might be avoided "if the ultimate purpose of divorce were submitted to by arrangement." Agreeing that divorce required satisfactory proof of adultery, the prince asked if the proposed separation would not require the same. He urged the cabinet to consider "whether the party who would propose the one would accept the other"—and if separation short of divorce would not "sacrifice important public interests" along with the regent's private feelings.[6]

The prince regent had misread Brougham just as Brougham overestimated Caroline's willingness to compromise. Indeed, she began complaining of attacks on her character and threatening a return to England. Liverpool and the cabinet repeated their longstanding position against a divorce. The Milan Commission's report in July did nothing to change their stance. Evidence provided by foreigners, mostly menial servants, carried little weight with British opinion. So long as

Caroline remained abroad and held no station higher than Princess of Wales they thought any public proceeding inexpedient.[7] Both conditions, however, merely delayed the question. Referring the prince regent to his own legal advisors bought time, especially since the cabinet expected their views would be unchanged. Leach indeed reported the unanimous opinion that no proceedings to secure the prince's aim could be advisable in any court of law and "the only eligible mode was by parliamentary inquiry with a view of a bill of divorce."[8] Brougham meanwhile tried to manipulate both sides by using the threat of legal proceedings to frighten Caroline into a settlement and warning Liverpool she might arrive in London to make her own public case.

A different crisis eclipsed the royal divorce when unrest returned amidst a sharp economic downturn. The prosperity that had muted discontent gave way to a trade slump that revived the protest cycle from 1816 on a larger scale. Depressed wages brought strikes while unemployment raised poor rates on localities. A bad harvest brought high bread prices the next year.[9] Radical agitators like Henry Hunt seized the opening with a more effective national organization and strategy than before. James Watson, a London Spencean, had formed the "Union of Non-Represented People" in 1818 to promote a national movement for electing "people's representatives" who would demand admission to parliament. Although it collapsed by the year's end, his effort identified a community of interest among otherwise disparate groups. Radicals picked up Watson's strategy the next year. Thomas Paine had proposed a national convention elected by universal male suffrage in 1793 and the fact that other radicals took the idea further alarmed observers as a threat to parliament's authority.[10]

Radicalism joined a theoretical critique of revealed religion and an institutional critique of the Established Church with a political attack on the Church's main support: the unreformed parliament, the crown, and landlords. Sweeping reform to shatter that nexus, radicals insisted, would end national debt and high taxes. It offered an easier answer to the distress from economic dislocation and trade slumps than anything the propertied classes could provide without challenging property ownership itself. Grounded in a philosophy by William Cobbett out of Thomas Paine, the charge reinforced a larger critique of elite parasitism in Church and state urged more forcefully since Waterloo. Cheap publications, traveling agitators, and the new phenomenon of monster meetings presented radical arguments to a wider plebeian audience more systematically than before.[11] Agitation dormant since the 1790s had revived with a sharper edge and greater reach beyond London. The new cycle of provincial meetings began as the public felt the economic downturn of 1819. Assembling groups, mostly strangers to the area where they met, and parading men in formation under banners with music marked an alarming new development. Besides nationalizing previously local protests, their disciplined action, however peaceable, raised an alarming specter of organized resistance absent in 1817.

Henry Hunt pushed the reform movement toward platform agitation with a strategy of mass meetings rather than conspiring revolution as Spencean radicals did.[12] A large gathering for parliamentary reform in Birmingham on July 12 named Sir Charles Wolesley "legislatorial attorney" with instructions to claim admission as their representative when parliament next met. By defying the law against electing an MP without the king's writ, the meeting implicitly challenged parliament. Others went further. A June meeting in Oldham called people to organize themselves as petitioning parliament was useless. The Revered Joseph Harrison told another gathering that with corruption as a barrier holding back the people "they must blow it up or blow it down." Wolesley, noting his own presence at the storming of the Bastille, declared that he "was not idle on that glorious day." Other meetings declined to follow Birmingham by electing a "legislatorial attorney," but the pattern in June and July threatened to make popular meetings in provincial towns a rival to parliament. Agitation spread to London with a mass meeting at Smithfield on July 21 that declared parliament's acts would cease to be binding in January 1820. Since the Commons, as the radical John Jebb had argued in the 1780s, sat as a proxy for the public rather than in its own right, like the king and nobility, the proxy might be regarded as annihilated once its principal's voice had been heard directly. Concerns grew among both ministers and local authorities. The Home Office and crown legal officers advised on the legality of meetings and measures to address unrest or peaceful gatherings that violated the law. Discretion remained with local authorities who relied on ministers supporting their actions taken in good faith. A proclamation in the prince regent's name on July 30 condemned seditious meetings and libels, along with unauthorized military drilling.[13]

Tension peaked on August 16 with a meeting at St Peter's Fields outside Manchester. Magistrates had forced its postponement twice by declaring illegal any gathering to follow Birmingham by naming a "legislatorial attorney." The government told Manchester radicals that any such meeting would be unlawful. Their own legal advisors warned it would subject them to sedition charges. Instead, the meeting assembled to petition for parliamentary reform. Between 20,000 and 60,000 men, women, and children met to hear speakers, including Hunt, demand universal suffrage and annual parliaments. Although peaceful, their numbers and arrival in formations that resembled troops on parade unnerved local authorities. Sidmouth, who sought to minimize charges of a confrontation, had urged magistrates not to intervene for any reason short of violence. Panicked magistrates, however, ordered yeomanry cavalry aided by regular hussars to disperse the crowd and arrest the speakers. Ensuing chaos left eleven dead and hundreds injured.[14] A local journalist for the *Manchester Observer*, James Wroe, called it the Peterloo Massacre as an ironic counterpoint to Wellington's famous victory. The name stuck.

Peterloo brought into focus the challenge authorities faced. Intelligence reports from a network of informers the government had built after the failure to convict

Illus. 10. Isaac Cruikshank, "Massacre at St. Peter's or 'Britons Strike Home'!!!" Likening the dispersal of a radical meeting outside Manchester to Wellington's victory at Waterloo cast the authorities as the people's enemy while playing to fears about the army's role in protecting public order. It also reinforced a political narrative Liverpool struggled to change.

men charged following the 1816 Spa Fields Riot kept ministers informed of radical conspiracies, but that information could not be shared beyond the cabinet.[15] Public reports still provided enough news to alarm. Lord Redesdale, a veteran of Sidmouth and Pitt's administrations, told Sidmouth "that the measures of the radical reformers must terminate in blood & that the sooner the crisis arrived the less dreadful it would be." Their efforts "amounted to a general conspiracy against the existing form of government." Redesdale called it high treason, even if aimed at the government rather than the king's person.[16] Although the Manchester magistrates had stopped the radical meetings, their actions were certain to spark controversy. Sidmouth promptly conveyed the prince regent's thanks to the magistrates and yeomanry for preserving the peace on a critical occasion.[17] Anything less would have thrown full responsibility upon local authorities. Wellington remarked that had Sidmouth not supported them, others in future would not act at all. Canning thought letting down magistrates would invite their resignation. Lord Sheffield asked how they could be expected to act unless assured of support, even high-handed support. If the executive shrank "from encouraging, approving, and supporting the magistracy," he warned, "there will be an end to all subordination."[18] Events at Manchester threatened the vital partnership between local authorities and government that enabled the British state to preserve order at minimal cost.

Liverpool thought the magistrates were "substantially right," even if he declined to affirm their course as entirely prudent. Upon reviewing the case, legal authorities, including Eldon as Lord Chancellor, considered them justified. A Lancashire grand jury effectively sanctioned magistrates by rejecting charges against the yeomanry while confirming others against Hunt and his associates. Its report also established that part of the county had been in a state little short of actual rebellion. Still, Liverpool noted that unrest, however alarming, had been confined largely to manufacturing regions in Northern England and Scotland. Without material distress or other practical grievances to aid them, radicals had accomplished nothing in London.[19] Peterloo had escalated tensions and turned many radicals from persuasion to acquiring weapons in self-defense. The news convinced John Gale Jones, as he later wrote, "that *the time for Reform was past and the hour of Revolution come.*" Men who plotted to assassinate the cabinet the next year called it high treason against the people, and ministers had reports of other more immediate conspiracies.[20] Disaffection presented a deeper challenge—and one harder to meet—than open violence. Blaming distress on Church and state threatened to divide the public from institutions. Liverpool worried a crisis of authority would start the cycle of revolution he had witnessed in France. Indeed, the combination of disaffection with organized and disciplined protest on a large scale struck many among the respectable, propertied classes as a warning echo of the French Revolution.[21]

Although the cabinet agreed on the need for legal measures against sedition, they differed on calling parliament back early to consider them. Sidmouth urged immediate action. Believing the present danger greater than any since the Hanoverian accession in 1714, he complained that the country suffered from the want of such decisive and efficient measures as the crisis demanded.[22] Liverpool sought a sense of parliamentary opinion, especially in the Commons. He thought it essential to avoid setbacks that might embolden radicals—and parliamentary opposition – while dampening the confidence of authorities. Until their political friends arrived in London, Liverpool told an absent colleague, it would be impossible to determine how far government could venture with a prospect of support.[23] Framing measures also took time, especially ones beyond a temporary response to a passing emergency. Canning, like Sidmouth and Eldon, saw the need for more powers than present laws afforded to repress "evils of modern growth, but too apparently of deep root & thriving malignity." He rightly warned that calling parliament without substantive proposals would let critics press awkward questions about the Manchester incident.[24]

Fitzwilliam forced Liverpool's hand by joining a county meeting of Yorkshire freeholders on October 14 that demanded an inquiry into the events at Manchester. The resolutions, which Fitzwilliam had drafted, affirmed the right of public assembly and charged ministers directly with prejudging the case by approving illegal action by the magistrates.[25] Liverpool saw the meeting as a provocation that demanded a firm response, though he, with the prince regent's concurrence, awaited reports before acting. Fitzwilliam had so identified himself with an attack on the government – despite serving as the king's representative in Yorkshire's West Riding – that Liverpool believed "forbearance would be ascribed to nothing but timidity." Supporters would find such weakness demoralizing and slacken their efforts. After a cabinet meeting on October 20, Sidmouth informed Fitzwilliam his services as Lord Lieutenant would no longer be required. Fitzwilliam, the prince regent said, "had drawn upon himself his own dismissal."[26] By giving the lead for other Whigs to organize county meetings, Fitzwilliam also prompted Liverpool to call parliament in late November so the government could face critics and test its own support. Delay now risked ceding initiative to the Whigs and their appeals to provincial opinion.[27]

Grey believed Whigs would benefit by occupying a middle ground condemning the extra-parliamentary activity by radicals like Hunt while opposing government measures that curtailed popular liberties. Moderate and reasonable men, he told Brougham, including "a great proportion of the property of the country" would endorse that stance. Indeed, the *Leeds Mercury* had warned in June that the danger to the country arose from extremes on both sides – ultra- reformers and ultra-royalists – and urged moderate figures to interpose themselves and avoid a choice between revolution or military despotism. Grey and other Whigs held back right after Peterloo to avoid either being co-opted by radicals or charged with being their accomplices.[28] Fitzwilliam, a protégé of Burke who opposed any parliamentary reform, could never be seen as a friend to radicalism. Having long thought radicals less threatening than claimed, he rather feared military encroachment on civil government under the pretext of containing subversion. "The wicked and foolish abuse of great and constitutional rights" by radicals, Fitzwilliam later wrote, gave ministers an opening to abridge public liberties.[29] His intervention enabled Brougham, Grey, and other Whigs to organize their own county meetings and take the issue from radicals who had lost public sympathy since August. Whigs now hoped to benefit. Their efforts posed a challenge within the political elite Liverpool could not ignore, particularly since it reinforced the charge his government served privileged interests at the public's expense.

Parliament's opening on November 23 left only a short time to frame and consider the measures that Liverpool intended as a test of parliamentary support. Merely recounting plots and conspiracies as in 1817 would not suffice. Legal advisors worked to translate proposals into good law, a process that reinforced doubts about coercion. Ministers struggled to define what separated exercising inalienable rights from disturbing public peace. The cabinet agreed on three measures to curb intimidation and violence, two on incitement through the press, and one directed at agitators themselves. Besides restricting meetings to a parochial level – thereby limiting their size and excluding itinerant orators – they banned unauthorized military training and empowered magistrates to seize caches of arms. The presence among radicals of former soldiers and their parading in disciplined formation prompted the latter. Raising the penalty for blasphemous and seditious libel while ordering publishers to post a bond guaranteeing payment of fines upon conviction deterred the pauper press. Taxing cheap publications raised their cost to cut circulation. A final measure kept those charged with conspiracy or libel from delaying their trial to the next assizes after entering a plea.[30] None of these proposals, as Liverpool privately told Grenville, interfered with petitioning, discussing politics and religion, or reading uncensored publications. They simply ended mass meetings that troubled even Brougham and fellow Whigs while dampening agitation directed at the distressed poor and giving local authorities a stronger hand. What critics later called "gagging acts" limited public meetings to what Liverpool described as the scale common fifty years earlier and applied the established stamp duty to cheap publications.[31]

When parliament met, Liverpool rejected calls for an inquiry into the proceedings at Manchester as that step would require suspending the course of law and silencing all subordinate tribunals. Indeed, he condemned those recent public meetings "where one county sat in judgment upon another" as exciting a feeling of terror. Whatever distress burdened the country, the only good parliament could do at present "was to give their confidence to the loyal part of the community" and ensure that magistrates and property alike felt protected.[32] Grenville scored an important point by arguing the present danger involved more than just economic distress and likened it to the beginnings of the French Revolution with its "servile, yet ostentatious imitation." Blasphemous and seditious publications had brought Church, state, and society into disrepute with local groups formed to spread "these impious and destructive doctrines." They gathered the discontented into "large and tumultuous bodies" where "they were invited to test their strength." Grenville accordingly urged immediate action to avoid open insurrection that would compel "those means of repression and defense at the thought of which every British heart bleeds." The speech, later published as a pamphlet, outlined a view Grenville had shared privately with Liverpool.[33]

The French Revolution offered an easy and rhetorically forceful parallel, albeit one Whigs and the press called alarmist. Liverpool cited his own experience watching the attack on the Bastille in seconding Grenville's argument. Desperate conduct by a few active leaders and fears of the many had brought revolution to France. An escalating cycle of violence had accustomed people to scenes of devastation from which before they would have recoiled.[34] Liverpool returned to the analogy in warning against blasphemous libels. Publications attacking religion "brutalize the human mind" even among "a religious and moral people" like the English. "Cheap tracts circulated for half-pence and farthings throughout the country" sought deliberately to weaken "all those principles of morality and religion by which the state was upheld."[35] Liverpool here echoed his father's 1773 warning against "skeptical infidelity" and defended ties linking Church and state. Despite their forceful warnings, Liverpool and his colleagues made clear they proposed limited restrictions to address specific problems even critics recognized. They accepted several amendments on details. Much of the debate saw both sides arguing over who best protected constitutional liberty. Parliament approved most of the legislation before Christmas and then adjourned until February on December 29. A new year offered brighter prospects as disturbed areas remained quiet while revenue and the harvest suggested improving economic conditions.[36]

George III's death on Saturday, January 29, 1820 ended an era. Liverpool hastened to Windsor on hearing of the old king's rapid decline amidst the coldest winter anyone living could remember. Half the kingdom seemed to have colds. William Wordsworth remarked how many old people the winter had carried away.[37] The poignancy of the impending moment could not have been lost upon Liverpool. George III had profoundly shaped politics over his life while befriending the Jenkinson family. Liverpool had been guided by him as much as by Pitt and almost his own father. The old king's principles had been a lodestar for loyal opinion while his steadfast probity offered a sharp contrast with his heir. Ministers were his servants in spirit along with name. Sidmouth captured how insiders felt by lamenting "how much better it is to weep over departed excellence in the nearest and dearest connections than to be harassed by living profligacy!"[38] If a regency lasting nearly a decade suggested "nothing would be new but the name of the sovereign," matters quickly showed otherwise when the new king demanded a divorce.

A storm brewing since before Waterloo crashed over the political landscape. The king and his ministers dispatched the formalities incumbent upon a new reign even though he was so agitated he could hardly go through with them.[39] Arrangements respecting his estranged wife upset him even more. What had been a personal matter became the question of whether a woman of Caroline's repute should be accorded the honors and privileges of a queen consort. Since her annuity lapsed on George III's death, a new grant also had to be settled. Unless ministers resolved matters, parliament could take them up with unpredictable consequences. Liverpool had to negotiate a separation to keep Caroline abroad. Unfortunately, it proved harder than ever as the parties became intransigent and the king demanded a divorce his cabinet flatly opposed.

What seemed a minor point involving prayers for the royal family in the Anglican liturgy obsessed George IV who demanded her exclusion and flatly insisted she not be recognized as queen. Praying for Caroline, as Croker privately remarked, would settle matters in her favor:

> If she is fit to be introduced as Queen before God Almighty, she is fit to be received by men & if we are to *pray* for her in church, we may surely bow to her at court. The praying for her will throw a sanctity round her which the good & pious people of this country will never afterwards bear to have withdrawn.

A point argued "as a mere matter of civil propriety & expediency" took on a religious and social aspect when the king used Croker's view to bolster his demands.[40] Distinguishing between such privileges as coronation and mention in the liturgy that remained in the king's gift and rights pertaining to a queen consort, Liverpool conceded the point while still opposing a divorce. A January 17 report by the king's advocate, the attorney general, and solicitor general had confirmed earlier objections. The king's personal advisor, Leach, concurred. Liverpool hoped a crumb of consolation with the liturgy would make the king more amenable. Abject submission had often followed a brief tantrum and prolonged sulk. Instead, George IV redoubled his insistence on a divorce. Leach told Eldon that the king would change his ministers and, if still checked, go to Hanover where he could be divorced.[41]

Liverpool gave the cabinet's view in a long February 10 minute. Canning qualified his concurrence by adding that he could not have agreed to omit her from the liturgy "if any *penal* process had been in contemplation" as divesting the queen of privileges attaching to her station before trial would have prejudiced the case. Divorce remained the sticking point behind the minute's conciliatory tone and belabored arguments. Since anything resembling a secret trial would revolt public feeling, a secret committee of parliament could not hear evidence. Caroline's defense would introduce "with every degree of exaggeration and in the most invidious colors" any circumstance to argue in mitigation. Even if rejected as evidence, nothing could prevent those points being made in speeches, motions, and petitions with a more injurious effect. There would be no way to contradict them. Success in a divorce proceeding "might be won with such personal discomfort to the king as would more than outweigh any advantage." Failure, must bring "the triumphant establishment in the country of one who would in that event be represented as the intended victim of persecution." The cabinet therefore preferred to negotiate a financial provision stipulating the queen remain abroad. While it might not prevent all the evils of a public dispute, trying for an agreement diminished the risk. Responsibility would rest upon Caroline and her advisors if they rejected it.[42]

George IV called Liverpool, Eldon, and Sidmouth to his presence after a Privy Council meeting to give them written observations and reiterate his insistence upon a divorce. His paper argued that a proceeding in the Lords could sit behind closed doors to at least delay the publication of testimony before the case had gone through. The qualified measure proposed offered no advantages over a divorce.[43] With the divorce now a point of honor, George IV quoted his late father's statement that "he might be driven to live in a cottage, but could not be driven to consent to that from which his conscience revolted." Recruiting Whig ministers as a new government to propose the necessary measures remained an unspoken threat as conversation became increasingly strained. The king crassly told Eldon that "I know your conscience always interferes except where your interest is concerned." He then ordered Liverpool from the room after asking if he knew to whom he spoke. Liverpool replied "Sir, I know that I am speaking to my sovereign and I believe addressing him as it becomes a loyal subject." When afterwards called back, Liverpool refused at first and only returned after a second request. George IV tried to make amends by saying they had both been too hasty.[44]

Despite those second thoughts, the audience damaged Liverpool's relationship with the king beyond easy repair. It would have taken an exceptionally deft touch to manage George IV's intense feelings on the divorce, but Liverpool's own nervous irritability made him both personally sensitive and ill-attuned to the sensibilities of others. He had always read personal differences badly, often missing the small cues that convey meaning beyond words. Harriett Arbuthnot, while praising Liverpool's qualities in 1821, noted his cold manner and "a most querulous, irritable temper" that made him difficult to act with.[45] It certainly impeded his efforts to convince the king of unpleasant realities. The temperamental gap separating an emotional, weak-willed, and self-indulgent monarch from the sensitive, morally serious prime minister who became more stubborn when pressed made differences harder to mend. George IV complained persistently of Liverpool's deficiencies in manner and tried to undermine him with colleagues. Rather than having the sovereign's personal favor as an asset, Liverpool now had the added liability of a hostile court as he struggled with the volatile state of parliament and popular opinion. Handling the king's "huffs and pets" fell mainly to Sidmouth, Castlereagh, and Wellington.[46]

Castlereagh thought the government effectively dissolved after the king's outburst. He expected to receive Metternich as a Kentish farmer rather than foreign secretary. Sir Benjamin Bloomfield, George IV's private secretary, had urged the cabinet to delay responding to the king's memorandum and couch its reply in conciliatory tones. Hearing Metternich's remark that "crowned heads could bear crime better than slander" also made him suggest an audience where Castlereagh reviewed tactfully, but at length, the recriminatory matter that would include connections starting with the king's clandestine marriage to Maria Fitzherbert in 1785. Significantly, Croker warned Bloomfield that clergy and gentry would side with Liverpool to create a formidable Tory opposition.[47] A cabinet minute on February 14 begged the king "not to impute to them an unreasonable prejudice in favor of their own opinions" while urging an arrangement to avoid public scandal. Brougham's earlier overture made them confident of securing one. George IV made what he called a great and painful sacrifice on February 17 in a reply emphasizing both the crown's dignity and his own personal honor and feelings.[48] It marked a complete surrender since the king's stipulation to Castlereagh the day before that an inquiry urged by the queen's advisors should lead to a divorce made the cabinet insist on exercising their own discretion.[49]

Resolving differences with George IV enabled Liverpool to raise continuing the queen's allowance under new terms with Brougham. He asked whether the principles in Brougham's overture last June might be the basis for an arrangement. Brougham replied that circumstances had changed "as the queen might be said now to be in *possession*" of her rights as consort. Proposing to give up what she now enjoyed differed greatly from conceding what then had not belonged to her. Liverpool noted the argument cut both ways since Caroline's income of £35,000 had ceased upon George III's death leaving her destitute without some new arrangement. Brougham admitted the point. Acquiescing in altering the liturgy to remove her name, he proposed meeting Caroline in France to discuss a settlement. A warning that he could not answer for her following his advice foreshadowed trouble ahead.[50]

Other matters intruded. Arthur Thistlewood, a Spencean who had been repeatedly jailed before, organized a plot to assassinate the cabinet during a dinner at Harrowby's on February 22. The attack was part of a larger plan to spark an uprising in London by afterwards displaying their heads on Westminster Bridge. Ministers had advance warning, but they were careful to conceal the knowledge to prevent compromising larger surveillance efforts. Indeed, Sidmouth took steps to bring the conspiracy to a head before it slipped beyond view.[51] Despite "an idea of going there to dinner and receiving their attack," Castlereagh told his brother "we thought it better to stay away from the festive board and not suffer it to go to single combat between Thistlewood and Marshall Liverpool."[52] Magistrates instead sprang a trap on the conspirators. Harrowby, who had sent his wife and daughters to safety, dined at Fife House with the Liverpools before other ministers arrived to await news. Louisa became hysterical and fainted when she learned the whole story.[53] A wave of horror ran through London society. Ministers knew that despite the conspirators' mishaps and the fact that their plot had been uncovered, they had contacts with London's radical underground and that provincial groups stood by for an uprising on news of their success. What seemed to be relative peace owed much to the way bitter cold kept people indoors. Radical agitation may have peaked the year before, but public order remained fragile enough to alarm ministers and keep troops on alert.[54]

News of the Cato Street Conspiracy broke just a few days after Liverpool determined on an early parliamentary election required by a new monarch's accession. Although the 1707 Act of Succession allowed parliament to remain in session for six months after the sovereign's demise, ministers gained nothing by delay. Business, especially financial estimates and the civil list, would face difficulty with the Commons focused on upcoming elections.[55] Tierney feared Thistlewood's plot might prejudice the public in the government's favor. Ministers cast it as a vindication of the Six Acts, but radicals, including Hunt who stood unsuccessfully for a seat to have a legal platform, demanded their repeal. Poll results largely indicated the same rough balance in 1818, but election violence even more boisterous than customary at the hustings showed unrest beyond parliament. Holland, who perceived a general indisposition to ministers and the court, doubted opposition would regain support lost in 1819. Instead, disaffection had raised a growing spirit "against the nature and practice of our government" that divided the upper and middling classes.[56] Liverpool saw "but two parties in the country: the church and king party and the radicals." Now "truly formidable," radicals presented a greater threat than the Whig opposition.[57]

Liverpool's assessment justified caution preparing estimates for the new parliament. A loss of support, particularly given tensions with George IV, might drive ministers from office and replace them with a weak government unable to check extra-parliamentary radicals. The civil list voted at the start of every reign to finance the crown risked obvious trouble. Liverpool determined to keep the amount at the reduced level set in 1816. When royal officials submitted estimates not less than £65,000 per annum beyond it, ministers held their ground. George IV accepted their decision after meeting with Sidmouth, but he later reopened the matter by demanded revisions to the speech opening parliament. Liverpool called a cabinet meeting upon an answer from the king "such as I think should lead to the dissolution of the government."[58] Colleagues, however, deemed talk of resigning premature. They backed Liverpool in a formal minute insisting the proposed income would fully "maintain the personal comfort, dignity, and splendor of the sovereign." George IV promptly accepted the original estimate with only a minor change to save face, though Eldon believed him disposed to part with the whole government. The king indeed complained to Sidmouth that the minute had been Liverpool's work signed by the cabinet as a matter of course.

Time now had come to determine whether ministers were his servants or those of Lord Liverpool. He drew back when Sidmouth replied that ministers were the king's servants, but would remain so only while they enjoyed his confidence.[59]

Attention to economy kept the opposition at bay when the parliamentary session opened on April 27. Support remained fragile as a narrow majority of twelve on a May 15 division over a motion involving the Scottish Court of Exchequer demonstrated. As the votes were tallied, Castlereagh begged those who had sided with ministers to stay as another division was expected that night.[60] The narrow margin showed difficulty in holding support or even securing regular attendance. While a Grenvillite described the want of attendance by government friends as "the *feature*" of the new parliament, the problem had been longstanding. Ministers lacked either the patronage that once purchased active support or the party discipline that later compelled it. Liverpool and Arbuthnot speculated about recruiting opposition figures, but the latter's wife thought they would do better to avoid mismanagement that needlessly antagonized country gentlemen.[61] Loyalism rooted in Church and king sentiment was a valuable reservoir of support in extremis, but did not help on financial questions. Huskisson noted "a soreness on every subject connected with expense, a clamor for economy" sharpened among yeoman farmers by the contrast between their wartime prosperity and present straitened circumstances. If that resentment found direction, ministers would need "to secure the affection & cordial good will of some great class in the state."[62]

Liverpool accordingly turned to merchants and manufacturers, many of whom shared his views on commercial reform. Following his father on the importance of trade, he increasingly looked to promote it by a laissez-faire approach rather than regulation. Expanding Britain's access to foreign markets, especially in the re-export trade which leveraged its global reach, benefitted trading companies and the shipping interest. It also enabled manufacturers to tap greater demand for their goods than home consumption alone could provide. Free trade provided an alternative political economy to the fiscal–military state and the old corruption which accompanied it.[63] While he certainly understood the critique of mercantilist policy that had developed since Adam Smith's *Wealth of Nations* appeared in 1776, practical experience and close observation guided him.[64] Abstraction never suited his temperament. Despite being well read in political economy and among the few politicians with the knowledge to apply it, Liverpool did not draw upon theory to offer a general intellectual analysis. His approach to feeling the way forward matched a tendency to act strategically rather than think or reason that way. It also reflected his awareness that many conservatives distrusted political economy on principle. Even Huskisson, recognized as a specialist on trade and finance, disliked being called a political economist as observers linked the term to Whigs and radicals.[65] Liverpool understood the need for a pragmatic approach grounded in experience that could avoid controversy.

Robinson had told the Commons in 1817 that he wished the country had never adopted a restrictive system and believed now that abandoning it would prove advantageous. Liverpool and his closest economic advisors quietly agreed. Robinson defended the government in May 1820 by arguing it had considerably relaxed commercial regulation and repealed duties on 300 articles over the past few years. [66] Liverpool never openly avowed the approach or pursued it systematically in the turmoil of postwar adjustment. Reform had been piecemeal and unobtrusive as many who accepted in principle the benefits of free trade still demanded exceptions for their own case. Despite growing talk of commercial reform, Liverpool realized he stood well ahead of opinion. Navigating the crosscurrents posed risks along with opportunities that called upon the prime minister's indirect approach of working through sympathetic individuals outside the government itself.[67]

Liverpool privately told London merchants led by Thomas Tooke that he entirely concurred in the principle expressed by their petition for a freer trade, but warned them not to expect immediate change given the vested interests tied to the existing system. Despite the qualification, Tooke read his words as an endorsement.[68] Alexander Baring, a financier and Whig MP, presented the petition to a very full House of Commons on May 8 with much support. Robinson backed the principle of free trade while pointing out the difficulties in transforming the commercial system. Ministers, he insisted, had already worked towards freeing trade. David Ricardo's call for a gradual end to the restrictive system along the lines of the phased resumption of cash payments helped deflect Baring's motion.[69] Other petitions from Glasgow and Manchester soon followed. Liverpool gave his own view in a speech published later as a pamphlet where he acknowledged "the great advantage resulting from unrestricted freedom of trade." Although Britain had risen to greatness under a different system, its rise came in spite of and not as a result of protection. Emphasizing the difficulty of modifying a complicated regulatory system allowed Liverpool to endorse free trade in principle without taking specific action. He argued that the fewer laws on commerce the better and denounced "a meddlesome disposition" among legislators that left the terms of trade uncertain year to year from constant change.[70]

Outside agitation helped Liverpool turn debate toward the liberalizing policy he preferred. Endorsing free trade took momentum from critics and kept Whigs from using the issue against ministers. Support for the principle combined with a pragmatic approach to its application won backing from free traders without antagonizing the more cautious. A Lords committee on foreign trade called trade restrictions an evil only justifiable by some great political expediency. Unless that point was clear, the restrictions ought to be removed. The report pointed to rationalizing commercial regulation and even gradually relaxing the Navigation Acts. Free trade now seemed a practical goal rather than a theoretical proposition with an important shift that became more apparent over the next few years.[71] Working through a parliamentary committee muted opposition and helped Liverpool draw backing beyond government supporters. He had adapted an important part of Pitt's early program with greater success. The debate over free trade enabled him to engage public opinion while not appearing subservient to it. Cultivating the impression of a concerned and diligent administration worked to counter the unpopularity the cabinet viewed with increasing alarm. Reforms Liverpool began showed that the existing political system could adapt while strengthening Britain as a great entrepôt for trade to bolster the whole economy.[72]

Queen Caroline's arrival on June 5 unleashed a crisis that quickly dominated the public scene. Liverpool had assumed she would prefer comfortable exile to public scandal and that Brougham could bring her to accept a settlement. While Brougham spent March electioneering in Westmorland, Caroline grew angry at slights during a sojourn in Rome. The refusal of foreign authorities and British diplomats to recognize her as queen enraged her. She took exclusion from the liturgy – "as if she was no longer for this world" – as an affront that betrayed Castlereagh's public assurances she would be treated with every consideration and no harshness.[73] Matthew Wood, a radical London alderman newly elected to parliament, had joined, if not supplanted, Brougham in her circle. He played to her resentments with hopes she would provide a rallying point for popular opposition to the government. William Cobbett's daughter Anne shrewdly observed in February the beginnings of a queen's party as her situation drew public comment.[74]

Emergence of a party around the queen marked an ominous sign. The cultural weight of royalism legitimized agitation and gave it subversive power. Thomas Hodgskin, a young associate of the London radical Francis Place, noted "something poetical and chivalrous and at the same time loyal in contending for a Queen and woman." Agitation for her politicized the hitherto apathetic. Moral questions raised by Caroline's appeal as a scorned queen reinforced standing charges of corruption against the overall political system.[75] The queen's case also had implications for parliamentary politics. Opposition politicians had often treated an heir to the throne who quarreled with his father as a path for their ambitions. Frederick, Prince of Wales and George IV, and, to a lesser degree, Princess Charlotte had shown the pattern at work. Caroline threatened to join established ways of exploiting divisions within the royal family with a new round of popular agitation and extend the conflict beyond the metropolitan political elite. Insiders knew enough to see fault on both sides, but the wider public read her plight as a woman scorned by a debauched husband. The danger recent experience had shown explains Liverpool's eagerness to stop the crisis before it began.

By April, Canning wondered if Brougham might have decided he had a better game fighting the queen's battle than helping ministers keep the peace.[76] Brougham seemed to be playing a complex game for his own advancement with an object less clear than the risks. Grey likened his conduct to Sheridan's earlier intrigues, as he thought a compromise would discredit all those involved while leaving the sense Brougham had betrayed his client. Indeed, Croker noted talk that he had "sold the queen." Caroline herself seemed increasingly suspicious.[77] But Liverpool had no alternative to working through Brougham. He raised the stakes on April 15 by pointing out that the queen's arrival in England would make a proceeding against her in parliament unavoidable. Liverpool also noted that a lawsuit involving the alleged forgery of the Duke of Brunswick's name could hurt Caroline's public standing. His warnings were a stick to accompany the carrot of £50,000 a year on condition of not coming into any British dominions and taking a title other than queen.[78] Hutchinson, who joined the discussions at the king's suggestion, had been alarmed since late March by the influence of her other advisors and thought Brougham had been subjected to a chain of events nobody could control.[79] Delays ran into May. Liverpool pressed Brougham to meet Caroline at Geneva as agreed. Caroline then forced the matter by requesting ministers to provide conveyance to England and calling Brougham to meet her in France at St Omer near Calais.

When Brougham and Hutchinson arrived they found Caroline determined to continue her journey. Although Brougham warned of the consequences and urged a settlement, he dared not, he told Liverpool, hint at renouncing her title. Doing so would have only made her depart immediately for England.[80] He instead brought Hutchinson forward in an abortive effort to open negotiations that won a slight delay. The attempt, hampered by not having the April 15 memorandum with the exact wording, drew a short refusal. Hutchinson finally concluded Brougham had deceived himself and everyone else about his influence over the queen.[81] Brougham admitted to Liverpool he had not advised her to accept, but rather to offer her own terms for staying abroad while being recognized as queen. He insisted that he always sought to avoid "discussions unnecessary in themselves & hurtful to the country." Public duty could not have carried him further, considering what he owed his client. Despite these equivocations, Brougham warned Caroline against advisors "who will be found very feeble allies in the time of difficulty" and urged she "proceed in the most private & even secret manner possible." While it might be very well for a candidate at an election to be drawn through town by the populace, such exhibitions risked the queen's dignity.[82] As Caroline landed with Wood at Dover on June 5 to a cheering crowd, Brougham still hoped to cut a deal his client would accept.

Liverpool's warning left no choice besides laying the question before parliament. The cabinet agreed to present evidence of the queen's misconduct abroad to secret committees of both houses in the notorious green bag. Precedent, as far as it could avail, guided them, but Liverpool admitted no precedent bore directly upon the present case. Leaving the committee "to point out whether any and what proceeding is fit to be adopted" bought further time.[83] Castlereagh faced more resistance in the Commons, where his announcement drew immediate

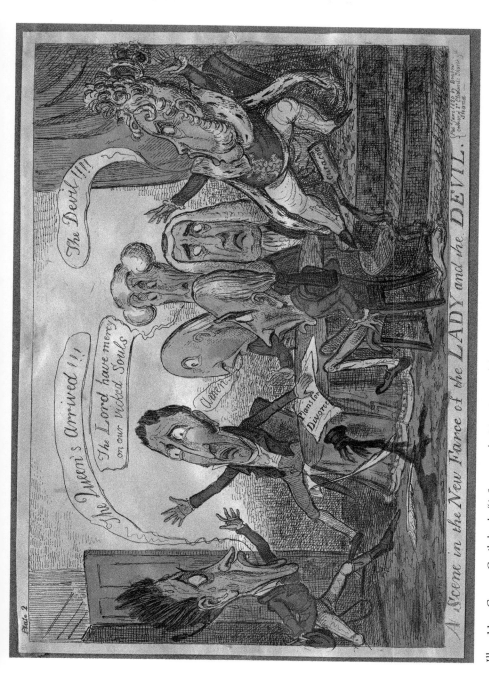

Illus. 11. George Cruikshank, "A Scene in the New Farce of the Lady and the Devil." Queen Caroline's arrival detonated a long-feared crisis that made 1820 the hardest year of Liverpool's career

comment even before he moved for an inquiry. Brougham presented a message from the queen on June 7 stating the measures pursued against her abroad by secret agents had compelled her to defend her character and just rights against the prospect of a secret tribunal.[84] Castlereagh denied that the cabinet approached the case "with a tone or persecution or prosecution," but he did not win support for a secret committee. Brougham instead urged a private arrangement to spare the country as "prevention was better than cure." Wilberforce's motion for a week's adjournment passed without a division.[85]

A new round of exchanges began. Caroline, having now seen the April 15 memorandum, deemed it inconsistent with her dignity and honor. Acquitting its authors of intending offense, she declared herself open to an arrangement that recognized her rank and privileges as queen. Other differences could be adjusted on that basis.[86] Liverpool replied that calling upon her to refrain from exercising certain rights and privileges did not mean she renounce them: whatever appertained to her by law continued unless parliament abrogated it. Ready to hear Caroline's suggestions, he made residence abroad an absolute condition. She then told Brougham to state that, as the government admits her recognition as queen, "persons of high station & character" could settle particulars subject to parliamentary approval. Liverpool cautiously noted that ministers could not advise the king to arbitrate a matter involving the crown's dignity and honor plus other public interests. But sensible of the advantages in an unreserved personal discussion, they would advise the king to appoint two of their number to join the queen's representatives to frame an arrangement.[87] Caroline looked first to Lord Fitzwilliam and the Earl of Sefton, but the former declined unless she were first restored to the liturgy. Instead, she named Brougham and Thomas Denman, her legal counsel, to confer with Wellington and Castlereagh. Talks broke down when Caroline insisted her name be restored to the liturgy as a sine qua non.[88]

Other trouble arose with the king over Canning, who had opposed any punitive measure toward the queen. Although Canning entirely concurred in the cabinet's decision to present evidence before parliament, his friendly relations with a woman who had stood godmother to his eldest son made him unwilling to take a strong part against her even as he wished to avoid disappointing colleagues. Liverpool persuaded him to withdraw his proffered resignation as it would embarrass the government. Canning seconded Castlereagh in the June 7 debate on a committee of inquiry, but joined his able defense of the government with flattering remarks about the queen that the opposition cheered.[89] George IV took offense and demanded an explanation from Liverpool who called the speech "honorable to himself and substantially useful to your majesty and your government." Refusing to convey what amounted to a censure, Liverpool stated that his own resignation would follow Canning's. After some uproar, including a renewed offer to resign that the king himself declined, Canning settled matters for the moment with a personal apology.[90]

Speculation Canning had been among Caroline's lovers explained the king's personal animosity, but the larger question involved George IV's relationship with Liverpool. His insistence Liverpool not compromise honor for political expediency reflected a deeper anger. Sidmouth peremptorily declined an offer from the king to lead a government and insisted on the need to retain Liverpool.[91] George IV also approached the Whigs through Leach, Hutchinson, and Lord Donoughmore. If Grey, Holland, and Grenville were willing to take office, Donoughmore told Lansdowne, the king "was prepared to dismiss his present administration instantly." No conditions would bind the new ministry. Tierney reported a similar overture, adding that George IV no longer felt personal hostility toward Grey. George IV sounded Wellesley himself. Whig leaders saw the difficulty of forming a government that could hold majorities in the Commons, while Grey had warned earlier against "incurring all the ridicule of disappointed hopes."[92] Nothing came of the overtures, which still highlighted the threat George IV's anger posed.

Popular responses amplified by the press brought dangers of their own. Cheering crowds that greeted Caroline in London soon turned violent, demanding the illumination of houses and breaking windows of dwellings that did not comply. By likening her arrival to the landings of William the Conqueror, Henry VII, and William of Orange, albeit armed with only native courage and "conscious innocence," *The Times* posed an implicit challenge three nights of rioting underlined. Even if, as Eldon suggested, few among the middling or upper classes sided with Caroline besides the profligate and those "endeavoring to acquire power through mischief," they were material enough for a queen's party, especially if plebeian radicals used her as a figurehead or the Whig opposition played for office.[93] Sir Thomas Lawrence, who thought Caroline aimed at revolution, feared "what strumpet audacity may be able to do supported by a headstrong mob."[94] Others likened her to Catherine II of Russia or the Duke of Orleans who had undermined Louis XVI as France slipped into revolution.

Exaggerated as such parallels seemed, they showed growing unease. Discipline among guards regiments in London faltered as soldiers protested against extra duty keeping order. Liverpool sent Wellington a report in late June that agitators in public houses zealously preached the Spanish army's example of aiding a coup against their king. The Foxite *Morning Chronicle* praised a revolution in Naples for "being achieved by the *soldiery*, since *whenever* they raise their voice it is *imperative*," while the *Leeds Mercury* lauded its goal of a representative constitution. Events made 1820 seem a year of revolution, particularly since the heir to the French throne had been assassinated in January, while handbills by the radical printer William Benbow reached to a wider plebeian audience beyond newspaper readers.[95] Although the army had been reliable during unrest in 1816 and 1819, even guards regiments now defiantly toasted the queen's health. Disaffection among soldiers liable to be influenced by popular sentiment unless kept disciplined and apart from civilians threatened to remove a brake on the mob. As one wit quipped, the extinguisher seemed to have caught fire.[96] Not surprisingly, parliament wanted the controversy ended without an inquiry.

Talks broke down, however, as Brougham and Denman insisted that ministers dispel inferences arising from Caroline's self-imposed exile by restoring her to the liturgy or officially introducing her as queen to foreign courts. Either step required Liverpool and the cabinet to repudiate all their previous actions in the case. Such a reversal would impugn their personal character and public judgment. A queen determined on vindication, a king seeking condemnation, and a government committed to upholding its own consistency left scant room for compromise. Wilberforce, quietly encouraged by cabinet and backbenchers, tried to break the deadlock with a resolution urging Caroline to accept terms. Ministers indicated they would resign if parliament censured their refusal to disavow past actions. An amendment to restore Caroline to the liturgy failed, but the motion itself passed by 391 to 124.[97] Wilberforce led a delegation to present the resolution two days later. Caroline rejected it disdainfully through a reply Brougham read. Her supporters jeered the delegation, mocking the evangelical Wilberforce as "Dr. Cantwell." Caroline's decision left no choice beyond proceeding, but Liverpool seemed quietly confident.[98]

The queen's case now became a party issue, though some government supporters opposed proceedings against her on moral grounds for publicizing adultery. Whigs argued for restoring her to the liturgy, even though Castlereagh had described her exclusion "as that species of neutral measure which could not be considered a stigma." Grey seized upon the resolution's wording to give notice of a motion to drop further inquiry.[99] Before the motion came to a debate, Caroline brought a petition protesting any secret inquiry and sought time for her counsel to prepare a defense. Speaking further on the petition, Brougham challenged evidence gathered without the queen's knowledge or representation to warn against a one-sided judgment.[100] Liverpool thought it his duty to secure time for considering the arguments, but he remained convinced that their original course remained the best. Grey then gave what an observer called "a speech for office" against the inquiry that sharply criticized Liverpool's conduct.[101] Liverpool called Grey's remarks one of the most inflammatory party attacks ever made in parliament. He replied in measured but firm tones that ministers had done all they could to avoid public scandal and warned that not proceeding could produce an even greater evil. While a legislative process in the Lords offered the best course, an inquiry first had to determine the grounds for action. Given the delicate matters involved, Liverpool insisted a secret committee would limit the risk that publicity might prejudice the case. Above all, he refused to be swayed by "clamor of the factious and discontented out of doors."[102]

Clamor grew, however. Unrest in the capital persisted even though ministers now believed troops loyal. Liverpool privately remarked that if George IV would not try to conciliate the public by showing himself it might be advisable he depart for Hanover until the storm passed. The country soon would be tranquil with the Duke of York as regent.[103] As the secret committee reviewed evidence, the cabinet determined to move a bill of pains and penalties depriving Caroline of her rights and privileges as queen and dissolving the marriage. The measure declared the offense and imposed punishment in a single act. Although procedures allowed evidence and counsel to be heard, along with cross examination in a quasi-judicial form, it was a legislative step where expediency carried weight. Political management to secure votes counted as much as legal skill. Passage required three readings in each house and royal assent. Having at first opposed the divorce clause, mainly to avoid being drawn into recrimination or religious arguments, Liverpool, Eldon, and Castlereagh included it as a logical consequence of the queen's degradation. Canning opposed the divorce, and his general discomfort brought a renewed offer to resign. The king, at Liverpool's insistence, again declined. Colleagues accepted his abstention and Canning went abroad to distance himself further from proceedings.[104]

Liverpool offered the bill on July 5, a day after Harrowby presented the secret committee's report. What became known as Queen Caroline's trial began on August 17 when he moved the second reading. Eldon presided as Lord Chancellor. The Solicitor General Sir John Copley and Attorney General Sir Robert Giffard presented the government's evidence, while Liverpool, with Harrowby seconding him, spoke for it in debate. A cordon of troops and a warship in the Thames guarded parliament where a new gallery was built to accommodate spectators in the Lords. Of more than 340 peers required to attend on pain of fine without a reasonable excuse, 256 appeared. They were more than twice the number usually drawn to major debates. Liverpool faced a serious difficulty calculating how many of them would act.[105] Rightly, he anticipated Whigs giving trouble on collateral points since they could not alter the course of proceedings; he aimed to avoid trouble until evidence had its effect on both the Lords and public opinion. The damage to Caroline's reputation gave ministers little solace. Reports only increased popular dismay.[106] Many peers who normally sided with ministers blamed them for the crisis, while others opposed the trial as an affront to public morality.[107] Brougham's aggressive cross-examination, which made *non mi ricordo* (I don't recall) a catchphrase, justified Liverpool's concerns over how the public would treat evidence from the Milan Commission. The whole proceeding tended to discredit established institutions, especially when set in a familiar narrative of elite corruption and self-interest. Demonstrating Caroline's adultery did not even begin to address that line of criticism.[108]

Tension, along with his worries about Louisa's health, fed Liverpool's nervous irritability despite his public calm. Eldon's joke about the fashion for nightly, even hourly cabinets in June soured as the cabinet met daily to review proceedings. Ministers approached the trial as a military campaign. Each day was a battle with victory or setback that guided their next move. Never in his life, Liverpool told Canning in September, had he undergone such continued fatigue.[109] Matters worsened as pressure grew from both parliamentary opposition in the Lords and popular agitation in the streets. The strain took an increasing toll on Liverpool. Sensing resistance from both houses, he sought on his own discretion for the king to abandon the divorce clause. He had declared it earlier a point subordinate to the queen's degradation. Besides foreclosing recriminatory evidence, the concession would mark the bill as act of state rather than George IV's private application for relief. The king conceded the point regretfully, but he again insisted Liverpool not yield his honor to political expediency.[110] Animosity between them simmered.

Although Liverpool thought the evidence of guilt conclusive – Harriet Arbuthnot tartly remarked that Whig ladies might believe themselves very secure against divorce if their husbands did not "consider the disgusting details they have heard *proof*" – those deciding the case still had to overcome public sentiment and their own repugnance at an affair in which respectable opinion deemed both parties to blame.[111] Admitting that peers had to judge the expediency of passing the bill along with the queen's guilt or innocence, Liverpool insisted that having heard the evidence they stood bound to pronounce an opinion. At several points over two days, he argued that evidence proved adultery. Denying it made past court rulings and votes by the Lords themselves in divorce cases with the same level of proof "a code of the *greatest cruelty, oppression* and *injustice*." Rejecting the bill now simply on prudential grounds thus would be "a triumph of guilt."[112] It would also repudiate the government in a way Liverpool privately thought grounds for resigning. Besides Eldon and briefly Harrowby, no other ministers spoke to the question. Grenville declared that evidence proved adultery. He defined the immediate question as whether to pronounce judgment or leave the matter unsettled. While refusing to convict or acquit on the second reading would be unjust to the queen and unsettling to public affairs, Grenville left open the expediency of actually passing the bill. He privately urged Liverpool to withdraw it. Harrowby suggested the same course after the second reading passed with a slim majority on November 6. Indeed, Liverpool had proposed declaring his willingness to let the bill drop after the second reading, but the cabinet demurred before the vote.[113]

Grey shrewdly insisted upon retaining the divorce clause. Omitting the provision would degrade the king as well as the queen if the bill passed as divorce could not be honorably separated from degradation.[114] Including it, however, made the bill all the more objectionable to many peers and the wider public. Losing the vote by 67 on November 9 showed the government's weakness. Castlereagh already dreaded managing the bill in the Commons. The cabinet struggled over the next step. George IV, who cared nothing for their public stranding, now wanted the proceeding ended to spare himself further pain. Wellington feared that dropping it abruptly would expose ministers "as but a set of tricksters." Liverpool contemplated proceeding if the bill had a large majority as responsibility then would lie with the Commons. Strain showed behind the scenes. Liverpool broke down in the cabinet with a violent outburst at Eldon that ended in tears. It showed how fragile his temper had become. The next day he apologized in a note complimenting Eldon's intervention in the debate.[115] When the third reading passed by nine votes, Liverpool closed further debate by declaring the state of the country, and the narrow balance in the Lords determined him to proceed no further. Grey angrily charged ministers with betraying their king, insulting their queen, and shocking the morals of society with detestable and disgusting evidence. Liverpool's motion passed without a division.[116]

George IV greeted the news with dismay, complaining to Sidmouth that the crisis had so shattered his body and spirit that he could barely cope. Castlereagh archly remarked that the king now knew "what it is to contend with a desperate and malignant woman in a country full of treason and a licentious press, and in every stage of which questions spring up that shake not only the administration, but the throne itself to its foundation." Arbuthnot called George IV "wild" to have parliament meet on November 23 to settle Caroline's pension at once and thereby close matters even though his ministers thought it insanity given the present fervor.[117] The king asked whether radicals would not "work double tides to keep treason and tumult afloat" if he prorogued parliament until January as ministers requested. After pressure from Eldon and Sidmouth, he conceded, but without making the customary speech to close the session. It ended instead with an absurd scene as the Speaker brusquely adjourned the Commons amidst an uproar as Brougham tried unsuccessfully to bring forward a petition from the queen that would have opened a new debate.[118]

Delay allowed popular agitation to consume itself on what fuel remained after Liverpool ended the proceedings. A majority on the third reading, however slight, vindicated ministers enough. They had proven their mettle by persisting against fierce opposition and withdrawing the bill only as a prudential measure. Liverpool bolstered his reputation for evenhandedness even as he closed proceedings in a way that denied the opposition leverage to press further.[119] Once he recovered his equilibrium with a break at Walmer Castle, he put upcoming discussion on favorable ground by outlining his plans before parliament met. No further steps would be taken against Caroline and she would receive without condition a just and reasonable provision. Liverpool, however, insisted on excluding her from the liturgy. Besides implicitly censuring ministers, a resolution adding her name to the prayers would effectively whitewash Caroline. It could only be ascribed to a fear of popular agitation that would increase public danger. "If parliament should determine upon it," Liverpool warned Wilberforce, "the country must dispense with my humble services." He preferred retiring than sanctioning a step he believed would "give a deadly blow to the moral character of the nation." It would "be felt after the present heats are over to the latest posterity as an eternal disgrace to all who have participated in it."[120] Stressing moral concerns and the danger to public order he reached out to the government's supporters and independent gentlemen who had objected to its policy toward the queen. Liverpool quietly challenged parliament either to back his administration or replace it.

A January satire cast the forlorn Liverpool as the biblical figure Ahithophel who hanged himself after Absalom's rejection of his counsel doomed a revolt against King David.[121] But rather than defeat, ministers won successive majorities in the Commons on questions relating to the queen. Once Castlereagh declared the queen's case ended – thereby declining any opening for ministers to justify their conduct in it – blame for prolonging unpopular discussion fell upon the Whigs. Country gentlemen distrusted them for making the case a party question, urging on the radicals who stirred commotion, and dragging the country onto a rack of popular commotion. Lord Tavistock's motion to censure the government's conduct failed by 146 votes on February 6. A motion for restoring Caroline to the liturgy won only 178 with 298 backing the ministry.[122] Even before then the Duke of Bedford assumed his fellow Whigs would not trouble "gentlemen who had six year leases to run" – the time before the next parliamentary elections – but rather let the matter make its own way out of doors. Queen fever, as Croker called it, began fading in early 1821. The result made the Whig Thomas Wishaw ruefully observe "that we live in a *Tory country*" where "the great majority of well-informed and respectable people whose sentiments ought to have weight in politics think very differently from ourselves." It also bolstered Liverpool's insistence "that all the thinking part of the country approved of the system on which the government was conducted" and saw any departure as leading to inevitable ruin.[123]

Agitation over the course of 1820 promoted a loyalist backlash in the country that government friends in the press encouraged. The shift contrasted with relative apathy in 1819 when attempts at forming civic associations to defend property or organize local declarations against radicals drew scant interest.[124] Just as radical activity in the 1790s fueled the loyalism that overwhelmed it, popular mobilization behind Caroline stirred meetings and addresses as controversy spilled into the provinces from London. Events belied Sidmouth's fear that "should the loyal remain inactive, they will be borne down by the disaffected" as government supports rallied early in 1821.[125] Tory newspapers, particularly the scurrilous *John Bull* published with Croker's help from late December, spread the case against Caroline and her political allies. Brougham later noted how gossip about Whig politicians and their ladies that *John Bull* spread with relish alarmed them enough to affect votes in parliament. Harriet Arbuthnot thought it did more than anything else towards putting down the queen.[126] As sentiment turned, Whigs and radicals saw their support dwindle. The loyalist rally drove home the consequence of their parliamentary defeat.

Illus. 12.   George Cruikshank, "And when Ahithophel saw that his Councel [sic] was not followed, he saddled his Ass, & arose, & went & hanged himself &c." Despite reinforcing his melancholy and careworn image, Queen Caroline's trial helped Liverpool's own standing. Withdrawing the bill of pains and penalties was less a defeat than it seemed at first.

The dangerous combination of parliamentary opposition and popular agitation that had kept ministers on the defensive since 1816 peaked in Queen Caroline's trial. Liverpool's management of the crisis confirmed his reputation for fairness and integrity. Francis Burton thought his conduct – "becoming a judge as well as a statesman" – had raised the premier's standing and "extorted compliments from the chief of his opponents." Lord Dacre remarked that he could always be trusted, saying that if Liverpool rose to reply in a debate "you may go out and leave your words in his hands and he will never misrepresent you."[127] The whole drama also showed that ministers could not check the robust expression of public sentiment. Richard Rush, the American minister in London, remarked on "the boundless rage of the press and liberty of speech" with fiery libels with caricatures hawked in all the streets. William Hone and others adapted traditions of elite ridicule for a much wider popular audience that amplified their effect. Laughter challenged authority more effectively than either reasoned debate or violent protest.[128] Sustained mockery certainly fueled crowd action in London and the provinces during the Caroline affair. Creevey pointed out at the height of the trial "the scene which caused such alarm at Manchester is repeated under the very nose of parliament and all the constituted authorities, and in a tenfold degree more alarming."[129] London had not seen disturbances on this scale since the 1780 Gordon Riots that had paralyzed the city.[130]

Repression could not check protest. Unprecedented deployments to keep peace during the trial had increased the garrison at the Tower of London to a full battalion and placed cavalry at five locations around the capital to handle unrest. Moving detachments to barracks outside where they could provide reinforcement at short notice reduced troops in Northern England by a fifth.[131] Even that had not secured the streets. Ministers had to avoid escalating an already dangerous situation by combining behind the scenes policing with an impassive public stance. Exercising the powers Wellington believed the Six Acts provided to punish libels and unauthorized meetings risked embarrassment. Insurgents never commanded majority support, but ministers at times feared the same was also true of the government and worried that whichever side looked like winning a confrontation might prevail.[132] They therefore faced agitation with calm resolve while trying quietly to peel away the popular support that sustained it. Liverpool displayed courage in persisting despite perils some thought verged on revolution, but he then with characteristic prudence gave up the case after justifying his actions. While his concession drained momentum behind opposition, it did not recapture the political initiative. Croker's warning during the Queen Caroline affair that "the ship that has weathered the gale will founder in the swell which follows it" captured the danger.[133]

The king's hostility became Liverpool's main problem in 1821. George IV had nearly dismissed the cabinet in November, but finally kept back the note telling Liverpool he wished to form a new administration.[134] Although Grey deemed

Illus. 13. George Cruikshank, "The Royal Extinguisher, or the King of Brobdingnag & the Lilliputians." As sentiment turned against Whigs and radicals who had supported Caroline, agitation faded and Liverpool's administration gained an increasingly stronger position.

it "quite impossible" he and his ministers would separate "however much they loathe one another," the king thought otherwise and criticized the opposition for not seizing the chance he gave them. Grenville refused a direct invitation to form a government during a five-hour audience on November 25. The meeting outraged Liverpool even though he remained unaware of the actual offer. Arbuthnot complained of the king "breaking down the strength of his government" by consulting men of great political consequence outside it.[135] Canning's resignation in December weakened the government at a critical time. According to Arbuthnot, Liverpool angrily described the step as "of a piece with all his former conduct." Canning had "no moral principle in public life" and looked only to himself.[136] Peel declined an offer to join the cabinet. Both men had friends more eager than they to press their claims, which raised the prospect of factional crossfire from Canning, Peel, and the Grenville connection while the king undermined Liverpool.[137]

Firm support from colleagues who doubted they could go on without him was a vital advantage. The government still needed debating talent in the Commons. Liverpool's efforts to solve that longstanding problem while draining the venom from faction by co-opting its leaders brought other problems. Londonderry, as Castlereagh became on succeeding to his father's Irish marquisate, thought moving Peel to the exchequer in Vansittart's place would diminish his own standing in the Commons. Interestingly, he now saw Canning as no threat.[138] Peel declined an offer of the India Board and withheld comment on any other post without a direct offer. More seriously, the king refused to accept Canning's return. Liverpool contemplated resigning over Canning's exclusion. His colleagues reluctantly determined not to break up the government, especially if the king framed his objection as a matter of timing. It was the sole point of difference. Liverpool agreed not to force an immediate confrontation. Refusing, however, to concede the principle of allowing the king to exclude a man permanently on personal grounds, he insisted appointments be made solely upon public grounds. George IV's pique toward the man he believed had cuckolded him would not deter Liverpool.[139]

Louisa's death on June 11 left Liverpool nearly prostrate with grief. A letter from the king shortly before she died drove him into a paroxysm of rage tearing apart the note and shouting he would resign.[140] Louisa had been the center of his emotional world. Outside politics, she was his life. They were rarely apart for more than brief periods, which made their final separation all the more painful. She reportedly had instructed that nobody else touch her body. The ailing widower nearly fainted lifting her into a coffin. Blinded by tears through the funeral service in the family church at Hawkesbury, Liverpool seemed oblivious to all else. He only returned to London on June 26 after staying at Coombe Wood to recuperate. Never had Arbuthnot seen a man so affected by loss.[141] Strain had already brought uncharacteristic talk of retirement amidst nervous outbursts. Sidmouth,

Harrowby, and even Londonderry had spoken during stressful times of retiring, but Liverpool was harder to replace. Nobody in the Lords could match either his authority or capacity in debate. Londonderry, the logical successor as premier, could not expect the same backing from the Church or among loyalist English Tories. In February, Wellington revealingly thought keeping Liverpool as leader in the Lords with Londonderry prime minister and Canning foreign secretary the best option.[142] Despite his talk, Liverpool drew back. Bereavement made the occupation public life gave him all the more vital, while retirement would pull out the keystone upholding whole the political edifice.

Sidmouth and Castlereagh warned the king in April that he could not dismiss Liverpool without breaking up the whole administration. Wellington asked him brusquely in July after hearing further complaints "if you do not like us, why do you not turn us out?" The king sat grinding his teeth in silence. Only the lack of a viable alternative kept him from acting. Liverpool discerned an effort "not to destroy the government at present, but to have the means of destroying it whenever the opportunity may be more convenient." The king's disdain coupled with the premier's resentment and prickliness heightened friction. George IV denied wishing to replace the administration, but still described Liverpool as a "captious, jealous, & impractical" minister "who objects to everything & even when he gives way, which is nine times in ten, he does it with so bad a grace that it is worse than an absolute refusal." A remark during his successful visit to Ireland in late August querying the legality of staying there and sending a Lord Lieutenant to England in his place showed more of the king's feelings than he intended.[143]

Liverpool contemplated bringing the king "to some distinct explanation" before his journey to Hanover, but the trial of will between them continued until he returned. The trip calmed feelings on both sides.[144] Londonderry, with Metternich's aid, brokered a reconciliation that came to fruition in November. Liverpool accepted household appointments the king had sought and endorsed sending Canning to India as governor general. The king deemed reconciliation with Liverpool the happiest day of his life, a response Harriet Arbuthnot likened to a child being granted a new plaything. Londonderry saw advantage in the outcome "for the king will learn that it is not so easy to dismiss a minister and the prime minister will learn that it must be remembered above all things that the king is master."[145] The former lesson, however, stood out more strongly. Unable to sack Liverpool without putting himself in the hands of Whigs likely to demand unpalatable changes in foreign policy and on the Catholic Question, the king had little choice beyond granting his confidence. Even at the height of his anger in late November, George IV had seen the dilemma and the result strengthened Liverpool's hand in their relationship. Noting the striking levity with which ministers had come to treat the king – that, regardless of his own failings, heightened the monarch's pique toward them – Croker thought "no reformers, if they knew the whole secret, would wish to reduce the monarch lower in real & effective state & power than his ministers place him."[146]

Mending the quarrel enabled Liverpool to proceed with the changes strengthening the government in the Commons. Appointments, he told one of the Grenville connection, would be grounded on that point alone.[147] Peel took the Home Office, replacing Sidmouth who had sought to retire since April but agreed to remain in the cabinet without office. Wellesley accepted the Irish Lord Lieutenancy with Peel's friend Henry Goulburn as chief secretary. The pairing balanced Wellesley's support for Catholic relief with Goulburn's opposition while making Ireland's government more effective against disorder that had loomed there in 1820. Charles Williams Wynne, the Grenville spokesman in the Commons, joined the cabinet as president of the India Board – the office Canning earlier had vacated – while the faction's leader received a promotion in the peerage as Duke of Buckingham and Chandos. William Plunket, a Grenville ally, became Irish attorney general with the understanding he would support ministers in Commons debates. Since Grenville had declined an overture two years earlier and passed the effective lead to his nephew Buckingham, Liverpool gained the Grenville connection without the elder statesmen himself. Wynne stipulated that office would not preclude him from countenancing, promoting, or even originating any measure of Catholic relief. The balance within the government on the question raised concerns as Grenville thought Sidmouth, Peel, and Goulburn on the Protestant side checked any weight Wellesley's appointment carried. Liverpool acquiesced at Londonderry's urging.[148]

While the appointments did less than Liverpool hoped for the government's debating strength in the 1822 session, they ended the prospect of factional crossfire. Broadening the administration's parliamentary basis helped reunite the old party that Pitt had led even if Canning remained excluded and Grenville kept personally aloof. Men separated by the schism of 1801 had joined with Liverpool as Pitt's acknowledged heir. Besides drawing Grenvillites' from the Whigs, their support diminished the middle ground between government and opposition from which an administration could be built.[149] Liverpool increased his hold over George IV when a Whig government including Brougham, whom the king truly hated after his defense of Caroline, and backed by radicals was the only alternative. The same point applied to country gentlemen and others in parliament who generally supported ministers while reserving the privilege of attacking them on particular questions, notably finance. Now they could only push the government so far without risking a greater change than they could accept. Popular agitation faded too once Caroline, who died on August 7, no longer provided a focus for discontent.

The political temperature receded from the fever of 1820 when the storm brewing since before Waterloo finally broke. Weathering it tested Liverpool's capacity, along with his nerve. The government lost control over events at several points, but Liverpool kept sufficient authority to avoid opening a political vacuum others might have filled. Despite private anxiety and outbursts in the cabinet, his public performance remained impressive throughout the crisis. Having faced down Caroline, violent protests by the London mob, and parliamentary opposition, he overcome George IV's antagonism to mend relations at court and strengthen his administration. Autumn 1821, like the months following Waterloo, had a touch of anti-climax. Liverpool's success in gathering the political factions aligned with Pitt before 1801 marked an overlooked coda to the drama that provided a chance to move beyond reacting to events and instead pursue an agenda on the government's own terms.

CHAPTER 9

Reform and Stabilization

A S TENSIONS GREW in early 1820, Peel reflected whether the public had become more liberal than Liverpool's government could accommodate. Never more influential, public opinion seemed more than ever dissatisfied with the power it now held. Sustained discontent, Peel feared, might force a choice between sweeping concessions on essential points or handing Whigs and Radicals power.[1] Liverpool, however, crafted an approach that defused pressure for political reform and reduced the popular discontent that gave it force. What historians later called liberal Toryism sought to promote economic growth and raise living standards while separating particular reforms from restructuring the entire political system.[2] Showing ministers could govern in the public interest under the existing constitution gave them the political initiative while denying critics leverage. Measures worked to stabilize political authority and contain pressures on existing boundaries of inclusion and exclusion, a central challenge of the period with the revival of a mass politics linked only tenuously with the political elite.[3] Liberal Toryism ensured reforms would come on terms that kept the essential fabric intact. Moving beyond the defensive management that had weathered the past five years, Liverpool took advantage of the shifting tide to pursue commercial reform within an agenda that consciously aimed to secure the constitutional order.

Defending obvious abuses and failings with a high hand, Liverpool realized, only invited opposition. Correcting them without conceding faults in the system as a whole avoided the trap Peel identified. It bolstered a case against wider reform. Liberalism as it later became understood differed from the liberal reforms Liverpool used to preempt it. The term liberal, which Peel considered "an odious but intelligible phrase," only acquired political meaning from the later 1810s, partly in the context of resistance to established authority in Spain.[4] Seeing Liverpool's policies from the perspective of developments after 1832 distorts their intent as he sought to deflect the kind of sweeping changes that followed his resignation in 1827. Instead of breaking with earlier policy, liberal Toryism brought a more active and systemic approach to a line Liverpool had pursued as circumstances allowed. His efforts to promote trade adapted a much older emphasis on securing market share to post-1815 realities. Liverpool drew upon long practical experience and wide reading from his early years. Reductions in expenditure and the size of government weakened charges of elite parasitism, while aiding private enterprise as the infrastructure developed to finance war came instead to serve commerce and manufacturing.[5] Plaudits from merchants strengthened the government's political hand, both against critics and restive supporters among the landed interest. Differences within the cabinet over specific questions – which involved personality as much as principle – tended to reinforce Liverpool's authority even as he shared public credit with colleagues. Reform showed Liverpool acting strategically as he gradually took the initiative.

Controversial issues still enabled critics to embarrass Liverpool's government. The depression in agricultural prices unsettled country gentlemen, who then, by making their support unreliable, put ministers on a defensive that impeded consistent financial policy. Wellington understood that "given the temper of the times, men may find themselves obliged to follow the torrent rather than stem it," but he sharply objected to their acting in concert against the government they professed to support.[6] Arbuthnot detected a very unpleasant temper in the Commons, along with pressure to reduce taxes further. Economic reforms that had abolished salaried offices had left him and the prime minister without patronage to buy support.[7] They had to persuade instead. Liverpool noted at the outset of the 1822 parliamentary session that government had cut almost £2,000,000 from its 1821 budget and planned more reduction for 1822. He further argued that reducing expenditure, however right in itself, gave agriculture no relief. Claiming otherwise only misled the public with false hopes. He looked instead to the growth of trade to relieve the landed interest since prosperity in commerce and manufacturing would naturally improve conditions for agriculture. Great interests within the community, he insisted, could not be separated or placed in hostility to one another.[8] Liverpool's words echoed longstanding arguments, but now ministers defended their achievements more forcefully to break a political deadlock that had long constrained them.

Liverpool used his response to a petition on agricultural distress with a February speech to discuss his general economic policy. Given the effort put into circulating the text as a pamphlet, it reflected the argument he wished to set before the country.[9] The undeniable depression in agriculture marked a broader pattern across Europe and North America. Noting the growth of population since 1800, an increase of revenue secured with a lower tax burden than earlier, and a considerable extension of Britain's foreign commerce, Liverpool forcefully refuted the longstanding argument that high taxation caused public distress. Countries suffered the same problem regardless of how they were taxed. Nearly a quarter of British taxes had been remitted since the war. The increase in general national wealth showed that remaining taxes had not limited the capital or resources available to the public, a tendency Liverpool called taxation's chief evil. Added revenue from duties on consumer goods, including candles and tea, indicated a rise in consumption that demonstrated higher living standards especially among all the poorest classes.[10]

Agriculture suffered not from high taxes, Liverpool argued, but a weak market diminished by the end of wartime demand and general overproduction. Earnings had fallen with the drop in prices. Parliament could not intervene to provide agriculture a more favorable market without harming other numerous interests. Invoking principles drawn from Adam Smith and others who later amplified his critique of market regulation, Liverpool insisted "the thing must be left to set itself right." Low prices would raise demand and cut production so the two sides could meet at fair mutual advantage. Language drawn from political economy framed his analysis, though Liverpool always valued practice over theory. The drop in prices gave other classes outside agriculture a material advantage by lowering food costs. Besides noting a drop in poor rates, which fell upon farmers and landowners, Liverpool argued that the lower orders in London had never enjoyed a higher living standard. While conceding that advantage to the consumer may go too far, he reiterated that the natural working of trade offered the best corrective. Strengthening public finances would not only lower interest rates, but also enable a further tax cut.[11] Liverpool left unsaid his preference for lowering indirect taxes on consumption to stimulate trade which improved all economic sectors. A quiet retreat from agricultural protection moved towards trade liberalization and reducing the national debt. Liverpool saw bringing the economy fully onto a peacetime footing while expanding commerce as the best path to recovery.

Even before the parliamentary session, ministers had sought to justify their conduct with a pamphlet entitled *The State of the Nation*.[12] Although it lacked an official stamp, *The Times* called it a manifesto of sorts. The publication applied the broad view reinforced by statistics and other evidence in Liverpool's speech to the whole range of policy. It spoke of the need to show attention to the public good and the consequent benefit of "concurrent effort between the people and their governors."[13] Appealing directly for public support met old complaints that the ministers had not received the acclaim their accomplishments deserved with a new assertiveness. A clear question of confidence on economic matters in May 1822 brought a majority that gave minsters scope they hitherto lacked for policy initiatives. Harriet Arbuthnot thought no government might choose to be so arbitrary as Liverpool's because weakness among the Whigs and the danger of their principles made it impossible to replace. Liverpool had only to take a firm line with country gentlemen to have them at his feet. Although she had a point, headwinds generated by agrarian distress had made the task difficult until ministers forced recalcitrant backbenchers to make a choice.[14]

Strain had taken a severe toll, especially on Londonderry who succeeded to his father's marquisate in April 1821 and still led the Commons while managing increasingly difficult relations with the Continental powers. He privately wished to escape the burdens of office. One of Sidmouth's protégés thought Canning rested his hopes of returning to the cabinet on the assumption that the failing health of both Liverpool and Londonderry would clear his path.[15] Londonderry crumbled in August 1822 fearing imagined conspiracies and accusing friends of turning against him. George IV, horrified by his foreign secretary's distraught manner, warned Liverpool in person and urged Londonderry not be left alone for an instant. Liverpool went to his colleague's house only to find he and his wife had left for the country. Lady Londonderry wrote that her husband's physician, Dr. Bankhead, had arrived. Liverpool planned to join them a few days later. Bankhead, however, brought the news Londonderry had killed himself with a penknife on the morning of August 12.[16]

It came as a staggering blow even as Liverpool and colleagues retrospectively pieced together the signs. Collapse, the king said, fell hardest on the strongest minds. Ministers agreed that Londonderry died in the country's service no less than had he fallen in battle. Liverpool had lost an old friend and perhaps his closest ally. He hardly exaggerated in telling Melville that "Londonderry's death strikes off from us the right hand of the administration." Since the government would be considered recast whether with more or fewer changes, Liverpool contemplated appointments blocked earlier.[17] Anticipating him, George IV insisted that plans for Canning's departure for India proceed. Peel, who had accompanied the king to Scotland, declined offering an opinion when pressed and reported the exchange.[18]

Liverpool knew where he stood with the king. Many in the cabinet, particularly Eldon and Sidmouth, distrusted Canning. Wellington, however, saw the need for him to replace Londonderry as foreign secretary, a post for which Peel lacked experience and fluency in French. The duke refused to accept the Foreign Office himself, telling Princess Lieven that doing so would end his independence as a soldier–statesman and bind him to his colleagues' opinions. Wellington claimed to lack the habit of parliamentary speaking a foreign secretary required. He also, very significantly, thought it impossible to veer from the line of foreign policy already set. Wellington's pivotal decision was the great refusal of his public life. Unwilling to accept that his active military career was over he declined to embrace a role as politician and cabinet minister. Canning took the Foreign Office instead. Bathurst and Melville accepted despite their suspicions, while Buckingham had threatened to withdraw Grenvillite support if Canning or another equally prominent advocate of Catholic Emancipation did not join the cabinet. Peel, unwilling to oppose what colleagues thought best to strengthen the government, agreed to serve alongside Canning as he had with Londonderry.[19]

Liverpool realized he lacked a sufficiently deft touch to bring George IV to accept the appointment. The prospect of an audience at Carlton House brought nervous agitation. Arbuthnot urged him not to press anything like an ultimatum.[20] Wellington, largely sidelined by an illness, handled the negotiation, knocking down successive objections. His insistence that the king's honor "consists in acts of mercy and grace" which might safely be extended to Canning removed the main objection. George IV still described the concession as "the greatest sacrifice of my opinions and feelings" he ever made. Liverpool thought the king's letters respecting Canning "ought to answer every purpose we can desire."[21] A note written for Canning's perusal alluded to an offense in terms framed to invite a response, but he let it pass without comment and took up the seals of office on September 21. Liverpool gained his object, albeit indirectly. The exchange showed difficulty with George IV remained. Wellington took over managing relations with the king. Canning's return also underlined how Liverpool had overtaken his old friend along with Grenville and Wellesley while reuniting the old Pittite group as the foundation of a conservative party. The tortoise had outrun more than a few hares.

Tensions with Canning's return involved personalities more than policy or political differences. Canning had long ago yielded precedence to his old rival Londonderry. Their outlook on critical issues of the day, including foreign policy, had converged. Both had been leading advocates of Catholic Emancipation under the arrangement that had guided Liverpool's government from its formation in 1812.[22] Peel stated directly that he had no political difference with Canning besides the Catholic question, which had caused no problem before. Wellington too downplayed any disagreements. Although Eldon warned that he would seek to replace all the king's old servants, Canning demanded no changes and only pressed Huskisson's longstanding claim. Canning's reputation for intrigue and habit of making things unduly complex was the real problem. Cyril Jackson, the Dean of Christ Church, once had observed that Canning "would always take the crooked road towards his object, even though the straighter one were easier and pleasanter as well as shorter." His "perpetually doing & undoing" exasperated colleagues who saw a trick behind every turn. Fear Canning would acquire an ascendancy over Liverpool's opinion reinforced suspicions. Rather than pitting liberals against reactionaries, differences split those repelled by Canning from others attracted to him. Liverpool held the balance more than ever. Neither side could manage without him, but tensions from keeping them in balance gave him greater trouble than before.[23]

Other arrangements completed the general restructuring. Londonderry's protégé Robinson, who combined eloquence and popularity in the Commons with an indolent manner, replaced Vansittart at the exchequer. With a peerage to salve his feelings, Vansittart became Chancellor of the Duchy of Lancaster. The ailing Bragge Bathurst's retirement opened a parliamentary seat at Harwich that enabled Canning to give up Liverpool in Huskisson's favor.[24] Promoting Robinson satisfied Vansittart if not Huskisson, who once aspired to the exchequer himself. More importantly, it gave Liverpool a better spokesman on finance in the Commons than Vansittart, whom Grenvillites had long thought the government's greatest liability. As Croker noted, "it is important to have a Chancellor of the Exchequer who commands the respect as well as the esteem of the house. Van had only the latter." Though satisfied with the measures Robinson proposed, country gentlemen in the Commons seemed even more pleased with the man whose speech won their applause.[25]

Placing Huskisson over the Board of Trade created trouble over his touchiness at lacking an office he felt commensurate with his abilities and a leading place among Liverpool's economic advisors. Feeling unappreciated for "pulling the laboring oar" while others rested idle, he thought it unfair to himself and injurious to the government that he should take a part belonging properly to responsible and efficient office while "I appear permanently doomed to a situation neither responsible nor official."[26] Huskisson unsurprisingly felt it a slight that Liverpool offered the post without the cabinet seat Robinson had held with it. That set him on the same level as the Board's vice president, Liverpool's Oxford friend Thomas Wallace. Nobody, he insisted to Arbuthnot, could perform the office's duties out of the cabinet. Liverpool's point that his father had once held the same post outside the cabinet did not console.[27] Bringing him around took Canning and Wellington more than a fortnight. The promise of admission to the cabinet at the earliest moment failed to mollify. Liverpool, deeply provoked himself, complained that nothing could be in "worse taste than a man endeavoring to force himself into a cabinet against the wishes of the king & his own friends." His aim had been to keep the unpopular Huskisson in a post where his valuable expertise could contribute effectively without exciting general notice and drawing criticism.[28]

Considering Huskisson's appointment over him as a demotion, Wallace predictably took offense. Accepting his old friend's argument, Liverpool scrambled to resolve the matter by pressing Arbuthnot to take the vice-presidency Wallace now wished to resign and open for him Huskisson's old post as commissioner of woods, forests, and land revenue. Arbuthnot, who had sought that job as a retreat from the burdensome work as patronage secretary at the Treasury, exploded at the suggestion. Taking a post thought beneath Wallace seemed poor return for his loyal service as Liverpool's political fixer. Liverpool quickly dropped the idea and did his best to conciliate Arbuthnot while trying vainly to find Wallace another post.[29] Arbuthnot's uncharacteristic anger faded, but Wallace left the government entirely. As Croker put it disdainfully, Liverpool had contrived to set Wallace "his dearest and earliest friend, Arbuthnot his chief confident, & Huskisson his principle advisor…the three men he most wished to serve & oblige…at variance with each other and with him." Arbuthnot's wife thought Liverpool meant no unkindness, but saw the episode as another sign of his inability "to consider other people's feelings."[30]

Despite Liverpool's failings managing touchy personalities – including the acerbic Croker – the government could now take advantage of the improving economy. The 1823 budget marked an important turning point. Anticipating a £5 million surplus of revenue over expenditure even while reducing assessed (i.e. direct) taxes by £2 million, Liverpool determined that ministers should concede on their own initiative as much as they believed prudent and take their stand there. He saw the best chance of saving the £5 million in "giving up all whatever may exceed it." Lowering the costs of agriculture and trade by tax cuts would provide significant relief by raising profits as consumption increased.[31] Taking a stand, as Liverpool phrased it, also called wavering supporters' bluff. Robinson outlined the country's financial situation in a February 21 speech described, perhaps with hyperbole, as eloquence not seen in the Commons since Perceval's death. He proposed lowering duties while placing £5 million into a new sinking fund to reduce the debt and strengthen public credit. Given, as Liverpool pointed out, that the government had remitted £22,000,000 per annum in taxes since 1816 – a sum comprising a third of the taxation levied during the latter stages of the war – keeping back revenue to reduce public debt brought scant resistance.[32]

The proposals gave the opposition little to question beyond technical details and won over those whose wavering support had caused so much uncertainty. Demonstrating command of public finances enabled ministers to marginalize Whigs and radicals alike. Growing prosperity reinforced a welcome trend as agriculture began recovering amidst a general improvement in trade. Noting that England's political climate remained as variable as its weather, Croker remarked in October that he had never known the country in better humor with the Whigs unpopular, radicals discredited, and Tories for the first time in a century unashamed of their name.[33] The shift had important consequences. Lower taxes weakened radical accusations that minsters transferred wealth from productive social groups to holders of public debt. Two longstanding themes – reform and "tax eating" – almost disappeared from print satires between 1822 and 1827, especially from 1823 through 1825. What had been a wave of reform petitions since Waterloo abruptly diminished to a trickle with only five submitted to the Commons between January 1824 and early summer 1827.[34] Now Liverpool could pursue a more active policy adumbrated earlier in his administration.

Liverpool sought to make Britain "the entrepôt of the merchandise of the world" while extending its own export trade. Besides securing the pure profit from re-export, shipping, and drawing foreign capital, Britain would sell more of its own manufactures as merchants made up assortments of cargo from local goods. A large proportion of the manufacturing population, Liverpool noted, now depended on foreign demand.[35] Prosperity also would benefit agriculture by stimulating demand as consumer incomes rose. Higher profits for agriculture would ease the political difficulty of adjusting the Corn Laws without unduly antagonizing the landed interest. The policy established to meet concerns raised by scarcity in the 1790s and its effects on social tensions clashed with the new program of political economy which met concerns about food supplies more effectively. Discussions and a report by the trade committee Wallace had chaired in 1820 pointed the way for more effective action in 1822 when Liverpool's government reformed the Navigation Acts to streamline regulation and encourage trade through Britain. Changes promoted British trade while dropping the principle that advantage could be gained from limiting the trade of others. Liverpool justified them on the ground that the increasing trade of foreign countries "provided the best guarantee against the distress of our manufacturers."[36] Freeing trade allowed markets to find their natural level – an equilibrium of supply and demand at sustainable prices – without the disruptions of war or some other temporary circumstance. It also reduced commercial imbalances that undercut demand for British goods.

A revenue surplus combined with revived employment in 1823 removed a break on commercial reform by lowering the need for indirect levies on consumption that had provided the main revenue stream over the long eighteenth century since 1688. Robinson's 1824 budget cut duties on rum, coal, wool, and silk to encourage legal trade and remove the smuggler's premium that fueled a serious problem of coastal lawbreaking. His proposal aimed to stabilize foreign trade by removing impediments, rather than create markets, but the step complimented reforms to the Navigation Acts. A shift toward reciprocity also met concerns Thomas Took had raised that foreign governments would retaliate by raising barriers of their own.[37] The structure of indirect taxes changed to reduce the burden on general consumption even as revenue grew with the increase of trade subject to customs duty. While customs duties fell to 38 percent of the value of imports by 1825 from 63 percent in 1822, they comprised a larger share of indirect taxation than excises on domestic goods. Over the long run consumers paid less duty on both imports and domestic goods.[38]

Lowering costs raised living standards, including among the London poor who paid less for coal, to undermine the charge of elite parasitism. More reductions followed the next year once Robinson established the principle. British subjects, Liverpool noted with satisfaction, paid fewer direct taxes in proportion to the overall revenue than the subjects of any other European country. Nonetheless, he preferred direct taxation over levies on consumers. Despite warnings against direct taxation as a check on investment and the argument that paying levies on many consumables like beer and tobacco was a matter of choice which also ensure the whole community paid into the national treasury, political economists had long tied the excise on necessities with a high wage economy. David Ricardo argued that they raised wages and thereby reduced profit.[39] Liverpool also realized lowering direct taxes blunted the popular discontent behind radicalism. The income tax, which Peel revived in 1842, would have tapped growing economic sectors more effectively and with less burden, but the sting of its defeat in 1816 made it too risky. If not for the political difficulties, he would have proposed

raising direct taxes to reduce indirect taxes by twice the amount. Commerce
then would receive considerable relief without the government losing revenue.[40]
Increased trade and lower burdens on the consumer furthered Liverpool's aim of
showing the existing political order could promote the public good.

Liverpool had opposed Grey's motion for parliamentary reform in 1793, arguing that the flaws it purported to address were in human nature itself rather than
the electoral system. Instead of who should be electors, he saw the fundamental
question as what kind of people ought to be elected. Lord John Russell revived
parliamentary reform in 1820 with a proposal to transfer seats from Grampound,
a notoriously corrupt borough where an election in 1818 had been overturned
for gross bribery, to Leeds which lacked its own representatives.[41] Russell's plan
set a precedent of enfranchising populous manufacturing towns that strengthened the case for broader reform. Liverpool, by contrast, worked to fix the
specific grievance with minimal change to legitimate the system. He believed
giving the right of election to populous manufacturing towns would spark turbulence among inhabitants subject to a perpetual canvass. It would also elect men
the least likely to show steady attachment to the good order of society. Existing
populous borough constituencies offered some advantage "as part of a mixed
and comprehensive representation," but Liverpool thought only on a limited
scale. The usual practice of making an electorate too large for effective bribery
by transferring a corrupt borough's seats into the surrounding area could not be
done with Grampound as the region already contained four other parliamentary
boroughs. Liverpool instead proposed transferring its members to a larger county
where elections were the least corrupt. "If you destroy something corrupt," he
observed, "the natural course seems to be to substitute something sound and safe
in place of it."[42]

The phrase expressed Liverpool's general view. He differed from colleagues
like Eldon and Bathurst who rejected any remedial measure. Arguing not
as "a parliamentary reformer but as an enemy of all plans of general reform,"
Liverpool insisted that "when an evil was clearly proved to exist nothing could
be worse than shutting the door against the remedy."[43] The British constitution,
with its balance of monarchical, aristocratic, and democratic elements, secured
ordered liberty while avoiding the extremes of absolutism or radical democracy.
Correcting failings or abuses defended the constitution by removing grounds on
which others might demand changes likely to give ambition and folly free rein.
As he had argued in 1793, "institutions must be adapted not only to the virtues,
but to the weaknesses and passions of mankind."[44] Liverpool's Augustinian view
of human nature stressed the need to check popular sentiment and momentary
enthusiasm. Preserving elite authority meant that public concerns must be met
without being swayed by undue pressure. As he told Canning with regard to
taxes "nothing should be yielded to clamor," but what could not be maintained
"should be conceded voluntarily as soon as possible." Timely concession helped

keep the political initiative while avoiding prolonged, useless contests that made the government appear odious without advantage.[45] Here was an insight guiding his political arts.

Resisting Catholic Emancipation posed more difficulty than deflecting parliamentary reform. It caught Liverpool between the risk of appearing odious to little advantage and his determination to defend the established order in Church and state. He saw the Catholic question as a matter of allegiance rather than theology because Catholic subjects offered the crown a divided loyalty. Securing a Protestant state also required a Protestant establishment. Agitation the issue fueled, particularly from 1823 when Daniel O'Connell transformed it into a mass movement in Ireland with the Catholic Association, worried Liverpool more than the religious question itself. Liverpool had contemplated giving way when Plunket's motion came before the Lords in 1821 with an opposing majority of only four lay peers, but Sidmouth pressed him to stand by his earlier views rather than accept emancipation with securities for the Established Church. Changing a long-held position would have opened him to charges of inconsistency. Liverpool had foreseen the problem in 1805 when he warned about commitments made under pressure to a position thoughtful men otherwise might not have taken but which they would find hard to abandon honorably. While accepting that some arrangement inevitably would be made, deep loyalty to the Church of England and his view of the constitution kept him from being the instrument of such a change.[46]

Liverpool thus argued the case against Catholic Emancipation forcefully while accepting small concessions that avoided what he considered threatening precedents. Canning's proposal in 1822 to allow Catholic peers to sit in the Lords showed the danger of having him outside the government. The measure might have been a parting shot before his expected departure for India. Liverpool attacked it as a most impolitic and dangerous concession that distinguished between peers and commoners of a particular church without settling the larger question.[47] He supported, however, an 1823 measure granting English Catholics the franchise already enjoyed in Ireland, describing them as "a highly respectable body" of "uniform loyalty." The matter differed entirely with Ireland's circumstances where granting forty shilling freeholders the vote in 1793 had given the Catholic majority political influence disproportionate to their property.[48]

Opening certain offices to Catholics the next year also did not threaten the Protestant establishment, but instead strengthened it by removing a cause of discontent. "By conceding these little things," Liverpool argued, the establishment "acquired strength to resist greater encroachments."[49] On the same principle, Irish tithe reform addressed a longstanding grievance he thought more serious than religious exclusion. An 1823 measure commuted tithes on a voluntary basis from a percentage of agricultural yield to a monetary payment reasonable in proportion to income of those liable to pay while adequate to supporting the Established Church. Eldon backed it. Harrowby called it "worth what gold could never buy" for removing "some of the most galling circumstances in the situation of Ireland." Liverpool reported the next year that the voluntary measure had been executed in 279 cases with 23 more since the current parliamentary session and 39 applications underway. Success in more than a tenth of Irish parishes exceeded the most sanguine hopes.[50] It did not, however, lower social tensions in Ireland or neutralize the Catholic question even as other difficulties faded.

1823 through 1825 were the halcyon years of Liverpool's administration. Having withstood the storm Queen Caroline's trial unleashed and the crushing loss of Louisa, he used growing prosperity and the collapse of effective opposition to strengthening the existing order by targeted reforms.[51] Marriage to his late wife's friend Mary Chester in September 1822 restored the domesticity Liverpool craved. While never quite lifting his sense of bereavement from Louisa's death, it marked a private turning point that paralleled the shift in political fortunes. Nonetheless, the toll showed. Canning thought the agitation Liverpool felt over cabinet arrangements in late 1822 "amounted almost to illness."[52] Outbursts and even tears were more common from 1820, although they never affected Liverpool's public reputation. Colleagues and other intimates remarked upon them, but many like Melville took the irritability as part of his personal manner when hard worked.[53] Illness his behavior reflected had eroded the self-control on which his calmer manner from 1809 through 1820 rested. A sedentary life-style exacerbated vascular degeneration that made his legs painful and swollen. George IV's secretary, a former physician, reported Liverpool in severe pain whenever he sat with his legs down. Observers described him resting them on the bench during parliamentary debates. While the degree varied, Liverpool suffered continual discomfort which made patience harder to maintain.[54]

Two portraits by Sir Thomas Lawrence capture Liverpool in his fifties while showing how he had aged. George IV commissioned the first in 1820 for the Waterloo Room at Windsor. Harriet Arbuthnot thought nothing "more exqui-sitely like or where the character & *manière d'être* of the individual is more perfectly caught" than the three-quarter-length figure on a plain ground with hands clasped before him. Besides having "exactly his untidy look & slouching way of countenance" the portrait captured Liverpool's "profound & penetrat-ing expression of countenance."[55] It showed qualities behind his public repu-tation, with quiet authority replacing the nervous intensity of youth. Lawrence began work on the second portrait in June 1826 for Peel who, sharing Liverpool's informed appreciation for art, wished to record his political friendships. The full-length painting of the now balding premier showed the same penetrating gaze as he held a rolled parchment beside an open dispatch box (see Fig. 14). Alert as Liverpool remained, his features showed the effects of age and care. Peel intended the series to record what political friends under Liverpool had accomplished.[56]

Lawrence alluded to a major achievement by painting Liverpool with a document referring to the National Gallery's establishment in 1824. Sir John

Illus. 14. Lord Liverpool by Sir Thomas Lawrence (c.1826). Liverpool's portrait at age fifty-six captures his authority as prime minister along with the weariness his long tenure had brought. The papers beside him refer to his role in establishing the National Gallery.

Beaumont, who opened his private collection to artists for study, had long urged enabling people of all ranks to enjoy great art in Britain. When John Julius Angerstein, a London financier and noted collector, died in January 1823, Beaumont told the government that if it bought Angerstein's collection "I will give you mine."[57] Liverpool seized the chance, when Austria settled a wartime loan by a £2,500,000 lump sum, to purchase thirty-eight paintings for £57,000 and lease a building to display them. He shared Beaumont's aim of displaying outstanding canvases to the public. As Liverpool told Louisa's sister Elizabeth, while small pictures could be as well shown in private collections, scarcely any houses in London could feature larger paintings at advantage. Consequently such works were either not bought or sent to country houses where few saw them. The National Gallery opened in May 1824 to receive 24,000 visitors in its first six months. A further £9,000 two years later added works by Titian and Carracci. Liverpool's support for the project reflects a long history of patronage the president of the Royal Academy recognized in offering a toast for the recovery of his health at its first meeting in May 1827. Along with literature, art was Liverpool's main outside interest. Literature, however, usually involved politics or political history with stylistic assessments reflecting his moral judgment.[58]

Funds from the Austrian loan payment, which the government considered a windfall, also covered both further tax relief and a £500,000 grant for church building to supplement the 1818 initiative. Liverpool thought further parliamentary discussion on the grant unnecessary as the case had been made already, but the expenditure underlined his religious commitment. As a major investment in consolidating the church establishment, the grant bolstered confidence among churchmen who believed its revival would restore the body politic to a sound and wholesome state.[59] The 1818 church building initiative had owed much to the High Church Hackney Phalanx, a counterpart to the evangelical Clapham Sect. Liverpool took advice on clerical appointments from one of its leaders, Henry Handley Norris. He certainly expressed in his understated style an abiding commitment to an Anglican spiritual basis for public life that resonated among supporters in the country who included many clergy. The premier also gave more personal attention to religious observance than stalwart political defenders of the establishment like Eldon and the Duke of Cumberland, let alone the essentially indifferent Pitt. A visitor to Coombe Wood described Liverpool attending morning service on Sunday and then gathering the household for prayers that afternoon from the liturgy in the *Book of Common Prayer*.[60] Liverpool had linked the case for new churches in 1818 with extending the benefits of instruction to all classes. Nothing in his mind separated religious from practical education or useful knowledge as a public service. Indeed, Liverpool sought the king's permission to subscribe from Treasury funds to a memorial for James Watt in one of the nation's cathedrals as a sign of royal encouragement "to the important interests of science and literature."[61]

Liverpool received an unaccustomed tribute of his own in January 1825 when the mayor and corporation of Bristol presented him the freedom of the city along with Canning. The celebration marked the only major occasion when he gave a speech outside parliament. Election speeches before he entered the Lords had been modest affairs since he had never faced a significant challenge. George IV had been enrolled as a freeman of Bristol as prince regent, but the last similar celebration had honored Wellington soon after Waterloo. Although the sheriff of Bristol invited Liverpool and Canning, the foreign secretary told his wife they really wanted Liverpool and would not take a refusal. Besides the fact that he had long represented a rival commercial city, Canning's position on Catholic Emancipation set him at odds with Bristol Tories. The prime minister, however, had staunchly defended both the Protestant constitution and commerce while enjoying a distant local connection through his forebear Anthony Jenkinson.[62] Honoring Liverpool and Canning expressed Bristol's appreciation for the government's efforts to bring the country through a difficult transition after 1815.

The visitors arrived on January 12 with great ceremony in a procession to the Mansion House for a banquet that brought notables from the surrounding counties together with Bristol merchants and tradesmen. They received the freedom of the incorporated society of Merchant Venturers along with that of the city and an address from the Bristol Chamber of Commerce. Liverpool gave four short speeches in reply during the long day's events. One struck a typically self-deprecating note by declaring his only merit lay in good intentions and best efforts that would have availed little without "the talents of my excellent and able colleagues."[63] Downplaying his own part and sharing credit over the years had built a reputation that raised Liverpool's public standing and bolstered his reputation among political insiders. More substantively, his description of the leading interests within the realm as *"links in a great social chain,* all connected and all dependent on each other for the mutual welfare he was pleased to witness" accommodated commercial society with a much older view of social relations.[64] Expanding trade brought prosperity to the landed and manufacturing interests while benefitting the community as a whole. Reforms aimed at promoting commerce strengthened the social and constitutional order rather than straining it by setting different interests at odds. Liverpool long sought to bring various interests behind the establishment so they would not align themselves against it and thereby aid those pressing for sweeping change. The acclaim for his government's accomplishments, even from the local opposition press, shows at least partial success.

Perhaps Liverpool missed a step in not appealing more directly to provincial opinion, especially since his facility as a parliamentary speaker would have been a significant asset. Croker also regretted the premier's indifference to actively managing the press. Besides the personal inconvenience it gave him in handling editors sympathetic to the government, Croker thought ministers had to write down their critics and make a positive case to the larger public.[65] Liverpool, however, lacked both Croker's urgency and the energy after 1820 to pursue the point. Canning was the only minister to make a point of speaking outside parliament on occasions besides elections. His practice of "going round the country *speechifying*," as Harriet Arbuthnot caustically phrased it, marked an innovation on the government side that aroused indignation from George IV and other ministers that Liverpool had to allay.[66] Although he eschewed such public appeals, Liverpool still gained credit for liberal measures that reduced taxation and promoted commerce. Even a provincial Whig paper that used the Bristol visit to denounce Pitt's system and take swipes at Canning and Castlereagh praised Liverpool for taking a more enlarged and enlightened view.[67]

The way Liverpool framed policies over recent years had raised his standing even among critics. Foreign affairs had returned to the agenda in 1820 as revolts in Spain and Naples revived old debates about national self-determination while dividing Britain from other great powers. A state paper of May 1820 the cabinet drew up from Castlereagh's draft insisted that Spanish unrest, despite the pernicious example of a military revolt, did not menace other states enough to justify external interference. The Quadruple Alliance that liberated Europe from Napoleon and secured the peace was never intended to supervise the internal affairs of other states. Guarding against revolutionary power, the paper argued, meant opposing the military character it had taken in France rather than democratic principles spread through Europe. Foreign action itself raised dangers, and the delicate questions intervention raised in specific cases made generalizing impractical. Nor could Britain act upon "abstract and speculative principles of precaution."[68]

Despite his oft-stated disdain for popular sentiment, Castlereagh realized the public would not back intervention without a clear link to the national interest. Foreign governments deceived themselves, he warned his brother, if they "press us to place ourselves on any ground John Bull will not maintain."[69] Principles expressed in the Troppau Protocol that November diametrically opposed Britain's political and constitutional system. Castlereagh's sharp reaction to attempts at winning over George IV – "if the king were to sanction them he would be on the road to abdication" – echoed Liverpool's 1815 reaction to the Holy Alliance. Wellington, who stood closest to Castlereagh on the importance of good relations with the European powers, dismissed as "wild schemes of establishing a general police" the idea raised at Troppau of sending troops from one country to keep order in another. Further discussions at Laibach made Liverpool bemoan the Congress System's very existence.[70]

Liverpool deliberately claimed a prudential middle ground during 1821. Describing Foxite Whigs and their friends in the press as seemingly determined to "uphold all revolutions, not looking to their causes or justifications" struck a chord familiar since the 1790s. Liverpool noted while that Grey and his colleague denounced legitimate monarchs, they "never complained of the acts perpetrated by usurpers." But the prime minister also opposed the disposition to crush all revolutions without reference to circumstances or their causes. What critics called the weak tone of his reply came largely from its effort to avoid justifying British policy at the allies' expense.[71] Liverpool's preference for disengagement reflected longstanding Tory concerns about the cost and risk of Continental involvement, especially where Britain had little direct stake. Peace strengthened public finances and muted popular discontent. Convinced from his long experience that revolution sprang at least partly from failed governance, Liverpool had no wish to rescue hapless rulers from their own folly. Britain, as Canning privately noted, had been gradually backing out of the alliance since 1818. Rather than striving to avoid "the éclat of a public difference," now it had to regain an insulated position to command "a view of passing events & either keep aloof from them altogether or descend to mix with them only at the moment when we are required & can hope to do good."[72] Liverpool shared his view.

Londonderry's suicide brought Canning to the Foreign Office as his successor, but Wellington represented Britain at the Congress of Verona. Allied leaders decided over his objections to bring down the revolutionary government in Madrid by joint pressure. Believing outside intervention in Spain both impractical and impolitic, Liverpool insisted British opposition could not be stated too directly. Canning formally instructed Wellington to declare peremptorily that Britain would not join any interference. Aside from the larger question, Liverpool saw the practical difficulties operations in Spain presented and the limited influence outsiders could exert unless the populace sided with them. The instructions only slightly hardened the position in the 1820 state paper, but still cut Britain out of effective deliberations. Metternich's efforts to hold the four Continental powers together by severing relations with Spain's government while delaying further action irritated Wellington and freed Liverpool to make a clearer break.[73] Wartime circumstances, he told Arbuthnot, had brought the country "into a course which was quite right at the time, but which (with our different prejudices and form of govt.) we could never expect to adhere inevitably."[74] As the prime minister made clear when parliament met in February 1823, the government saw "the question of Spain as one clearly and purely Spanish."[75]

The imminent prospect of a French army crossing into Spain revived parliamentary discussion in some of the session's most vigorous debates. Liverpool rejected what he called the false choice Whigs posed between walking in the train of despotism or appearing as protector of constitutional liberty. Insisting that the British constitution marked a compromise between the principles of monarchy and democracy, he urged a middle ground of neutrality "in this conflict of opinion."[76] Grey implied that ministers now held France to a different standard by permitting what had justified war against Louis XIV and Napoleon. Had Liverpool, he challenged, abandoned the commitment to the European balance of power defended in his maiden speech decades ago as the foundation of British security? Liverpool replied that opposing French intervention meant a war with steep costs and no compensating advantage. Since France could accomplish nothing against the wishes of the Spanish people, Britain had little to fear.[77] Privately he distinguished a Spain without its American colonies from the whole Spanish empire taking a French line in external relations. French influence over a Spain without South America had less effect on the balance of power. Indeed, Canning had worked with Liverpool's support to keep France and other European powers from aiding Spain's failing effort to regain breakaway colonies.[78] There, Britain had far more leverage than in Spain itself.

While British foreign policy effectively followed the same line Liverpool and the cabinet had taken since 1820, Canning introduced a sharper, less emollient tone. It irritated colleagues and the king who thought he went too far in repudiating the wartime alliance. Lingering suspicions over Canning's integrity made them suspect he imposed policy on Liverpool, whom Dorothea Lieven claimed, "no longer thinks or moves without his consent." Wellington angrily declared at a party following a parliamentary debate that "My Lord Liverpool is neither more nor less than a common prostitute." His embarrassment at such an outburst with ladies present failed to check the duke's anger. He complained that Liverpool and Canning always had some *arrière pensée* in dealing with him that made him feel "like a man who, going into a crowd, thinks it prudent to button up his pockets."[79] George IV thought Liverpool exercised too little control over what he disparaged as a "government of departments" in which ministers and officials outside the cabinet acted too much on their own initiative and urged him to correct a situation that compared unfavorably with Pitt's day.[80] Arbuthnot, on Wellington's advice, warned Liverpool in October the king considered him under Canning's influence and might even accept the foreign secretary as prime minister in his place. Dislike and distrust of Canning now bothered George IV less than his conviction that real power already rested with him and Liverpool led in name alone.[81]

Liverpool, however, could not see the grounds on which the king rested his belief in Canning's "unbounded influence over my mind and opinions." Managing public business required a good understanding and confidence between the premier and whichever minister led the other house of parliament. Liverpool's relations with Canning were no different than earlier with Perceval and Castlereagh. He remained unaware of a single instance where Canning assumed an influence or authority not belonging to him. Having denied the charge, he warned that George IV must not presume that other ministers would continue "if he dismissed me because it was his *royal will & pleasure*" or on some spurious pretext. Were Liverpool to determine he could not go on with honor and credit, it remained with him "to consider *when* I can most easily retire." The king should take care not to create a political storm likely to overshadow the closing years of his reign.[82]

Coincidence of opinion between Liverpool and Canning gave a false impression of the latter's ascendancy since the prime minister kept a close hold over the Foreign Office. Castlereagh's absence on missions abroad had given him wider scope for independent action than Canning enjoyed. Liverpool no more hesitated questioning an old friend than any other colleague or even the king, but disputes over foreign policy show how political tensions had shifted from parliament and public to within the government itself. Conflict there proved much harder and stressful to manage. Personal differences also made handling disagreement over policy more difficult.

Spain's American colonies raised an especially vexatious issue that split the cabinet. Openly recognizing the Latin American republics before Spain acknowledged their independence gave the appearance of sanctioning rebellion against lawful authority and governments founded upon revolutionary principles. Their effective independence, however, forced British policy to adapt, if only to handle commercial relations and keep the United States from dominating a valuable market. Britain had sought to open South American markets throughout the eighteenth century, and Liverpool set promoting trade as a top priority. A revision to the Navigation Acts in 1822 gave South American republics the commercial rights of independent states without formal recognition and the legal standing it provided. Rather than take that larger step, Liverpool preferred "the handsome, the gentleman-like course" of giving Spain the lead in recognizing its former colonies' independence.[83] The cabinet, however, remained at odds while outside pressure for a decision grew. Canning and Huskisson urged recognition, not least because they faced insistent requests from merchants. Wellington and Sidmouth objected to a step likely to provoke the Continental powers. Indeed, Wellington insisted that, having spent his life fighting against revolutionists and their principles, he would never agree to ally with democratic governments in America against Europe's monarchies. The dispute exasperated a weary Liverpool, particularly since 1824 had otherwise seen the shortest and quietest parliamentary session in years.[84]

Pragmatism guided Liverpool. He told Parliament in March 1824 that Britain would never follow the example the Bourbons had set in the 1770s by aiding the North American colonies. Were the contest settled and "the general body of the population" in favor of "the new state of things," however, foreign powers had a positive right to acknowledge an accomplished fact.[85] By autumn, Liverpool privately asked whether any external considerations justified further delay. Leaving so large a region "in a state of outlawry" presented a problem. The new states could also force recognition by imposing excessive duties on ships of any country withholding it. Deferring either to Spain or to the Continental powers, he argued, subordinated British concerns to foreign states unable to sustain their prejudices. Since they had refused to sacrifice their own views on other occasions, Britain had no obligation to defer now. He urged recognition to keep other powers, especially France and the United States, from gaining influence at British expense. Liverpool saw the United States as Britain's most formidable rival for trade in South America. He also realized the possibility of a Franco-American junction at its expense as had occurred in the 1770s and again during the closing years of the Napoleonic Wars. The War of 1812 shaped his thinking on that threat, which ministers had quietly taken steps to counter. "Sooner or later," he warned, "we shall probably have to contend with the combined maritime power of France and of the United States." A favorable disposition by South American states toward Britain offered a golden opportunity to establish "a fair counterpoise to that combined maritime power" which once lost may never be recovered.[86]

Wellington remained opposed, though he told Harriet Arbuthnot that Liverpool had been the only person to give a good reason to negotiate with the South American states.[87] Bathurst complained in July 1824 that Liverpool "had completely and entirely changed his politics and was become quite a liberal." Other disgruntled colleagues agreed over the following months. George IV openly charged Liverpool with adopting the liberalism it had taken all Pitt's talent and firmness to repress in the 1790s. Ironically, what colleagues and king disparaged as liberal served Liverpool's conservative project of defending the existing order. Ultra Tories viewed Continental legitimists with disdain; they sought to defend Britain's balanced order in Church, state, and society rather than monarchical authority per se. Seeking a middle ground between what Liverpool disparaged as the doctrinaire approaches of legitimists and liberals neatly matched the sentiments of his government's supporters in the country. Tory sentiment long had set commercial and overseas interests over close involvement with Continental disputes. Liverpool sought the freedom to promote British interests from a detached, secure position, not to promote liberalism abroad. Recognizing the South American republics further denied Whigs any room for criticism and raised the government's popularity.[88] Unfortunately, it also heightened personal tensions among ministers. Wellington's irritability, Bathurst's unease with change, and Canning's sheer busyness generated frictions Liverpool found increasingly difficult as circumstances worsened in 1825.

The challenge now involved renewed agitation in Ireland rather than debates over a liberal turn in foreign policy. Wellesley claimed that but for activity by O'Connell's Catholic Association and "polemical clamor of conflicting religious zealots," the greatly improved Irish conditions over the past year would have allowed him to give parliament "the gratifying tribute of Ireland tranquilized."[89] Founding the Catholic Association in 1823, whose Dublin premises critics disparaged as the "Popish Parliament," enabled O'Connell to push aside the patrician moderates who had hitherto led agitation to repeal Catholic disabilities. Admitting priests as members free of payment in 1824 and then inaugurating a penny monthly rent collected at churches made the association a mass organization with a structure that conferred a quasi-representative legitimacy. Conscious imitation of the Westminster parliament became more marked from November 1824 when the association began using a chamber with facing rows of benches for its discussions.[90] The situation in Ireland resembled the radical agitation for parliamentary reform that upset England in 1819, but with better organization, wider support, and more effective leadership. O'Connell deliberately thwarted the government's conciliation policy and agitated the Catholic question in a way that risked splitting the government.

Liverpool determined to suppress the Catholic Association as a possible rival to the government that might claim popular legitimacy. O'Connell raised the stakes in a speech on December 20 by hoping that if parliament did not satisfy Catholic claims "some Bolivar will arise to vindicate their rights." Peel pressed sedition charges, but George IV thought it ridiculous to prosecute a man for holding up the example of someone with whom the government intended to negotiate a treaty. A Dublin grand jury threw out the charge on New Year's Day.[91] When parliament met on February 3, Liverpool separated the Catholic Association's legality from Catholic disabilities and petitions for their repeal. How could a body which levied an unauthorized tax and constantly strove to evade the spirit of the laws be thought consistent with the British constitution or the country's peace? Liverpool cited "the spirit of political and religious dissension" as the reason Ireland had not matched England's prosperity despite a lower tax burden. The measure against unlawful societies in Ireland, which covered Protestant groups along with the Catholic Association, faced little opposition after the motion to consider it passed the Commons by a considerable majority.[92] Henry Hobhouse speculated that parliamentary advocates of Catholic Emancipation, having been pressed against their judgment by the Irish to bring it forward again, preferred the ban to pass quickly so they could proceed with their case.[93]

Liverpool sharply denied rumors in March 1825 the government would concede Catholic Emancipation and that he would bring in the bill himself.[94] Nonetheless, he felt the awkwardness of being caught between his convictions and how he read the political landscape. A settled Commons majority for Catholic Emancipation meant defeating the present bill in the Lords only delayed an eventual concession that would abandon a position he had held on principle and defended at length. Upon reflection, Liverpool determined he could not in conscience agree to such a reversal, let alone work to secure emancipation. Resignation provided the only honorable escape from what he now considered an impossible situation.[95]

Liverpool had shown more flexibility earlier, despite his consistent public line since George III declared against Catholic Emancipation. Several factors hardened his stance in 1825. Tory opinion, both elite and popular, had moved from an earlier neutral or even sympathetic view of Catholicism to seeing a resurgent post-Napoleonic Church as a threat to Britain's Protestant constitution.

Harriet Arbuthnot's remark that Liverpool considered the question religiously points to his belief that an intertwined relationship between Church and state was essential to upholding temporal order, public morality, and Christian teaching. Conceding the Established Church's political monopoly severed those links along with the basis of principled resistance to wider reforms.[96] His sharper line in 1825 also reflected a temper fraying under strain and a suspicion the balance within the government had turned against him. He risked closing a long political life with disgrace, he told Bathurst, if he appeared now "to be clinging to office when my opinions have been overruled in the House of Commons and when I cannot expect to be able to defend the Protestant cause much longer in the House of Lords."[97]

Wellington believed the time had come to settle the question, but on terms that would secure the Protestant establishment and bring along the king. He looked to a concordat with the Pope vesting clerical appointments in the crown with regular salaries for priests to make them independent of their parishioners. Arrangements in Hanover and the Netherlands offered reliable precedents. The principle of timely concession behind Wellington's reasoning matched Liverpool's general stance and it would become a standard conservative approach. Liverpool might well have been open to such a settlement earlier to stifle agitation, and Wellington thought he could bring him and Peel around. Instead, he and Bathurst spent May struggling to talk them both out of resigning.[98] Arbuthnot warned the premier that his resignation would bring the Whigs into power, especially if Peel and Eldon joined him. Liverpool could hold together a government from which Wellington resigned because the duke's influence was military rather than civil. Others would not follow him out of office. A government under Canning as Liverpool's successor, however, would be thrown to the opposition because then a break with Wellington on any major question would produce a larger split. Bathurst warned that resignation would leave the Protestant side outraged that Liverpool abandoned their cause and the king complaining he had been abandoned. With an entire change of councils in prospect, "it will not be your Protestant friends alone who will reproach you." Bathurst again warned of the consequences and insisted that "it will require a very strong proof of your resignation having been necessary before you can stand excused."[99]

The public would have found Liverpool's departure puzzling since the crisis had apparently ended when the Lords rejected the bill on May 17 by forty-eight votes. Liverpool argued forcefully against the measure in what Gash rightly deemed "the most vehement anti-Catholic speech he had ever made."[100] He insisted straightforwardly that "Catholics were not entitled to equal rights in a Protestant country." While "all subjects in a free state were entitled to the enjoyment of equal rights upon equal conditions," the Catholic who divided his allegiance "between a spiritual and a temporal master" did not afford such equal conditions in demanding his rights. Doubtless with Ireland and the Catholic

Association in mind, Liverpool objected to the temporal and practical power Catholic priests exercised. If the present laws deprived Catholics "of all share in the advantages of our free constitution," they still enjoyed "more civil and political liberty than the Protestants residing in any Catholic state in Europe." Liverpool found curious the willingness of those "who talked so much of natural rights" to sacrifice the franchise of five hundred thousand Irish voters to end disabilities which affected only thirty or forty men. He reacted more strongly to another companion measure intended to remove the danger from Catholic Emancipation with a provision for Catholic clergy by law that would bind their interest to the state. That step went beyond removing disabilities. It established the Catholic religion legally as a rival to the Anglican establishment the crown was sworn to uphold. Setting Catholics and Protestants upon the same footing, Liverpool concluded, would bring "religious dissension and not religious peace."[101]

The speech nailed Liverpool's colors to the mast on Catholic Emancipation. English opinion beyond parliament largely agreed. Along with opposition to radical politics, resistance to Catholic demands indicated a shift toward popular Toryism.[102] George IV congratulated Liverpool on a most powerful intervention, but the premier replied that the majority in the Lords, while satisfactory, remained a hollow one that could not be relied upon in the future. Even with the bill rejected, Liverpool thought the Catholic question essentially decided. His speech alarmed Canning enough to insist the cabinet take up the issue on which it had been neutral since 1812. Liverpool's reply that doing so would change the whole basis upon which the government stood put Canning and those who shared his view into a corner. Nobody dared take responsibility for destroying the ministry. Canning, after private hints from Wellington on where blame would fall, declared himself satisfied with having merely raised the matter. Liverpool and Peel then lost any grounds for resigning. The whole crisis underlined the premier's authority. Colleagues realized that neither of the two wings in his administration could stand alone without him to keep them in balance. He also carried weight in parliamentary debates hardly any colleagues in either house could match. By accident or design – and Liverpool is too opaque a figure for it to be quite clear – he had blocked any intrigue to displace him. He now led the strongest and most successful government since the 1790s, with decisions kept quietly in his own hands.[103] Managing his colleagues remained a stressful chore.

Differences on the Catholic question spilled over into discussions over the timing for elections. Liverpool faced the choice between calling an election in 1825 or delaying until the parliament expired at its full life after next year's session. Public business and the harvest made September 1825 the earliest point for a decision.[104] Besides the government's popularity, Wellington believed the current state of public opinion would return a parliament more sympathetic to the Protestant constitution and prevent a reprise of the recent tensions. Liverpool, however, rejected such a direct appeal on the Catholic question. While recognizing the advantages of an autumn election, he remained indifferent to an immediate dissolution "if we can *all* agree to keep the Catholic question and the Corn question in abeyance during the next session." [105] The agreement to postpone two difficult issues that divided ministers and their supporters provided an advantage. A concession to Canning and others on the Catholic side – along with borough-owners including Lonsdale and the Duke of Rutland who wished to delay the inevitable trouble of electioneering – kept peace within the government and secured Liverpool's aim on Corn Law reform as well as Catholic Emancipation. [106]

Henry Hobhouse wondered if Liverpool would have listened to the borough-owners had he anticipated the economic crisis in late 1825. The year had opened on a high note with trade flourishing and a budget surplus enabling Robinson to offer his second free trade budget reducing duties and other taxes which added to the stimulus earlier tax cuts had provided. Expansion had already turned into speculation that raised share prices to a peak in February 1825. Liverpool warned on March 25 that speculators could expect no parliamentary relief if a downturn embarrassed them. Without speaking to any particular measure, he noted "that general spirit of speculation which was going beyond all bounds and was likely to bring the greatest mischief." [107] Traders ignored the hint. The expansion of both foreign trade and overseas investment had drawn specie from the Bank of England. A loss of public confidence when the boom crashed joined with efforts to check the external drain on specie to throw domestic capital markets into a contraction.

Crisis hit hard on December 12 when Pole, Thornton, and Co. of London failed, bringing down with it forty-three corresponding country banks. Liverpool and other ministers held hourly consultations with Bank of England officials and London financiers urging inflationary measures to ease contraction of the money supply, but they refused to suspend cash payments. Canning thought the bank sought to force the suspension it wanted by leaving no alternative. After a dramatic five-hour cabinet meeting on December 16 with soldiers deployed to guard the bank at Threadneedle Street, ministers determined not to concede suspension. Liverpool had support from Wellington, along with Huskisson, Robinson, Canning, and Peel. Denied their request, bank directors instead agreed to buy exchequer bills, issue small notes, and extend discounts. Gold procured from abroad by Rothschild and a pledge by London merchants to exercise mutual trust and confidence stemmed panic even though Bank of England stock continued falling until it hit a low on December 24. Inflationary measures short of suspension propped up the market to narrowly avert another crisis as it became clear that floating exchequer bills would be presented for payment. Issuing banknotes enabled the bank to purchase exchequer bills on December 20 and lower the discount rate to par by the next day. Besides stabilizing the capital market, the government had quietly secured its own liquidity as the year closed.[108]

Was Liverpool to blame for the crisis by promoting commercial expansion? His policies to improve the general economy by increasing trade reflected widespread concern about pain from the postwar slump and the social tension it brought. It bears noting that he warned against speculation. Checking a rising trade cycle without imposing a recession or other collateral damage has been difficult outside an economist's classroom even since the 1920s. It was certainly beyond the tools available in the 1820s. Managing the situation had exhausted Liverpool, who complained before Christmas that strain had ruined his health and questioned his ability to cope with further difficulties. Physicians treating his bad leg doubted whether Liverpool had the stamina to continue in office, especially with a difficult parliamentary session ahead. A careless remark by Lord Westmorland at the cabinet dinner on January 25 to discuss the king's speech opening parliament threw Liverpool into a rage. Westmorland, a longtime critic of liberal policies known for his crude manner, had not come to London for deliberations amidst the December crisis. Liverpool angrily told him that having stayed idle in the country he had no business faulting colleagues who made the necessary decisions and then charged him with spreading malicious gossip in London clubs. Westmorland quietly replied that in a friendly cabinet he had not thought it necessary to measure every word so carefully and that he had no intention to give offense. Revealingly, Liverpool declared he would not remain in office if colleagues opposed him.[109]

Merchants demanded an issue of exchequer bills on precedents from 1798 and 1811 to relieve the financial squeeze the crash imposed. Liverpool refused categorically. Referring back to his warnings from the previous March, he insisted that those caught up in distress and ruin by their rash speculations could not expect the help afforded before under very different circumstances.[110] A wave of bankruptcies revived distress as credit tightened after the brief period of liberal discounting in December. The diarist Greville claimed that "the terror of all the bankers and merchants, as well as all owners of property, is not to be conceived but by those who witnessed it."[111] Liverpool, backed by Huskisson and Peel, still refused to waver. They preferred the bank to discount current exchequer bills and thereby afford the desired relief by expanding the circulation. Liverpool told Canning that any other policy "would have to be undertaken by a different administration."[112] Croker expected a mutiny among government supporters when a petition backed by London merchants and some of the Bank of England's directors came before the Commons on February 23, but ministers held to Liverpool's position. Robinson said the proposed relief would "offer a bonus to extravagant speculation." Canning effectively told the Commons that they would have to place the government in other hands if they insisted on the issue of exchequer bills. Twisting the knife, he pointed out that the Bank of England's authority to make advances on mortgages and merchandise allowed it to alleviate the squeeze on commercial credit without government intervention.[113]

Although Canning may have interpreted Liverpool's words more sharply than they were intended with a warning that surprised the cabinet and king, his threat enforced the premier's authority in the face of both private cabal and public pressure. Liverpool treated the issue as a choice between returning to postwar fiscal expedients or continuing efforts to place finances on a stable basis that would allow trade to reach its natural level. Securing the foundations for commercial growth after the upheavals of war showed the political system could govern without major reform. The moral hazard of relieving speculators troubled Liverpool, but other reasons underpinned his refusal to issue exchequer bills. As Peel told Wellington, the proposed £5 million issue risked either a dramatic discount in existing bills if the rate were lower or a much greater charge on the exchequer if it were higher. The bank would have to cash bills for the measure to have any effect, and Liverpool preferred it issue notes on the security of goods rather than exchequer bills. Nothing short of the government's threat to resign, Canning said, would overcome the bank's resistance.[114] Liverpool's brinksmanship worked, especially when the demand for credit did not exceed available resources as many feared.

Legislation could not cure the effects of rash speculation, but Liverpool accepted the need for corrective and palliative measures. The answer, he believed, was to stabilize the currency by checking paper circulation and placing banking on a more firm security.[115] Besides the economic reasons for the stability of a metallic currency, Liverpool knew radicals like Cobbett denounced paper money and loans as transferring earnings of the poor to the well-connected. Circulation of notes from country banks with less capital to back their issues had doubled between 1824 and 1826 even as the Bank of England withdrew its own notes. Facilitating the speculation that brought the present distress, small notes country banks issued also injured the poorer classes who had no part in it. "A poor man could not refuse a one-pound bank note" Liverpool observed, and, needing to spend on his daily needs, he could not retain it as others might to recover its value later. The falling value of paper money imposed a tax on the poor that Liverpool sought to end by replacing small notes with coin, although he extended the stamping of new notes until October. While the concession surprised Canning, who had defeated a motion in the Commons for the extension, it kept country bankers from withdrawing notes at once in protest.[116] Enabling the Bank of England to open provincial branches and legalizing joint stock companies with a larger capital than existing country banks complemented Liverpool's currency policy. He thought the present law absurd because it allowed individuals or a group not exceeding six to open a country bank while excluding a larger number better able to finance their operation.[117] Scotland and Ireland were exempted from the limit on small notes after some lobbying, but Liverpool carried the overall remedial plan.

Illus. 15.   Robert Cruikshank, "The National Pop-Shop in Threadneedle Street." Having refused demands for an issue of exchequer bills during the 1825 financial crisis, Liverpool forced the Bank of England to relieve commercial distress by making advances.

Social tension revived in 1826 as repercussions from the crash brought a manufacturing depression on the heels of a bad harvest. Rising food prices and the drop in wages and employment hit industrial districts especially hard with petitions and then violent protests growing into the spring. Machine breaking in Lancashire showed the potential for a return to the problems of 1819. Liverpool acknowledged that nobody could see the situation in manufacturing districts without being appalled at the prevailing distress. The prospect another poor harvest would raise food prices alarmed him. Even though ministers had kept their pledge to postpone debate on the Corn Laws, he sought the release of bonded grain in warehouses along with authority to permit further imports. Circumstances, he told the Lords, can "form an exception to a general principle" that justifies steps otherwise to be avoided.[118] He carefully sidestepped discussing principles relating either to the permanent price of corn or the propriety of granting the executive discretion over imports. The expedience of alleviating distress and preserving social peace outweighed those separate questions until a more permanent system could be adopted.[119]

Liverpool had always been concerned to secure an adequate food supply. Motives that had prompted the Corn Laws in 1815 had led him to contemplate their reform, but any change stirred political trouble from the landed interest and risked another round of differences within the cabinet. Wellington and other Tories saw the landed interest – along with bishops and clergy, the great aristocracy, county magistrates, and leading merchants and bankers – as the country's *parti conservateur*. Anything touching on its concerns involved for them more than practical considerations.[120] Reforms Liverpool had in mind to protect consumer and producer alike through a sliding scale required a deft touch to mollify fears that support for agriculture would be ended. Likely political trouble made him delay until other matters forced the issue under increasingly difficult circumstances.

Parliament adjourned on May 24 with elections starting in English boroughs a few weeks later and continuing through June. Canning and Eldon both anticipated in January gains for their respective sides on the Catholic question. Lord Carlisle thought a June election would be less favorable for ministers than last year, but he saw little party spirit in March except against Catholics. The previous year's agitation over Catholic Emancipation had stirred English opinion to a degree felt in the constituencies. Controversy over the Corn Laws, along with Liverpool's May statement on the temporary relaxation of duties to relieve distress, made it another topic of discussion, but one that lacked a clear focus as sentiment regarding agricultural protection did not fall along such sharp lines as the Catholic question.[121] Hobhouse described the English returns as "decidedly friendly to ministers and particularly to the Protestants." Whigs fared badly in populous constituencies, but the influence Catholic priests exerted over forty shilling freeholders in Ireland struck an ominous note. Peel warned that party animosities there never stood higher. O'Connell and his associates realized the potential of the electoral weapon the Catholic Association now had available.[122] Liverpool upheld the government's neutrality on the Catholic question, but that meant denying an angry Palmerston support when several Protestant colleagues stood against him for Cambridge University. Palmerston's consequent reliance on Whig votes for reelection and his growing belief that "the stupid old Tory party" who resisted the government comprised the real opposition indicated trouble ahead.[123]

Renewed concern about the harvest underlined the need to reform the Corn Laws, particularly when the government issued an order in council that opened ports for certain foodstuffs at a duty to be specified later.[124] The step exceeded the authority Liverpool had secured in May and required a subsequent indemnity along with fixing the duty on the goods imported. Critics suspected that Liverpool, Peel, Huskisson, and Canning had used momentary panic to undermine protection. Allegations Huskisson had promised Liverpool voters an imminent free trade in grain led Wellington to protest what he called an attempt to limit the cabinet's discretion. Liverpool thought newspaper reports erroneous, but pointed out that he had committed himself to revising the policy during the previous session even though he was not bound on the principles of that change. The deflationary effects on agriculture of reducing taxes and returning the currency to gold made necessary some adjustment.[125]

Distrust kept dissension simmering below the surface of cabinet discussions. Huskisson, increasingly attacked by Tory journalists as a crypto-Jacobin, aroused an almost pathological hatred. Realizing what he called "the unjust prejudice which prevails respecting Huskisson," Liverpool kept him largely in the background of early deliberations. He and Canning would introduce the eventual changes to the Corn Laws as the government's proposal rather than a departmental one.[126] When he circulated Huskisson's October 18 memorandum to select colleagues, including Peel, Liverpool noted sharing it with the whole cabinet would be imprudent. Accepting the need to protect agriculture from prices falling too low while securing consumers from shortage and excessive price, he believed country gentlemen would accept a productive duty up to the price of fifty-five or sixty shillings a quarter of wheat. Sixty shillings was the remunerative price. Above that rate Liverpool took Huskission's suggestion to propose lowering the duty on a sliding scale to permit controlled imports.[127] Huskisson welcomed the change. Although Westmorland expressed predictable outrage, the cabinet as a whole accepted the plan by late November. It struck a compromise, as Canning noted by casting "the balance of principle in favor of trade and the balance of price in favor of agriculture."[128] Liverpool had found a typically pragmatic solution, but now the issue had taken on symbolic meaning for competing factions that made it harder to manage.

A foreign crisis occupied Liverpool, Wellington, and Canning as Portugal sought British support against a Spanish-backed insurgency. Since the Portuguese had adopted liberal institutions that Spain rejected, Liverpool considered their army's efficiency the best guarantee of peace, but internal tensions raised doubts Portugal could protect its independence. When the Portuguese requested that William Beresford, who had reorganized and led their army during the Peninsular War, again take command, the triumvirate considered whether to agree and on what terms. Besides dispatching Beresford, the government organized a British expeditionary force under Sir William Henry Clinton to underline its commitment to Portuguese independence while avoiding escalation.[129] Canning forcefully defended the government's approach of combining preparations with a measured diplomatic tone as "enabling Spain to preserve peace without dishonor." He went further, however, in a famous rhetorical flourish by declaring that to check French predominance earlier he had "called the New World into existence to redress the balance of the Old."[130] Those impromptu words, certain to annoy Wellington and revive differences over the recognition of South America, drew more attention than the main arguments of his speech and became a lasting phrase.

Wellington had picked a quarrel of his own with Liverpool over his brother Gerald's appointment to an Irish bishopric. It drove Liverpool to distraction by late December despite Arbuthnot's valiant efforts to mend relations. Liverpool had rejected Gerald's elevation to an Irish bishopric on the ground he had refused to divorce an adulterous wife despite public scandal. Wellesley drew Wellington into the matter when the premier had rejected his overture in August. The more Wellington considered it the more convinced he became that Liverpool took a narrow and shortsighted view. He believed any other man whose brothers held such high offices would have received ample preferment. Almost inevitably, given the circumstances and subject of clerical appointments, Liverpool took the moral ground and reiterated his objections to promoting a clergyman living apart from his wife. Wellington, who laid the entire blame on Gerald's wife, accused Liverpool of hypocrisy.[131] Arbuthnot tried to mediate, pointing out that Wellington believed himself Liverpool's firmest supporter in the government and felt great pressure from his family. Liverpool replied angrily that Arbuthnot's letter had made him physically sick. While pained to think he had made Liverpool ill, Arbuthnot insisted that he considered it his duty to keep him and Wellington together. It had become impossible to calm Wellington's galled feelings over the immediate point and his anger threatened a break with their differences on foreign and domestic policy.[132] Bathurst thought the evidence justified Liverpool and believed him more conciliatory to Wellington than before, but lamented the tone he had taken. The whole exchange left both men dissatisfied and defensive.[133]

Increasing strain contributed to the illness that kept Liverpool from parliament in early December. He took the enforced absence "as a hint I am better fitted now for repose than for the labors and still more for the anxieties of the situation which I have held for so many years." With the Catholic question as it stood and controversy over the Corn Laws in prospect, Liverpool expected the government would break up during the coming year. At present, he told Robinson, it "hangs by a thread."[134] Harriet Arbuthnot thought Liverpool's talk of resigning differed now from his habitual complaints as he spoke of his latest illness having left him greatly shaken. The premier also dreaded the mail with its prospect of hectoring missives from Canning. Her bias showed in a judgment that also reflected an informed sense of the toll the past year had taken. Liverpool's talk that extending his life a few more years would require "care & attention & above all *repose*" showed his own realization that he had reached a limit. As he later told Peel, "no man knew what it was like to have been prime minister for fifteen years and never in all that period to have opened his morning letters without a feeling of apprehension."[135] Canning thought Liverpool planned to retire when the parliamentary session closed, but he and his private secretary discovered on joining the premier in Bath that his health and spirits had improved. Reminiscing about earlier days occupied an evening. Liverpool never spoke of retiring.[136]

Indeed, he soon returned to business in London while Canning was confined at home through February with rheumatic fever. Canning had quipped to Wellington that whoever made arrangements for the Duke of York's recent funeral must have taken a bet or insurance on the lives of the mourners who had stood upon a cold damp floor that left both of them and several others sick afterward.[137] Besides confirming the government's neutrality on the Catholic question against pressure on both sides, Liverpool proceeded with plans to introduce a revised corn bill along the lines agreed in November. He moved the address of condolence to the king on the Duke of York's death on February 12, 1827. Two days later he proposed an increased grant for the Duke of Clarence who now stood next in line to the throne. Friends thought he handled the latter business with an uncharacteristic lack of efficiency. Eldon and the Treasury secretary, Joseph Planta, who both spent time with him on February 16, nevertheless believed they had never seen Liverpool in better health and spirits. His real state remained hard to assess.[138]

After opening the morning post with his private secretaries on Saturday, February 17, Liverpool carried some of the letters to read over breakfast. The servant who brought the meal noticed him sitting oddly and later remarked that he made no attempt at conversation. Nothing, however, seemed to him particularly out of order. On returning twenty minutes later, he found Liverpool collapsed unconscious and inert on the floor with a crumpled letter in his hand. Although physicians treated him promptly, Liverpool only regained consciousness a few days later and remained unable to speak. Not until the second week of March could he control his right side enough to walk with difficulty. Liverpool's speech remained semi-articulate. Improvement, as Harriet Arbuthnot wrote, did not "amount to a return of reason." Although he moved from Fife House in

London to the quieter surroundings of Coombe Wood, a cerebral hemorrhage had left Liverpool an invalid with doubtful prospects.[139] Only two days after the stroke, *The Times* declared it rendered Liverpool "politically, if not literally dead." The *Morning Chronicle* deemed it "extremely unlikely that he will ever again submit to the toils and anxieties from which it is understood he has long been anxious to free himself."[140]

The news caused a great sensation among Liverpool's colleagues, though some remarked how little anybody seemed to care about the man himself rather than the political consequences of his illness.[141] Peel convened those ministers available for a cabinet meeting the evening of the stroke and then brought word to the king at Brighton. Upon returning the following Monday he went at the king's command to Canning, himself still recuperating. They agreed to do nothing for the moment and await indications whether or not their colleague would recover sufficiently to continue in office. George IV concurred. Matters stood on hold for some weeks even as rumors, conjectures, and projects for reconstructing the government circulated. Early accounts expressed guarded optimism, but as one insider remarked that "the few who could speak with the most knowledge & with the greatest authority on the subject either decline to speak at all or use very guarded language."[142] When his wife spoke encouragingly of his return to business on March 23 and told him the king had kept his post open, Liverpool movingly replied, "no, no, not I...too weak." A few weeks later the king's private secretary informed her that a successor had to be named. Her husband seemed to acquiesce.[143]

Events quickly overshadowed Liverpool even as the president of the Royal Academy drew a cheer with a toast for his recovery at a dinner in May.[144] The blow-up Croker had long predicted came when George IV chose Canning to succeed Liverpool. Peel, Wellington, and others refused to serve under him. The king accepted their departure as a chance to assert his own authority. Canning's appeal to sympathetic Whigs only alienated his Tory rivals further even though it also split the opposition between those willing to back him and others like Grey who refused.[145] His death in August did not mend Tory divisions. Had Canning died before Liverpool, the government may have survived a transition to the leadership of Wellington and Peel. If he had lived a few years longer, the coalition Canning formed would have enjoyed a fair trial either to reshape the political landscape or collapse in failure. Instead, the timing of his death left the eggs broken with the proverbial omelet still unmade.[146] Robinson, ennobled as Lord Goderich, briefly led Canning's administration before giving way in January 1828 to Wellington. Recent differences, however, made it impossible to reconstruct an administration embracing as broad a spectrum of Tory opinion as Liverpool's government had done. Canning's friends operated as a semi-detached group. Repealing the Test and Corporation Acts set a wedge dividing Tories that Catholic Emancipation drove home. Conceding it also removed the last principled argument for preserving the representative system as it was. Liberal and high Tories alike embraced a position on parliamentary reform Wellington could not accept.

By then, Liverpool seemed largely forgotten as a secluded invalid. Although lucid enough in late August, 1827 to sign a codicil to his will authorizing a few personal and charitable bequests, a further stroke had rendered him a mental and physical shadow. Liverpool died on December 4, 1828 in the presence of his wife, brother, and trusted steward. A funeral cortege smaller than that for Louisa carried the former premier's remains from Coombe Wood with a crowd paying its respects at neighboring Kingston, where Liverpool had long been active in the parish. On December 18, Liverpool was laid to rest at Hawkesbury Church in Gloucestershire alongside Louisa and his parents with a quiet interment. No memorial marked the spot for another thirty years, until Sir George Samuel Jackson erected a tablet on the church wall commemorating the man who had governed Britain for fifteen years.[147]

CONCLUSION

Weathering the Storm

D RAMATIC EVENTS OVER the years after Liverpool's stroke eclipsed his public reputation. The political crisis ending with the 1832 Reform Act marked a watershed that set the terms on which he would be remembered. Conflicts over issues that had made Liverpool essential for holding a revived Tory party together ironically pushed him into the background even before he died. The split gave Whigs an opening they had lacked since 1783 as personal differences and policy disputes upset the parliamentary base of Liverpool's administration. Repealing the Test and Corporation Acts and then passing Catholic Emancipation also began a constitutional revolution that swept away the balanced constitution Liverpool had upheld through his long career. Instead, "parliamentary government" transferred powers over executive government formerly held by the Crown to ministers as members of a cabinet answerable to parliament, primarily the Commons.[1] The shift made Liverpool seem a figure of a bygone age with scant relevance to politics from the 1830s. What had been pressing controversies – Walter Bagehot took Catholic Emancipation as an obvious case from 1856 – were no longer even political questions. Doubts about them seemed absurd to younger generations. Harriet Martineau revealingly described parliament in 1816 as closer to its predecessor a hundred years before than to her own readers in the 1840s.[2] Liverpool became a relic of that much earlier world.

The way Liverpool quickly faded from view raises questions about both his legacy and the larger narrative that framed nineteenth-century British history. Brougham noted in retrospect that blame never fell directly upon Liverpool: "while others were the objects of alternate excretion and scorn, he was generally respected, never assailed." A prime minister spared criticism marked a "singular spectacle" that Brougham attributed to Liverpool's mediocrity. Praise, like blame, fell to those seen as responsible while Liverpool merely oversaw their actions. "Respectable mediocrity," Brougham dismissively observed, "offends nobody." Spencer Walpole, who wrote a popular history of the decades after Waterloo, deemed Liverpool "respectable in everything," but "eminent in nothing." Martineau considered his role "something like the station which a quiet and prudent king may fill in other countries" at the head of the nation's councils while others determined policy and

managed business. She thought Liverpool "a good balance-wheel when the move-
ments of parties might otherwise be going too fast" but his main accomplishment
was "choosing and conciliating able men, and keeping them together in sufficient harmony to get through their work." With Bathurst and Sidmouth, he was
neither envied nor feared "for the force of their characters or the splendor of their
talents."[3] The hostile verdict that marginalized Liverpool stuck.

It also served a larger purpose of validating an emerging liberal consensus on
the early nineteenth century. Historians, publicists, and politicians who had seen
their aims repeatedly thwarted had a considerable stake in framing the period
before 1830 as stagnant and reactionary. Their rhetorical strategy encompassed
culture and politics to make the recent past seem like a different world operating on
premises that no longer mattered or even made sense. Liberals, particularly those
like Palmerston who had changed their allegiance, pressed the case for decades to
bolster their standing on the right side of history. George Cornewall Lewis, the
Edinburgh Review editor Palmerston briefed in the 1850s, described Whigs of
Liverpool's day as "not only more liberal and tolerant than the Tories," but also
"more enlightened and philosophical" on finance, economic affairs, legal reform,
and foreign policy. As Liverpool's government lost its hold upon the public, Lewis
insisted that the opposition rose steadily in popular esteem.[4] Bagehot thought
the French Revolution had left the wealthy and comfortable "afraid of catching
revolution" like "an infectious disease, beginning no one knows how, and going
no one knows where."[5] Their anxieties fueled reflexive opposition to reform and
what liberals deemed a thoughtless approach to public questions. Tories from the
1790s, William Lecky claimed, adopted Burke's dread of organic change in state,
church, and society without his disposition toward administrative reform.[6] The
result brought stagnation ended by a wave of reform held back too long.

Complaints that "old corruption" had diverted an undue portion of the country's wealth to the well-connected whether as salaried officials, clergy, or holders of government debt gave credence to Lecky's view. But the charge ignored
Liverpool's part in dismantling the system that provided the patronage so vocally
denounced. Claims of elite parasitism that bolstered a critique of the Established
Church as a pillar of the temporal order reinforced a standard view of the eighteenth-century constitution as an oppressive, unresponsive system incapable
of adapting without sweeping reform. Thomas Babbington Macaulay called
the 1832 Reform Act "the revolution which brought parliament into harmony
with the nation" just as the Glorious Revolution had "brought the Crown into
harmony with parliament."[7] Liverpool, from that standpoint, had overseen the
final, stagnant years of disharmony. Martineau unsurprisingly considered reform
as "that vital renovation of our representative system which will be to thoughtful
students of a thousand years hence what Magna Charta is to us."[8]

The politicians and publicists who cast the closing decades of the long eighteenth century that closed in 1832 as an era of darkness only then dispelled by

enlightenment and progress set a lasting narrative that guided historians as their subject developed as an academic discipline from mid-century. Liberal historians rearranged English political history into a benign, teleological pattern of unfolding parliamentary liberties and representative government. Anyone outside that narrative they dismissed as an impediment to welcome change. Social historians focusing on the plebeian experience during the age of agricultural enclosure and industrial urbanization rendered their own critical verdict on Liverpool's era as a time of hardship worsened by elite indifference or exploitation. Scholars like E. P. Thompson formed by the impact of Marxism between the twentieth-century world wars reinforced that verdict even as they challenged or modified the liberal consensus.[9] Diplomatic historians and scholars of international relations, particularly Sir Charles Webster who advised British officials in both twentieth-century World Wars, offered a reassessment of British foreign policy during the Napoleonic Wars and their aftermath that rehabilitated its architects. Liverpool still remained a minor, supporting character in works that did not change the larger narrative of early nineteenth-century British history until the second half of the twentieth century.

Even those who inherited the revived Tory party that formed during Liverpool's career rarely turned to its leading figures for guidance. The early nineteenth century fell into neglect as a transitional period between a heroic age dominated by the Younger Pitt and then Peel's turn to reform as leader of a rebranded Conservative party. A Conservative revival under Derby, Disraeli, and later Salisbury further overshadowed Liverpool and his mature career. Taking Disraeli as an inspiration, the party turned away from Peel, Liverpool, and lessons drawn from the 1820s. Despite sharing much of Liverpool's outlook, Salisbury thought him too preoccupied with the kind of political management Disraeli satirized with the characters of Tadpole and Taper in *Coningsby* at the expense of principled engagement with larger issues.[10] Salisbury's view reflected the standard assumption that the country seemed to govern Liverpool more than he governed it. Despite filling an important place, Liverpool was not himself an important man; keystone of the arch, in Lewis' evocative phrase, rather than capital or column. Conservatives never built a politically useful narrative around Liverpool or the early nineteenth century as they had earlier done around Pitt, whose suitably revised persona became a cornerstone of the second Tory party.[11] Nobody had a stake in defending Liverpool's legacy or saw much advantage in trying before well into the twentieth century.

Regardless of their own political outlook, historians by the 1970s turned increasingly to the early nineteenth century to understand developments in the 1830s and 40s. Debates over questions ranging from Poor Laws and Corn Laws to the structure of the laissez-faire state took form during Liverpool's career. Boyd Hilton's study of Tory economic policy from 1815 through 1830 led him to engage with the period's cultural and intellectual trends. Others, including Richard Brent and Jonathan Parry, acknowledged the post-Waterloo years' importance for understanding decades that followed.[12] Victorian liberalism emerged partly in reaction to Liverpool's policies and certainly with a growing attention to the notion of public opinion driven by middle class politicization. Conservatives also struggled to adapt even before controversy over parliamentary reform swept them from office. Where E. P. Thompson argued famously that the years from 1790 and 1830 saw the making of an English working class, James Sack presents compelling evidence for a resilient conservative ethos forming over a period extending from the publication of Burke's *Reflections* and James Boswell's *Life of Johnson* to Peel's Tamworth Manifesto in 1834.[13] The decades that preceded the Reform era provided a better understanding of liberal – and radical – thinking along with a bridge linking Pitt's era with that of Peel. It follows logically that Norman Gash, who made a career of politics during the age of Peel and showed notable attention to the Conservative party, turned in his retirement to a study of Liverpool that Margaret Thatcher took up for her holiday reading.

Reading Liverpool's story forward from the eighteenth century brings out important continuities that shaped his career. A perspective that sets his outlook and formative experience into sharper focus also makes intelligible key aspects of the political and institutional context in which he operated. As Gash rightly points out, Liverpool led the last great eighteenth-century administration in structure and length while facing challenges that made it the first great nineteenth-century government.[14] Martineau captured more than she knew in calling Liverpool a good balance wheel because he managed both to check escalating pressures at key moments and press ahead with reforms that carried the public behind his administration. Bringing opinion ahead of what it might otherwise contemplate involved leadership that served the deeply conservative aim of upholding the established constitution in Church and state by drawing to its support new interest groups within the realm. Far from opposing administrative reform as Lecky alleged, Liverpool used it effectively in a Burkean sense to prove the system could respond and adapt on its own terms. Dampening social tension and striving to secure a broadly based prosperity validated the government's legitimacy while demonstrating its responsiveness to popular opinion. Liverpool showed considerable imagination with the politics of addition that drew support to his administration while denying opposition Whigs and radical groups the backing they needed to challenge it. Even with ominous clouds gathering in early 1827, he shaped the political environment quite effectively. Only after his departure from public life did the administration split irrevocably.

Liverpool avoided personal blame as discontent boiled over, but the fact that colleagues bore the brunt of outrage did not make his situation easy. Brougham's suggestion that the couch of office "so thorny to others, was to him of down" ignores the strain Liverpool felt behind the scenes.[15] It does capture, however, the advantage he enjoyed working out of sight as the fulcrum of his government who scrupulously maintained a balance among its component parts while holding respect in both parliament and beyond its doors.[16] Liverpool managed not by conciliation or exercising a charisma he obviously lacked, but rather by seeing a step or two ahead when he set policy and directed the strategy to implement it. Knowledge and experience gave an advantage with colleagues. He used political tactics effectively to deflect conflict where possible, contain it when not, and secure outcomes he preferred. Final decisions on appointments and patronage – along with the difficulties they aroused – also fell to Liverpool. The lead colleagues took often reflected the demands of parliamentary business and relations with George IV. Clement Atlee's much later remark during his tenure as premier after 1945 that "if you have a good dog, don't bark yourself" captures part of the difference between the image politics often presents from outside and the reality of how cabinet government worked.[17] Relying upon the strengths and public standing of colleagues while guiding policy was among Liverpool's talents. It helped make him the keystone of the political architecture that had weathered the storm of war and its aftermath.

The Catholic question marked the great failure of Liverpool's career that foreshadowed problems looming in 1827. It could neither be avoided nor settled in the 1820s on terms Liverpool could accept. Resolving the issue much earlier with Act of Union or through the kind of concordat with Rome that Wellington favored would have prevented O'Connell from building the Catholic Association into a mass movement across Ireland backed by the clergy that posed exactly the danger seen from plebeian radicals in England during the summer of 1819. Liverpool had checked unrest in England to uphold order within a constitutional framework by rallying the propertied classes and allowing plebeian agitation to fade. Ireland presented a very different situation during the 1820s where circumstances dealt O'Connell a much stronger hand that enabled him in 1828 to force Wellington into an unwelcome choice between concession and repression.

Liverpool's commitment to the Church of England reinforced by George III's refusal to accept Catholic Emancipation with the Act of Union drew the future premier into an increasingly entrenched stance. Here loyalty worked as a tragic flaw by narrowing options and denying Liverpool the flexibility he showed elsewhere. Tory sentiment largely sympathized with Catholicism in the 1790s, as did many politicians until George III declared his own views.[18] A concordat regularizing Catholicism in Ireland need not have affected the Established Church's constitutional position in England any more than a Presbyterian Kirk in Scotland had under the 1707 Act of Union. The prospect of securing Catholic loyalty in Ireland underlay support for emancipation by Castlereagh, Canning, and Croker. Liverpool himself realized that economic relations formed the real grounds of Irish discontent – and that those relations could not be adjusted without costly upheaval – but settling the Catholic question earlier when Tory opinion took a less hostile view might have lowered tension without envenoming mainland politics. Instead, Catholic Emancipation split the Tory party after Liverpool's stroke and turned the disgruntled on both sides of the question to parliamentary reform. That step reinforced divisions which created the opening that the Whig opposition seized decisively in late 1830.[19]

It also focuses attention back to assessing Liverpool's record and legacy. His administration almost split in 1826, raising the prospect that renewed conflict would break up the government. Events following his departure from public life swept aside much of the political structure he sought to uphold along with the Tory ascendancy that had taken root since 1783. Measures to break the Anglican political monopoly and restructure parliamentary representation that Liverpool had determinedly resisted brought the sweeping change he feared. What Peel aptly described as a "moral storm" broke upon Westminster with a struggle over relations between the Established Church, Protestant Nonconformists, Catholics, and political institutions culminated in a crisis of parliamentary agency and then brought reforms to local government.[20] The new demands those changes involved set a very different political dynamic to which parties and their leaders responded. A small but telling example came in 1842 when Peel rejected the suggestion he follow Liverpool's precedent with a parliamentary grant for church building on the ground that taxpayers would object. He thought responsibility for the expense rested now with each church and its parishioners rather than the state.[21] On Liverpool's own terms, his career might well seem a failure. The Whigs and radicals who opposed him and their defenders among the intelligentsia who shaped the nineteenth-century consensus on his era certainly thought so.

Viewing Liverpool's career through the prism of 1827–1832, however, gives a distorted perspective on his accomplishments. The oft-quoted remark that "all political lives, unless they are cut off in midstream at a happy juncture, end in failure, because that is the nature of politics and human affairs" captures Liverpool's situation as the problems before him outran available solutions.[22] Much of what he sought to resist came after an incapacitating stroke pulled him from the scene. Until then, he successfully contained pressures for change and channelled them to minimize their impact on the established order. Viewing his career through later changes distorts his accomplishments. Having won the war against Napoleon, as Gash notes, Liverpool also won the peace and set a line of conservative policy.[23] To adapt the formula he used with Castlereagh on foreign affairs in 1814, a return to the settled order of things meant economic shocks or other crises need not spark revolution. Averting upheaval, implementing reforms, and rallying the propertied classes to his government after 1821, Liverpool provided a model for including rising new interests within the established order that showed considerable promise. His conception of a balanced political order with economic and social interests cooperating to secure ordered liberty and property offered an alternative to sweeping organic reform that held its own. Liverpool showed how the system could adapt on its own terms and secure a prosperity and rising living standards that checked political opponents.

Liverpool also had a legacy, albeit often unacknowledged, beyond the reform era. Salisbury articulated a conservative politics during the 1850s and 60s that despite his sharp tone echoed Liverpool's approach. Much the same was true on foreign policy under the 14th Earl of Derby's leadership of the Tory party. Both took a pragmatic approach that limited British involvement with questions where the country lacked direct interest or political leverage.[24] Fiscal and financial policies, including the shift from indirect levies on consumption to direct taxation, in Liverpool's later years set the prototype for Peel's bolder, more integrated program from 1841. The concept he laid out in those policies guided a free trade revolution that Peel promoted and then Gladstone continued. Points regarding the interdependence of commerce, manufacturing, and agriculture, safeguarding plebeian living standards, and pursuing national rather than sectional or class interests that Peel argued in the 1840s had been made in Liverpool's parliamentary speeches of the 1820s.[25] Those remarks themselves drew upon long experience in governing and insight drawn from reading and reflection on eighteenth-century developments. Liverpool displayed considerable imagination by building upon Pitt's legacy and other influences as he adapted to challenges in the early nineteenth century. The conservative trajectory he set testifies to the scale of his accomplishment in office.

Liverpool's achievements over his career and the legacy they established demonstrate his capacity. While neither charismatic nor heroic, he earned the respect of contemporaries and the loyalty of colleagues who appreciated his strengths. Inner steel and trust in his own judgment never pushed him into the overconfidence all too prevalent among successful politicians. Common sense and humility instead gave him the flexibility to adapt when needed, but hold fast under pressure. Personal resilience coupled with an invaluable all-round ability guided both Liverpool's policies and the political arts by which he pursued them. The challenges of war and peace during the early nineteenth century made that task especially difficult. Low points in the struggle against Napoleon and successive political crises from the 1816 parliamentary session through the Queen Caroline Affair in 1820 rendered the outcome anything but certain. Looking back from the placid world of mid-Victorian Britain obscures the tension those who lived through the period felt. Amidst growing tension between Addington's government and those of Pitt's friends on the cusp of directly opposing it, Canning penned an accolade to their lost leader for a banquet on May 28, 1802 honoring the late premier's birthday.[26] The song lauding Pitt as "the pilot that weathered the storm" became a staple of Tory occasions even as the principles celebrated drifted away from those Pitt actually held during his life. Liverpool deserves the description much more for his success after claiming Pitt's mantle in guiding Britain through the storm and strife of a transitional era and toward the calmer weather of mid-Victorian prosperity.

NOTES

INTRODUCTION

1. Stephen M. Lee, *George Canning and Liberal Toryism, 1801–1827* (Woodbridge: 2008), 123; Norman Gash, *Lord Liverpool: The Life and Political Career of Robert Banks Jenkinson, Second Earl of Liverpool, 1770–1828* (Cambridge: 1984), 228–9; *Bristol Mercury*, January 17, 1825; *Felix Farley's Bristol Journal*, January 15, 1825; *Bath Chronicle*, January 20, 1825.
2. *Bristol Mercury*, January 17, 1825.
3. *Bath Chronicle*, January 20, 1825.
4. J. E. Cookson, *Lord Liverpool's Administration: The Crucial Years, 1815–1822* (Edinburgh: 1975), 1.
5. John Derry, "Governing Temperament under Pitt and Liverpool" in *The Whig Ascendancy: Colloquies on Hanoverian England*, ed. John Cannon (New York: 1981), 119.
6. Gash et al., *The Conservatives: A History from their Origins to 1965* (London: 1977), 52.
7. Angus Hawkins, *Victorian Political Culture: "Habits of Heart in Mind"* (Oxford: 2015), 8–9; *Croker Papers*, II:124–5.
8. Cookson, 396; Gash, *Liverpool*, 254, 7.
9. Richard A. Gaunt, *Sir Robert Peel: The Life and Legacy* (London: 2010), 154. A Tory party shaped by Disraeli and Salisbury downplayed Peel's legacy, leaving him to their rivals until the 1930s.
10. Muir, *Wellington*, I:viii.
11. Boyd Hilton. "The Political Arts of Lord Liverpool," *Transactions of the Royal Historical Society* 5th ser. 38(1988): 147–70.
12. Walter L. Arnstein, "Norman Gash: Peelite" in *Recent Historians of Great Britain: Essays on the Post 1945 Generation*, ed. Arnstein (Ames: 1990), 165; Brian Harrison and Theodore Hoppen, "Norman Gash," *Biographical Memoirs of Fellows of the British Academy* 40 (2012):215.
13. Harrison and Hoppen, 206, 217–18.
14. Gash, *The Conservatives*, 38.
15. Hilton," Political Arts," 147–8, 250; Ibid., *A Mad Bad Dangerous People? England, 1783–1846* (Oxford: 2006), 311.
16. Malcolm Chase, *1820: Disorder and Instability in the United Kingdom* (Manchester: 2013), 21.
17. Roger Knight, *Britain Against Napoleon: The Organization of Victory, 1793–1815* (London: 2013), xxii, xxxviii.
18. Hawkins, 1.

19. Marilyn Morris, *Sex, Money and Personal Character in Eighteenth-Century British Politics* (New Haven: 2014), 5; Paul Langford, "Politics and Manners from Sir Robert Walpole to Sir Robert Peel," *Proceedings of the British Academy* 94(1996): 121.

20. J. C. D. Clark, *English Society, 1660-1832: Religion, Ideology and Politics During the Ancien Régime* (Cambridge: 2000), 123, 23–4.

21. H. T. Dickinson, *Liberty and Property: Political Ideology in Eighteenth-Century Britain* (New York: 1977), 143, 149–50; Hawkins, 34–5.

22. W. R. Brock, *Lord Liverpool and Liberal Toryism: 1820 to 1827* (Cambridge: 1941), 24–5.

23. *PH* 17 (February 6, 1772): 269–70; Ibid., 30 (May 6, 1793): 810–20.

24. *PH* 30 (May 6, 1793): 820.

25. Peter Jupp, *The Governing of Britain, 1688–1848: The Executive, Parliament and the People* (London: 2006), 137.

26. Lee, 151; Philip Harling, *The Waning of "Old Corruption": The Politics of Economical Reform in Britain, 1779–1848* (Oxford: 1996), 51–5.

27. Webster, *Foreign Policy*, II:14; *Croker Papers*, I:231.

28. Langford, "Politics and Manners," 118.

29. Jupp, 123–6, 143.

30. Lady Bessborough to Granville Leveson-Gower. February 1802. *Leveson-Gower*, I:329.

31. Brock, 32.

32. Arbuthnot to William Huskisson. December 2, 1822. Add MSS 38743.

33. Sydney Smith to Bishop Bloomfield. September 5, 1840. *The Letters of Sydney Smith*, ed. N. C. Smith, 2 vols. (Oxford: 1953), II:709. Noting that the "Hungry Forties" saw much greater social tension than a later era of mid-Victorian prosperity only underlines Smith's point.

34. David Eastwood, "The Age of Uncertainty: Britain in the Early Nineteenth Century," *Transactions of the Royal Historical Society* 8(1998): 113.

1. ANTECEDENTS AND UPBRINGING

1. Wordsworth, "My Heart Leaps Up When I Behold" (1802).

2. Anthony Addington to Charles Jenkinson. July 23, 1770. Add MSS 38469; Amarantha Jenkinson to Charles Jenkinson. July 19, 1770. Loan 72/58.

3. Jean-Marc Alter, "The Life and Early Career of Robert Banks Jenkinson, the Second Earl of Liverpool, 1770–1812" (University of Wales: Ph.D. Diss., 1988), 2.

4. Sushil Chaudury, "All the Main Conspirators – The Making of the Plassy Revolution," *Indian Historical Review* 24.1–2(1997–8): 104–33; William Watts, *Memoirs of the Revolution in Bengal, Anno. Dom. 1757. By Which Meer Jaffeir was Raised to the Government of that Province together with Those of Babar and Orixa* (London: 1760).

5. Lucy S. Sutherland, *The East India Company in Eighteenth-Century Politics* (Oxford: 1952), 125; Charles Jenkinson to Richard Wolters. [1764] Add MSS 38304 f. 20.

6. Portugal's settlement in Goa had created a hybrid world of overlapping cultures from the sixteenth century and marriage with Indian women had been encouraged. William Dalrymple, *White Mughals: Love and Betrayal in Eighteenth-Century India* (New York: 2002), 7–10.

7. Gash, *Liverpool*, 10.

8. Nicholas K. Robinson, *Edmund Burke: A Life in Caricature* (New Haven: 1996). One of the most caricatured figures of his day, Burke is the sixth person most often featured among the British Museum's satirical prints from 1778–97, after the king, his eldest son, and three prime ministers.

9. Dalrymple, 39–40.

10. Charles Jenkinson [then Lord Liverpool] to G. Chalmers. July 7, 1797. Add MSS 38310.

11. *The Voyage of Master Anthony Jenkinson, made from the City of Mosco in Russia, to the City of Boghar in Bactria, in the year 1558; Written by Himself to the Merchants of London of the Muscovy Company* in Richard Hakluyt, *The Principal Navigations, Voyages, Traffiques, and Discoveries of the English Nation*, 12 vols. (Glasgow: 1903–5), II:449–79.

12. T. S. Willen, *The Early History of the Russia Company, 1553–1603* (New York: 1968), 91–2, 118–24.

13. Gash, *Liverpool*, 9.

14. Margaret Banks to Charles Jenkinson. In Ninetta S. Jucker, ed., *The Jenkinson Papers, 1760–1776* (London: 1949), 64–5.

15. B. D. Henning, ed., *History of Parliament: The Commons, 1660–1690*, 3 vols. (London: 1983), II:645.

16. Eveline Cruickshanks, Stuart Handley, and D. W. Hayton, eds., *The House of Commons: 1690–1715*, 5 vols. (Cambridge: 2002), II:467–8, IV:490; Henning, II:645; Romney Sedgewick, ed., *The House of Commons: 1715–1754*, 2 vols. (Oxford: 1970), I:302.

17. Cruickshanks, IV:491; Richard Pares, *George III and the Politicians* (Oxford: 1953), 15.

18. Cruickshanks, IV:490–1; Linda Colley, *In Defiance of Oligarchy: The Tory Party, 1715–60* (Cambridge: 1982), 153.

19. Cruickshanks, IV:491.

20. Peter B. Nockles, *The Oxford Movement in Context: Anglican High Churchmanship 1760–1857* (Cambridge: 1994), 25–6.

21. Colley, 21.

22. Dickinson, *Liberty and Property*, 153; Reed Browning, *Political and Constitutional Ideas of the Court Whigs* (Baton Rouge: 1982), 206.

23. Lord Edward Fitzmaurice, *Life of William, Earl of Shelburne, Afterwards First Marquess of Lansdowne*, 2 vols. (London: 1875), I:45.

24. J. A. W. Gunn, *Beyond Liberty and Property: The Process of Self-Recognition in Eighteenth-Century Political Thought* (Kingston and Montreal: 1983), 191.

25. Richard Price, *British Society, 1680–1880: Dynamism, Containment, Change* (Cambridge: 1999), 241–2.

26. Colley, 124.

27. Fitzmaurice, I:49; Colley, 7.

28. James J. Sack, *From Jacobite to Conservative: Reaction and Orthodoxy in Britain c. 1760–1832* (Cambridge: 1993), 46; William Reginald Ward, *Georgian Oxford: University Politics in the Eighteenth Century* (Oxford: 1958), 131.

29. Robert Tombs, *The English and their History* (New York: 2015), 306, 273.

30. Keith Graham Feiling, *The Second Tory Party, 1714–1832* (London: 1951), 58; Gunn, 149; Dickinson, *Liberty and Property*, 43; Browning, 197.

31. Lord Liverpool to John Wilson Croker. December 7, 1845. *Croker Papers*, III:177.

32. *Croker Papers*, III:178; *Jackson's Oxford Journal*, December 8, 1753 and March 2, 1754.

33. Horace Walpole, *Memoirs of the Reign of King George III*, 4 vols. (Freeport: 1970), I:192.

34. *Grenville Papers*, I:180.

35. Ibid., I:359; Ninetta Jucker, *The Jenkinson Papers* (London: 1949), xi.

36. John Brewer, *Party Ideology and Popular Politics at the Accession of George III* (Cambridge: 1976), 223, 225; Jenkinson's list is in Add MSS 38334; Feiling, 78; Lord John Russell, ed., *Memorials and Correspondence of Charles James Fox*, 2 vols. (Philadelphia: 1853), I:61; Charles Jenkinson to Sir James Lowther. October 30, 1762. Loan 72/51.

37. Charles R. Ritcheson, *British Politics and the American Revolution* (Norman: 1954), 19, 20–1, 25–6; Add MSS 38339 ff. 131–5.

38. *Grenville Papers*, III:393.

39. Jucker, xiv; Pares, 4; Feiling, 104, 101, Ritcheson, *British Politics*, 68–9; Black, *George III*, 68.

40. John Morley, *Edmund Burke: A Historical Study* (New York: 1924), 13.

41. Henry B. Wheatley ed., *The Historical and Posthumous Memoirs of Sir Nathaniel William Wraxall, 1772–1784, Edited with Notes and Additional Chapters from the Author's Unpublished Manuscripts*, 5 vols. (London: 1884), I:417–18.

42. *Gentleman's Magazine* (1770), 598–9.

43. *Burke's Correspondence*, III:89; Pares, 12.

44. Clark, *English Society*, 123; Black, *George III*, 25, 56–7.

45. Jupp, 117.

46. Brewer, 132–3.

47. Frank O'Gorman, *The Rise of Party in England: The Rockingham Whigs, 1760–82* (London: 1975), 28–9, 182; Walpole, II:66.

48. James Vaughn, "The Politics of Empire: Metropolitan Socio-Political Development and the Imperial Transformation of the British East India Company, 1675–1775" (University of Chicago: Ph.D. diss., 2009), 349–50, 317, 515.

49. Pares, 107; Brewer, 50.

50. *PH* 17 (April 5, 1773): 830; Ibid. (April 5, 1772): 650.

51. *PH* 17 (March 14, 1774):1176; Ibid., 18 (May 12, 1775): 646.

52. *PH* 19 (March 17, 1778): 948; Liverpool to Lord Bristol. November 27, 1799. Add MSS 38311; Jenkinson to John Robinson. July 22, 1780. *HMC Abergavenny* (London: 1887), 32.

53. A. M. C. Waterman, "The Nexus Between Theology and Political Doctrine in Church and Dissent" in *Enlightenment and Religion: Rational Dissent in Eighteenth-Century Britain*, Knud Haakonssen (Cambridge: 1996), 194–5; Clark, *The Language of Liberty: Political Discourse and Social Dynamics in the Anglo-American World, 1660–1832* (Cambridge: 1994), 166–7.

54. *PH* 17 (February 23, 1773): 752–3.

55. *PH* 17 (February 6, 1772): 269–70.

56. Waterman, 194–5; Clark, *Language of Liberty*, 166–7.

57. Nockles, 25–6; Clark, *English Society*, 44, 316; Sack, *Jacobite to Conservative*, 76–7.

58. Feiling, 102; Russell, *Fox*, I:51–2.

59. Sutherland, 215; Mackesy, 247–8.

60. Charles Jenkinson to Lord Harcourt. December 29, 1777. Jucker, xxv.

61. *PH* 20 (November 25, 1775): 1138.

62. *London Evening Post*, December 30, 1775.

63. Jenkinson to George III. January 22, 1782. Fortescue, V:338.

64. North to George III. January 21, 1782. Fortescue, V:336–7.

65. *Life and Letters of Sir Gilbert Elliot, First Earl of Minto, 1751–1806*, ed. Countess of Minto, 3 vols. (London: 1874), I:76–7.

66. Charles Jenkinson to John Robinson. June 13, 1782. Add MSS 38309; John Norris, *Shelburne and Reform* (London: 1963), 170.

67. John Eden, Lord Auckland, *Journal and Correspondence of William, Lord Auckland* (London:1862), I:33; Cannon, *The Fox–North Coalition: Crisis of the Constitution, 1782–4* (Cambridge: 1969), 29; Robinson to Jenkinson. October 12, 1782. Add MSS 38567.

68. Lord Thurlow to George III, March 10, 1783. Fortescue, VI:269–71; Memorandum by George III. March 30, 1783. Ibid., VI:321–7. Cannon, *Fox–North Coalition*, 77–8; George III to Lord Weymouth. March 25, 1783. Fortescue, VI:310.

69. Draft of a Message from the King to Parliament. March 28, 1783. Fortescue, VI:316–7; George III to Lord Temple. April 1, 1783. Fortescue, VI: 329–30.

70. Russell, *Fox*, II:71, 90.

71. Jenkinson to Robinson. September 24, 1783. HMC Abergavenny, 63.

72. Robinson to Jenkinson. December 1, 1783. BL Loan 72/29; Jenkinson to Robinson. December 5, 1783. HMC Abergavenny, 61; R. Atkinson to Robinson. December 8, 1783. Ibid.

73. Feiling, 156.

74. George III to North. December 18, 1783. Fortescue, VI:476.

75. Gibbon to Lord Edward Eliot. October 27, 1784. *Letters of Edward Gibbon*, III:20.

76. Jenkinson to Mrs. Johnson. February 1784. Add MSS 38309.

77. Lord John Russell called the split between Pitt and Fox "another evil consequence of the struggle of 1784." *Fox*, II:202–3; Feiling, 160.

78. Black, *George III*, 268; *LC* I:xxxvii; Hilton, *Dangerous People*, 30.

79. Jenkinson to Robinson. December 24, 1783. HMC Abergavenny. 64.

80. Robinson to Jenkinson. BL Loan 72/29. December 22, 1783.

81. Feiling, 158.

82. Jenkinson to J. Horne. November 16, 1784. Add MSS 38309.

83. Cornwall to Jenkinson; December 1785. Loan 71/59; Pitt to Jenkinson. April 17, 1786. Loan 72/38.

84. Michael J. Turner, *Pitt the Younger: A Life* (London: 2003), 101; *Elliot Letters*, I:106.

85. Stanhope, Philip Henry, Earl of, *Life of the Right Honorable William Pitt*, 4 vols. (London: 1862), I:306. Hawkesbury also received the sinecure as chancellor to the Duchy of Lancaster "during pleasure" rather than for life as he had sought. Pitt made the post a surety for Jenkinson's loyalty.

86. *The Rolliad, in Two Parts; Probationary Odes for the Laureatship; And Political Ecologues and Miscellanies*, 2nd edition (London: 1812), 499–501.

87. *The Extraordinary and Facetious History of the Immaculate Boy: Who, John Gilpin Like, Ran a GreaterRrisk than he Intended, and Came Home Safe at Last. / As read at the Cockpit-Royal, and received with uncommon applause* (London: 1785).

88. *Wraxall Memoirs*, III:220.

89. *PH* 26 (June 1, 1786): 81.

90. Mackesy, *War Without Victory: The Downfall of Pitt, 1799–1802* (Oxford: 1984), 11.

91. William Woodfall to Eden. February 3, 1787. *Auckland Journal*, I:171

92. *Wraxall Memoirs*, III:351.

93. Amarantha Jenkinson to Charles Jenkinson. October 16, 1770. Loan 72/58.

94. Sir Bankes Jenkinson to Charles Jenkinson. October 4–12, 1771. Loan 72/46; John Jenkinson to Charles Jenkinson. June 6, 1775. BL Loan 72/54; Alter, 4.

95. Gash, *Liverpool*, 11.

96. Charles Wolfram Cornwall to Charles Jenkinson. March 31, 1777. Loan 72/59.

97. Paul Langford, *A Polite and Commercial People: England, 1727–1783* (Oxford: 1989), 4; Vic Gatrell, *City of Laughter: Sex and Satire in Eighteenth-Century London* (New York: 2006), 160.

98. Mrs. Eugenia Stanhope, ed., *Letters Written by the Late Right Honorable Philip Dormer Stanhope, Earl of Chesterfield, to his Son, Philip Stanhope Esq*, 2nd edn, 4 vols. (London: 1774), 155; Clark, *English Society*, 221–2.

99. James Boswell, *Life of Johnson*, ed. R.W. Chapman (Oxford: 1980), 188, 610; Adam Smith, *Theory of Moral Sentiments*, ed. D. D. Raphael and A.L. Macfie (Indianapolis: 1982), 388–9.

100. Peter Waldo to Charles Jenkinson, February 22, 1779. Add MSS 38306.

101. Robert Banks Jenkinson to Charles Jenkinson. October 20, 1779 Add MSS 59772; ibid., May 9, 1781. Add MSS 38580.

102. Jenkinson to Frances Johnson. April 21, 1780. Add MSS 38307.

103. Charles Wolfram Cornwall to Charles Jenkinson. September 9, 1781. Loan 72/59.

104. Alter, 7; Sir Bankes Jenkinson to Charles Jenkinson. January 13, 1779. Loan 72/46.

105. Gash, *Liverpool*, 11.

106. Charles Jenkinson to Lord Percy. May 21, 1791. Add MSS 38310.

107. M. V. Wallbank, "Eighteenth-Century Public Schools and the Education of the Governing Elite," *History of Education* 8.1 (1979), 1–3, 6: Clark, *English Society*, 225.

108. Gibbon, *Memoirs of My Life*, ed. G. A. Bonnard (London: 1966), 38.

109. Wallbank, 11–2, 15; Browning, 214–15; Clark, *English Society*, 223.

110. Charles Jenkinson to Frances Johnson. June 8, 1784. Add MSS 38389.

111. Charles Jenkinson to Robert Banks Jenkinson. November 4, 1784. Loan 72/51.

112. *Gentleman's Magazine* (1828) part 1, 81; Mokyr, *The Enlightened Economy: An Economic History of Britain, 1700–1850* (New Haven: 2009), 70.

113. Charles Jenkinson to Robert Banks Jenkinson. November 4, 1784. Loan 72/51.

114. Peter Waldo to Charles Jenkinson. February 22, 1779. Add MSS 38210; Elizabeth Cornwall to Charles Jenkinson. December 10, 1782. Loan 72/59; S. J. DuRosel to Charles Jenkinson. August 23 1781. Add MSS 38471; Elizabeth Cornwall to Charles Jenkinson. January 10, 1784. Loan MSS 72/59.

115. Sir Bankes Jenkinson to Charles Jenkinson. January 31, 1786. Loan MSS 72/47; Charles Jenkinson to Robert Banks Jenkinson. November 27, 1784. Loan MSS 72/51.

116. Charles Jenkinson to Robert Banks Jenkinson. November 15, 1784. Loan MSS 72/51

117. Robert Banks Jenkinson to Charles Jenkinson. October 2, 1785. October 2, 1785. Add MSS 59772.
118. Cornwall to Hawkesbury. December 2, 1786. Add MSS 38221; Hawkesbury to Cornwall. December 5, 1786. BL Add MSS 38309.
119. Hawkesbury to Frances Johnson. November 30, 1786. Add MSS 38309.
120. Gash, *Liverpool,* 12–13; Knight, xxxiii; Jenkinson to Hawkesbury. April 26, 1787. Add MSS 59772.
121. Hawkesbury to Cyril Jackson. April 25, 1786. Add MSS 38309.
122. Jackson to Hawkesbury. May 6, 1787. Add MSS 38580.
123. Jenkinson to Hawkesbury. June 4, 1787. Add MSS 59772.
124. *Autobiography of Edward Gibbon, Esq. Illustrated From His Letters with Occasional Notes and Narration,* ed. Lord Sheffield (New York: 1846), 101–2.
125. Lucy S. Sutherland and Leslie Mitchell, eds., *The History of the University of Oxford: Vol. V. The Eighteenth Century* (Oxford: 1986), 3, 408–1.
126. Lady Stafford to Granville Leveson-Gower. May 14, 1787. *Leveson-Gower,* I:8.
127. Jenkinson to Hawkesbury. December 14, 1787. Add MSS 38471.
128. Black, *A Subject for Taste: Culture in Eighteenth-Century England* (London: 2005), 58; G. Cecil White, *A Versatile Professor: Reminiscences of the Rev. Edward Nares, D.D.* (London: 1903), 101–2.
129. Jenkinson to Hawkesbury. December 2, 1787. Add MSS 38471; Jenkinson to Hawkesbury. January 9 and January 19, 1788. Loan 72/35; Nathaniel Wetherell to Hawkesbury. January 29, 1788. Add MSS 38471.
130. Jenkinson to Hawkesbury. February 21, 1788. Loan 72/53.
131. Gash, *Liverpool,* 15.
132. Gash, "The Tortoise and the Hare: Liverpool and Canning," *History Today* (March 1982): 12–13; Wendy Hinde, *George Canning* (New York: 1973), 15.
133. J. F. Newton, *The Early Days of the Right Honorable George Canning, First Lord of the Treasury and Chancellor of the Exchequer, and of Some of his Contemporaries with an original Letter Written by Him in the Year 1788* (London: 1828), 6–7, 21.
134. Hinde, 17–18; Gash, *Liverpool,* 15.
135. Newton, 30.
136. Cyril Jackson to Canning. February 18, 1801. Canning MSS.
137. Alter, 20–1.
138. Jenkinson to Hawkesbury. November 2, 1788. Loan 72/53.
139. Hawkesbury to Cornwallis. January 6 and April 22, 1789 and April 18, 1790. Add MSS 38310; William Wyndham Greville to Marquess of Buckingham. December 11, 1788. Duke of Buckingham and Chandos, *Memoirs of the Court and Cabinets of George III,* 2 vols. (London: 1853), II:54; Hawkesbury to Duke of Dorset. March 13, 1789. Sackville MSS.
140. Jenkinson to Hawkesbury. November 9, 1788; Jenkinson to Canning. January 1, 1789. Canning MSS.
141. Thorne, I:292; Jenkinson to Hawkesbury. February 8, 1789. Loan 72/54.
142. Jenkinson to Hawkesbury. November 25, 1788 and February 15, 1789. Loan 72/53.
143. Jenkinson to Hawkesbury. December 8, 1788 and February 1, 1789. Loan 72/53; Hall to Hawkesbury. March 1, 1789 and July 9, 1789. Add MSS 61818 and April 1, 1789. Loan 72/10.

2. APPRENTICESHIP AND PUBLIC LIFE

1. Black, *France and the Grand Tour* (Houndmills: 2003), 137; Brewer, "Whose Grand Tour?" in *The English Prize: The Capture of the Westmorland, an Episode of the Grand Tour,* ed. Maria Dolores Sánchez-Jáuregui and Scott Wilcox (New Haven: 2012), 50.
2. Martin Sherlock, *New Letters from an English Traveller* (London: 1781), 147. Sherlock had been tutor to Jenkinson's future father-in-law.
3. Hawkesbury to Boutin. April 5, 1789. Add MSS 38310.
4. Hawkesbury to Dorset. July 2, 1789. Sackville MSS; Bankes Jenkinson to Hawkesbury. May 15, 1789. Loan 72/47.
5. Their father had been receiver general of the finances. Simon-Charles became treasurer of the French navy while Charles-Robert built the Tivoli gardens after serving as an intendant and commissioner of the French East India Company. Despite their age, both men fell victim to the guillotine.
6. Hawkesbury to Dorset. May 6, 1788. Sackville MSS.
7. Dorset to Nathaniel William Wraxall. January 5 and January 29, 1789. Beinecke MSS.
8. Hawkesbury to Duke of Dorset. July 24, 1789. Add MSS 38310.
9. Simon Schama, *Citizens: A Chronicle of the French Revolution* (New York: 1989), 399–405.
10. Jenkinson to Hawkesbury. July 23, 1789. Loan 72/47; *PD* 1st ser. 41 (November 30, 1819): 500.
11. Jenkinson to Hawkesbury. September 23, 1789. Loan 72/47; Yonge, I:13; Jenkinson to Hawkesbury. October 5, 1789. Loan 72/53.
12. David Hackett Fisher, *The Great Wave: Price Revolutions and the Rhythm of History* (Oxford: 1996), 146, 136.
13. Jenkinson to Canning. Undated. Canning MSS.
14. Franklyn to Hawkesbury. October 30, 1798. Loan 72/35; Gash, *Liverpool,* 16.
15. William Eden to Hawkesbury. September 22, 1789. Add MSS 38471.
16. Jenkinson to Hawkesbury. July 1 and July 19, 1790, and March 1, 1791. Loan 72/53.
17. See Paul Seaward's introduction to Edward Hyde, Earl of Clarendon's *History of the Rebellion: A New Selection,* ed. Seaward (Oxford: 2009), xv–xvi.
18. Jenkinson to Hawkesbury. December 3, 1790. Loan 72/53.
19. Jenkinson to Hawkesbury. December 13, 1790. Loan 72/53.
20. Jenkinson to Hawkesbury. December 18, 1790. Loan 72/53.
21. Hawkesbury to Cornwallis. April 18, 1790. Add MSS 38310.
22. Gibbon to Lord Sheffield. December 15, 1789. *Letters of Edward Gibbon,* ed. J. E. Norton, 3 vols. (New York 1956), III:184.
23. PH 29(February 17, 1792):826.
24. Jenkinson to Hawkesbury. January 8, and 27, 1791. Loan 72/53.
25. Jenkinson to Hawkesbury, February 16. Loan 72/53.
26. Jenkinson to Hawkesbury, February 7, 1791. Loan 72/53; quoted in Brewer, 52.
27. Sir William Hamilton to Hawkesbury. February 8, 1791. Loan 57/12.
28. Jenkinson to Hawkesbury. February 23 and March 8, 1791. Loan 72/53.
29. Jenkinson to Hawkesbury. May 7, 1791. Loan 72/53.
30. Jenkinson to Hawkesbury. July 19, 1790, Loan 72/53; Jenkinson to Lowther, July 11, December 14 and 19, 1791. Add MSS 38310.
31. Jenkinson to Hawkesbury. December 3, 1790. Loan 72/53; Ibid., March 15, 1791.

32. Grenville to Hawkesbury. November 25, 1790. Loan 72/12.

33. Jenkinson to Canning. May 19, 1791. Canning MSS.

34. Jenkinson to Canning. June 17, 1791. Ibid.

35. Granville to Lady Stafford. [undated] *Leveson-Gower*, I:35.

36. *PH* 29 (February 29, 1792): 917.

37. Ibid., 918–26.

38. Ibid., 929, 944.

39. *The Times*, March 1, 1792; Robinson to Hawkesbury. March 1, 1792. Add MSS 38567.

40. Burke to Hawkesbury. March 2, 1792. BL Add MSS 38227; Jane Long to Hawkesbury. March 1, 1792. Add MSS 38566; Pitt to George III. March 1, 1792. *LC* III. I:584; Pitt and Dundas to Hawkesbury. February 29, 1792. Add MSS 38566.

41. Thorne, IV:301; Morris, 90; Turner, 137; William Hague, *William Pitt the Younger: A Biography* (New York: 2005), 262.

42. Leeds to James Bland Burgess. May 21, 1789, Ibid. May 22, 1789, and Burgess to Leeds. May 22, 1789. Burgess MSS.

43. Black, *George III*, 333

44. Feiling, 177; David Lambert, "The Counter-Revolutionary Atlantic: White West Indian Petitions and Proslavery Networks," *Social and Cultural Geography* 6.3(2005): 405–20; Christer Petley, "'Devoted Islands' and 'That Madman Wilberforce': British Proslavery Patriotism During the Age of Abolition," *Journal of Imperial and Commonwealth History* 39.3(September 2011): 393–415.

45. Hawkesbury to Dorset. July 4, 1788. Sackville MSS.

46. *PH* 29 (April 2, 1792): 1124–33.

47. Elliot to his wife. April 3, 1792 and April 27, 1793. *Elliot Letters*, II:4–5,135.

48. *PH* 29 (April 2, 1792):1128, 1132.

49. *PH* 29 (May 21, 1792): 450.

50. *The Times*, July 19, 1792; *Leveson-Gower*, II:48.

51. Jenkinson to Hawkesbury. July 15, 1792. Loan 72/53.

52. Granville to his mother. August 1, 1792. *Leveson-Gower*, I:49.

53. Jenkinson to Hawkesbury. July 22, 1792. Loan 72/53.

54. Jenkinson to Hawkesbury. July 26, 1792. Loan 72/53.

55. Jenkinson to Hawkesbury. August 8, 1789. Loan 72/53.

56. Jenkinson to Hawkesbury. August 23, 1789. Loan 72/53.

57. Paul W. Schroeder, *The Transformation of European Politics, 1763–1840* (Oxford: 1994), 67–71; John Clarke, *British Diplomacy and Foreign Policy, 1782–1865: The National Interest* (London: 1989), 81.

58. Burgess to Auckland. September 7, 1792. *Auckland Journal*, II:441.

59. Henry Erskine to Sir Gilbert Elliot. June 14, 1792. *Elliot Letters*, II:58; Gibbon to Sheffield. May 30, 1793. *Gibbon Letters*, III:258.

60. *PH* 30 (December 15, 1792): 86–90.

61. Ibid., 89.

62. Burke, *Letters on a Regicide Peace* in *Select Works of Edmund Burke*, 4 vols. (Indianapolis: 1999), III:182–4.

63. *PH* 30 (January 4, 1793): 204–6.

64. *PH* 30 (February 18, 1793): 441–2; *The Times*, February 19, 1793; Pitt to George III. February 19, 1793. *LC* II:8.

65. *PH* 30 (May 6, 1793): 809.

66. Elliot to David Carnegie. January 1793. *Elliot Letters*, II:102–3.
67. *PH* 30 (May 6, 1793): 810–20.
68. While Jonathan Clark describes "ministerial Whig ideology" as the intellectual structure for defending the English state in *English Society*, 238–9, Sack's *Jacobite to Conservative* traces the persistence of Tory ideas and networks. Differences, as Harry Dickinson points out, did not preclude overlap between them. Dickinson, *Liberty and Property*, passim.
69. John Ehrman, *The Younger Pitt: The Reluctant Transition* (Stanford: 1983), 230.
70. A.V. Beedell, "John Reeves' Prosecution for a Seditious Libel, 1795–6: A Study in Political Cynicism," *Historical Journal* 36.4(December 1993): 799–824.
71. Sheffield to Auckland. October 21, 1792. *Auckland Journal*, II:458; Kirsty Carpenter, *Refugees of the French Revolution: Émigrés in London, 1789–1802* (Houndmills: 1999), fn. 45.
72. *The Times*, May 29, 1793.
73. Alter, 42.
74. *PH* 31 (May 30, 1794): 636.
75. *PH* 31 (May 30, 1794): 643.
76. Gillray, "Promised Horrors of the French Invasion, – Or – Forcible Reasons for Negotiating a Regicide Peace." October 20, 1796. Print 8,826. *Catalog of Political and Personal Satires Preserved in the Department of Prints and Drawings in the British Museum*, ed. M. D. George.
77. Canning to Lord Crewe. November 24, 1792. George Canning MSS. Clements Library; Canning to Lady Crewe. December 25, 1792. Ibid.
78. *The Letter Journal of George Canning*, ed. Peter Jupp (London: 1991), 55–9; Canning to Boringdon. March 26, 1794. Add MSS 48219. Grey's hatred for Canning persisted as observers remarked when Canning became prime minister in 1827.
79. Morris, 91–2, 83.
80. *Letter Journal*, 88, 261.
81. Gash, *Liverpool*, 26.
82. *Letter Journal*, 92.
83. Ibid., 109–3, 115–16, 123–4.
84. Cookson, *The British Armed Nation, 1793–1815* (Oxford: 1997), 211–13; Austin Gee, *The British Volunteer Movement, 1794–1814* (Oxford: 2003), 230, 248–9.
85. Knight, 79.
86. Hawkesbury to Liverpool. August 28, 1796. Loan 72/54.
87. W. S. Childe-Pemberton, *The Earl-Bishop: The Life of Frederick Hervey, Bishop of Derry, Earl of Bristol*, 2 vols. (New York: 1924), I:291.
88. *Letter Journal*, 42.
89. Ibid., 164.
90. Ibid., 165–6; Canning's Diary. December 17 and 18, 1794 and January 5, 1795. Canning MSS.
91. Jenkinson to Canning. December 27, 1794. Canning MSS.
92. Jenkinson to Canning. January 17, 1795. Canning MSS.
93. *Letter Journal*, 210, 224, 228–9.
94. *Lady Holland's Journal*, I:242.
95. Ibid., I:257; *Letter Journal*, 239–40.
96. Morris, 84; Langford, "Politics and Manners," 119.
97. Mornington to Henry Addington. November 19, 1799. Sidmouth MSS.

98. Lady Hawkesbury to Liverpool. August 30, September 4, and September 9, 1797. Loan 72/57; Hawkesbury to Liverpool. September 8, 1797. Loan 72/54.

99. Hawkesbury to Liverpool. September 19, 1797. Loan 72/54.

100. Hawkesbury to Liverpool. September 14, 1796. Loan 72/54.

101. Roger Wells, *Wretched Faces: Famine in Wartime England, 1793–1801* (New York: 1988), 34, 55; Ehrman, *Reluctant Transition*, 443–4.

102. Hilton, *Dangerous People*, 72; Quintin Crawford to Auckland. February 14. 1794. *Auckland Journal*, III:185.

103. *PH* 31 (April 10, 1794): 248–9; *Letter Journal*, 78.

104. David A. Bell, *The First Total War: Napoleon's Europe and the Birth of Warfare as We Know It* (New York: 2007), 169.

105. Ehrman, *The Younger Pitt: The Consuming Struggle* (Stanford: 1996), 227; Jenkinson to Hawkesbury. July 21 1794. Add MSS 38229; Sheffield to Auckland. January 5, 1794. *Auckland Journal*, III:168.

106. Michael Duffy, "British War Policy: The Austrian Alliance, 1793–1801" (Oxford University: D.Phil. Thesis, 1971), 2–3, 453.

107. Schroeder, 151.

108. *Letter Journal*, 194–5; Mornington to Addington. July 27, 1794. Sidmouth MSS.

109. Jenkinson to Hawkesbury. February 23, 1795. Loan 73/54.

110. Hawkesbury to Canning. February 23, 1796. Canning MSS.

111. Hawkesbury to Addington. August 27, 1796. Sidmouth MSS; Hawkesbury to Liverpool. August 28, 1796. Loan 72/54.

112. Knight, 83–4; Hilton, *Dangerous People*, 91–2.

113. Ehrman, *Consuming Struggle*, 56–8.

114. Hawkesbury to Liverpool. October 4, 1797. Loan 73/54; Hawkesbury to Canning. September 8, 1797. Canning MSS.

115. Hawkesbury to Canning. October 2, 1798. Canning MSS.

116. Hawkesbury to Liverpool. January 29, 1798. Loan 73/54; Morton Eden to Auckland. November 16, 1793. *Auckland Journal*, III:145.

117. *The Diary of the Right Honorable William Windham, 1784 to 1810*, ed. Cecilia Anne Baring (London: 1866), 358; Hawkesbury to Liverpool. October 7, 1798 and October 12, 1798. BL Loan 72/54.

118. Hawkesbury to Liverpool. October 16, 1799. Loan 72/54.

119. Hawkesbury to Canning. October 17, 1799. Canning MSS.

120. Auckland to Lord Henry Spencer. November 20, 1794. *Auckland Journal* III:261.

121. Ehrman, *Reluctant Transition*, 408, 191.

122. David Wilkinson, *The Duke of Portland: Politics and Party in the Age of George III* (Houndmills: 2003), 107.

123. Ritcheson, *Aftermath of Revolution: British Policy Toward the United States, 1783–1795* (Dallas: 1969), 276; minutes dated January 21, 1793 in Add MSS 83852; Hawkesbury to Pitt. October 12, 1791. Add MSS 38351.

124. Ehrman, *Consuming Struggle*, 14.

125. Ritcheson, *Aftermath*, 345–8; Memorandum dated August 29, 1794. Add MSS 38310.

126. Hawkesbury declined a cabinet summons in October as his presence "may occasion discussion which cannot now be of any use." Hawkesbury to Grenville. October 17, 1794. Add MSS 38230. The note in Add MSS 38354 f.101 mentions two conversations between father and son.

127. Jenkinson to Hawkesbury. July 27, 1794. Loan 72/53.

128. Walter M. Stern, "The Bread Crisis in Britain, 1795–96," *Economica* 31.122 (May 1964):181; Jennifer Mori, *William Pitt and the French Revolution, 1785–1795* (New York: 1997), 249–52.

129. Wilkinson, 116–17.

130. Grenville to Pitt October 18, 1800. Quoted in Mori, 258; Ehrman, *Consuming Struggle*, 277; Liverpool to Dundas. October 11, 1800. Add MSS 38311.

131. *PH* 35 (July 5, 1800): 460.

132. Hawkesbury to Pitt. July 5, 1800. Loan 72/54.

133. Draper Hill, *Mr Gillray the Caricaturist* (London: 1965), 58.

134. *Thomas Lawrence: Regency Power & Brilliance*, ed. A. Cassandra Albinson, Peter Funnell, and Lucy Peltz (New Haven: 2010), 122, 115–16.

135. Langford, "Politics and Manners," 110, 118

136. Ehrman, *Consuming Struggle*, 14–15.

137. Hawkesbury to Liverpool. March 10, 1799. Loan 72/54.

138. *PH* 35 (December 5, 1800): 713–16.

139. Ibid., 416–18.

140. Hilton, *Corn, Cash, Commerce*, 18–21.

141. *Diaries of Sylvester Douglas, Lord Glenbervie*, ed. Francis Bickley, 2 vols. (London: 1928), I:221–2.

3. POLITICS AND WAR

1. Pares, 91–2; Gibbon to Dorothea Gibbon. July 15, 1785. *Gibbon Letters*, III:29; Knight, 214.

2. Ehrman, *Reluctant Transition*, 138, 261, 267–8.

3. Piers Mackesy, *War Without Victory*, 12–13.

4. Auckland to Lord Henry Spencer. July 24, 1794. *Auckland Journal*, III:223; *Elliot Letters*, II:196fn.

5. Grenville to Thomas Grenville. September 15, 1794. *Court of George III*, II:301.

6. Hawkesbury to Liverpool. November 18, 1799. Loan 72/54; Hawkesbury to Canning. December 1, [1799]. Canning MSS; Hawkesbury to Liverpool. August 23, 1800. Loan 72/54.

7. George III to Grenville. June 27, 1800. *LC* III:368; Canning to John Hookham Frere. June 26, 1800. Add MSS 38833; Cooke to Castlereagh. June 26, 1800. *CC* III:341.

8. Pitt to Dundas. November 8, 1792. Pitt Family MSS. Clements Library.

9. Douglas, *Glenbervie*, I:36; Glenbervie to Dundas. April 26, 1794. Melville MSS. Clements Library.

10. Ehrman, *Consuming Struggle*, 509–12.

11. Edmund Burke, "A Letter to Richard Burke on Protestant Ascendancy in Ireland" (1792) in *On Empire, Liberty, and Reform: Speeches and Letters*, ed. David Bromwhich (New Haven: 2000), 428–9.

12. Hawkesbury to Mornington. September 23, 1798. Add MSS 37308.

13. Cooke to Cornwallis. April 22, 1800. *CC* III:285; Douglas, *Glenbervie*, I:157.

14. Sack, *Jacobite to Conservative*, 227–8.

15. Black, *George III*, 374; Ehrman, *Consuming Struggle*, 508, 177, 511.

16. Turner, 214.

17. Douglas, *Glenbervie*, I:398, 147.
18. Ibid., I:294–5.
19. Mackesy, *War Without Victory*, 16–18, 92–3, 139; Hague, 385.
20. Lord Rosebery, *Pitt* (London: 1915), 230; *Farington*. October 20, 1800. I:293.
21. Lady Malmesbury to Lady Minto. February 8, 1801. *Elliot Letters*, III:198.
22. *Colchester*, I:258–9.
23. *LC* III:xx.
24. Black, *George III*, 389, 384.
25. *PH* 35 (February 11, 1801): 962–3.
26. Gash, *Liverpool*, 38.
27. *PH* 35 (February 9, 1801): 944 and (February 11, 1801): 848.
28. *Colchester*, I:122; Douglas, *Glenbervie*, I: 244; *Diaries and Correspondence of James Harris, First Earl of Malmesbury*, Ed. James Howard Harris, Second Earl of Malmesbury, 4 vols. (London: 1844), IV:6–6; Douglas, *Glenbervie* 156–8. As Lord Harrowby, Ryder succeed Hawkesbury as foreign secretary in 1804.
29. George III to Hawkesbury. May 14, 1801. Loan 72/1; Douglas, *Glenbervie*, I:179, 205; *PH* 30 (March 25, 1801): 1114.
30. Douglas, *Glenvbervie* I:209; Foster, ed., *The Two Duchesses*, 167.
31. Canning to John Hookham Frere. July 30, 1801. Add MSS 38833; Leveson-Gower to his mother. February 20, 1801. *Leveson-Gower* I:298–9; I:Frere to Canning. February 18, 1801. Canning MSS.
32. Gillray, "Lilliputian-Substitutes, Equiping [sic] for Public Service." May 28, 1801. Print 9722 (see Fig. 3).
33. Grenville to Hawkesbury. February 11, 1801. *HMC Dropmore*, VI:443.
34. *Colchester* [March 1, 1801]; Douglas, *Glenbervie*, I:193–4; *PH* 35 (March 27, 1801): 1225.
35. Memoir by Gentz. [November 1800]. *HMC Dropmore*, VI:375.
36. Clarke, 92; C. A. Bayly, *Imperial Meridian: The British Empire and the World, 1780–1830* (London: 1989), 72–3; A. D. Harvey, *Collision of Empires: Britain in Three World Wars* (London: 1992).
37. Hawkesbury to Liverpool. July 31, 1800. Loan 72/54
38. Mackesy, *War Without Victory*, 133–5, 143, 183, 202; draft cabinet minute in *LC* III:510 fn; Lord Carysfort to Grenville. January 21, 1801. Cited in Mackesy, 184.
39. Schroeder, 220.
40. Whitworth to Grenville. April 16, 1801. *HMC Dropmore*, VII:4; John D. Grainger, *The Amiens Truce: Britain and Bonaparte, 1801–1803* (London: 2004), 27; Hawkesbury to Grenville. April 13, 1801. *HMC Dropmore*, VII:3.
41. Hawkesbury to George III. April 23, 1801, and George III to Hawkesbury. April 24, 1801. *LC* III:518–19; Hawkesbury to George III. May 8, 1801. Ibid., III:531.
42. Grenville to Hawkesbury. July 15, 1801. *HMC Dropmore*, VII:30–3; Grenville to Addington. May 8, 1801. Ibid., VII:16.
43. Douglas, *Glenbervie*, I:195.
44. Hawkesbury to Paget. February 28, 1801. BL Add MSS 48389.
45. *LC* III:511fn; Lady Hawkesbury to Liverpool. February 28, 1801. Loan 72/57.
46. Grenville to Hawkesbury. April 14, 1801. *HMC Dropmore*, VII:4; *PH* 35 May 18, 1801): 1420–1.
47. Liverpool to Lord Frederick Hervey. Saturday evening [1801]. Hervey MSS.

48. Ehrman, *Consuming Struggle*, 334–5, 336.

49. Addington to George III. March 19, 1801. *LC* III:512.

50. *The Times*, July 4, 1801.

51. Liverpool to Hawkebsury. March 23, 1801. Loan 72/51.

52. Duffy, 451; Schroeder, 225–6.

53. Hawkesbury to Canning. October 17, 1799. Canning MSS.

54. Clarke, 108–9.

55. Grainger, 37–9.

56. Hawkesbury's memorandum. April 12, 1801. Add MSS 38316.

57. Hawkesbury to Otto. April 14, 1801. Add MSS 38316.

58. Otto to Hawkesbury. June 1, 1801. Add MSS 38312; Hawkesbury to Otto. June 6, 1801. Add MSS 38316; Grainger, 38.

59. Hawkesbury to Otto. June 25, 1801. Add MSS 39316.

60. Hawkesbury to Otto. July 20, 1801. Add MSS 38316; George III to Hawkesbury. July 25, 1801. Loan 72/1.

61. Otto to Hawkesbury. July 26, 1801. Add MSS 38312.

62. Hawkesbury to George III. [August 28], 1801. Loan 72/1; George III to Hawkesbury. August 30, 1801. Loan 72/1.

63. Hawkesbury's project. September 19, 1801. Add MSS 38312; Hawkesbury to Otto. September 22, 1801. Add MSS.

64. Hawkesbury to Otto. September 29, 1801. Add MSS 38316.

65. Grainger, 46–7.

66. Hawkesbury to George III. September 29, 1801. *LC* III:612–13; George III to Hawkesbury. Ibid. III:613; George III to Hawkesbury. May 1801. Loan 72/1.

67. Dundas to Grenville. October 10, 1801. *HMC Dropmore*, VII:57–8; Mulgrave to Grenville. Ibid., VII:62.

68. Pitt to Canning. October 20, 1801. Canning MSS; Pitt to Bathurst. October 2, 1801. *HMC Bathurst*, 25; Grenville. October 5, 1801. *HMC Dropmore*, VII:49–50.

69. Grenville to Bathurst. October 15, 1801. *HMC Bathurst*, 25; Grenville to George III. October 19,1801. Aspinall, *LC* III:616–17; Grenville to Pitt. October 6, 1801. *HMC Dropmore*, VII; Grenville to Addington. October 14, 1801. Ibid., VII:59–60; Addington to Grenville. October 15, 1801. Ibid., VII:60.

70. Douglas, *Glenbervie*, I:254–5; Smart, *EA*, I:46.

71. Cornwallis to Charles Ross. September 17, 1801. *The Correspondence of Charles, First Marquis Cornwallis*, ed. Charles Ross, 3 vols. (London: 1859), III:328.

72. *Holland Memoirs*, I:186; *PH* 36 (October 29,1801): 17.

73. *PH* 36 (November 3, 1801): 36–7.

74. Ibid., 37–40.

75. Ibid., 38–48.

76. Douglas, *Glenbervie*, I:278.

77. *PH* 36(November 4, 1801): 86; Ibid., (November 3, 1801):57.

78. James Gilray, "Political Dreamings! Visions of Peace! Perspective Horrors." Print 9735; *PH* 36 (October 26, 1801); Ibid. (November 4, 1801).

79. *PH* 36 (November 13, 1801): 267–8, 268–9.

80. Ibid., 270–5.

81. Hawkesbury to George III. October 5, 1801. Loan 72/1; George III to Hawkesbury. October 6, 1801. Ibid.

82. Granger, 79, 52–3.
83. Hawkesbury to Cornwallis. November 14, 1801. PRO 30/11/267.
84. "Draft of Official Instructions." [undated] FO 27/59; Hawkesbury to Cornwallis. November 1, 1801. Ibid.
85. Hawkesbury to Cornwallis. November 16, 1801. FO 27/59.
86. Littlehales to Charles Abbot. November 21, 1801. *Colchester*, I:387; Cornwallis to Ross, December 7, 1801. *Cornwallis*, III:406.
87. Cornwallis to Hawkesbury. December 3, 1801. FO 27/59; Grainger, 58.
88. Cornwallis to Hawkesbury. December 30, 1801 and December 31, 1801. FO27/59.
89. Liverpool to Hawkesbury. March 1, 1802. Loan 72/51; Hawkesbury to Cornwallis. March 22, 1802. FO 27/60.
90. Hawkesbury to Cornwallis. March 14, 1802. FO 27/60; George III to Hawkesbury. March 14, 1802. Loan 72/1.
91. Bradford Perkins, *The First Rapprochement: England and the United States, 1795–1805* (Philadelphia: 1955), 89, 133–8.
92. *PH* 36 (May 13, 1802): 761–4, 757, 767.
93. Eldon to Addington. October 1801. Sidmouth MSS; Sir John McPherson to Addington. August 14, 1801. Ibid.
94. Yonge, I:68; *Malmesbury* IV:64.
95. Carpenter, 178–9.
96. Pitt to Addington. February 17, 1802. Sidmouth MSS.
97. Hilton, *Dangerous People*, 100–1; Charles J. Fedorak, *Henry Addington, Prime Minister, 1801–1804: Peace, War, and Parliamentary Politics* (Akron: 2002), 90–3; *EA* I:52–3, 56; Canning to J. H. Frere. April 11, 1802. Add MSS 38833.
98. Gash, *Liverpool*, 46.
99. Grainger, 121.
100. Perkins, 133, 5.
101. Thomas Grenville to Grenville. March 13, 1802. *HMC Dropmore*, VI:89–90; *The Diaries and Correspondence of the Right Hon. George Rose*, ed. L. V. Harcourt, 2 vols. (London: 1860), II:46–51; *Malmesbury*, IV:69.
102. Hill, *Fashionable Contrasts: Caricatures by James Gillray* (London: 1966), 13–14; George, VIII:24.
103. Rose, II:157.
104. Robert Gascoyne-Cecil, 3rd Marquess of Salisbury, "Lord Castlereagh," *Quarterly Review* 111 (January 1862): 206.
105. Hilton, by contrast, calls Hawkesbury "a capable and level-headed foreign secretary." *Dangerous People*, 99.
106. Merry to Hammond. April 28, 1802. FO 27/60; Hawkesbury to George III. April 11, 1802. Loan 72/1; Merry to Hawkesbury. May 7, 1802. FO 27/62; Hawkesbury to Merry. May 20, 1802. Add MSS 38318.
107. Merry to Hammond. June 19, 1802. FO 27/63; Paget to Hawkesbury. June 23, 1802. FO 7/66.
108. Liverpool to Hawkesbury. May 24, 1802. Loan 72/51; Fedorak, *Henry Addington*, 115.
109. Hawkesbury to Merry. August 13, 1802. FO 27/63.
110. Liverpool to Hawkesbury. August 18, 1802. Loan 72/51.
111. Hawkesbury to Merry. August 28, 1802. FO 27/63.
112. George III to Hawkesbury. August 29, 1802. Loan 72/1.

113. Grainger, 125–8; Hawkesbury to Otto. October 10, 1802. Add MSS 48389.

114. Hawkesbury to Liverpool. November 9, 1802. Add MSS 38236; Hawkesbury to Liverpool. November 11, 1802. Loan 72/55.

115. Pitt to Addington. November 10, 1802. Sidmouth MSS.

116. Hawkesbury to Whitworth. November 25, 1802. Whitworth Papers. FO/323/4; Liverpool to Whitworth. December 6, 1802. Ibid.

117. Whitworth to Hawkesbury. November 20, 1802. FO 27/67.

118. *PH* 36 (November 4, 1801):100.

119. George III to Hawkesbury. January 28, 1803. Loan 71/1; Grainger, 152–3.

120. Hawkesbury to Whitworth. February 9, 1803. FO 323/4.

121. Grainger, 158–9; Hawkesbury to Whitworth. March 4, 1803 FO 323/4; Ibid., April 4, 1803.

122. Hawkesbury to Whitworth. March 23, 1803. FO 323/4.

123. Whitworth to Hawkesbury. February 7, 1803. FO 27/67.

124. Hawkesbury to Whitworth. April 4, 1803. FO 27/68; Whitworth to Hawkesbury. April 25, 1803. Ibid.

125. Schroeder, 226, 229–30.

126. Robert Liston to Whitworth. February 3, 1803. FO 323/4; Political rhetoric during the Seven Years War had cast Anglo-French rivalry as an exterminatory war and Napoleon embraced the analogy with fantasies of destroying the new Carthage as Romans had done the old. Bell, 80, 233; Hawkesbury to Whitworth. May 19, 1803. FO 324/4.

127. *Morning Chronicle*, November 19, 1801.

128. Rose, I:489–90; Pitt to Hawkesbury. November 21, 1802 Loan 72/38; Liverpool to Hervey. 6 September, 1802. Hervey MSS.

129. Liverpool to Whitworth. December 6, 1802. FO 323/4; Tierney to Lady Holland. December 26, 1802 Add MSS51585; Hawkesbury to Liverpool. January 9, 1803. Loan 72/55.

130. See Fig. 5: Gillray, "Bat-Catching," January 19, 1803. Print 6694.

131. Fedorak, *Henry Addington*, 130–1; Melville to Addington. March 22, 1803. Sidmouth MSS.

132. Fedorak, *Henry Addington*, 182–4 ; *Malmesbury*, IV:185, 187.

133. Alter, 240; *PH* 36 (May 23, 1803): 1377–85, 1385–6.

134. *PH* 36 (June 3, 1803):1560–4.

135. Fox to Lord Holland. June 6, 1803. Add MSS 47575; *PH* 36 (June 3, 1803):1564–70.

136. Hawkesbury to Liverpool. [June 5, 1803]. Loan 72/55; Liverpool to Hawkesbury. June 7, 1803. Loan 72/49.

137. Thomas Grenville to Buckingham. January 12, 1803. Buckingham, *Court of George III*, III:245; Douglas, *Glenbervie*, I:332–3; Hawkesbury to Liverpool. May 21, 1803. 72/55.

138. Liverpool to Hawkesbury. June 1, 1803. Add MSS 38236.

139. Liverpool to Mrs. Johnson. November 23, 1803. Add MSS 38311.

140. Hawkesbury to Canning. October 17, 1799. Canning MSS.

141. Fedorak, "In Search of a Necessary Ally: Addington, Hawkesbury and Russia, 1801–1804," *International History Review* 13(1991): 223, 230–1, 236.

142. Schroeder, 254–5; Hawkesbury to Liverpool. July 16, 1803. Loan 72/55.

143. Gash, *Liverpool*, 52–3.

144. Cornwallis to Ross. February 13, 1804. *Cornwallis*, III:511–12; Fedorak, *Henry Addington*, 197–200.

145. Schroeder, 244.

4.   POLITICAL BROKER

1. Charles Philip Yorke to Lord Hardwicke. May 11, 1804. Add MSS 35706.

2. Pitt to Eldon. May 2, 1804. Stanhope, IV:iv–viii.

3. Rose, I:122–4.

4. Grenville to Pitt. May 8, 1804. *HMC Dropmore* VII:222; Horace Twiss, *The Public and Private Life of Lord Chancellor Eldon with Selections from his Correspondence*, 3 vols. (London: 1844), I:449.

5. The original sketch is the frontispiece of Stanhope, IV; Buckingham to Grenville. November 1, 1802. *HMC Dropmore*, VII:118.

6. Liverpool to the Bishop of Hertford. July 9, 1804. Loan 72/51.

7. Liverpool to Sir Joseph Banks. May 18, 1804. Add MSS 38311; Liverpool to Mrs. Johnson. June 5, 1804. Ibid.

8. Canning to his wife. May 13, 1804. Canning MSS.

9. *PD* 1st ser. 2 (June 18, 1804): 722.

10. *PD* 1st ser. 2 (June 18, 1804): 723, 729, 731–4.

11. Hawkesbury to Pitt. June 20, 1804. Add MSS 38571.

12. Douglas, *Glenbervie*, I:410.

13. Liverpool to Hawkesbury. June 21, 1804. Loan 72/51.

14. Hawkesbury to Liverpool. June 24, 1804. Loan 72/55; Liverpool to Hawkesbury. June 24, 1804. Loan 72/51.

15. Canning to Hawkesbury. January 11, 1805. Loan 72/24.

16. Hawkesbury to Canning. January 11, 1805. Loan 72/24.

17. Canning to Reverend John Sneyd. February 9, 1805. Canning MSS. Clements Library.

18. Hinde, 129; Dorothy Marshall, *The Rise of George Canning* (London: 1938), 288–91.

19. *P of W* IV:6; Liverpool to the Bishop of Hertford. July 8, 1804. Loan 72/51; Dundas to Pitt. April 3, 1804. Add MSS 40102.

20. Hawkesbury to Liverpool. June 30, 1804. BL Loan 72/55; Ibid., August 14, 1804. Loan 72/55.

21. *P of W* V:5–8.

22. Liverpool to the Bishop of Hertford. July 8, 1804. Loan 72/51.

23. E. A. Smith, *George IV* (New Haven: 1999), 101.

24. Hannah Smith, *Georgian Monarchy: Politics and Culture, 1714–1760* (Cambridge: 2006), 243; Liverpool to Hawkesbury. September 2, 1804. Loan 72/51.

25. Alter, 312; Memorandum by Sir Robert Wilson in *P of W* IV:112–18; *Leveson-Gower*, I:462; Rose, II:157.

26. Hawkesbury to Liverpool. November 17, 1804. Loan 72/55.

27. Hawkesbury to Liverpool. November 21, 1804. Loan 72/55; Ibid., November 22, 1804.

28. Hawkesbury to Liverpool. November 6, 1804. Add MSS 38236; Hawkesbury to Hardwicke. November 15, 1804. Loan 72/55.

29. Liverpool to Hawkesbury. July 16, 1804. Loan 72/51; Liverpool to Bishop of Hertford. July 16. 1804. Ibid.

30. Addington to Hiley Addington. July 10, 1804 and October 11, 1804. Sidmouth MSS.

31. Addington to Hiley Addington. November 1, 1804. Ibid.

32. Hawkesbury to Liverpool. November 22, 1804. Loan 72/55.

33. Hawkesbury to Liverpool. December 11, 1804. Ibid.

34. Hawkesbury to Pitt. December 12, 1804. Ibid.

35. Hawkesbury to Liverpool. December 19, 1804. Loan 72/55; Hawkesbury to Addington. December 19, 1804. Sidmouth MSS.

36. John Ehrman, *Consuming Struggle*, 724–5.

37. Foster, *The Two Duchesses*, 194.

38. Hawkesbury to Addington. December 19, 1804. Sidmouth MSS.

39. Ireland to Liverpool. December 26, 1804. Add MSS 38263; Pellew, *Life and Correspondence of the Right Honorable Henry Addington, First Viscount Sidmouth*, 3 vols. (London: 1847), II:131; Bathurst to Harrowby. February 3, 1805. Harrowby MSS.

40. Pellew, II:134–5, 140–9; Yonge, I:182. A fall had left Harrowby seriously injured.

41. Alter, 237–8.

42. J. W. Croker to Vesey Fitzgerald. December 20, 1821. *Croker Papers*, I:219.

43. George III to Hawkesbury. Add MSS 38190.

44. Hawkesbury to Liverpool. August 14, 1804. Loan 72/55; Gash, Liverpool, 60.

45. R. R. Nelson, *The Home Office, 1782–1801* (Durham: 1969), 22–3, 95–8, 102, 136–7.

46. Perceval to Hawkesbury. October 5, 1804. Yonge, I:166–9.

47. Alter, 339; George III to Hawkesbury. February 3, 1805. Loan 72/1.

48. *Memoirs of Lady Hester Stanhope*, 3 vols. (London: 1846), I:189–90.

49. Hawkesbury to Hardwicke. November 15, 1804. Add MSS 35209.

50. Hawkesbury to Hardwicke. January 26, 1805. Loan 72/55.

51. Hawkesbury to Hardwicke. February 2, 1805. Add MSS 35710; Hardwicke to Hawkesbury. February 16, 1805. Add MSS 38241; Hawkesbury to Hardwicke. March 17, 1805. Add MSS 35756.

52. Pitt to George III. January 8, 1805. *LC* IV:275; Hawkesbury to Liverpool. January 8, 1805. Loan 72/55.

53. *PD* 1st ser. 2 (January 15, 1805): 20.

54. Ehrman, *Consuming Struggle*, 746–8.

55. *PD* 1st ser 3 (February 13, 1805): 503–10, 516–17.

56. Ehrman, *Consuming Struggle*, 752–5; Knight, 97fn, 224–5.

57. William Windham to Captain Lukin. March 9, 1805. *The Windham Papers: The Life and Correspondence of the Rt. Hon. William Windham*, ed. Earl of Rosebery, 2 vols. (London: 1913), II:253; *Colchester*, I:546–7; Gash, *Liverpool*, 62.

58. *Malmesbury*, IV:338; Thorne, III:5, 347n.

59. Pitt to George III. May 5, 1805. *LC* IV:324; Knight, 349.

60. Hawkesbury to Liverpool. April 17, 1805. Loan 72/55; Cobbett to Windham. April 19, 1805. Add MSS 37853.

61. Liverpool to Hawkesbury. Undated. Loan 71/51; Hawkesbury to Liverpool. April 21, 1805. Loan 72/55; Knight, 226.

62. Sidmouth to Pitt. April 22, 1805 and April 25, 1805. Sidmouth MSS; Sidmouth to Hawkesbury. April 27, 1805. Add MSS 38241; Sidmouth to George III. April 28, 1805. *LC* IV:318–19.

63. *PD* 1st ser. 4 (March 25, 1805): 104.

64. Ibid. (May 10, 1805): 672–3.

65. John Ireland, *The Letters of Fabius to the Right Hon. William Pitt, on his Proposed Abolition of the Test in Favor of the Roman Catholics of Ireland* (London: 1801); Ibid., *Vindicae Regiae: or a Defense of the Kingly Office in Two Letters to Earl Stanhope* (London: 1797); Ireland to Liverpool. May 17, 1805. Add MSS 38236; Hawkesbury to Ireland. May 29, 1805. Add MSS 38473.

66. *PD* 1st ser. 4 (May 10, 1805): 673–4.

67. Ibid., 673–80.

68. Ibid., 681–91.

69. Ibid., 710, 174.

70. Hawkesbury to George III. May 14, 1805. *LC* IV:328; George III to Hawkesbury. May 15, 1805. Add MSS 38564.

71. Gilray, "The End of the Irish Farce of Catholic Emancipation," May 17, 1801. Print 10,404; William Anthony Hay, *The Whig Revival, 1808–1830* (Houndmills: 2005), 10–11.

72. Hawkesbury to Liverpool. June 15, 1805. Loan 72/55.

73. Hawkesbury to Liverpool. June 19 and July 5, 1805. Loan 72/55.

74. *Malmesbury*, IV:388–9; Sidmouth to Bathurst. July 10, 1805. Sidmouth MSS.

75. Hawkesbury to Liverpool. July 7, 1805. Loan 72/55.

76. Thomas Grenville to Grenville. June 25, 1805. *HMC Dropmore* VII:280; Buckingham to Grenville. June 27, 1805. Ibid., VII:281–3; Grenville to Buckingham. June 25, 1805. Buckingham, *Court of George III*, III:426–7.

77. Liverpool to Bristol. July 17, 1805. Hervey MSS.

78. Williams, "Political Astronomy," May 1805. Print 10.411.

79. Lady Hawkesbury to Liverpool. June 22, 1805. Loan 72/57; Hawkesbury to Liverpool. July 5, 1805. Loan 72/55.

80. Sidmouth to Buckinghamshire. September 19, 1805. Sidmouth MSS.

81. Hawkesbury to Liverpool. September 24, 1805. Loan 72/55; PD 1st ser. 3 (February 15, 1805): 517; Liverpool to Hawkesbury. Undated. Loan 72/55.

82. PD 1st ser. 3 (February 15, 1805): 517.

83. Pitt to Bathurst. September 27, 1805. Loan 57/2; Spencer Perceval to Lord Arden. September 28, 1805. Add MSS 49188.

84. John Ireland to Liverpool. November 24, 1805. Add MSS 38236.

85. Hawkesbury to Liverpool. November 6, 1805. Loan 72/55; Hawkesbury to Flaxman. December 11, 1805. Add MSS 39791.

86. Gash, *Liverpool*, 63.

87. Stanhope, IV:370.

88. Ehrman, 824–5; *PD* 1st ser. 6 (January 21, 1806): 8–10; Gash, *Liverpool*, 66.

89. Lord Aberdeen's Diary. January 25, 1806. Add MSS 43337; Hawkesbury to Liverpool. 8 a.m. January 23, 1806 and later that day. Loan 72/55; *PD* 1st ser. 6 (January 28, 1806): 75.

90. John Allen's Journal. January 24, 1806. Add MSS 52204A; Aberdeen Diary. January 25, 1806. Add MSS 43337.

91. Hawkesbury to Liverpool. January 23, 1806. Loan 72/55; Cabinet Minute. January 24, 1806. *LC* 382.

92. Gash, *Liverpool*, 66; Lady Bessborough to Leveson-Gower. January 27, 1806. *Leveson-Gower*, II: 168; *Colchester*, II:36.

93. Aberdeen Diary. February 2 and 4, 1806. Add MSS 43337.

94. Knight, 338.

95. Ilchester, *Lady Holland Journals*, II:123.

96. Pellew, II:417; Aberdeen's Diary. March 20, 1806. Add MSS 43337.

97. Black, *George III*, 390.

98. *The First Lady Warncliffe and Her Family*, ed. Caroline Grosvenor and Lord Stuart of Wortley, 2 vols. (London: 1927), I:119.

99. Foster, *The Two Duchesses*, 309; Holland, *Memoirs*, I:208.

100. Liverpool to Louisa. August 12, 1806. Loan 72/51; Sheffield to Auckland. January 28, 1806. *Auckland Journal*, IV:269.

101. Black, *George III*, 396; Aspinall, *LC*, xxix.

102. Alter, 366–7.

103. *PD* 1st ser. 6 (March 3, 1806): 253–60, 265, 274–7, 284.

104. Aberdeen Diary. Undated. Add MSS 43337.

105. *PD* 1st ser. 6 (April 23, 1806): 884–5.

106. Alter, 388; *PD* 1st ser. 7 (May 12, 1806): 97; Hawkesbury to Liverpool. July 18, 1806. Loan 72/55.

107. *PD* 1st ser. 7 (June 11, 1806): 604–5, 607; Ibid. (June 13, 1806): 655.

108. Ibid. (July 8, 1806): 962; Ibid. (July 18, 1806): 1189.

109. Ibid. (May 7, 1806): 33.

110. Ibid. (May 16, 1806): 234; Ibid. (June 24, 1807): 805–6; 8 (February 5, 1807): 671–2.

111. Liverpool to Louisa. August 12, 1806. Loan 72/51.

112. Canning to Rose. September 9, 1806. Add MSS 42773.

113. Hardwicke to Yorke. September 16, 1805. Add MSS 45034.

114. Denis Gray, *Spencer Perceval: The Evangelical Prime Minister, 1762–1812* (Manchester: 1963), 77–90.

115. Hawkesbury to Liverpool. August 27, 1806. Loan 72/56; Liverpool to Hawkesbury. September 8, 1806. Loan 72/51.

116. Louisa to Liverpool. August 11, 1806. Loan 72/55; Liverpool to Louisa. August 12, 1806. Loan 72/51; Hawkesbury to Liverpool. August 14, 1806. Loan 72/55.

117. Hawkesbury to Liverpool. October 7, 1806. Loan 72/56; Ibid., October 19, 2006.

118. Thorne, I:183–6; Hawkesbury to Liverpool. November 26, 1806. Loan 72/56.

119. Gray, 70.

120. Bathurst to Grenville. March 1807. Loan 57/3; Grenville to Bathurst. March 11, 1807. Ibid.

121. Portland to Hawkesbury. March 8, 1807. Add MSS 38191; Grenville to Bathurst. March 18, 1807. Loan 57/3.

122. Ilchester, *Lady Holland Journals*, II:223–4.

123. Hawkesbury to Canning. March 19, 1807. Canning MSS; Hawkesbury to Liverpool. March 19, 1807. Add MSS 38236; Liverpool to Mrs. Johnson. April 1807. Add MSS 38241.

124. Camden to Bathurst. December 10, 1806. *HMC Bathurst*.

125. Hawkesbury to Liverpool. March 19, 1807. Add MSS 38236; *Malmesbury*, IV:373; Portland to George III. March 20, 1807. *LC* IV:529; Wilkinson, 163; Hawkesbury to George III. March 20, 1807. *LC* IV:530.

126. Perceval to Arden. March 19, 1807. BL Add MSS 49188; Portland to George III. March 23, 1807. *LC* IV:536–9.

127. *PD* 1st ser. 9 (March 26, 1807): 231–7, 239–40.

128. Ibid., 247–52, 258.

129. Hawkesbury to George III. March 26, 1807. *LC* IV:544–5; Sidmouth to George III. April 8, 1807. Ibid., IV:557; George III to Sidmouth. April 9, 1807. Ibid., 557–8.

130. *PD* 1st ser. 9 (April 13, 1807): 351–4, 366–7, 385–6.

131. Ibid., 389–99, 403.

132. Ibid., 411.

133. Ibid., 420–1.

134. Hawkesbury to George III. April 14, 1807. *LC* IV:563; George III to Hawkesbury. April 14, 1807. Ibid., 563; Perceval to George III. April 16, 1807. Ibid., 564–5.

135. Portland to George III. April 24, 1807. *LC* IV:571–2; George III to Portland. April 25, 1807. Ibid., 572; *Malmesbury*, IV:385.

136. Thorne, I:188–9.

137. Sir Arthur Wellesley to Hawkesbury. April 27, 1807. *WSD* V:13. Wellesley sought Hawkesbury's authority in May to support John Wilson Croker's attempt to carry Downpatrick, a seat Croker later secured on petition. The next year, Croker deputized as chief secretary while Wellesley took military command of an expedition to Iberia. Wellesley to Hawkesbury, May 9, 1807. Ibid., V:41–2; Muir, *Wellington*, I:190.

138. Hawkesbury to Liverpool. May 20, 1807 and June 29, 1807. Loan 72/56; Liverpool to Harrowby. June 21, 1807. Harrowby MSS.

5.   PILLAR OF STATE

1. Wilkinson, 163; Perceval to Huskisson. August 21, 1809. Cited in *LC* V:x–xi.

2. Grosvenor and Stuart, eds., *Lady Warncliffe*, I:136.

3. Liverpool to Auckland. April 4, 1807. *Auckland Journal*, IV:309; Liverpool to Hawkesbury. May 24, 1807 and May 31, 1807. Loan 72/51.

4. Alter, 400–2; Liverpool to Hawkesbury. June 30, 1807. Loan 51.

5. Thorne, II: 446, III:299–300, 113.

6. Liverpool to C. Arnold. April 27, 1807. Loan 72/51; Liverpool to Hawkesbury. May 7, 1807. Ibid.

7. Yonge, 244–6; Prince of Wales to Queen Charlotte. May 5, 1807. *P of W* VI:167–8.

8. Alter, 404.

9. Dominic Lieven, *Russia Against Napoleon: The True Story of the Campaigns of War and Peace* (New York: 2010), 16; *EA* I:118–20.

10. Muir, *Wellington*, I:208–9.

11. George III to Castlereagh. July 18, 1807. *LC* IV:607; Canning to his wife. August 26, 1807. Canning MSS; Twiss, II:60–1.

12. Muir, *Wellington*, I:220.

13. Harvey, *Collision of Empires*, 101.

14. Liverpool to Hawkesbury. July 28, 1807. Loan 72/51; Hawkesbury to Liverpool. August 9, 1807. Loan 72/56; Vice Admiral George Berkeley to Bathurst. August 13, 1807. HMC Bathurst, 63–4.

15. Memorandum to the cabinet. October 12, 1807. Add MSS 49177.

16. Hawkesbury to Perceval. [October, 1807.] Add MSS 49177; Castlereagh to Perceval. Ibid.

17. Hawkesbury to Liverpool. November 15, 1807. Loan 72/56.

18. Knight, 401.

19. Hawkesbury to Wellesley. April 27, 1807. Wellington MSS.

20. Wellesley to Hawkesbury. May 7, 1807. *WSD* V:28–36; James Traill to Wellesley. 16 July, 1807. Ibid., V:119–21.

21. Hawkesbury to Sir Arthur Wellesley. October 22, 1807. Wellington MSS.

22. Wellesley to Hawkesbury. October 22, 1807 and April 22, 1808 *WSD* V: 142, 403; Hawkesbury to Wellesley. October 29, 1807. Wellington MSS; Yonge, II:260–3. Lord Wellesley, Sir Arthur's brother, supported Catholic Emancipation.

23. Muir, *Wellington*, I:198–9, 202, 307.
24. Hawkesbury to Liverpool. October 31, 1807. Loan 72/56; Hawkesbury to George III. *LC* November 2, 1807.
25. Carpenter, 179.
26. Yonge, II: 246; Hawkesbury to Canning. November 7, 1807. Canning MSS.
27. Hawkesbury to Wellesley. November 12, 1807. Wellington MSS.
28. Charles Esdaile, *The Peninsular War: A New History* (London: 2002), 5, 26–8; Ian Robertson, *An Atlas of the Peninsular War* (New Haven: 2010), 16–17.
29. Hawkesbury to Canning. November 7, 1807. Canning MSS; Hawkesbury to Sir Arthur Wellesley. November 12, 1807. Wellington MSS; Alter, 407; Hawkesbury to Wellesley. December 23, 1807. Wellington MSS.
30. Thomas Grenville to Grenville. January 9, 1808. *HMC Dropmore*, VIII:171; Hawkesbury to Mr. North. January 8, 1808. Add MSS 38242.
31. Hawkesbury to Canning. January 9, 1808; Douglas, *Glenbervie*, II:12.
32. *PD* 1st ser. 10 (January 21): 18, 24–5.
33. Ibid. (February 8, 1808): 368–75.
34. Ibid. (January 27, 1808): 150.
35. Ibid. (February 4, 1808): 312-13.
36. Ibid., (February 4, 1808): 312; Ibid. (February 26, 1808): 786; Ibid. (March 22, 1808): 1242.
37. Ibid. (March 29, 1808): 1270, 1272.
38. Ibid. (March 29, 1808): 1280–3; Hawkesbury to Liverpool. March 20, 1808. Loan 72/56.
39. Liverpool to Hawkesbury. April 25, 1808. Loan 72/56.
40. Alter, 409–10.
41. Liverpool to Hawkesbury. April 28, 1808. Loan 72/56.
42. Liverpool to Hawkesbury. June 9, 1808. Add MSS 38473; Hawkesbury to Liverpool. June 3, 1808. Loan 72/56.
43. Muir, *Napoleon*, 37–9; *PD* 1st ser. 11 (June 15, 1808): 890–1; Gillray, "The Spanish Bull Fight or the Corsican Matador in Danger," July 11, 1808. Print 10, 997.
44. Sidmouth to Hiley Addington. September 4, 1808. Sidmouth MSS; Hawkesbury to Liverpool. August 9, 1808. Loan 72/56.
45. Castlereagh to Wellesley. June 30, 1808. *WD* IV:16–18; Muir, *Napoleon*, 46–7; Castlereagh to Wellesley. July 15, 1808. *WD* IV:30–1; Wellesley to Charles Stewart. August 25, 1808. Ibid., 118–20; Robertson, 28–31; Memorandum to Sir Hew Dalrymple. August 23, 1808. *WD* IV:120–1.
46. Sidmouth to Hiley Addington. September 4, 1808. Sidmouth MSS; Hawkesbury to Liverpool. August 9, 1808. Loan 72/56; *Farington*, V:100; Michael Roberts, *The Whig Party, 1807–1812* (London: 1939), 120.
47. *Morning Chronicle.* November 28, 1808.
48. Hawkesbury to Canning. September 18, 1808. Canning MSS.
49. Hawkesbury to Liverpool. September 15, 1808 and October 7, 1808. Loan 72/56; Muir, *Napoleon*, 59.
50. Liverpool to Wellington. February 1812. Yonge, I:378.
51. *LC* V:xi.
52. Hawkesbury to Liverpool. August 20, 1808. BL Loan 72/56; Giles Hunt, *The Duel: Castlereagh, Canning, and Deadly Cabinet Rivalry* (London: 2008), 99–101.

53. Hawkesbury to Canning. September 15, 1808. Canning MSS.
54. Schroeder, 337; Hawkesbury to Canning. October 21, 1808. Canning MSS; Hawkesbury to Liverpool. October 26, 1808. Loan 72/56; Liverpool to Hawkesbury. November 21, 1808. Ibid.
55. Liverpool to Hawkesbury. [December 7, 1808.] Loan 72/51.
56. Alter, 415.
57. Arbuthnot to Huskisson. December 2, 1822. Add MSS 38477.
58. Cecil Jenkinson to John Pemberton. December 18, 1808. Cited in Alter, 415–16.
59. Hawkesbury to George III. December 17, 1808. *LC* V:160; George III to Hawkesbury. December 18, 1808. Ibid.
60. Perceval to Canning. January 19, 1809. *LC* V:168.
61. *PD* 1st ser. 12 (January 19, 1809): 6–9.
62. Ibid., 12–13, 20.
63. Ibid., 22–3.
64. Ibid. (January 25, 1809): 135–7.
65. Ibid. 14 (April 21, 1809): 122–4, 150–64.
66. Ibid. 12 (February 7, 1809): 326.
67. Wilkinson, 164–5.
68. Knight, 344.
69. Liverpool to Artois. March 2, 1809. Yonge, I:276–7.
70. Hunt and John Bew's *Castlereagh: A Life* (New York: 2012) give the most recent accounts.
71. Liverpool to George III. July 11, 1809. *LC* V:310–12.
72. Canning to his wife. July 12 and July 16, 1809. Ibid.
73. Hunt, 127–39.
74. Thomas Grenville to Grenville. October 3, 1809. *HMC Dropmore*, IX:333; Liverpool to Wellington. October 20, 1809. *WSD* VI:413; Wellington to Castlereagh. October 14, 1809. Ibid.
75. Cabinet Minute. September 18, 1809. *LC* V:357–62; Perceval to Yorke. September 23, 1809. Add MSS 45036; Perceval to Arden. September 23, 1809. Add MSS 49188.
76. Tierney to Grey. September 15, 1809. Grey MSS; Grenville to Auckland. September 25, 1809. Add MSS 34457; Grey to Perceval. September 26, 1809. Add MSS 38243.
77. Liverpool to Wallace. September 25, 1809. Add MSS 38243; Rose, II:397; Grenville to Auckland. September 25, 1809. Add MSS 34457.
78. Perceval to Arden. September 30, 1809. Add MSS 49188; George III to Perceval. October 2, 1809. *LC* V:385–6.
79. Liverpool to Wellesley. October 5, 1809. Loan 72/20; Rose, II:402–3.
80. Perceval to Yorke, October 24, 1809. Add MSS 45036; Perceval to George III. October 26, 1809. *LC* V:423; Perceval to Arden. October 24, 1808. Add MSS 49188.
81. Liverpool to George III. October 28, 1809. *LC* V:428; Ibid., 423n; George III to Liverpool. October 29, 1809. Ibid., V:428–9.
82. *Ward*, I:289; Feiling, 262; Liverpool to Wellington. October 20, 1809. *WSD* VI:413.
83. Harvey, *Britain in the Early Nineteenth-Century*, 286.
84. Alter, 430–1; Holland, *Further Memoirs*, 41.
85. Liverpool to Hall. October 26, 1809 and November 2, 1809. Add MSS 38321.
86. Grenville had 406 votes against Eldon's 393. Yonge, I:299. Eldon regretted Beaufort had not stood alone, but, once committed, he could not withdraw unless his supporters volunteered to back Beaufort. Eldon to George III. December 15, 1809. *LC* V:470–1.

87. Knight, 423; Muir, *Wellington*, I:349.

88. Carl von Clausewitz, *On War*, ed. and trans. Michael Howard and Peter Paret (New York: 1993), 99, 118–19. Clausewitz's theory of strategy and command sprang from his experience in this era.

89. Liverpool to Wellington. October 20, 1809. *WSD* VI:413.

90. Wellington to Liverpool. November 19, 1809. Ibid., VI:423–4.

91. Liverpool to Wellington. November 1, 1809. Ibid., VI:413.

92. Joshua Moon, *Wellington's Two-Front War: The Peninsular Campaigns at Home and Abroad, 1808–1914* (Norman: 2010), 4–9.

93. Gash, *Liverpool*, 82–-97; Knight, 288–9. 334–5, 339.

94. Gray, 342–4; Huskisson's Memorandum on War Finance. August 13, 1809. Add MSS 37416; Muir, *Napoleon*, 111–12.

95. Knight, 392–3.

96. Liverpool to Wellington. December 15, 1809. *WSD* VI:439–41; Liverpool to Wellington. December 15, 1809. Add MSS 38325.

97. Wellington to Liverpool. April 26, 1810. *WSD* VI:516; Muir, *Wellington*, I:372.

98. Wellington to Liverpool. June 6, 1810. *WSD* VI:531.

99. Wellington to Liverpool. June 6, 1810. *WSD* VI:531; Liverpool to Wellington. July 5, 1810. Ibid., VI:552.

100. Wellington to Liverpool. April 2, 1810. *WD* VI:5–10.

101. Wellington to Berkley, April 10, 1810. *WD* VI:22; Wellington to Wellesley-Pole. May 9, 1810. *Camden Miscellany*,79, ed. C. K. Webster (1948), 34; Wellington to Wellesley-Pole. October 22, 1809. Ibid., 29.

102. Moon, 99; *The Times*, March 2, 1811, Muir, *Napoleon*, 154; Gash, *Liverpool*, 85–6.

103. *PD* 1st ser. 15 (January 23, 1810): 9.

104. Gray, 288–9; Canning to his wife. January 27 and February 8, 1810. Canning MSS; Perceval to George III. January 27, 1810. *LC* V: 500.

105. *PD* 1st ser. 15 (January 26, 1810): 131–4.

106. Ibid., 141–54; Ibid. (January 29, 1810): 210–11; Liverpool to Wellesley. January 14, 1810. Add MSS 37295.

107. *PD* 1st ser. 15 (February 22, 1810): 512–21.

108. Ibid.

109. Ibid., 16 (March 2, 1810): 2–3.

110. Ibid. (May 7, 1810), 846–7.

111. Ibid., 17 (June 15, 1810): 567.

112. Wellesley's unsigned draft. March 13, 1810. Add MSS 37297; Wellesley to Perceval. May 12, 1810. Ibid.

113. Perceval to Yorke. April 23, 1810 Add MSS 45036; Perceval to Wellesley. April 28, 1810. Add MSS 37295.

114. Alter, 436; Twiss, II:91; Mulgrave to Perceval. September 11, 1810. Add MSS 37295.

115. Bew, 275; Wellington to Wellesley-Pole. September 5, 1810. *WSD* VI:358–9; Muir, *Wellington*, I:402–3.

116. Liverpool to Wellington. April 25, 1810. *WSD* VI:551; Liverpool to Wellington. August 2, 1810. Ibid., VI:567; Liverpool to Wellington. September 10. Ibid., VI:567.

117. Black, *George III*, 407; Liverpool to Wellington. October 17, 1810. *WSD* VI:618.

118. Liverpool to Bathurst. October 27, 1810. Loan 57/4.

119. *P of W* VII:58–9; Ryder to Bathurst. November 3, 1810. Loan 57/4.

120. *P of W* VII:61.

121. Liverpool to Wellington. November 19, 1810. *WSD* VI:642.

122. *PD* 1st ser. 18 (November 29, 1810): 44–6, 53–4.

123. Liverpool to Wellington. December 4, 1810. *WSD* VI:647.

124. *PD* 1st ser. 18 (December 13, 1810):120.

125. Perceval to Prince of Wales. December 19, 1810. *P of W* VII:109; *Colchester*, II:298.

126. McMahon to Northumberland. *P of W* VII:115; Protest of the Royal Dukes. December 19, 1810. Ibid. VII:114.

127. *PD* 1st ser. 18 (December 27, 1810): 387–402.

128. Ibid., 428–38, 447–9.

129. Wellington to Wellesley-Pole. December 15, 1810. Camden Miscellany.

130. William Adam's memorandum. January 5, 1811. *P of W* VII:139–46.

131. Grey and Grenville to Prince of Wales. January 11, 1811. Ibid. VII:158–9; William Adam's memorandum. [c. January 11, 1811.] Ibid. VII:160–4; Sheridan to Holland. January 15, 1810. Ibid. VII:171–6; Holland, *Further Memoirs*, 72; *Ward*, I:367, 380–1.

132. Liverpool to Wellington. January 17, 1811. *WSD* VII:45–6.

133. *Colchester*, II:319 ; Alter, 441; Prince of Wales to Perceval. February 4, 1811. *P of W* VII:200–1.

134. Wellington to Sir Thomas Graham. May 3, 1810. *WD* IV:49–50.

135. Moon, 67–8.

136. Robertson, 52–5; Muir, *Wellington*, I:413.

137. Liverpool to Wellington. April 11, 1811. *WSD* VII:104–5, 102.

138. Wellington to Arbuthnot. May 28, 1811. *AC* 6.

139. Muir, *Wellington*, I:415; Liverpool to Wellington. May 29, 1811. *WSD* VII:145.

140. Esdaile, 338.

141. Moon, 68.

142. Liverpool to Wellington. February 16, 1811. *WSD* VII:61–2; Wellington to Liverpool. March 16, 1811. *WD* VII:368–9.

143. Liverpool to Wellington. May 7, 1811. *WSD* VII:120–1; Moon, 95; Sack, "Wellington and the Tory Press, 1828–30" in *Wellington: Studies in the Military and Political Career of the First Duke of Wellington*, ed. Gash (Manchester: 1990), 159–92.

144. Liverpool to Wellington. April 11, 1811. *WSD* VII:103.

145. Black, *George III*, 407–8; Colonel James Willoughby to McMahon. November 15, 1811. *P of W* VIII:221–4.

146. Twiss, II:196–8; Prince Regent to Duke of York. February 13, 1812. *P of W* VIII:370–1.

147. *P of W* VIII:311–12 quotes at length from Canning's account of a conversation with Wellesley.

148. Liverpool to Wellington. January 20, 1812. *WSD* VII:257; John Severn, *Architects of Empire: The Duke of Wellington and His Brothers* (Norman: 2007), 348–9, 352–3; *Ward*, I:424–5.

149. Prince Regent to the Cabinet. February 13, 1812. *George IV*, I:5–6; Perceval to Prince Regent. February 18, 1812. Ibid., 19.

150. *Ward*, I:473; Gray, 48–9.

151. Salisbury, "Lord Castlereagh," *Quarterly Review* 111 (January, 1862): 205.

6. PRIME MINISTER AND PEACEMAKING

1.   Gray, 457; *The Times*, May 22, 1812.
2.   Twiss, 210–11.
3.   *PD* 1st ser. 23 (May 11, 1812): 165–7.
4.   Twiss, II:204; Bathurst's notes. May 11, 1812. Loan 57/5; *PD* 1st ser. 23 (May 11, 1812): 163–4, 168, 174.
5.   Bew, 304; Gray, 459–60; Gordon Pentland, "'Now the great Man in the Parliament House is dead, we shall have a big Loaf!' Responses to the Assassination of Spencer Perceval," *Journal of British Studies* 51(2012): 340–63.
6.   Cabinet minute. May 13, 1812. *George IV*, I:74–5; Twiss, II:211–12; Canning to Wellesley. May 16, 1812. Add MSS 37296.
7.   Précis of conversation on May 17, 1812. Add MSS 37269.
8.   Précis of conversation. May 18, 1812. Add MSS 37269.
9.   Canning to Liverpool. May 18, 1812. Add MSS 37296; Wellesley to Liverpool. May 18, 1812. Ibid.; Liverpool to Wellesley. May 19, 1814. Ibid.
10. *The Times*, May 20, 1812; Charlotte to Prince Regent. May 21, 1812. *George IV*, I:81; *Farington*, VII:85.
11. *Colchester*, II:383; Cabinet Minute. May 22, 1812. *George IV*, I:83.
12. Holland to Wellesley. May 23, 1812. Add MSS 37296; Lansdowne to Wellesley. May 23, 1812.
13. Liverpool to Canning. May 23, 1812. Canning MSS; Liverpool to Canning. May 24, 1812. Ibid.; Wellesley to Prince Regent. May 24, 1812. *George IV*, I:85-7; Arbuthnot to Huskisson. Undated. Add MSS 38738.
14. John Allen's Journal. May 26, 1812. Add MSS 52204b; Cabinet minute. May 27, 1812. *George IV*, I:90–1.
15. Liverpool to Prince Regent. May 28, 1812. Yonge, I:393.
16. Sidmouth to Prince Regent. May 28, 1812. *George IV*, I:92–3; Eldon to Prince Regent. May 28, 1812. Ibid.
17. Grey to Grenville. June 1, 1812. *HMC Dropmore*, X:277; Richmond to Bathurst. June 7, 1812. Loan 57/5.
18. Grenville to Buckingham. May 27, 1812. *Regency Memoirs*, I:329–30; *Creevy Papers*, I:158.
19. Moira to Charles Hastings. June 4, 1812. *HMC Rawdon Hastings*, III:295.
20. Holland, *Further Memoirs*, 149, 147; Thomas Grenville to Buckingham. May 24, 1812. *Regency Memoirs*, I:318; Aberdeen to Liverpool. June 23, 1812. Loan 73/7.
21. Pellew, III:78; Gash, *Liverpool*, 94.
22. Neville Thompson, *Earl Bathurst and the British Empire, 1762–1834* (Barnsley: 1999), ix, 1, 52–3.
23. *Colchester*, II:396.
24. Canning to Liverpool. July 19, 1812. Loan 72/24; Liverpool to Canning. July 19, 1812. Canning MSS; Canning to Liverpool. July 1812. Ibid.
25. Liverpool to Canning. July 22, 1812. Canning MSS.
26. Canning to Liverpool. July 25, 1812. Loan 72/27; Castlereagh to Liverpool. July 26, 1812. Ibid.; Arbuthnot to Huskisson. July 26, 1812. Add MSS 38738.
27. Canning to Liverpool. July 27, 1812. Canning MSS; Liverpool to Canning. July, 27, 1812. Ibid.

28. Lady Bessborough to Granville Leveson-Gower. August 7, 1812. *Leveson-Gower*, II:443; Robert Isaac Wilberforce and Samuel Wilberforce, *Life of William Wilberforce*, 5 vols. (London: 1838), IV:33–4.

29. Cookson, 7.

30. Quenelle, 170.

31. Liverpool to Wellington. August 19, 1812. *WSD* VII:402.

32. Wellington to Liverpool. June 19, 1812. Ibid., VII:343.

33. Hay, 28.

34. Holland, *Further Memoirs*, 132; Hay, 32–3.

35. Michael R. Watts, *The Dissenters: Volume II, The Expansion of Evangelical Nonconformity* (Oxford: 1995), 285, 349, 68; Tombs, 289.

36. David Hempton, *Methodism and Politics in British Society, 1750–1850* (Stanford: 1984), 99; Michael A. Rutz, "The Politicizing of Evangelical Dissent, 1811–13," *Parliamentary History* 20.2(2001):197.

37. Hempton, 102–3.

38. *PD* 1st ser. 23 (July 23, 1812): 1193.

39. Waterman, "Theology and Political Doctrine," 212–14.

40. Yonge, I:433–4; Gash, *Liverpool*, 95.

41. Watts, 531; Hempton, 104–5.

42. Watts, 387–9; Cannon ed., *The Whig Ascendancy*, 137.

43. Liverpool to Wellington. August 19, 1812. *WSD* VII:401–2.

44. Arbuthnot to Huskisson. August 17, 1812. Add MSS 38738; Dorothy Stuart, *Dearest Bess: The Life and Times of Lady Elizabeth Foster, afterwards Duchess of Devonshire, from Her Unpublished Journals and Correspondence* (London: 1955), 190.

45. Liverpool to Peel. September 10, 1812. Add MSS 40181; *EA* I:332.

46. Thorne, I:226–7; Gash, *Liverpool*, 96; Canning to Huskisson. August 12, 1812. Add MSS 39738.

47. Croker to Peel. September 28, 1812. Add MSS 40183; Liverpool to Peel. September 22, 1812. Add MSS 40181.

48. Liverpool to Peel. November 1, 1812. Add MSS 40181; Thorne, I:236.

49. Liverpool to Peel. November 1, 1812. Add MSS 40181.

50. *PD* 1st ser. 24 (November 30, 1812): 20–32.

51. Ibid., 37–42.

52. Muir, *Napoleon*, 219; *PD* 1st ser. 25 (March 12, 1813): 88.

53. *Colchester*, II:440; Gash, *Liverpool*, 106.

54. Hinde, 265.

55. *Leveson-Gower*, II:470.

56. Gash, *Liverpool*, 101–2; *AJ* I:121.

57. Richard W. Davis, *A Political History of the House of Lords, 1811–1846: From the Regency to Corn Law Repeal* (Palo Alto: 2007), 47.

58. Liverpool to Peel. October 10, 1812. Add MSS 40181; Gash, *Liverpool*, 101.

59. Jupp, 126, 143.

60. Liverpool to Wellington. January 20, 1812. *WSD* VII:257.

61. Hilton, "Political Arts," 155–6.

62. Bew, 287; *HMC Dropmore*, X:220–3.

63. Princess Charlotte to Miss Mercer Elphinstone. August 14, 1813. Aspinall, *Letters of the Princess Charlotte, 1811–1817* (London: 1949), 63.

64. Gash, *Liverpool*, 104–5.

65. *BD*, xxx.

66. Gash, *Liverpool*, 104–5,

67. Muir, *Napoleon*, 198–9.

68. Liverpool to Wellington. April 1812. Add MSS 38326.

69. Moon, 103.

70. Wellington to Bathurst. July 4, 1812. *WD* V:733.

71. Bathurst to Wellington. August 31, September 9, and October 13, 1812. *WSD* VII:412–13, 415–16, 457–8; Liverpool to Wellington. October 7, 1812. Ibid. VII:445.

72. Bathurst to Harrowby. September 16, 1812. Harrowby MSS; Harrowby to Bathurst. September 17, 1812.

73. Wellington to Bathurst. July 21, 1812. *WD* V:761; Liverpool to Wellington. August 19, 1812. *WSD* VII:401–2.

74. Yonge, I:442–3.

75. Muir, *Napoleon*, 231; Bathurst to Wellington. October 12, 1812. *WSD* VII:455–6; Liverpool to Wellington. October 27, 1812. Ibid. VII:463.

76. Liverpool to Wellington. December 22, 1812. *WSD* VII:502–3.

77. Lieven, 70–1, 288–9; Schroeder, 460–1; Muir, *Napoleon*, 249–51.

78. Liverpool to Wellington. February 17, 1813. *WSD* VII:555–6.

79. Castlereagh to Aberdeen. August 6, 1813. *BD* 94.

80. Schroeder, 457, 472–4; Lieven, 362, 327; Adam Zamoyski, *Rites of Peace: The Fall of Napoleon and the Congress of Vienna* (New York: 2007), 63.

81. Castlereagh to Cathcart. September 18, 1812. *BD* 19–25.

82. Muir, *Napoleon*, 294–5.

83. Liverpool to Wellington. July 7, 1813. *WSD* VIII:64–5.

84. Bathurst to Wellington, September 9, 1813. Ibid., 245.

85. Liverpool to Bathurst. October 10, 1813. Ibid., 302.

86. *PD* 1st ser. 27 (November 4, 1813): 19.

87. *Foreign Policy*, I:187–8.

88. Muir, *Napoleon*, 296; *Foreign Policy*, I:223.

89. *BD* 123–8.

90. Wellington to Bathurst. November 21, 1813. Harrowby MSS.

91. Castlereagh to Liverpool. December 30, 1813 and December 31, 1813. *CC* IX:123.

92. Bathurst to Harrowby. December 30, 1813. Harrowby MSS.

93. Liverpool's Cabinet Memorandum. January 4, 1814. Yonge, I:483–8; Liverpool to Castlereagh. December 30, 1813 and January 6, 1814. *Foreign Policy*, I:511–12; Stuart, 203–4.

94. Aberdeen to Harrowby. September 23, 1813. Harrowby MSS; Castlereagh to Liverpool. January 22, 1814. *CC* IX:185; Bew, 337–8.

95. Castlereagh to Liverpool. January 30, 1814. *CC* IX:212; Quenelle, 484, 477.

96. Liverpool to Castlereagh. February 12, 1814. *Foreign Policy*, I:520–2; Muir, *Wellington*, I:575.

97. Zamoyski, 153–4; Castlereagh to Liverpool. February 18, 1814. *CC* IX:266; Liverpool to Castlereagh. February 17, 1814. *Foreign Policy*, I:523–4; Castlereagh to Liverpool. March 5, 1814. *CC* IX:311.

98. Castlereagh to William Richard Hamilton. March 10, 1814. Ibid. 335.

99. Liverpool to Castlereagh, March 22, 1814. Ibid. 529–30; Castlereagh to Liverpool. March 30, 1814. *BD* 173; Muir, *Napoleon*, 232–5.

100. Liverpool to Castlereagh. March 17, 1814. *Foreign Policy*, I:529

101. Liverpool to Castlereagh. November 25, 1814. *WSD* IX:285.

102. Liverpool to Castlereagh. April 9, 1814. *Foreign Policy*, I:531.

103. Castlereagh to Liverpool. April 19, 1814. *CC* IX:472.

104. Wilberforce to Liverpool, April 12, 1814. Loan 72/39; Liverpool to Wilberforce April 12, 1814. Ibid.; Liverpool to Castlereagh. April 14, 1814. *Foreign Policy*, I:533–4.

105. Wilberforce to Liverpool. April 11, 1814. Loan 72/30; Liverpool to Wilberforce. April 12, 1814. Ibid.; Castlereagh to Liverpool. May 19, 1814. *BD* 183–4.

106. Smith, 148; *Foreign Policy*, I:251–2; Liverpool to Castlereagh. April 26, 1814. Ibid., 537–8.

107. Castlereagh to Liverpool. April 20, 1814. *CC* IX:478; Liverpool to Castlereagh. April 26, 1814. *Foreign Policy*, I:537; Muir, *Napoleon*, 330–1.

108. Yonge, I:432–57; Smith, 155–6; Princess Charlotte to Elpinstone. October 28, 1812. Aspinall, *Princess Charlotte*, 28–31; *PD*. 1st ser. 24 (March 2, 1813): 983.

109. Aspinall, *Princess Charlotte*, 38–40, 57, 95.

110. Smith, 159.

111. Grey to Princess Charlotte. October 19, 1813. Aspinall, *Princess Charlotte*, 80–2.

112. Muir, *Napoleon*, 330.

113. Smith, 161–3; Yonge, II:12–15; Grey to Elphinstone. July 7, 1814. Aspinall, *Princess Charlotte*, 123–4; *PD* 1st ser. 27 (July 19, 1814): 755–8.

114. Bew, 362, 365; Muir, *Napoleon*, 330–1.

115. Knight, 451.

116. Gash, *Liverpool*, 109; Grosvenor and Wortley, eds., *Lady Warncliffe*, I:206–7.

117. Yonge, 6–8.

118. Ibid., 9–11.

119. Liverpool to Wellington. September 15, 1814. *WSD* IX:259.

120. Liverpool to Castlereagh. December 23, 1814. Yonge, II:87.

121. *PD* 1st ser. 27 (May 10, 1814): 768–75; 790–1.

122. Liverpool to Wellington. September 2, 1814. WSD IX:211–13; Liverpool to Castlereagh. September 2, 1814. Ibid., 213–14.

123. Troy Bickham, *The Weight of Vengeance: The United States, the British Empire and the War of 1812* (Oxford: 2012), 234–6; Webster states Castlereagh "had only a small share in the negotiations," *Foreign Policy*, I:viii.

124. Liverpool to Wellington. September 27, 1814. *WSD* IX:290–1; Liverpool to Bathurst. September 15, 1814. Loan 57/8; Wellington to Liverpool. November 9, 1814. *WSD* IX:426.

125. Liverpool to Harrowby. October 10, 1814. Harrowby MSS; Liverpool to Bathurst. September 11, 1814. Loan 57/8; Liverpool to Wellington. October 28, 1814. *WSD* IX:384.

126. Bickham, 237–8.

127. Liverpool to Castlereagh. November 2, 1814. *WSD* IX:401–2.

128. Liverpool to Castlereagh. November 25, 1814. *WSD* IX:285.

129. Mark Jarrett, *The Congress of Vienna and its Legacy: War and Great Power Diplomacy After Napoleon* (London: 2013), 105.

130. Liverpool to Castlereagh. October 28, 1814. *WSD* IX:382; Bathurst to Castlereagh. November 27, 1814. *BD* 247–8.
131. Castlereagh to Liverpool. November 11, 1814 and December 5, 1814. Ibid. 229–33, 251–4.
132. Liverpool to Castlereagh. Yonge, II:90.
133. Liverpool to Wellington. December 23, 1814. *WSD* IX:494.
134. Mulgrave to Bathurst. January 18, 1815. Loan 72/15; Liverpool to Bathurst. January 21, 1815. Loan 57/9; Liverpool to Bathurst. January 16, 1815. Ibid.
135. Bickham, 252; Knight, 448.
136. Castlereagh to Liverpool. January 5, 1815 *WSD* IX:527; Liverpool to Castlereagh. December 23, 1814. Ibid. 495.
137. Apsley to Bathurst. January 2, 1815 and January 5, 1815. Loan 57/9; Liverpool to Bathurst. January 16, 1815. Ibid.
138. Liverpool to Castlereagh. November 2, 1814. *WSD* IX:401; Castlereagh to Wellington. December 1814. Ibid., 459.
139. Liverpool to Canning. January 6, 1815. Canning MSS; Yonge, II:132; Liverpool to Castlereagh. January 16, 1815. *WSD* IX:539; Apsley to Bathurst. January 30, 1815 Loan 57/9.
140. *George IV*, II:27–8.
141. Liverpool to Castlereagh. February 20, 1815. *WSD* IX:573; Ibid., January 16, 1815. *WSD* IX:538.
142. Hilton, *Corn, Cash, Commerce*, 11–15; *PD* 1st ser. 30 (March 15, 1815): 181; Prince Regent to Queen Charlotte. March 8, 1815. *George IV*, II:27–8.
143. Wellington to Castlereagh. October 4, 1814. *WSD* IX:314–16; Wellington to Liverpool. November 9, 1814. Ibid., 424–5.
144. Liverpool to Wellington. November 4, 1814. *WSD* IX: 409; Liverpool to Canning. April 19, 1815. Ibid. X:105–6.
145. Castlereagh to Wellington. March 28, 1815. *WSD* IX:263–8.
146. Castlereagh to Wellington. March 16, 1815. *WSD* IX:597.
147. Castlereagh to Wellington. April 3, 1815. *WSD* X:17–18; Harrowby to Castlereagh. April 7, 1815. Ibid., X:31–5; Liverpool memoranda. April 1, 1815. Ibid., X:35–7.
148. Huw Davies, *Wellington's Wars: The Making of a Military Genius* (New Haven: 2012), 230, 225–6; Muir, *Napoleon*, 253.
149. *PD* 1st ser. 30 (April 7, 1815): 363.
150. Ibid. (April 27, 1815): 886.
151. Muir, *Napoleon*, 350; Liverpool to Canning. June 13, 1815. *WSD* X:465.
152. *PD* 1st ser. 31 (May 23, 1815): 316–32.
153. Ibid., 333–59, 363–5, 371.
154. Liverpool to Canning. June 13, 1815. *WSD* X:465.
155. Davies, 235–47; Schroeder, 551–3.
156. Muir, *Napoleon*, 364–5; Prince Regent to Wellington. June 22, 1815. *WSD* X:553–4.
157. Bathurst to Wellington. June 29, 1815. *WSD* X:625; Castlereagh to Wellington. June 26, 1815. Ibid. X:590–1.
158. Wellington to Sir Charles Stuart. June 28, 1815. *WD* VIII:175–6.
159. Liverpool to Castlereagh. July 1815. *WSD* XI:47.
160. Muir, *Napoleon*, 367–8; Croker to Mrs. Croker. July 20, 1815. *Croker Papers*, I:68–9.
161. Liverpool memorandum. June 30, 1815. *WSD* X:630–1.

162. Harrowby memorandum. April 1815. *WSD* X:37–40.
163. Liverpool to Canning. August 4, 1815. *WSD* XI:94–6.
164. Castlereagh to Bathurst. July 14, 1815. *WSD* XI:29; Castlereagh to Liverpool. July 14, 1815. Ibid., XI:28–9.
165. Muir, *Wellington*, II:94–5.
166. Liverpool to Castlereagh. August 18, 1815 and September 19, 1815. *WSD* XI:130–1, 164–5; Muir, *Wellington*, I:96.
167. Castlereagh to Liverpool. September 28, 1815. *WSD* XI:175–7; Schroeder, 557–9.
168. Liverpool to Castlereagh. October 3, 1815. *WSD* XI:183.
169. Liverpool to Bathurst. October 12, 1815. *HMC Bathurst*, 388–9; Liverpool to Castlereagh. September 15, 1815. *WSD* XI:158–9.
170. Liverpool to Louisa. November 15, 18, 21, and 23, 1815. Add MSS 38474; Liverpool to Prince Regent. November 23, 1815. *George IV*, II:135.

7. THE CHALLENGES OF PEACE

1. Cookson, 1.
2. Hilton, *Dangerous People*, 275–6.
3. Martin Daunton, *Trusting Leviathan: The Politics of Taxation in Britain, 1799–1914* (Cambridge: 2001), 32–3.
4. Philip Harling, "Rethinking 'Old Corruption,'" *Past & Present* 147 (May 1995): 127–8; R. Seymour, "State of the Nation," June 10, 1829. Print 15,799; Watts, 384.
5. W. W. Rostow, "Trade Cycles, Harvests and Politics: 1790–1850" in *The British Economy of the Nineteenth Century* (Oxford: 1948), 123–5.
6. Liverpool to Castlereagh. December 23, 1814. *WSD* IX:495.
7. Brougham described it as "in fact, a tax upon income, and not a property tax." *PD* 1st ser. 32 (February 19, 1816): 673; Patrick K. O'Brien, "The Political Economy of British Taxation, 1660–1815," *Economic History Review* 2nd ser. 41.1 (1988):13, 21–2.
8. Hilton, *Corn, Cash, Commerce*, 11; Canning to Liverpool. January 14, 1815. Add MSS 38293; Liverpool to Canning. February 16, 1815. Canning MSS; Arbuthnot to Huskisson. February 4, 1815. Add MSS 38740; *PD* 1st ser. 29 (February 20, 1815): 853; O'Brien, 22.
9. Canning to Liverpool. March 17, 1815. Add MSS 38293; Canning to Huskisson. March 17, 1815. Add MSS 38740.
10. *PD* 1st ser. 30 (May 23, 1815): 686–7, 695–700.
11. Hay, 54–5.
12. Liverpool to Peel. January 28, 1816. Add MSS 40181; *EA* I:435.
13. *PD* 1st ser. 32 (February 1, 1816): 11–12.
14. Ibid., 36–40, 58–9.
15. Cookson, 45–50.
16. *PD* 1st ser. 32 (February 14, 1816): 510–22.
17. Ibid. (February 28, 1816): 1016–1017; Bew, 422.
18. Cookson, 55–6; Huskisson to Canning. March 13, 1816. Canning MSS.
19. Davis, 70.
20. See William Alexander Mackinnon, *On the Rise: Progress and Present State of Public Opinion* (London: 1828) for a contemporary analysis; Hilton, *Dangerous People*, 311.
21. *PD* 1st ser. 32 (February 22, 1816):809–10; Ibid (February 26, 1816): 836–7.

22. *The Times*, February 15, 1816; *PD* 1st ser. 33 (March 7, 1816): 26; Ibid. (March 8, 1816): 74–5.

23. George Cruikshank, "The British Atlas, or John Bull Supporting the Peace Establishment," June 1816. Print 12,786 and "State Physicians Bleeding John Bull to Death!!" Print 12,756; *Morning Chronicle*, February 23, 1816.

24. Liverpool to Castlereagh. August 11, 1815. *CC* X:476–7.

25. Liverpool to Canning. February 13, 1816. Canning MSS.

26. Biancamaria Fontana, *Rethinking the Politics of Commercial Society: The Edinburgh Review, 1802–1832* (Cambridge: 1985), 124, 137.

27. *PD* 1st ser. 33 (March 22, 1816): 518–19.

28. Ibid. (March 14, 1816):8–14.

29. Yonge, II:255; Castlereagh to Prince Regent. March 18, 1816. *George IV*, II:648.

30. Hilton, *Corn, Cash, Commerce*, 32; Cookson, 77–8, 67; O'Brien, 21.

31. Cruickshank, "The Death of the Property Tax," March 1816. Print 12,752; Castlereagh to Prince Regent. March 18, 1816. *George IV*, II:648.

32. *PD* 1st ser. 33 (March 20, 1816): 460–1.

33. Bew, 421, 423.

34. *PD* 1st ser. 33 (March 20, 1816): 479, 496–7.

35. Hay, 61.

36. Liverpool to Sir Benjamin Bloomfield. March 21, 1816. Yonge, II:270; Prince Regent to Liverpool. March 24, 1816. Ibid., 271.

37. Liverpool, Castlereagh, and Vansittart to Prince Regent. March 15, 1816. *George IV*, II:158–9.

38. *Examiner*, March 22, 1812.

39. Cookson, 75–6.

40. *PD* 1st ser. 33 (March 25, 1816): 567–76.

41. Ibid., 577.

42. *Croker Papers*, I:81–4; *PD* 1st ser. 33 (March 25, 1816): 585–7, 594.

43. *Ward*, II:4–5.

44. Muir, *Wellington*, II:135.

45. Thorne, I:306–17.

46. Tony Hayter, *The Army and the Crowd in Mid-Georgian England* (London: 1978).

47. *PD* 1st ser. 32 (February 14, 1816): 321; Ibid., 33 (April 5, 1816): 592; Ibid., 34 (May 13, 1816): 486.

48. Bew, 528–9; Earl of Illchester, ed., *Elizabeth, Lady Holland to Her Son, 1821–1845* (London: 1946).

49. Liverpool to Prince Regent. February 8, 1816. *George IV*, II:146–8; Prince Regent to Liverpool. February 9, 1816. Ibid., II:148.

50. Liverpool to Canning. February 13, 1816. Canning MSS; Canning to Liverpool. March 8, 1816. Ibid.; Canning to Huskisson. March 22, 1816. Add MSS 38741.

51. Cookson, 85–8.

52. Sir Charles Webster thought Liverpool an even-tempered figure of great tact and persuasion, and "not a man who wished to impose his ideas on others." *Foreign Policy*, 34–5. Brock also stressed his equanimity and amiable manner. Brock, 32. Hilton rightly shows how Liverpool's capacity to give and take offense made him anything but "the cool and calculating unruffler of other men's feathers." Hilton, "Political Arts," 147–8.

53. Black, *George III*, 369.

54. Bew, 413–14; Brougham to William Vizard. July 14, 1816. *George IV*, II:164–5.

55. Count Münster to Prince Regent. June 2, 1816. Box 8/7. RA.

56. Castlereagh to the Prince Regent. March 13, 1816. *George IV*, II:644.

57. Cabinet Minute. August 1816. Box 8/7. RA; Bathurst to Harrowby. August 21, 1816. Harrowby MSS.

58. "Paving the War for a Royal Divorce," October 1, 1816. Print 12,808.

59. Gash, *Lord Liverpool*, 128; Bloomfield to Liverpool. September 13, 1816. *George IV*, II:169; Liverpool to Peel. October 18, 1816. Add MSS 40181; Liverpool to Sidmouth. October 28, 1816. Sidmouth MSS.

60. Cookson, 90; *EA* I:489–92.

61. Liverpool to Peel. October 18, 1816. Add MSS 40181.

62. Cookson, 98, 91–2; Liverpool to Castlereagh. October 28, 1816. Yonge, II:281–2; Liverpool to Sidmouth. October 29, 1816. Sidmouth MSS.

63. Liverpool to Sidmouth. October 22, 1816. Sidmouth MSS; Pellew, III:152–3.

64. Liverpool to Peel. October 18, 1816. Add MSS 40181; Sidmouth to Liverpool. November 5, 1816. Sidmouth MSS; Pellew, 149, 161.

65. Peel to Whitworth. January 29, 1817. Parker, I:237–8.

66. *PD* 1st ser. 35 (February 4, 1817): 193, 197–8.

67. Ibid. (January 29, 1817): 57–8; Ibid. (February 24, 1817): 608.

68. *PD* 1st ser. 35 (February 5, 1817): 215.

69. Thomas Grenville to Grenville. January 20, 1817. *HMC Dropmore*, X:421–2; Sack, *The Grenvillites, 1801–29: Party Politics and Factionalism in the Age of Pitt and Liverpool* (Urbana: 1979), 165–7.

70. *PD* 1st ser. 35 (February 18, 1817): 411.

71. Ibid., 419–20.

72. Ibid., 480, 483–4.

73. Ibid. (February 21, 1817): 489, 491; Ibid. (February 24, 1817): 531–3.

74. Ibid., 554, 568–73.

75. Cookson, 111; Aspinall, "The Social Status of Journalists at the Beginning of the Nineteenth Century," *Review of English Studies* 21(1945): 216, 220–5.

76. Southey's Memorandum to Liverpool. March 19, 1817. Yonge, II:298–9; Cookson, 112–14.

77. Thomas Grenville to Grenville. January 10, 14, and 20, 1817. *HMC Dropmore*, X:418–22.

78. *PD* 1st ser. 35 (February 25, 1817): 673, 687.

79. Cookson, 118–23.

80. Harling, *Waning of "Old Corruption,"* 168.

81. Langford, "Politics and Manners," 109.

82. Morris, 145.

83. *PD* 1st ser. 35 (February 24, 1817): 608.

84. Cookson, 125–8.

85. Castlereagh to Wellington. March 31, 1817. *WSD* XI:661.

86. Harling, "The Law of Libel and the Limits of Repression, 1790–1832," *Historical Journal* 44(2001): 107–32; Edward Royle, *Revolutionary Britannia? Reflections on the Threat of Revolution in Britain, 1789–1848* (Manchester: 2000), 48.

87. *Hobhouse*, 69; *British Monitor*, June 21, 1818.

88. Royle, 48–9.

89. Croker to Viscount Exmouth. November 6, 1817. Croker MSS; *Lady Warncliffe*, I:227; Henry Brougham, *The Life and Times of Henry Brougham, Written by Himself*, 3 vols. (London: 1871), II:332.

90. Croker to Peel. November 17, 1817. Croker MSS.

91. *Creevey Papers*, I:268–71

92. Prince Regent to Queen Charlotte. December 16, 1817. *George IV*, II:222–6; Liverpool to Peel. November 10, 1817. Yonge, II:321–2.

93. *Creevey Papers* I:277.

94. *PD* 1st ser. 38 (April 13, 1818): 3; Ibid. (April 14, 1818):42; Ibid. (April 15, 1818): 97–8.

95. Cookson, 141.

96. Watts, 113.

97. Ibid.,38 (May 20, 1818): 831–3.

98. Ibid. (May 15, 1818): 713.

99. Bew, 515; *AJ* I:76.

100. Hilton, *The Age of Atonement: The Influence of Evangelicalism on Social and Economic Thought, 1795–1865* (Oxford: 1988), 227–8; Watts, 1; David W. Bebbington, *Evangelicalism in Modern Britain: A History from the 1730s to the 1980s* (London: 1989), 2–3.

101. Reider Payne, *Ecclesiastical Patronage in England, 1770–1801: A Study of Four Family and Political Networks* (Lewiston: 2010), 221; *Hobhouse*, 32.

102. Gash, *Pillars of Government and Other Essays on State and Society, c. 1770–1880* (London: 1986), 21–4.

103. Thorne, I:253–4.

104. Canning to Liverpool. June 25, 1818. Canning MSS.

105. Huskisson to Liverpool. July 3, 1818. Add MSS 38191.

106. Schroeder, 592–3; Muir, *Wellington*, II:114; Jarrett, 180.

107. Liverpool to Wellington. February 10, 1818. Yonge, II:332–4; *Foreign Policy*, II:86–7.

108. Castlereagh to Liverpool. October 20, 1818. *CC* XII:54–5; Bathurst to Castlereagh. October 20, 1818. Ibid., XII:55–8, Jarrett, 205.

109. Bew, 454–5.

110. Liverpool to Castlereagh. October 23, 1818. *CC* XII:54–5; Muir, *Wellington*, II:121–2.

111. Hilton, "Political Arts," 156; Wellington to Liverpool. November 1, 1818.

112. Liverpool to Peel. January 23, 1818. Add MSS 40181.

113. Arbuthnot to Liverpool. November 1, 1818. Loan 57/7.

114. Thorne, II:330.

115. Hay, 92.

116. Liverpool to Bathurst. September 27, 1818. *HMC Bathurst*, 456.

117. Cookson, 145–50; Melville to Liverpool. July 28, 1818. Add MSS 38272.

118. Arbuthnot to Liverpool. November 1, 1818. Loan 57/7; Harrowby to Bathurst. December 26, 1818. *HMC Bathurst*, 466.

119. Wynn to Buckingham. [undated] *Regency Memoirs*, II:315.

120. *Colchester*, III:73.

121. *PD* 1st ser. 39 (March 2, 1819): 845; *AC* 15–16; *PD* 1st ser. 40 (May 6, 1819): 197.

122. Liverpool to Prince Regent. May 9, 1819. *George IV*, II:289–90; Prince Regent to Liverpool. May 10, 1819. Ibid., II:290–1; Liverpool to Prince Regent. May 11, 1819. Ibid., II:292.

123. Twiss, II:329.

124. John Rickman to Colchester. [1819] *Colchester*, III:72.

125. *PD* 1st ser. 40 (May 18, 1819): 502, 549; *Colchester*, III:76; *PD* 1st ser. 40 (June 7, 1819): 974.

126. Hilton, *Corn, Cash, and Commerce*, 48–9; Liverpool to Huskisson. September 29, 1820. Add MSS 38742.

127. Price, 105–6.

128. *PD* 1st ser. 33 (March 28, 1816): 668; Ibid., 38 (May 26, 1818): 928.

129. *Ibid.*, 1st ser. 40 (May 26,1818): 920–5; Cookson, 152; Hilton, *Corn, Cash, Commerce*, 39.

130. Huskisson to Mrs. Huskisson. February 3, 1819. Add MSS 39949.

131. Hilton, *Corn, Cash, Commerce*, 45.

132. *PD* 1st ser. 40 (May 21, 1819): 610–28.

133. Hilton, *Corn, Cash Commerce*, 40, 57–9.

134. Price, 42–3.

135. Harling, *Waning of "Old Corruption,"* 177–8.

8.   REVOLUTION RESISTED

1. Twiss, II:304–6; *George IV*, II:252.

2. Vice-Chancellor's Statement. January 31, 1821. Box 23/32. RA; John Allen Powell's Milan Commission Diary. August 5, 1818. Box 23/40. Ibid.

3. Jane Robbins, *The Trial of Queen Caroline: The Scandalous Affair that Nearly Ended a Monarchy* (London: 2006), 77–8; James Brougham to Henry Brougham [March 1819]. *George IV*, II:280–5.

4. Brougham to Lord Hutchinson. June 14, 1819. Box 8/8. RA.

5. Prince Regent to Liverpool. June 16, 1819. Box 8/8. RA.

6. Answer to the Cabinet Minute of June 17, 1819. June 22, 1819. Box 8/8. RA.

7. Cabinet Minute. July 24, 1819. Add MSS 38368.

8. Leach to Bloomfield. November 15, 1819. Box 8/8 RA.

9. *EA* I:689–90; Chase, 6.

10. T. M. Parsinnen, "Association, Convention, and Anti-Parliament in British Radical Politics, 1771–1847," *English Historical Review* 88(1973): 515–16, 511.

11. Clark, *English Society*, 499–500, 494; W. D. Rubinstein, "The End of 'Old Corruption' in Britain, 1760–1860," *Past & Present* 101(1983): 57–8, 62–3.

12. Royle, 52.

13. Read, *The English Provinces, c. 1760–1960: A Study in Influence* (London: 1964), 74–5; Muir, *Wellington* II:144; Reade, *Peterloo* 116–17; Parsinnen, 509.

14. Reade, *Peterloo*, 119–20; Parsinnen, 516–17.

15. Chase, 54–5.

16. Redesdale to Sidmouth. August 19, 1819. Sidmouth MSS.

17. Bloomfield to Sidmouth. August 19, 1819. Sidmouth MSS.

18. Muir, *Wellington*, II:145; Canning to Huskisson. September 14, 1819. Add MSS 38741; Sheffield to Sidmouth. November 1, 1819. Pellew, III:263.

19. Liverpool to Canning. September 23, 1819. Yonge, II:407–11.

20. Royle, 53–4; Chase, 52.

21. Cookson, 180–1.

22. Sidmouth to Liverpool. October 1, 1819. Sidmouth MSS.

23. Liverpool to Melville. September 24, 1819. Add MSS 38279.

24. Canning to Liverpool. October 14, 1819. Canning MSS.

25. E. A. Smith, *Whig Principles and Party Politics: Earl Fitzwilliam and the Whig Party, 1748–1833* (Manchester, 1975), 349–50; *Courier*, October 16, 1819.

26. Liverpool to Sidmouth. October 14, 1819 and October 17, 1819. *HMC Bathurst*, 479–80.

27. Liverpool to Canning. October 10, 1819. Yonge, II:411.

28. Hay, 102; *Leeds Mercury*, June 26, 1819.

29. Smith, *Whig Principles*, 347–52.

30. Cookson, 191.

31. Liverpool to Grenville. November 14, 1817. Yonge, II:430–4.

32. *PD* 1st ser. 41 (November 29, 1819): 44–8.

33. Ibid., (November 30, 1819):448–73; Grenville to Liverpool. November 12, 1819. Yonge, II:418–30.

34. *PD* 1st ser. 41 (November 30, 1819): 494–506.

35. Ibid. (December 6, 1819): 738–42.

36. Cookson, 200.

37. Chase, 9–11.

38. Sidmouth to Talbot. February 13, 1820. Sidmouth MSS.

39. Croker to Sir George Warrender. February 3, 1820. Croker MSS; *Hobhouse*, 3; *AJ* I:1.

40. Croker Journals. February 10, 1820. Croker MSS.

41. Cookson, 207–8, 211; *Hobhouse*, 6; Eldon to Liverpool [undated] Yonge, III:24.

42. Cabinet Minute. February 10, 1820. Box 8/10. Royal Archives.

43. Undated memorandum. Add MSS 38866

44. *Hobhouse*, 8; *Greville*, I:89.

45. *AJ* I:121.

46. Cookson, 212.

47. Castlereagh to his brother. February 13, 1820. *CC* XII:213–14; *Hobhouse*, 8–9; Croker Journals. February 14, 1820. Croker MSS.

48. Cabinet Minute. February 14, 1820. Add MSS 38866; Royal memorandum. February 17, 1820. Ibid.

49. *Hobhouse*, 9.

50. Liverpool's undated Memorandum. Add MSS 38566.

51. Chase, 78–9.

52. Bew, 471–4.

53. Gash, *Liverpool*, 154–5.

54. Chase, 82–3.

55. Cookson, 215.

56. Chase, 92–4.; D. R. Fisher ed., *The House of Commons, 1820–1831*, 7 vols. (Cambridge: 2009), I:217.

57. Liverpool to Canning. March 23, 1820. Canning MSS.

58. Liverpool to Bathurst. April 23, 1820. *HMC Bathurst*, 488.

59. *Hobhouse*, 18–21; Cabinet Memorandum. April 24, 1820; Buckingham, *Memoir of the Court of George IV*, I:12.

60. *PD* 2nd ser. 1 (May 15, 1820): 385–6.

61. Buckingham, *George IV Memoir*, IV I:19; *AJ* I:18–19.

62. Huskisson to Arbuthnot. March 24, 1820. Add MSS 38742.

63. Price, 116.

64. Mokyr, 70.

65. Sack, *Jacobite to Conservative*, 180–90; Fontana, 105.

66. *PD* 1st ser. 1 (March 13, 1817): 1051; Ibid. (May 15, 1820): 183.

67. Cookson, 223–5; Hilton, "Political Arts," 151, 158–9.

68. Henry Newmarch and Thomas Took, *A History of Prices and of the State of the Circulation during the Years 1703–1856*, 6 vols. (London: 1838–57), VI:337–41.

69. *PD* 2nd ser. 1 (May 15, 1820):165–85, 191–3; *George IV Memoir*, I:19.

70. *PD* 2nd ser. 1 (May 26, 1820): 565–94.

71. *EA* 754–9.

72. Cookson, 227.

73. Caroline to Liverpool. March 16, 1820. Loan 73/3.

74. Robbins, 106–7, 93.

75. Jonathan Fulcher, "The Loyalist Response to the Queen Caroline Agitations" *Journal of British Studies* 34(October 1995): 484, 486; Thomas Lacquer, "The Queen Caroline Affair: Politics and Art in the Reign of George IV," *Journal of Modern History* 54(1982): 458; Tamara Hunt, "Morality and Monarchy in the Queen Caroline Affair," *Albion* 23(1991): 697–722.

76. Canning to Liverpool. April 2, 1820. Add MSS 28193

77. Grey to Lady Grey. May 20 and June 7, 1820. Grey MSS; Croker Journals. April 12, 1820. Croker MSS.

78. Liverpool's undated Memorandum. Add MSS 38566.

79. Hutchinson to Bloomfield. March 31, 1820. RA. 8/10; Hutchinson to Bloomfield. April 19, 1820. Ibid.

80. Brougham to Liverpool. June 3, 1820. Yonge, III:65–7.

81. Hutchinson to Liverpool. June 5, 1820. Yonge, III:72–4

82. Brougham to Liverpool. June 4, 1820. Loan 72/3; Brougham to Caroline. June 4, 1820. Ibid.

83. *PD* 2nd ser. 1 (June 6, 1820): 870.

84. Ibid. (June 7, 1820): 905–6.

85. Ibid. (June 7, 1820): 908, 845. 982.

86. Caroline to Liverpool. June 10, 1820. Loan 72/3.

87. Liverpool to Caroline. June 11, 1820. Loan 57/3; Caroline to Liverpool. June 12, 1820. Ibid.; Liverpool to Caroline. June 13, 1820. Ibid.; Brougham to Liverpool. June 14, 1820. Ibid.

88. *AJ* 23; *Hobhouse*, 25.

89. *PD* 2nd ser. 1 (June 6, 1820): 973.

90. Bloomfield to Liverpool. June 10, 1820. Add MSS 38547; Liverpool to George IV. June 11, 1820. Add MSS 38565.

91. *Hobhouse*, 27.

92. Lansdowne to Grey. June 12, 1820. Grey MSS; Tierney to Grey. June 12, 1820. Ibid.; George IV to Wellesley. *George IV*, II:346; Grey to Holland. February 20, 1820. Add MSS 51553.

93. *The Times*, June 6, 1820; Twiss, II:372.

94. *Farington*, VIII:252–3.

95. Muir, *Wellington*, II:159–60; Chase, 166.

96. Memorandum to Liverpool. June 1820. *WND* I:127–9; *Greville*, I:100.
97. Cookson, 239–41.
98. Robbins, 128–9; *Greville*, I:99; Gash, *Liverpool*, 161.
99. *PD* 2nd ser. 1 (June 22, 1820):1313; Ibid. (June 23, 1820): 1315–16.
100. Ibid. (June 26, 1820): 1329–36
101. Ibid. (June 27,1820): 1–15; *Greville*, I:100.
102. *PD* 2nd ser. 1 (June 27, 1820): 15–22.
103. *AJ* I:26.
104. Rose Melikan, *John Scott, Lord Eldon, 1751–1838: The Duty of Loyalty* (Cambridge: 1999), 280; Cookson, 246; Hinde, 299–300.
105. Cookson, 253–4.
106. Liverpool to Harrowby. August 11, 1820. Harrowby MSS.
107. Edward Wilbraham to Liverpool. August 9, 1820. Loan 72/3; Kenyon to Liverpool. July 1, 1820. Add MSS 38566; Liverpool to Kenyon. July 8, 1820. Yonge, III:105–6.
108. Cookson, 258–9.
109. Twiss, 372 ; *Greville*, I:106; Liverpool to Canning. September 12, 1820. Yonge, III:106.
110. Liverpool to George IV. September 1, 1820. *George IV*, II:361–2; George IV to Liverpool. September 6, 1820. Ibid., II:366.
111. Liverpool to Canning. September 12, 1820 Yonge, III:106–7; *AJ* I:35, 44.
112. *PD* 3rd ser. 2 (November 3, 1820): 1574–5; Ibid. (November 4, 1820): 1601, 1612–15.
113. Ibid., 1683–8; Grenville to Liverpool. November 6, 1820. Add MSS 38288; *Hobhouse*, 37–8.
114. *PD* 2nd ser. 2 (November 3, 1820):1572; Ibid. (November 8, 1820):1723.
115. Ibid., 1726; Arbuthnot to Huskisson. November 5, 1820. Add MSS 38742; *AJ* I:51–2; Twiss, II:398–9.
116. *PD* 2nd ser. 2 (November 10, 1820):1746–7.
117. *Hobhouse*, 40; *George IV*, II:378n; Arbuthnot to Huskisson. November 17, 1820. Add MSS 38742.
118. George IV to Eldon. *George IV*, II:377–8; *Hobhouse*, 41–2;
119. *Ward*, II:91–4.
120. Liverpool to Wilberforce. December 29, 1820. Loan 72/3.
121. George Cruickshank, "And when Ahithophel saw that his Counsel was not followed, he saddled his Ass, & arose, & went & hanged himself &c." January 31, 1821 (see Fig. 12). Print 12, 116.
122. *PD* 3rd ser. 3 (February 6, 1821): 507; Ibid. (February 14, 1821): 665; Cookson, 296–8.
123. *AJ* I:66; Croker to Sir Graham Moore. February 6, 1821. Croker MSS; Lady Seymour, ed., *The "Pope" of Holland House: Selections from the Correspondence of John Wishaw and His Friends, 1813–1840* (London: T.F. Unwin, 1906), 209–10; *PD* 3rd ser. 3 (January 23, 1821): 12–13.
124. Fulcher, 495.
125. Sidmouth to Sir William Elford. December 17, 1820. Sidmouth MSS.
126. *AJ* I:89.
127. *Colchester*, III:180–1; *Ward*, II:57.
128. Gatrell, 521–31. Hone's 1817 acquittal on a charge of blasphemous libel made it harder to prosecute satire while presenting courts as a target for ridicule. Deterrence worked both ways.
129. *Creevey Papers*, I:332.

130. Royle, 55.
131. Chase, 177.
132. Royle, 157.
133. Muir, *Wellington*, II:165; Croker to Peel. August 9, 1820. Croker MSS.
134. George IV to Liverpool. November 16, 1820. *George IV*, II:380.
135. Grey to Holland. November 21, 1820. Add MSS 51553; *George IV*, II:389–91; Buckingham, *George IV Memoir*, IV I:80–1; Arbuthnot to Bathurst. November 29, 1820. *HMC Bathurst.*
136. Muir, *Wellington*, II:168.
137. Liverpool to Charles Bathurst. December 29, 1820. Add MSS 38288.
138. *AJ* 82–3.
139. *Hobhouse*, 65–6; Liverpool to Bathurst. June 27, 1820. *HMC Bathurst* 199–500; Bathurst to Liverpool. Ibid., 501.
140. *AJ* I:100.
141. Ibid., 103; Gash, *Liverpool*, 117.
142. *AJ* I:76.
143. *Hobhouse*, 52–3, 67; *AJ* I:105; Croker Journals. July 30 and August 26, 1821. Croker MSS.
144. Liverpool to Bathurst. August 31, 1821. *HMC Bathurst*, 517–18.
145. *AJ* I:126; Quenelle, 143.
146. Chase, 201; Croker Journals. September 16, 1821. Croker MSS.
147. Buckingham, *George IV Memoir*, I:232.
148. Liverpool to George IV. November 29 and December 1, 1821. *George IV*, II:473–6; Sack, *Grenvillites*, 188–90; Yonge, III:160–4.
149. Cookson, 339–40.

9.   REFORM AND STABILIZATION

1. Peel to Croker. March 23, 1820. *Croker Papers*, I:170.
2. Taylor, 152.
3. Price, 263.
4. *Croker Papers* I:170; Clark, *English Society*, 6–8.
5. Mokyr, 434.
6. Wellington to Buckingham. March 6, 1822. *WND* I:219.
7. Fisher, I:326; Harling, *Waning of "Old Corruption,"* 179–80.
8. *PD* 2nd ser. 6 (February 5, 1822): 14–15.
9. Published as *The Speech of the Earl of Liverpool: Delivered in the House of Lords on Tuesday, the 26ᵗʰ day of February, 1822 on the subject of the agricultural distress of the country and the financial measures proposed for its relief. With an appendix, containing several accounts therein referred to* (London: 1822) it went through several printings.
10. *PD* ser. 6 (February 26, 1822): 382–701.
11. Ibid., 701–16.
12. *The State of the Nation, at the Commencement of the Year 1822 Considered under the Four Departments of the Finance, Foreign Relations, Home Department, Colonies and Board of Trade &c.* (London: 1822).
13. Gash, *Pillars*, 26–9.
14. Cookson, 364–5; *AJ* I:146–7.

15. Bew, 510, 519; *Hobhouse*, 79.
16. Ibid., 89.
17. Liverpool to Melville. August 25, 1822. Yonge, III:197
18. George IV to Liverpool. August 17, 1822. Ibid., 194–5.
19. Cookson, 368; Muir, *Wellington*, II:186–7; Buckingham to Wellington. August 20, 1822. *WSD* I:261–2; Peel to Charles Manners-Sutton. September 2, 1822. Parker, I:332–3; Arbuthnot to Sidmouth. September 4, 1822. Sidmouth MSS.
20. Arbuthnot to Harriet Arbuthnot. September 2, 1822. *AC* 31.
21. Wellington to George IV. September 7, 1822 *WSD* I:274–6; George IV to Liverpool. September 8, 1822. Yonge, III:199; Liverpool to Wellington. September 8, 1822; Arbuthnot to Bathurst. September 12, 1822. HMC Bathurst, 532.
22. Bew, 531; Peel to Charles Manners-Sutton. September 2, 1822. Parker, I:332–3.
23. *Hobhouse* 87, 96; *AJ* I:209; Cookson, 392–4.
24. *Hobhouse*, 99–101; Yonge, III:208–11; Fisher, IV:215.
25. Croker to Sir William Knighton. February 11, 1823. Croker MSS; *Hobhouse*, 103.
26. Huskisson to Liverpool. May 12, 1822 and January 11, 1822. Add MSS 38742.
27. Huskisson to Canning. November 1822. Add MSS 38743; Huskisson to Charles Ellis. December 29, 1822. Ibid.; Huskisson to Arbuthnot. December 26, 1822. Ibid., Arbuthnot to Huskisson. December 2, 1822. Ibid.
28. Cookson, 387; Liverpool to Arbuthnot. December 30, 1822. *AC* 36–7; Bathurst to Harrowby. January 5, 1823. Harrowby MSS.
29. Canning to Arbuthnot. January 10, 1823. *AC* 38; Arbuthnot to Liverpool. January 12, 1823; Ibid., 39–41; Liverpool to Arbuthnot. February 17, 1823. Ibid., 43–4.
30. Croker to Sir Graham Moore. January 21, 1823. Croker MSS; *AJ* I:205–6.
31. Liverpool to Vansittart. January 7, 1823. Yonge, III:249–50.
32. Smart, *EA* II:150–3; *PD* 2nd ser. 8 (February 21, 1823): 194–213; *Hobhouse*, 103; *PD* 2nd ser. 8 (March 21, 1823): 636.
33. Croker to Bloomfield. October 5, 1823. Croker MSS.
34. Harling, *Waning of "Old Corruption,"* 185.
35. *PD* 2nd ser. 7 (June 17, 1822): 1121; Hilton, *Corn. Cash, Commerce*, 184–5; Liverpool to Grenville. November 14, 1819. Add MSS 38281.
36. *EA* II:103–6; *PD* 2nd ser. 7 (June 17, 1822): 1121.
37. *EA* II:195–8; O'Brien, 21–2; Hilton, *Corn, Cash, Commerce*, 178–9; Price, 119.
38. Harling, *Waning of "Old Corruption,"* 183–4.
39. Price, 139.
40. Liverpool to Canning. October 19, 1824. Loan 72/25.
41. Price, 288; Fisher, II:153–4.
42. Ibid.; Yonge, III:137–8.
43. *PD* 2nd ser. 5 (June 17, 1822): 1121.
44. *PH* 30 (May 6, 1793): 820.
45. Liverpool to Canning. October 18, 1824. Loan 72/25; *PD* 2nd ser. 11 (May 24, 1824): 842.
46. *Hobhouse*, 54; Hawkesbury to Hardwicke. November 15, 1804. BL Add MSS 35209.
47. Gash, *Liverpool*, 185; *PD* 2nd ser. 5 (June 21, 1822): 1250.
48. *PD* 2nd ser. 9 (July 9, 1823): 1487–9.
49. Ibid., 11 (May 24, 1824): 841.
50. Ibid. (April 2, 1824): 74.

51. Gash, *Liverpool*, 216.
52. Canning to Huskisson. January 3, 1823. Add MSS 38744.
53. Buckingham, *George IV Memoir*, I:419.
54. Gash, *Liverpool*, 205–6.
55. *AJ* I:121.
56. Albinson et al., eds., 17–21.
57. *"Noble and Patriotic," The Beaumont Gift 1828* (London: 1988).
58. Gash, *Liverpool*, 210–11.
59. *PD* 2nd ser. 11 (March 11, 1824): 880; Chase, 14, 205.
60. Sack, *Jacobite to Conservative*, 192–3, 256; *Farington*, VIII:241.
61. *PD* 1st ser. 38 (May 15, 1818): 713; Liverpool to George III. June 16, 1824. Yonge, III:288.
62. Lee, 123; *Bristol Mercury*, January 17, 1825; Gash, *Liverpool*, 228–9.
63. *Bath Chronicle*, January 20, 1825.
64. *Bristol Mercury*, January 17, 1825.
65. Portsmouth, 42, 52–3, 25.
66. *AJ* I:275.
67. *Bristol Mercury*, January 17, 1824.
68. *Foreign Policy*, II:234–40; Gash, *Lord Liverpool*, 198.
69. Jarrett, 230.
70. Bew, 503–4; Muir, *Wellington*, II:174–5.
71. *PD* 3rd ser. 4 (February 18, 1821): 762–71; Ibid. (March 2, 1820): 1723; *AJ* I:65.
72. Canning to Liverpool. March 1, 1821. Loan 72/25.
73. Schroeder, 264–5; Muir, *Wellington*, II:194–5; Liverpool to Canning. September 27, 1822. *WND* I:300.
74. Liverpool to Arbuthnot. December 29, 1822. *AC* 36.
75. *PD* 2nd ser. 8 (February 4, 1823): 31–2.
76. Ibid. (April 24, 1823), 247–9.
77. Ibid. (April 14, 1823): 829–68; Ibid. (April 24, 1823): 229–30, 239.
78. Liverpool to Bathurst. October 16, 1823. *HMC Bathurst*, 548–9; Schroeder, 634–5; Hinde, 350–7.
79. Quenelle, 274; *AJ* II:284.
80. George IV to Liverpool. November 6, 1823. *George IV*, III:38–9.
81. Arbuthnot to Liverpool. October 7, 1823. *AC* 46–57.
82. Liverpool to Arbuthnot. October 8, 1823. Ibid., 57–8.
83. *HMC Bathurst*, 526; *PD* 2nd ser. 10 (March 15, 1824): 1000.
84. *Hobhouse*, 110; *AJ* I: 285, 296–7.
85. *PD* 2nd ser. 10 (15 Mar, 1824): 999.
86. Yonge, III:297–304; Liverpool, with Canning, Wellington, and Peel, were among subscribers to William James' 1826 *Naval History of Great Britain, from the Declaration of War by France in February 1793 to the Accession of George IV in 1820* written partly as a rebuff to American claims about their navy's effectiveness during the War of 1812. Andrew Lambert, "Winning without Fighting: British Grant Strategy and its Application to the United States, 1815–65" in *Strategic Logic and Political Rationality: Essays in Honor of Michael I. Handel*, ed. Bradford Lee and Karl F. Walling (London: 2003), 174–7.
87. *AJ* I:366.

88. Sack, *Jacobite to Conservative*, 246; Muir, *Wellington*, II:200–201; Harling, *Waning of "Old Corruption,"* 184.
89. Wellesley to Liverpool. December 22, 1824. Loan 72/23.
90. Fisher, VI:530–2.
91. *AJ* I:369.
92. *PD* 2nd ser. 12 (February 3, 1825): 126–8.
93. *Hobhouse*, 113.
94. *Colchester*, III:372–4.
95. Gash, *Liverpool*, 233.
96. Sack, *Jacobite to Conservative*, 230–51; *AJ* I:392.
97. Liverpool to Bathurst. May 4, 1825. *HMC Bathurst*, 580–1.
98. *AJ* I:380–1; Muir, *Wellington*, II:223–6.
99. Arbuthnot to Liverpool. May 13, 1825. AJ 76–7; Bathurst to Liverpool. May 13, 1825. *HMC Bathurst* 581–2; Bathurst to Liverpool. May 23, 1825. Ibid., 584–5.
100. Gash, *Liverpool*, 234.
101. *PD* 2nd ser. 12 (February 3, 1825): 739–52.
102. Hempton, 117.
103. Muir, *Wellington*, II:205–6.
104. Liverpool to Wellington. June 23, 1825. *WND* II:465.
105. Wellington to Eldon. September 7, 1825. *WND* II:482–3; Liverpool to Wellington. September 16, 1825. Ibid. II:499.
106. Fisher I:221; *Hobhouse*, 118–19.
107. *EA* II:264–6; Hilton, *Corn, Cash, Commerce*, 207; *PD* 2nd ser. 12 (March 25, 1825): 1194–5.
108. Hilton, *Corn, Cash, Commerce*, 215–20.
109. Gash, *Liverpool*, 238; *AJ* II:6.
110. *PD* 2nd ser. 14 (February 26, 1826): 16.
111. *Greville*, I:154.
112. Hilton, *Corn, Cash, Commerce*, 225; Gash, *Liverpool*, 238.
113. Croker to Wellington. March 20, 1826. *WND* III:209–12; *PD* 2nd ser. 14 (February 26, 1826): 707, 726–8.
114. Peel to Wellington. March 3, 1826. *WND* III:143–5; Canning to Wellington. Ibid., III:209.
115. *PD* 2nd ser. 14 (February 9, 1826): 18.
116. Ibid. (February 17, 1826): 450–7, 465; Hilton *Corn, Cash, Commerce*, 221–2.
117. *PD* 2nd ser. 14 (February 17, 1826): 461–2.
118. *EA* II:331–2; *Hobhouse*, 120; *PD* 2nd ser. 15 (May 1, 1826): 461–2.
119. Ibid., 752.
120. Hilton, *Corn, Cash, Commerce*, 201.
121. Fisher, I:222.
122. *Hobhouse*, 121; Peel to Wellington. July 31, 1826. *WSD* III:383; Fisher, I:225.
123. Gash, *Liverpool*, 239–40; Fisher, 331.
124. *EA* II:389–91.
125. Wellington to Liverpool. June 23, 1826. *WND* III:342–3; Liverpool to Wellington. June 24, 1826. Ibid. 343.
126. Sack, *Jacobite to Conservative*, 206, 184–7; Liverpool to Canning. February 10, 1827. Yonge, III:451.

127. Huskisson Memorandum. October 18, 1826. Add MSS 38761; Liverpool to Huskisson. October 25, 1826. Add MSS 38748.
128. Huskisson to Robinson. November 20, 1826. Add MSS 38748; *AJ* II:55–7.
129. Gash, *Liverpool*, 240–1; Hinde, 412–20.
130. *PD* 2nd ser. 16 (November, 1826): 18.390–9.
131. Severn, *Architects of Empire*, 445–7.
132. Arbuthnot to Liverpool. August 25, 1826. Loan 72/7; Liverpool to Arbuthnot. Ibid.; Arbuthnot to Liverpool. September 5, 1826. Ibid.
133. Bathurst to Arbuthnot. September 13, 1826. *AC* 83; Liverpool to Arbuthnot. September 8, 1826. Loan 72/2.
134. Liverpool to Robinson. December 16, 1826. Yonge, III:438–9.
135. *AJ* II:65; Gash, *Liverpool*, 246.
136. Hinde, 434.
137. Canning to Wellington. January 29, 1827. *WND* III:574.
138. *Colchester*, III:463; Twiss, II:583; Gash, *Liverpool*, 246.
139. *AJ* II:81, 85; *Colchester*, III:463; Gash, *Liverpool*, 248.
140. *The Times*, February 19, 1827; *Morning Chronicle*, February 19, 1827.
141. *Greville*, I:168.
142. *AJ* II:82; Herries to Knighton. February 27, 1827. *George IV*, III:200.
143. Gash, *Liverpool*, 249.
144. *Colchester*, III:493.
145. Hay, 138–53.
146. Muir, *Wellington*, II:292–3.
147. Gash, *Liverpool*, 249–50.

CONCLUSION: WEATHERING THE STORM

1.   Hawkins, 131. The description of "parliamentary government" comes from an 1858 essay by the 3rd Earl Gray outlining how it worked.
2.   Walter Bagehot, "The Character of Sir Robert Peel" in *Works and Life of the Late Walter Bagehot*, ed. Mrs. Russell Barrington, 9 vols. (London: 1915), II:178; Harriet Martineau, *The History of England during the Thirty Years Peace, 1816–1846* (London: 1849), 11.
3.   Brougham, *Historical Sketches of Statesmen Who Flourished in the Time of George III*, 3 vols. (London: 1839–1843) II:133–4, 140; Spencer Walpole, *A History of England From the Conclusion of the Great War in 1815* (London: 1913), I:294; Martineau, 11–12, 433.
4.   George Cornewall Lewis, *Essays on the Administration of Great Britain from 1783 to 1830 Contributed to the Edinburgh Review*, ed. Sir Edmund Head (London: 1864), 418, 422. Lewis edited the *Edinburgh Review* before serving in Palmerston's Liberal cabinet.
5.   Bagehot, "Character of Sir Robert Peel," II:184.
6.   W. E. H. Lecky, *History of England in the Eighteenth Century*, 8 vols. (New York: 1878–90), III:225.
7.   Thomas Babbington Macaulay to Macvey Napier. July 20, 1838. *Letters of Thomas Babbington Macaulay*, ed. Thomas Pinney, 6 vols. (Cambridge: 1974–81), II:252.
8.   Martineau, 430.
9.   I borrow some of these categories from J. C. D. Clark, *Revolution and Rebellion: State and Society in England in the Seventeenth and Eighteenth Centuries* (Cambridge: 1986), 2.

10. Maurice Cowling, *Religion and Public Doctrine in Modern England* (Cambridge: 1980), 370.

11. Lewis, 432; Sack, "Memory of Pitt," 623–40.

12. Hilton, *The Age of Atonement*; Richard Brent, *Liberal Anglican Politics: Whiggery, Liberalism and Reform, 1830–1841* (Oxford: 1987); Jonathan Parry, *The Rise and Fall of Liberal Government in Victorian Britain* (New Haven: 1993).

13. E. P. Thompson, *The Making of the English Working Class* (Harmondsworth: 1980); Sack, "Memory of Pitt," 634–5.

14. Gash, *Liverpool*, 6.

15. Brougham, *Historical Sketches*, II:133.

16. Muir, *Fortunes of Peace*, 166.

17. I owe this reference to conversation with John Bew.

18. Sack, *Jacobite to Conservative*, 227–8, 239–40.

19. Hay, 161–3.

20. Hawkins, 8–9.

21. Gash, *Pillars of Government*, 24–5.

22. J. Enoch Powell, *Joseph Chamberlain* (London: 1977), 151.

23. Gash, *Liverpool*, 253.

24. Cowling, 368–73, 379; Angus Hawkins, "'A Calm, Temperate, Deliberate, and Conciliatory Course of Conduct': Mid-Victorian Conservative Foreign Policy," in *The Tory World: Deep History and the Tory Theme in British Foreign Policy, 1679–2014*, ed. Jeremy Black (Farnham: 2015), 167, 180–3.

25. Gash, *Lord Liverpool*, 253.

26. Canning to John Hookham Frere. April 26, 1802. BL Add MSS 38833. Folios 114 and 115 provide the verses of the "The Pilot that Weathered the Storm."

BIBLIOGRAPHY

MANUSCRIPTS

BEINECKE RARE BOOK AND MANUSCRIPT LIBRARY, YALE UNIVERSITY
> Canning Papers
> Dorset Papers
> Wraxall Anecdotes and Characters

BODLEIAN LIBRARY, OXFORD UNIVERSITY
> James Bland Burges Papers

BRITISH LIBRARY
Additional Manuscripts Collection:
> Aberdeen Papers
> Auckland Papers
> Canning Papers
> Dundas Papers
> Hardwicke Papers
> Holland House Papers

> Huskisson Papers
> Liverpool Papers
> Peel Papers
> Spencer Perceval Papers
> Wellesley Papers

Loan Manuscripts:
> Bathurst Papers
> Liverpool Papers

BRITISH NATIONAL ARCHIVES, KEW
> FO 7 (Austria)
> FO 27 (France)
> FO 323 Whitworth Papers
> PRO 30 Cornwallis Papers

DEVON RECORD OFFICE
> Sidmouth Papers

DURHAM UNIVERSITY LIBRARY
> Grey Papers

KENT HISTORY AND LIBRARY CENTRE
> Sackville Papers

ROYAL ARCHIVES, WINDSOR CASTLE
Private Papers of George IV_

SANDON HALL, STAFFORDSHIRE
Harrowby Papers

UNIVERSITY OF SOUTHAMPTON
Wellington Papers

SUFFOLK RECORD OFFICE, BURY ST EDMUNDS
Hervey Papers

WEST YORKSHIRE ARCHIVE SERVICE
Harewood (Canning) Papers

WILLIAM L. CLEMENTS LIBRARY, UNIVERSITY OF MICHIGAN
Canning Papers
Croker Papers
Melville Papers
Pitt Family Papers

NEWSPAPERS

Bath Chronicle

Bristol Mercury

British Monitor

Courier

Examiner

Felix Farley's Bristol Journal

Gentleman's Magazine

Jackson's Oxford Journal

Leeds Mercury

London Evening Post

Morning Chronicle

Quarterly Review

The Times

PUBLISHED PRIMARY SOURCES

Abbot, Charles, Lord Colchester. *The Diary and Correspondence of Charles Abbot, Lord Colchester.* Ed. Charles, Lord Colchester. 3 vols. London: 1861.

Anon., *The State of the Nation, at the Commencement of the Year 1822 Considered under the Four Departments of the Finance, Foreign Relations, Home Department, Colonies and Board of Trade &c.* London: 1822.

Arbuthnot, Harriet. *The Journal of Mrs. Arbuthnot, 1820–1832.* Ed. Francis Bamford and the Duke of Wellington. 2 vols. London: 1959.

Aspinall, Arthur, ed. *Letters of George IV.* 3 vols. Cambridge: 1938.

_____. *Correspondence of Charles Arbuthnot.* Camden 3rd ser. 65. London: 1941.

_____. *Correspondence of George, Prince of Wales, 1770–1812.* 8 vols. New York: 1963–71.

_____. *Diary of Henry Hobhouse, 1820–1827.* London: 1947.

_____. *Later Correspondence of George III.* 5 vols. Cambridge: 1962–70.

_____. *Letters of the Princess Charlotte, 1811–1817.* London: 1949.

Bagehot, Walter. *Works and Life of the Late Walter Bagehot.* Ed. Barrington Russell. 9 vols. London: 1915.

Brougham, Henry. *Historical Sketches of Statesmen Who Flourished in the Time of George III.* 3 vols. London: 1839–43.

_____. *The Life and Times of Henry Brougham, Written by Himself.* 3 vols. London: 1871.

Buckingham and Chandos, Duke of. *Memoirs of the Court and Cabinets of George III.* 2 vols. London: 1853.

_____. *Memoirs of the Court of England during the Regency, 1811–1820.* 2 vols. London: 1856.

_____. *Memoirs of the Court of George IV, 1820–1830.* 2 vols. London: 1856.

Burke, Edmund. *Letters on a Regicide Peace. Select Works of Edmund Burke.* Vol. 3. Indianapolis: 1999.

_____. *On Empire, Liberty, and Reform: Speeches and Letters.* Ed. David Bromwich. New Haven: 2000.

Castlereagh, Viscount. *Memoirs and Correspondence of Viscount Castlereagh, Second Marquis of Londonderry.* Ed. Charles William Vane, 3rd Marquis of Londonderry. 12 vols. London: 1848–53.

Cornwallis, Charles. *The Correspondence of Charles, First Marquis Cornwallis.* Ed. Charles Ross. 3 vols. London: 1859.

Correspondence of King George III from 1760 to December 1783. Printed from the Original Papers in the Royal Archives at Windsor Castle. Ed. J. W. Fortescue. 6 vols. London: 1927–8.

Creevey, Thomas. *The Creevey Papers: A Selection of the Correspondence and Diaries of Sir Thomas Creevey MP.* Ed. Sir Herbert Maxwell. 2 vols. London: 1903.

Croker, John Wilson. *The Croker Papers: The Correspondence and Diaries of the Late Right Honourable John Wilson Croker, Secretary to the Admiralty from 1809 to 1830.* Ed. Louis J. Jennings. 3 vols. London: 1885.

Douglas, Sylvester. *Diaries of Sylvester Douglas, Lord Glenbervie.* Ed. Francis Bickley. 2 vols. London: 1928.

Eden, Lord Auckland John. *Journal and Correspondence of William, Lord Auckland.* London: 1862.

Elliot, Sir Gilbert. *Life and Letters of Sir Gilbert Elliot, First Earl of Minto, 1751–1806.* Ed. Countess of Minto. London: 1874.

The Extraordinary and Facetious History of the Immaculate Boy: who, John Gilpin like, Ran a Greater Risk than he Intended, and Came Home Safe at Last. / As read at the Cockpit-Royal, and received with uncommon applause. London: 1785.

Fitzmaurice, Lord Edward. *Life of William, Earl of Shelburne, Afterwards First Marquess of Lansdowne.* 2 vols. London: 1875.

Foster, Lady Elizabeth. *Dearest Bess: The Life and Times of Lady Elizabeth Foster, Afterwards Duchess of Devonshire, from her Unpublished Journals and Correspondence.* London: 1955.

Foster, Vere, ed., *The Two Duchesses, Georgiana, Duchess of Devonshire, Elizabeth, Duchess of Devonshire: Family Correspondence [...].* London: 1898.

Fox, Charles James. *Memorials and Correspondence of Charles James Fox.* Ed. Lord John Russell. 2 vols. Philadelphia: 1853.

Gibbon, Edward. *Autobiography of Edward Gibbon, Esq. Illustrated From His Letters with Occasional Notes and Narration.* Ed. Lord Sheffield. New York: 1911.

_____. *Memoirs of My Life.* Ed. G. A. Bonnard. London: 1966.

Gower, Lord Granville Leveson. *Lord Granville Leveson-Gower (First Earl Granville) Private Correspondence, 1781 to 1821, Edited by his Daughter in Law Castalia Countess Granville.* 2 vols. London: 1916.

Greig, James, ed. *The Farington Diary*. 8 vols. London: 1923–8.

Greville, Charles. *The Greville Memoirs*. Ed. Roger Fulford and Lytton Strachey. 8 vols. London: 1938.

Grosvenor, Caroline, and Wortley, Lord Stuart, eds., *The First Lady Warncliffe and Her Family, 1779–1856*. London: 1927.

Holland, Henry Richard Vassall Fox, 3rd Lord. *Further Memoirs of the Whig Party 1807–1821 with Some Miscellaneous Reminiscences*, ed. Lord Stavordale. London: 1905.

_____. *Memoirs of the Whig Party during My Time*. Ed. Henry Edward Lord Holland. 2 vols. London: 1852.

Ilchester, Earl of, ed. *Elizabeth, Lady Holland to Her Son, 1821–1845*. London: 1946.

_____. *The Journal of Elizabeth, Lady Holland (1791–1811)*. 2 vols. London: 1908.

Ireland, John. *The Letters of Fabius to the Right Hon. William Pitt, on his Proposed Abolition of the Test in Favor of the Roman Catholics of Ireland*. London: 1801.

_____. *Vindicae Regiae: or a Defense of the Kingly Office in Two Letters to Earl Stanhope*. London: 1797.

Jucker, Ninetta S., ed. *The Jenkinson Papers, 1760–1776*. London: 1949.

Lecky, William Edward Hartpole. *History of England in the Eighteenth Century*. 8 vols. New York: 1878–90.

Lewis, George Cornewall. *Essays on the Administration of Great Britain from 1783 to 1830 Contributed to the Edinburgh Review*. Ed. Sir Edmund Head. London: 1864.

Liverpool, Robert Banks Jenkinson, 2nd Earl of. *The Speech of the Earl of Liverpool: Delivered in the House of Lords on Tuesday, the 26th day of February, 1822 on the subject of the agricultural distress of the country and the financial measures proposed for its relief. With an appendix, containing several accounts therein referred to*. London: 1822.

Lodge, Edmund. *Portraits and Memoirs of the Most Illustrious Personages of British History*. Vol. 13 (1829).

Mackinnon, William Alexander. *On the Rise: Progress and Present State of Public Opinion*. London: 1828.

Malmesbury, James Harris, First Earl of. *Diaries and Correspondence of James Harris, First Earl of Malmesbury*. Ed. James Howard Harris, Second Earl of Malmesbury. 4 vols. London: 1844.

Martineau, Harriet. *The History of England during the Thirty Years Peace, 1816–1846*. London: 1849.

Newmarch, Henry, and Took, Thomas. *A History of Prices and of the State of the Circulation during the Years 1703–1856*. 6 vols. London: 1838–57.

Newton, J. F. *The Early Days of the Right Honorable George Canning, First Lord of the Treasury and Chancellor of the Exchequer, and of Some of his Contemporaries with an Original Letter Written by Him in the Year 1788*. London: 1828.

Parker, Charles Stuart, ed. *Sir Robert Peel from His Private Papers*. 5 vols. London: 1891.

Pellew, George, ed. *Life and Correspondence of the Right Honorable Henry Addington, First Viscount Sidmouth*. 3 vols. London: 1847.

Phipps, Edmund, ed. *Memoirs of the Political and Literary Life of Robert Plumer Ward*. 2 vols. London: 1850.

Pinney, Thomas. *Letters of Thomas Babbington Macaulay*. 6 vols. Cambridge: 2008.

Quenelle, Peter, ed. *The Private Letters of Princess Lieven to Prince Metternich, 1820–1826*. London: 1937.

The Rolliad in Two Parts: Probationary Odes for the Laureatship; and Political Ecologues and Miscellanies. 2nd edition. London: 1812.

Rose, George. *The Diaries and Correspondence of the Right Hon. George Rose, Containing Original Letters of the Most Distinguished Statesmen of His Day.* Ed. L. V. Harcourt. 2 vols. London: 1860.

Royal Commission on Historical Manuscripts, Great Britain. *Report on the Manuscripts of the Earl of Abergavenny, Lord Braye, G. F. Luttrell Esq. &c.* London: 1887.

_____. *Report on the Manuscripts of Earl Bathurst Preserved at Cirencester Park* London: 1923.

_____. *Report on the Manuscripts of J. B. Fortescue Preserved at Dropmore.* 11 vols. London: 1892–1927.

_____. *Report on the Manuscripts of the Late Reginald Rawdon Hastings Esq. of the Manor House, Ashby de la Zouche.* London: 1934.

Sherlock, Martin. *New Letters from an English Traveller.* London: 1781.

Smart, William. *Economic Annals of the Nineteenth Century.* 2 vols. London: 1910 and 1917.

Smith, Nowell C., ed. *Letters of Sydney Smith.* 2 vols. Oxford: 1953.

Stanhope, Eugenia., ed. *Letters Written by the Late Right Honourable Philip Dormer Stanhope, Earl of Chesterfield, to his Son, Philip Stanhope Esq.* 2nd edition. 4 vols. London: 1774.

Stanhope, Lady Hester. *Memoirs of Lady Hester Stanhope.* 3 vols. London: 1846.

Stanhope, Philip Henry, Earl of. *Life of the Right Honourable William Pitt.* 4 vols. London: 1862.

Stuart, Dorothy. *Dearest Bess: The Life and Times of Lady Elizabeth Foster, afterwards Duchess of Devonshire, from Her Unpublished Journals and Correspondence.* London: 1955.

Twiss, Horace. *The Public and Private Life of Lord Chancellor Eldon with Selections from his Correspondence.* 3 vols. London: 1844.

Walpole, Horace. *The Last Journals of Horace Walpole during the Reign of George III from 1771 to 1783.* 2 vols. London: 1910.

_____. *Memoirs of the Reign of King George III.* 4 vols. Freeport: 1970.

Walpole, Spencer. *A History of England from the Conclusion of the Great War in 1815.* London: 1913.

Watts, William. *Memoirs of the Revolution in Bengal, Anno. Dom. 1757. By Which Meer Jaffeir was Raised to the Government of that Province together with Those of Barbar and Orixa.* London: 1760.

Webster, Charles K. *British Diplomacy, 1813–1815: Select Documents Dealing with the Reconstruction of Europe.* London: 1921.

Wellington, Arthur Wellesley, Duke of. *Dispatches, Correspondence and Memoranda of Field Marshall Arthur, Duke of Wellington K.G.* Ed. his son, the Duke of Wellington, in continuation of the former series. 8 vols. London: 1857–80.

_____. *The Dispatches of Field Marshall the Duke of* Wellington, during his Various Campaigns in India, Denmark, Portugal, Spain, the Low Countries and France. Ed. Colonel Gurwood. 8 vols. London: 1844.

_____. *Supplementary Dispatches, Correspondence and Memoranda of Field Marshall Arthur, Duke of Wellington K.G.* Ed. his son, the Duke of Wellington. 15 vols. London: 1858–72.

Wheatley, Henry B., ed. *The Historical and Posthumous Memoirs of Sir Nathaniel William Wraxall, 1772–1784. Edited with Notes and Additional Chapters from the Author's Unpublished Manuscripts.* 5 vols. London: 1884.

Wilberforce, Robert Isaac, and Wilberforce, Samuel. *Life of William Wilberforce.* 5 vols. London: 1838.

Windham, William. *The Diary of the Right Hon. William Windham, 1784 to 1810*. Ed. Cecilia Anne Baring. London: 1866.

_____. *The Windham Papers: The Life and Correspondence of the Rt. Hon. William Windham*. Ed. Earl of Rosebery. 2 vols. London: 1913.

Wishaw, John. *The "Pope" of Holland House: Selections from the Correspondence of John Wishaw and His Friends*. Ed. Lady Seymour. London: 1906.

Yonge, Charles Duke. *The Life and Administration of Robert Banks, Second Earl of Liverpool, K.G. Late First Lord of the Treasury. Compiled from Original Documents*. 3 vols. London: 1868.

SECONDARY SOURCES

BOOKS

Albinson, A. Cassandra, Funnell, Peter, and Peltz, Lucy, eds. *Thomas Lawrence: Regency Power and Brilliance*. New Haven: 2010.

Arnstein, Walter L. "Norman Gash: Peelite" in *Recent Historians of Great Britain: Essays on the Post-1945 Generation*. Ed. W. L. Arnstein. Ames: 1990.

Bayly, C. A. *Imperial Meridian: The British Empire and the World 1780–1830*. London: 1989.

Bebbington, David W. *Evangelicalism in Modern Britain: A History from the 1730s to the 1980s*. London: 1989.

Bell, David A. *The First Total War: Napoleon's Europe and the Birth of Warfare as We Know It*. New York: 2007.

Bew, John. *Castlereagh: A Life*. New York: 2012.

Bickham, Troy. *The Weight of Vengeance: The United States, the British Empire and the War of 1812*. Oxford: 2012.

Black, Jeremy. *France and the Grand Tour*. Houndmills: 2003.

_____. *George III: America's Last King*. New Haven: 2006.

_____. *A Subject for Taste: Culture in Eighteenth-Century England*. London: 2005.

_____, ed. *The Tory World: Deep History and the Tory Theme in British Foreign Policy, 1679–2014*. Farnham: 2015.

Boswell, James. *Life of Johnson*. Ed. R. W. Chapman. Oxford: 1980.

Brent, Richard. *Liberal Anglican Politics: Whiggery, Liberalism and Reform 1830–1841*. Oxford: 1987.

Brewer, John. *Party Ideology and Popular Politics at the Accession of George III*. Cambridge: 1976.

Brock, W. R. *Lord Liverpool and Liberal Toryism: 1820 to 1827*. Cambridge: 1941.

Brown, David. *Palmerston: A Biography*. New Haven: 2010.

Browning, Reed. *Political and Constitutional Ideas of the Court Whigs*. Baton Rouge: 1982.

Cannon, John. *The Fox–North Coalition: Crisis of the Constitution, 1782–4*. Cambridge: 1969.

_____, ed. *The Whig Ascendancy: Colloquies on Hanoverian Britain*. New York: 1981.

Carpenter, Kirsty. *Refugees of the French Revolution: Émigrés in London, 1789–1802*. Houndmills: 1999.

Chase, Malcolm. *1820: Disorder and Instability in the United Kingdom*. Manchester: 2013.

Childe-Pemberton, W. S. *The Earl-Bishop: The Life of Frederick Hervey, Bishop of Derry, Earl of Bristol*. 2 vols. New York: 1924.

Clark, J. C. D. *English Society, 1660–1832: Religion, Ideology and Politics During the Ancien Régime.* Cambridge: 2000.

————. *The Language of Liberty: Political Discourse and Social Dynamics in the Anglo-American World, 1660–1832.* Cambridge: 1994.

————. *Revolution and Rebellion: State and Society in England in the Seventeenth and Eighteenth Centuries.* Cambridge: 1986.

Clarke, John. *British Diplomacy and Foreign Policy, 1782–1865: The National Interest.* London: 1989.

Clausewitz, Carl von. *On War.* Ed. and trans. Michael Howard and Peter Paret. New York: 1993.

Colley, Linda. *In Defiance of Oligarchy: The Tory Party, 1715–1760.* Cambridge: 1982.

Cookson, J. E. *The British Armed Nation, 1793–1815.* Oxford: 1997.

————. *Lord Liverpool's Administration: The Crucial Years, 1815–1822.* Edinburgh: 1995.

Cowling, Maurice. *Religion and Public Doctrine in Modern England.* Cambridge: 1980.

Cruickshanks, Eveline, Handley, Stuart, and Hayton, D. W., eds., *The House of Commons: 1690–1715.* 5 vols. Cambridge: 2002.

Dalrymple, William. *White Mughals: Love and Betrayal in Eighteenth-Century India.* New York: 2002.

Daunton, Martin. *Trusting Leviathan: The Politics of Taxation in Britain, 1799–1914.* Cambridge: 2001.

Davies, Huw. *Wellington's Wars: The Making of a Military Genius.* New Haven: 2012.

Davis, Richard W. *A Political History of the House of Lords, 1811–1846: From the Regency to Corn Law Repeal.* Palo Alto: 2007.

Dickinson, H. T. *Liberty and Property: Political Ideology in Eighteenth-Century Britain.* New York: 1977.

————. *The Politics of the People in Eighteenth-Century Britain.* New York: 1995.

Ehrman, John. *The Younger Pitt: The Consuming Struggle.* Stanford: 1996.

————. *The Younger Pitt: The Reluctant Transition.* Stanford: 1983.

Esdaile, Charles. *The Peninsular War: A New History.* London: 2002.

Fedorak, Charles J. *Henry Addington, Prime Minister, 1801–1804: Peace, War, and Parliamentary Politics.* Akron: 2002.

Feiling, Keith Graham. *The Second Tory Party, 1714–1832.* London: 1951.

Fisher, David Hackett. *The Great Wave: Price Revolutions and the Rhythm of History.* Oxford: 1996.

Fisher, D. R., ed. *The House of Commons, 1820–1831.* 7 vols. Cambridge: 2009.

Fontana, Biancamaria. *Rethinking the Politics of Commercial Society: The Edinburgh Review, 1802–1832.* Cambridge: 1985.

Gash, Norman. *Lord Liverpool: The Life and Political Career of Robert Banks Jenkinson, Second Earl of Liverpool, 1770–1828.* London: 1984.

————. *Pillars of Government and Other Essays on the State of Society, c. 1770–1880.* London: 1986.

————, ed. *Wellington: Studies in the Military and Political Career of the First Duke of Wellington.* Manchester: 1990.

————, Southgate, Donald, and Dilks, David. *The Conservatives: A History from their Origins to 1965.* London: 1977.

Gatrell, Vic. *City of Laughter: Sex and Satire in Eighteenth-Century London.* New York: 2006.

Gaunt, Richard A. *Sir Robert Peel: The Life and Legacy.* London: 2010.

Gee, Austin. *The British Volunteer Movement, 1794–1814.* Oxford: 2003.

George, M. D., ed. *Catalogue of Political and Personal Satires Preserved in the Department of Prints and Drawings of the British Museum.* Vols. 5–11. London: 1933–54.

Grainger, John D. *The Amiens Truce: Britain and Bonaparte, 1801–1803.* London: 2004.

Gray, Denis. *Spencer Perceval: The Evangelical Prime Minister, 1762–1812.* Manchester: 1963.

Gunn, J. A. W. *Beyond Liberty and Property: The Process of Self-Recognition in Eighteenth Century Political Thought.* Kingston and Montreal: 1983.

Haakonssen, Knud, eds. *Enlightenment and Religion: Rational Dissent in Eighteenth-Century Britain.* Cambridge: 1996.

Hague, William. *William Pitt the Younger: A Biography.* New York: 2005.

Hakluyt, Richard. *The Principal Navigations, Voyages, Traffiques, and Discoveries of the English Nation.* Vol. 2. Glasgow: 1903–5.

Harling, Philip. *The Waning of "Old Corruption": The Politics of Economical Reform in Britain, 1779–1848.* Oxford: 1996.

Harvey, A. D. *Britain in the Early Nineteenth Century.* New York: 1978.

———. *Collision of Empires: Britain in Three World Wars.* London: 1992.

Hawkins, Angus. *Victorian Political Culture: "Habits of Heart and Mind."* Oxford: 2015.

Hay, William Anthony. *The Whig Revival, 1808–1830.* Houndmills: 2005.

Hayter, Tony. *The Army and the Crowd in Mid-Georgian England.* London: 1978.

Hempton, David. *Methodism and Politics in British Society, 1750–1850.* Stanford: 1984.

Henning, B. D., ed. *History of Parliament: The Commons, 1660–1690.* Vol. 2. London: 1983.

Hill, Draper. *Fashionable Contrasts: Caricatures by James Gillray.* London: 1966.

———. *Mr. Gillray the Caricaturist.* London: 1965.

Hilton, Boyd. *The Age of Atonement: The Influence of Evangelicalism on Social and Economic Thought ca. 1795–1865.* Oxford: 1988.

———. *Corn, Cash, Commerce: The Economic Politics of the Tory Government, 1815–1830.* Oxford: 1977.

———. *A Mad Bad Dangerous People? England, 1783–1846.* Oxford: 2006.

Hinde, Wendy. *George Canning.* New York: 1973.

Hunt, Giles. *The Duel: Castlereagh, Canning, and Deadly Cabinet Rivalry.* London: 2008.

Hyde, Edward. *History of the Rebellion: A New Selection.* Ed. Paul Seaward. Oxford: 2009.

Jarrett, Mark. *The Congress of Vienna and its Legacy: War and Great Power Diplomacy After Napoleon.* London: 2013.

Jupp, Peter. *The Governing of Britain, 1688–1848: The Executive, Parliament and the People.* London: 2006.

Knight, Roger. *Britain Against Napoleon: The Organization of Victory, 1793–1815.* London: 2013.

Lambert, Andrew. "Winning Without Fighting: British Grand Strategy and Its Application to the United States, 1815–65." in *Strategic Logic and Political Rationality: Essays in Honor of Michael I. Handel.* Ed. Bradford A. Lee and Karl Walling. London: 2003.

Langford, Paul. *A Polite and Commercial People: England, 1727–1783.* Oxford: 1989.

———. "Politics and Manners from Sir Robert Walpole to Sir Robert Peel." *Proceedings of the British Academy* 94(1996): 103–25.

Lee, Stephen M. *George Canning and Liberal Toryism, 1801–1827.* Woodbridge: 2008.

Lieven, Dominic. *Russia Against Napoleon: The True Story of the Campaigns of War and Peace.* New York: 2010.

Mackesy, Piers. *War Without Victory: The Downfall of Pitt, 1799–1802.* Oxford: 1984.

Marshall, Dorothy. *The Rise of George Canning.* London: Longmans Green & Co., 1938.

Melikan, Rose. *John Scott, Lord Eldon, 1751–1838: The Duty of Loyalty.* Cambridge: 1999.

Mitchell, Leslie, and Sutherland, Lucy S., eds., *The History of the University of Oxford: Vol. V The Eighteenth Century.* Oxford: 1986.

Mokyr, Joel. *The Enlightened Economy: An Economic History of Britain, 1700–1850.* New Haven: 2009.

Moon, Joshua. *Wellington's Two Front War: The Peninsular Campaigns at Home and Abroad, 1808–1814.* Norman: 2010.

Mori, Jennifer. *William Pitt and the French Revolution, 1785–1795.* New York: 1997.

Morley, John. *Edmund Burke: A Historical Study.* New York: 1924.

Morris, Marilyn. *Sex, Money and Personal Character in Eighteenth-Century British Politics.* New Haven: 2014.

Muir, Rory. *Britain and the Defeat of Napoleon, 1807–1815.* New Haven: 1996.

———. *Wellington: The Path to Victory, 1769–1814.* New Haven: 2013.

———. *Wellington: Waterloo and the Fortunes of Peace, 1814–1852.* New Haven: 2015.

Namier, Sir Lewis, and Brooke, John, eds. *History of Parliament: The House of Commons, 1754–1790.* 3 vols. London: 1964.

Nelson, R. R. *The Home Office, 1782–1801.* Durham: 1969.

"Noble and Patriotic:" The Beaumont Gift 1828. London: 1988.

Nockles, Peter B. *The Oxford Movement in Context: Anglican High Churchmanship 1760–1857.* Cambridge: 1994.

Norris, John. *Shelburne and Reform.* London: 1963.

O'Gorman, Frank. *The Rise of Party in England: The Rockingham Whigs, 1760–82.* London: 1975.

Pares, Richard. *George III and the Politicians.* Oxford: 1953.

Parry, Jonathan. *The Rise and Fall of Liberal Government in Victorian Britain.* New Haven: 1993.

Payne, Reider. *Ecclesiastical Patronage in England, 1770–1801: A Study of Four Family and Political Networks.* Lewiston: 2010.

Perkins, Bradford. *The First Rapprochement: England and the United States, 1795–1805.* Philadelphia: 1955.

Portsmouth, Robert. *John Wilson Croker: Irish Ideas and the Invention of Modern Conservatism.* Dublin: 2010.

Powell, J. Enoch. *Joseph Chamberlain.* London: 1977.

Price, Richard. *British Society, 1688–1880: Dynamism, Containment, Change.* Cambridge: 1999.

Read, Donald. *The English Provinces, c. 1760–1960: A Study in Influence.* London: 1964.

———. *Peterloo: The "Massacre" and Its Background.* Manchester: 1958.

Ritcheson, Charles R. *Aftermath of Revolution: British Policy Toward the United States, 1783–1795.* Dallas: 1969.

———. *British Politics and the American Revolution.* Norman: 1953.

Robbins, Jane. *The Trial of Queen Caroline: The Scandalous Affair that Nearly Ended a Monarchy.* London: 2006.

Roberts, Michael. *The Whig Party, 1807–1812.* London: 1939.

Robertson, Ian. *An Atlas of the Peninsular War.* New Haven: 2010.

Robinson, Nicholas K. *Edmund Burke: A Life in Caricature.* New Haven: 1996.

Rosebery, Lord. *Pitt.* London: 1915.

Rostow, W.W. *British Economy of the Nineteenth Century*. Oxford: 1948.

Royle, Edward. *Revolutionary Britannia? Reflections on the Threat of Revolution in Britain, 1789–1848*. Manchester: 2000.

Sack, James J. *From Jacobite to Conservative: Reaction and Orthodoxy in Britain c. 1760–1832*. Cambridge: 1993.

_____. *The Grenvillites, 1801–29: Party Politics and Factionalism in the Age of Pitt and Liverpool*. Urbana: 1979.

Sánchez-Jáuregui, Dolores, and Wilcox, Scott, eds. *The English Prize: The Capture of the Westmorland, an Episode of the Grand Tour*. New Haven: 2012.

Schama, Simon. *Citizens: A Chronicle of the French Revolution*. New York: 1989.

Schroeder, Paul W. *The Transformation of European Politics, 1763–1840*. Oxford: 1994.

Sedgewick, Romney, ed. *The House of Commons: 1715–1754*. 2 vols. Oxford: 1970.

Severn, John. *Architects of Empire: The Duke of Wellington and His Brothers*. Norman: 2007.

Smith, Adam. *Theory of Moral Sentiments*. Ed. D. D. Raphael and A. L. Macife. Indianapolis: 1982.

Smith, E. A. *George IV*. New Haven: 1999.

_____. *Whig Principles and Party Politics: Earl Fitzwilliam and the Whig Party, 1748–1833*. Manchester: 1975.

Smith, Hannah. *Georgian Monarchy: Politics and Culture, 1714–1760*. Cambridge: 2006.

Sutherland, Lucy S. *The East India Company in Eighteenth-Century Politics*. Oxford: 1952.

Thompson, E. P. *The Making of the English Working Class*. Harmondsworth: 1980.

Thompson, Neville. *Earl Bathurst and the British Empire, 1762–1834*. Barnsley: 1999.

Thorne, R. G. *The House of Commons: 1790–1820*. 5 vols. London: 1986.

Tombs, Robert. *The English and their History*. New York: 2015.

Turner, Michael J. *Pitt the Younger: A Life*. London: 2003.

Ward, William Reginald. *Georgian Oxford: University Politics in the Eighteenth Century*. Oxford: 1958.

Watts, Michael R. *The Dissenters: Volume II, The Expansion of Evangelical Nonconformity*. Oxford: 1995.

Webster, Charles K. *The Foreign Policy of Castlereagh, 1812–1815: Britain and the Reconstruction of Europe*. London: 1963.

_____. *The Foreign Policy of Castlereagh, 1815–1822: Britain and the European Alliance*. London: 1963.

Wells, Roger. *Wretched Faces: Famine in Wartime England, 1793–1801*. New York: 1988.

Willen, T. S. *The Early History of the Russia Company, 1553–1603*. New York: 1968.

Wilkinson, David. *The Duke of Portland: Politics and Party in the Age of George III*. Houndmills: 2003.

Zamoyski, Adam. *Rites of Peace: The Fall of Napoleon and the Congress of Vienna*. New York: 2007.

JOURNAL ARTICLES

Aspinall, Arthur. "The Social Status of Journalists at the Beginning of the Nineteenth Century." *Review of English Studies* 21(July 1945): 216–32.

Beedell, A. V. "John Reeves' Prosecution for a Seditious Libel, 1795–6: A Study in Political Cynicism." *Historical Journal* 36.4(December 1993): 799–824.

Bradley, James E. "The Anglican Pulpit, the Social Order, and the Resurgence of Toryism During the American Revolution." *Albion: A Quarterly Journal Concerned with British Studies* 21.3 (Autumn 1989): 366–7.

Chaudury, Sushil. "All the Main Conspirators – The Making of the Plassy Revolution." *Indian Historical Review* 24.1–2(1997–8): 104–33.

Eastwood, David. "The Age of Uncertainty: Britain in the Early Nineteenth Century." *Transactions of the Royal Historical Society* 6th ser. 8(1998): 91–116.

Fedorak, Charles J. "In Search of a Necessary Ally: Addington, Hawkesbury and Russia, 1801–1804." *International History Review* 13.2(May 1991): 223–36.

Fulcher, Jonathan. "The Loyalist Response to the Queen Caroline Agitations." *Journal of British Studies* 34.4(October 1995): 481–502.

Gash, Norman. "The Tortoise and the Hare: Liverpool and Canning." *History Today* (March 1982): 12–13.

Harling, Philip. "The Law of Libel and the Limits of Repression, 1790–1832." *Historical Journal* 44(2001): 107–32.

_____. "Rethinking 'Old Corruption.'" *Past and Present* 147(May 1995): 127–58.

Harrison, Brian and Theodore Hoppen. "Norman Gash." *Biographical Memoirs of Fellows of the British Academy* 40(2012): 199–236.

Hilton, Boyd. "The Political Arts of Lord Liverpool." *Transactions of the Royal Historical Society* 5th ser. 38(December 1988): 147–70.

Hunt, Tamara. "Morality and Monarchy in the Queen Caroline Affair." *Albion: A Quarterly Journal Concerned with British Studies* 23.4(Winter 1991): 697–722.

Lacquer, Thomas. "The Queen Caroline Affair: Politics and Art in the Reign of George IV." *Journal of Modern History* 54.3(September 1982): 417–66.

Lambert, David. "The Counter-Revolutionary Atlantic: White West Indian Petitions and Proslavery Networks." *Social and Cultural Geography* 6.3(2005): 405–20.

Langford, Paul. "Politics and Manners from Sir Robert Walpole to Sir Robert Peel." *Proceedings of the British Academy* 94(1996): 103–25.

O'Brien, Patrick K. "The Political Economy of British Taxation, 1660–1815." *Economic History Review* 41.1(1988): 1–32.

Parsinnen, T. M. "Association, Convention, and Anti-Parliament in British Radical Politics, 1771–1847." *English Historical Review* 88.348 (July 1973): 504–33.

Pentland, Gordon. "'Now the great Man in the Parliament House is dead, we shall have a big Loaf!' Responses to the Assassination of Spencer Perceval." *Journal of British Studies* 51(2012): 340–63.

Petley, Christer. "'Devoted Islands' and 'That Madman Wilberforce': British Proslavery Patriotism During the Age of Abolition." *Journal of Imperial and Commonwealth History* 39.3(September 2011): 393–415.

Ritcheson, Charles R. "Preparation of the Stamp Act." *William and Mary Quarterly* 3.10(October 1953): 543–59.

Rubinstein, W. D. "The End of 'Old Corruption' in Britain, 1760–1860." *Past & Present* 101(November 1983): 55–86.

Rutz, Michael A. "The Politicizing of Evangelical Dissent, 1811–1813." *Parliamentary History* 20.2(June 2001): 187–207.

Sack, James J. "The Memory of Pitt and the Memory of Burke." *Historical Journal* 30.3(September 1987): 623–40.

Stern, Walter M. "The Bread Crisis in Britain, 1795–96." *Economica* 31.122(May 1964): 181.

Wallbank, M. V. "Eighteenth-Century Public Schools and the Education of the Governing Elite." *History of Education* 8.1(1979): 1–3.

DISSERTATIONS AND THESES

Alter, Jean-Marc. "The Life and Early Career of Robert Banks Jenkinson, the Second Earl of Liverpool 1770–1812." Ph.D. diss., University of Wales, 1988.

Duffy, Michael. "British War Policy: The Austrian Alliance, 1793–1801." D.Phil. thesis, Oxford University, 1971.

Vaughn, James. "The Politics of Empire: Metropolitan Socio-Political Development and the Imperial Transformation of the British East India Company, 1675–1775." Ph.D. diss., University of Chicago, 2009.

Index